GETTING SAVED FROM THE SIXTIES

GETTING

SAVED

FROM

THE SIXTIES

Moral
Meaning
in Conversion
and Cultural
Change

Steven M. Tipton

Foreword by Robert N. Bellah

University of California Press
Berkeley   Los Angeles   London

University of California Press
Berkeley and Los Angeles, California

University of California Press, Ltd.
London, England

Library of Congress Cataloging in Publication Data

Tipton, Steven M.
    Getting saved from the sixties.

    Bibliography: p. 349
    Includes index.
    1. United States—Moral conditions.   2. Youth—
United States—Conduct of life.   3. Social ethics.
I. Title.
HN59.T58   973.92   81-3033
ISBN 0-520-03868-1   AACR2

Printed in the United States of America

123456789

FOR MY FIRST TEACHERS:

Claire Barbat Whittle
Benjamin Parker Tipton
Mary Whittle Tipton

CONTENTS

FOREWORD

Edward Shils has said that "the true calling of sociology is to contribute to the self-understanding of society." In this sense Steven Tipton's book is a fulfillment of what sociology ought to be. Tipton is himself a member of the generation here described and faced its conundrums and its choices. But he has brought to his participation in the common life the special sensitivities and awarenesses of the sociological tradition. Far from making him stand aloof, these resources for self-understanding have helped him make more vital contact with his contemporaries as he has refined his ideas and those of the people with whom he talked. As is true of the best sociology, the result is a collaborative product to which those he studied have contributed richly. It is a book from which we all have much to learn.

Getting Saved from the Sixties is not a book about "new religions" perched exotically on the margins of American society. It is a book about central issues in American society—moral and political issues as well as religious ones. It uses the three movements chosen for study as lenses to look at the larger society at a particularly poignant moment in its historical transformation. It asks how young Americans from mainstream backgrounds were attracted to such exotic movements in the first place and what they came to make of their society after they experienced their conversions. During the course of the book Tipton sheds light on changing conceptions of family, community, occupation, and politics, and on the problems we are experiencing in each of these spheres. The religious question is raised when all these other spheres have become problematic. Discrete problems of meaning accumulate and drive toward the general problem of meaning. They raise the question, "What do we go by?" as Tipton puts it. That is the question he leaves us with.

Peter Berger has said that good sociology "implies an ongoing communication" with history and philosophy. Shorn of that communication sociology soon becomes an esoteric technology. In this respect too Tipton's book is sociology as it ought to be. Chapter 1 sketches the historical framework necessary to make sense of the events of the sixties and seventies. Tipton shows that the disruptions of the sixties occurred along old fault lines in the American terrain, particularly those separating the biblical from the utilitarian tradition. It is this connection to older cultural cleavages which makes the events of the sixties significant long after the more effervescent effects have fadèd. And in chapter 5 Tipton points out the implications of his findings for the developmental problems that lie ahead of us. He offers us no easy solutions but he does point up the issues that our history, intensified by recent events, presents us with.

Throughout the book Tipton draws on moral philosophy for concepts and categories to sharpen his inquiry. He presumes that moral reasoning is not limited to philosophers and that philosophic concepts may help to illumine the preconceptions and conclusions of those he studied. In this, as the text shows, he was not mistaken. Tipton is clearly a gifted interviewer and some of the quotations in this book, transcribed directly from tapes, are stunning in their focus and clarity. But the level of discourse that Tipton's informants are able to sustain is not only the result of his ability to put them at ease but also the intellectual coherence of his questioning, informed as it is by philosophical reflection, that challenges them to rise to their best.

It is not accidental that the interview is the "method" of the book. It is integral to the kind of sociology that is being practiced. Shils has written:

> Sociology, in principle, takes the other man as he is; it tries to find out what he does, what he thinks and feels. This curiosity can be a perverse intrusion into privacy, it can be part of a program of acquiring information to be used to manipulate. It is also an acknowledgment of the other's right to an independent moral existence. In trying to acquire the interviewed person's account of his own past as he sees it and in his own words, the sociologist is introducing the interviewed person into science as a morally meaningful being. This is one of the partially realized possibilities.

That Tipton more than partially realizes this possibility reflects the fact that his questioning is philosophical at the same time that it is sociological. The open-ended interview as he employs it is not only archetypally sociological, it is also Socratic. Sociology for Tipton is not only a form of social self-understanding but also a form of moral reflection.

It is decisive for Tipton's inquiry that concepts, whether sociological or philosophical, are not ends in themselves but serve to return us better informed to social reality and moral practice. If people do not act only as a result of social pressures neither do they act on deductions from ethical theory alone. The moral life is indeed lived in the midst of social and historical exigencies, but these must always be interpreted before there can be a response. Interpretation is seldom a matter of deduction from abstract theory, though some degree of rational reflection is almost always involved. But tradition and precedent on the one hand, the charismatic exemplar on the other, are frequently involved. Tipton gives us much of the texture of the moral life as it is lived in America today with all its conflicts and unclarities. He sees his task not as describing inevitable trends nor as legislating an ethical theory but as helping us clarify our moral commitments in the face of the hard realities ahead. The book could be called an example of "practical reason," to resurrect a classical term for whose contemporary meaning we are groping. Tipton's work, in its combination of intellectual and moral responsibility, shows us what sociology as practical reason might be.

Even before the book was completed, *Getting Saved from the Sixties*, through a series of fortuitous happenings, led to the formation of a collective project involving Tipton and several others, including myself, which we have entitled "The Moral Basis of Social Commitment in America." Using the technique of sociology as moral inquiry, with a central focus on the interview as a place where sociologist and citizen engage in active and concerned exchange, we are talking to Americans in a number of communities in various parts of the country. This time our focus is neither on the young nor on exotic religious groups. We are approaching directly a variety of middle-class Americans in an effort to discover how they make sense of their society, how they view their participation in it, and what their hopes and fears are. We have found a remarkably warm response, for these are matters with which many of our fellow citizens are concerned and about which they welcome the chance to exchange views and clarify ideas. The books that this project will engender will all owe much to *Getting Saved from the Sixties*.

Getting Saved from the Sixties stands in the central tradition of sociology. It attempts to understand (*Verstehen*) the persons and groups that are its subjects. It attempts to use that understanding to clarify for us all the nature of the society we live in and some of the directions in which it seems to be going. But if this book stands securely in a sociological tradition that is by now almost a century old and in a philosophical tradition that is much older than that, it is also, with its freshness, its vitality, and its ability to talk easily about the ought and the is, a product of the sixties. Fortunately it avoids the least attractive features of the sixties generation—their lack of self-discipline, their self-righteousness, their anti-intellectualism. Perhaps the distance of a decade has helped us assimilate what was, for all its pathologies, a fresh turn in American history. If we were to lose entirely the optimism and enthusiasm of those days, our future would be ominous indeed.

Robert N. Bellah

PREFACE

. . . Watchman, what of the night? The watchman
said, The morning cometh, and also the night:
if ye will enquire, enquire ye: return, come.
Isaiah 21:11-12.

Religious movements arise and people join them for a number of reasons. Sixties youth have joined alternative religious movements basically, I will argue, to make moral sense of their lives. Their conversion may be an intensely personal and subjective change of heart, but it is also a change of mind which draws on and transforms the public, objectified resources for moral meaning carried by our culture. If we trace the cultural dynamics of their conversion and listen to their accounts of it as a shift in moral outlook, we should be able to see this process of change beginning with problems of right and wrong their earlier views cannot resolve and their later views can. We should be able to see how such problems are couched in the social situation of those who face them and how their solution turns on changes in that situation. This is what I have sought to do in the following study.

This study is an inquiry into the ways Americans understand right and wrong, into how they think out their morality and how they live it out. What shape do moral ideas take in persons' lives and in the life of a society? Why at times do they weaken and break down? How do they undergo change and find renewal? I have looked for answers to these questions in alternative religious movements, among persons seeking their own answers to immediate moral questions with felt urgency. That search is what I am most concerned to describe, not the formal beliefs of the movements themselves, nor their social organization. What results from this concern is a kind of moral anthropology, built around descriptive ethics and interpretive sociology. It is founded on the conviction that a humanistic sociology is more a redundancy than a hybrid, that a field of ethics focused on the actual conduct of life owes as much to Socrates, Moses, and Jesus as to any ethnographer.

This approach claims two chief characteristics. First, it is concretely grounded. It describes the way particular persons in particular social settings understand the society and their own lives within it. It hedges against overgeneralizing its findings by identifying ideas in relation to those who hold them. Second, this approach is holistic. It seeks to show the coherence of whole patterns of meaning, experience, and moral judgment. It asks how perceived facts, axiomatic assumptions, and felt loyalties come together in a mode of moral discourse. It refers to the texts of high culture to interpret contemporary popular culture. Thus, for example, it sees the "California culture" that nurtures these alternative religious movements as itself the youngest child of all-American parents, not an aberrant orphan. This approach contrasts with and seeks to complement the relatively piecemeal, precategorized results of conventional survey research into values and attitudes, on one hand, and the nonempirical sweep of cultural history, on the other. Let me next say something about the assumptions this approach makes and the methods it uses.

The coherence of social life rests on the convictions we share about its moral meanings. We can act and experience momentarily without conscious reference to these meanings, but we cannot *know* what we are doing or feeling without thinking about it in their light. Social and economic conditions influence our thinking, but they do not do it for us. Instead they intersect with culture in speech to provide the crux of social action. The moral sense we make of our lives, and of one another, takes the form of discourse about what is good, which acts are right, and who is virtuous. Concern for the actual content of this moral discourse and respect for its integrity as a living text mark the starting point of this study. I will take what people say about how they see, judge, and make sense of their lives as raw evidence for the way they make and change their culture.

Understood in ethical terms, the ideas we hold give us a model of and for social reality. They tell us what is so, and what we ought to do about it. They mirror the world we enter every day, and they point out the path we ought to take through it, so that we can justify self and society only in relation to each other. To hold moral discourse central to the study of social life is not to imagine ordinary persons as moral philosophers-writ-small, but rather to recognize that they, like us, ask themselves "What should I do now? Why?" And that their answers matter just as much to them as do ours to us.

This approach enables ideologically and socially distinct movements to respond to the same fundamental ethical questions:

What is good in itself?

What makes an act right?

What makes a person worthy of praise or blame?

What concrete cases decisively test these general views?

We can, then, ask philosophically unified questions both of different traditions in our culture and of individuals in different movements allied with given traditions. We can also analyze their answers in light of ethical theories tied to the sweep of western high culture, yet now being re-created or changed through the concrete experience of persons who live in a particular generation, time, and place in American society.

Such a binocular vision, coupling the cultural autonomy and inner logic of ideas with their specific social contours, leads to joining the methods of descriptive ethics and interpretive sociology. To apply these methods we need to know enough about the formal beliefs of a given movement to translate the general ethical terms of our inquiry into the peculiar patterns of meaning each movement affords its participants. (Not, "What is virtue?" for example, but "What does it mean to be born again and live like Jesus, to be Christ-like?") I have tried to spend enough time and effort in each of the movements studied to become familiar with the shared language and activity through which its members appropriate a public ideology and communicate their private experience. Aided by participant-observation and informal interviewing beforehand, I have sought to engage individual members of these groups in the sort of moral conversation that focuses the felt truth of their own lives upon the wider society and culture. By beginning with moral biography and fastening on the crucial events, relationships, situations, and background social structures that frame an ethic, I seek to distinguish the social location and contours of particular ideas. By developing a reflective, reason-giving dialogue about the meaning of the actual problems central to a person's life, I seek to elicit the mode of discourse, the logic of argument, and the constellation of symbols which hold moral ideas together. In tandem, moral biography and dialogue, carried out in the context of particular groups and institutions, are directed to the end of tracing out the process through which culture gives meaning to the very social experience that transforms it. (See Appendix IV for further comments on research methods.)

I describe the transformation of moral meaning for sixties youth who have joined a millenarian Pentecostal sect (The Living Word Fellowship), a Zen Buddhist meditation center (Pacific Zen Center), and a human potential training organization (Erhard Seminars Training, *est*). Each case study follows a similar format. The movement is first introduced by a short sketch of its institutions and history, its social organization and the composition of its membership. Its formal ethic is briefly presented in terms much like those the movement itself uses in presenting its ethic to newcomers. Second, this ethic *as appropriated by sixties youth in each movement* is analyzed according to categories of ethical evaluation this study brings to it. Third, the felt meaning of each ethic for sixties youth is followed out into different areas of their lives: (1) their inner experience of themselves; (2) their interpersonal relationships, gender roles, courtship, and marriage; (3) their education, work, and social status; (4) their politics and vision of society.

As representatives of the three major types of alternative religious movements that have flourished in our society since the 1960s (conservative Christian, neo-Oriental, and psychotherapeutic), these three cases can be identified as evaluative outlooks adopted by the young in response to their experience of discontinuous cultural change in America during the 1960s. In the study's last chapter, I will compare these three outlooks, the social audiences to which they appeal most specifically, and the organizational arrangements and ways of life they accompany most closely. I will ask how generalizable to the larger society are their solutions to its moral problems. In reply I will examine the new influence exerted by conservative Christian, neo-Oriental, and psychologized ethics on the civil religious rhetoric of American politics since the late 1970s. I conclude by reflecting on what the process of getting saved from the sixties tells us about the social nature of moral ideas and how they change.

Now, at the outset, I would like to consider the conflict between mainstream culture and the sixties counterculture, to which these religious movements as a class are successors, and in terms of which they acquire their special significance for their young members. I will interpret this conflict primarily on the level of religious meanings and moral norms, where it appears as a crisis of culture. I will base this interpretation on a set of distinctions made between different *styles* (not contents) of ethical evaluation. These ideal types are intended to provide no narrow, detailed field of vision for a recent chapter of our social history, but a wider, more general view of American morality in a social context. From this point of view, then, let us begin by looking backward at the sixties as an era of upheaval in which the moral authority and the rationale of established social institutions were questioned, found wanting, and opposed.

ACKNOWLEDGMENTS

I wish to thank all those who made this work possible. I can only begin to return their kindness by extending it to others.

To my advisers—Robert Bellah, Ralph Potter, Ann Swidler—goes my deepest gratitude for their research and teaching, their patience and inspiration, on all of which I have drawn heavily.

I am indebted to Arthur Dyck, Preston Williams, Nur Yalman, and to the late Talcott Parsons as teachers and mentors. They deserve much thanks, as do the following readers, critics, and friends of this work in its several versions and parts: James Luther Adams, Dick Anthony, Daniel Bell, John Coleman, Robert Coles, Harvey Cox, Clifford Geertz, William Hutchison, David McClelland, Richard Madsen, Masotoshi Nagotomi, Jacob Needleman, Benjamin Paul, David Riesman, Tom Robbins, Renato Rosaldo, Quentin Skinner, Don Stone, Philip Stone, and William Sullivan; Kobun Chino-roshi, Richard Baker-roshi, Lewis Richmond-sensei, Rev. Walter Willetts, and Victor Gioscia.

The Danforth Foundation supported the initial stages of my thesis research in 1973-1976, in conjunction with the Society for Values in Higher Education. The Ford Foundation and its Committee on Public Policy and Social Organization supported the 1977-1978 period, in which I did the great bulk of the writing. Dean Krister Stendahl and the faculty of Harvard Divinity School provided a scholarly home for me during this time. The New Religious Movements Program of the Graduate Theological Union enabled me to do follow-up research in the Bay Area of California in 1978. I am truly grateful to all of them, and to the Princeton Institute for Advanced Studies for its generous 1977-1978 invitation. I am also indebted to the Committee on the Study of Religion and the Department of Sociology at Harvard University, and to the Department of Sociology at the University of California, Berkeley, where I studied; and to Emory University and its Candler School of Theology, where I began teaching, while working on this book.

Parts of chapter 3, framed by material drawn from chapters 1 and 5, appeared in "New Religious Movements and the Problem of a Modern Ethic," *Sociological Inquiry*, vol. 49, nos. 2-3 (Summer 1979). Parts of chapter 4 likewise appeared in "The Moral Logic of Conversion and Cultural Change," *Daedalus*, vol. 110, no. 4 (Fall 1981). The illustrations and text on pp. 98-99 are drawn from Katsuki Sekida, *Zen Training* (John Weatherhill, 1975).

My special thanks to Pamela Chance, who typed the manuscript, and David Hackett who indexed it; to David French, who lived with its inception; and to Kristin Mann, who sustained its writing with the care of a true companion and the understanding of a fellow scholar.

Finally, I wish to thank all of those Pentecostal Christians, Zen students, and *est* graduates who have given something of their lives to the heart of this work.

CULTURE AND COUNTERCULTURE
Looking Backward at the Sixties

1

Each of us holds ideas of right and wrong. We ground them in our experience of life and through them we make sense of that experience. They enable us to regulate our behavior, to justify and criticize ourselves. Society instructs us in this activity and sanctions it. Culture gives us patterns of meaning to order it. These patterns are woven in distinct styles of ethical evaluation which turn out to be quite few in number, though each possesses great range and subtlety in its application. Thus culture allows us to respond to the diversity of our experience and circumstances even as it defines the integrity of their meaning. How does this process of response and definition actually unfold? How does it shift direction in times of social change? How do moral meanings come to be transformed?

To answer concretely, let us follow the course of sixties youth raised on traditional ethics they came to deny in favor of countercultural values, only to find these, too, impossible to live out, however hard they tried. And try they did—on drugs and in love, on communes and at work, at sit-ins and be-ins. "Nobody tried harder," one recalls, yet "life was a downer for me in the world." Why?

> I didn't know what I wanted. No, I wanted happiness, but I didn't know what it was. I thought it was being high twenty-four hours a day, and I couldn't get it. Now I know it's being contented. In the world that's impossible—there's always something wrong with you—but the Lord takes you just the way you are and if you've got something wrong in your heart, He'll deliver you from it. All you have to do is obey His Word.

At the end of their youth and the decade they converted to religious movements that have enabled them to resolve their moral dilemma, whether in the process of getting saved and being born again as charismatic Christians, seeking enlightenment along Eastern paths, or finding self-realization in the human potential movement.

These are the changing lives that focus the attention of this study, the voices that make up the heart of its text. But before we can grasp their moral meaning, we must look at the cultural traditions that fostered them, let them down, and then offered them the resources for their reintegration. Contrasting styles of ethical evaluation inherent in these traditions structured the conflict of values between mainstream culture and counterculture during the 1960s, and they have shaped its mediative transformation in alternative religions during the 1970s. These conservative Christian, neo-Oriental, and psychotherapeutic movements have resolved the problems this conflict framed, by recombining elements of its opposing sides into unified ethics that have given new meaning to a generation's experience and new purpose to their lives since the sixties.

With the storm of events that swept across America in the 1960s—a bitter war, racial strife, student protest—there occurred an underlying disaffection from traditional convictions of what this society and its way of life were about. This occurred among greater numbers of Americans than ever before and among more persons from different backgrounds than before—among the socially privileged as well as among the relatively deprived. An attitude of frustration and disillusionment with the society's seeming failure to enact its own highest ideals began to grow, particularly among the young. By many measures it has continued into the 1980s, spreading to an entire generation of youth and beyond, although expectations of radical change and actions of overt protest have diminished.[1] The cresting wave of the counterculture has passed, but the currents of America's meaning still remain confused in its wake.

Let us begin by examining those two interpretations of reality in America which have anchored traditional beliefs in our society and its way of life and have sustained loyalty to its ideals up until the 1960s: biblical religion and utilitarian individualism.[2]

Historically, the Protestant Christian variant of biblical religion began with the Reformation and arrived in America with the original colonists, particularly New England's Puritans. They understood themselves to be a nation elected by God and subject to his laws for a millennial purpose. Their vision of "God's new Israel" was validated for later generations by America's successful revolution and subsequent growth. Lincoln reaffirmed this vision in the Civil War. It found twentieth-century spokesmen in such figures as Woodrow Wilson and William Jennings Bryan, and latter-day defenders among the Fundamentalists.[3]

The second interpretation of reality in America, utilitarian individualism, began with the rise of the middle class in late medieval Europe and the concomitant development of a market economy. Its first great spokesman was Thomas Hobbes. For America its chief popularizers were John Locke and his followers in the tradition of the social contract. Utilitarian individualism as a cultural outlook has strong implicit ties with Anglo-American social science, from classical economics in the eighteenth and early nineteenth centuries to social Darwinism in the later nineteenth century to present-day social exchange theories. Its growing influence over American life derives in part from the compatibility of utilitarian individualism with the conditions of modernity: technological economic production, bureaucratic social organization, and empirical science.[4]

AMERICAN MORAL CULTURE I:
BIBLICAL RELIGION

Let us look at biblical religion as a cultural system that embraces religious meanings, moral norms, and ideas of the social order. In its revelational form, biblical religion traditionally conceives reality in terms of an absolute objective God who is the Creator and Father of all human beings. God reveals his will to them in sacred scripture and he commands them to obey him. God's commandment and man's obedience are themselves the basis of moral goodness, rather than God's goodness being the basis or reason for obeying his commandment. To be good, in short, obey God. Do so because he is God, not simply because he is good. Morality rests neither upon philosophical reason nor ecclesiastical casuistry but directly upon revelation and the grace of God that engenders faith. It is our duty to obey God's commandments, and we are guided in doing so by conscience. What matters is the action done or left undone and, even more, the faithful intention of the agent to obey God. *Freedom* means freedom to do the right act, the act one is obliged to do by God's commandment. To be free is to be free from sin, which is equivalent to being in a state of obedience to God and possessing a morally virtuous character.[5]

In typological terms biblical morality embodies an *authoritative* style of ethical evaluation. This style is oriented mainly to an authoritative moral source (God or Marx, for example). Its will is revealed to us directly or via some scripture or institution (Bible or *Kapital,* Papacy or Party), discerned by literal exegesis and by faith. An act is right because it is commanded by this authoritative source and to do it, therefore, is an act of obedience, the cardinal virtue of this ethic. Biblical religion poses the moral question, "What should I do?" in the form, "What does God command?" The ensuing answer specifies that act which is "obedient" and "faithful." Moral disagreement is resolved by further exegesis and greater familiarity with scripture and, ultimately, by conversion. The authoritative style of ethical evaluation prescribes and forbids particular acts more specifically than does any other ethical style. It does so by means of fixed commandments and regulations that can be applied to specific cases. (The typology of ethical evaluation is outlined on the following page and described more fully in Appendix 1.)

Biblical morality tells us, "Do that act which God commands." It asserts that there are features of an act itself (being commanded by God), besides the good or bad consequences it produces, that make it right. By judging that certain acts are right and obligatory in themselves, not only because of their consequences, biblical morality holds to a *deontological* theory of right action.[6] This stands opposed to utilitarian morality, which

STYLES OF ETHICAL EVALUATION

Style / Dimension	Oriented to	Mode of knowledge	Discourse	Right-making characteristic	Virtue
Authoritative	Authority (God)	Faith/ conscience	What does God command?	Commanded by God	Obedience
Regular	Rules	Reason	What is the relevant rule, principle?	Conforms to rules	Rationality
Consequential	Consequences	Cost-benefit calculation	What do I want?/What will most satisfy it?	Produces most good consequences	Efficiency
Expressive	Self and situation	Intuition/ feelings	What's happening?	Expresses self/ responds to situation	Sensitivity

(Adapted from Ralph Potter, *Nuclear Dilemma*; see n. 2.)

defines the rightness or wrongness of acts solely by the goodness or badness of their consequences.

Biblical religion, discussed thus far in its revelational form, also includes a rationalist line of development. This likewise holds to a deontological theory of right action, but is characterized by a rule-governed or *regular* style of ethical evaluation. It is oriented mainly to rules or principles of right conduct as discerned by reason. An act is right, not only by virtue of its consequences but because it conforms in itself to rules of action accepted as relevant by reason. It also accords with the regularity of nature and human existence. To do the act, therefore, is reasonable. In this sense the rationalist believer holds that God commands an act because it is right, not that an act is right because God commands it. The regular style poses the moral question, "What should I do?" by asking "What is the relevant rule, law, or principle?" It answers by specifying that act which is "right" and "obligatory." Moral disagreement is resolved by reasoning dialectically. That is, one moves from a particular problem (whether to take someone's life, for example) to its solution, which is generalized to principles ("It is wrong to kill.") that are then tested against other problems (self-defense, war, euthanasia), and so on, to increasingly abstract principles ("Treat all persons as ends in themselves and never merely as means.") that are internally consistent and prescriptively generalizable to the widest range of cases. *Rationality*, defined by canons of consistency and generalizability, is the cardinal virtue of the regular ethic. After the authoritative ethical style, the regular style gives the most specific prescription of right acts by ruling out certain acts in themselves, regardless of consequences, because they fail to meet prior fixed criteria of right conduct.

The regular style arises from an Aristotelian ethic that Aquinas Christianized and interpreted within a framework of law that has both Stoic and Hebraic origins. It runs through the rationalist strands of Enlightenment philosophy. It influences the viewpoints of liberal Christianity, Judaism, and philosophical humanism in American culture, and it informs American legal institutions.

Biblical Morality and Society

Protestant Christianity makes each person an *individual*. He stands alone before God, stripped of the ritual-sacramental and legal mediation of the Catholic church and of the hierarchical status and property-specific social ties of feudalism.[7] Every man is equal before God, because each man is alone before him. Because the Protestant Christian is always directly before God, abstracted from all his social relations, he no longer finds his moral duties fixed for him as a function of his social identity, as in a traditional society or in the classical ethic of Aristotle and its medieval modification by Aquinas. Now he is to be a sovereign moral agent, unbound by the duties of office, status, or political power and free to make his own commitments. At the same time, however, he is faced with absolute moral demands revealed as God's will, which are to be fulfilled by autonomous action within the world.

In this last respect and so in several others, the individualism of biblical religion differs from that of utilitarianism. In Protestant Christianity the individual leaves behind his place in society to stand before God, but his compliance with divine commands takes institutionalized form in the society at large. Luther severed the identification of the church with any concrete social organization and located the true church in the souls of the faithful. Thus the visible church was secularized, in effect, while the true church was invisibly expanded to include all of society within a holy community. Religious action now became identified with social life in its entirety, not just with one organizationally bounded sector of it. Calvin and the reformed church tradition elaborated an institutional structure to actualize religious convictions in society. This structure was invested with the control needed to insure the solidarity of the faithful and with the power needed to transform the earthly kingdom. Calvinism conceived of a "holy community destined by divine mandate, but implemented by *human agency*, to bring into being a kingdom of God on earth."[8] Church and polity cooperate to create a social order in which Christian charity and civic virtue foster each other. In this way ascetic Protestantism invested the layman's worldly work, including politics, with the value of a religious vocation. It institutionalized that work as a contribution to building a community whose ends were religious and moral.[9] The monastery was gone, but the rigor of the monastic ethic was carried into the society at large so that each man became a monk in the world.[10]

Individual voluntarism is, then, an important element of Protestant Christianity, but the collective and social idea of the holy community predominates. This idea gave rise to the Puritan understanding of America as "a nation under God," elected by God to be an exemplary "City upon a Hill," and held by him to a biblical covenant. To serve God and work out their own salvation, writes John Winthrop, these "members of Christ" must "followe the counsel of Micah, to do justly, to love mercy, and to walke humbly with our God. For this ende, wee must be knit together in this worke as one man, wee must entertaine each other in brotherly Affeccion. . . ."[11] Social life, in sum, goes on within the context of a religious and moral community. Social life is dedicated to religious ends. It is collectively bound by objective moral judgment regarding both the rightness of its actions and the goodness of its ends.

AMERICAN MORAL CULTURE II: UTILITARIAN INDIVIDUALISM

Where biblical religion begins with the notion of an absolute God, utilitarianism begins with the individual person as an agent seeking to satisfy his own wants or interests.[12] Where obedience to divine commands defines right action and thus moral goodness for the Christian, utilitarianism defines the rightness of actions by the goodness of their consequences in terms of satisfying one's wants. The utilitarian, then, really faces two questions in order to act, instead of the Christian's single question, "What does God command?" The utilitarian first asks, "What do I want?" or "What are my interests?" His answer to this first question defines the goodness of consequences. This, in turn, determines the answer to his second question, "Which act will produce the most good consequences, that is, will most satisfy my wants?" Utilitarianism is quite clear about which acts are right: those that produce the greatest amount of good consequences. It is less clear about what consequences are good, usually taking wants or interests as given or self-evident in a way that suggests notions like happiness, pleasure, or self-preservation to define what is good in itself.

Because self-interest determines right action, freedom for the utilitarian is freedom *from* restraint, freedom to pursue his own unspecified ends, whatever they may be. This stands opposed to the biblical or humanist freedom *to* do the right act as specified by divine command or dialectical reason.[13] For utilitarian individualism, self-interest replaces biblical commandment as a moral starting point. *Technical reason*—the rationalization of means to maximize given ends—replaces conscience as moral guide.[14] Because the right act is the one that *maximizes* good consequences, choosing the right act becomes an empirical question of accurately calculating consequences, not an evaluative question of conscientiously judging acts themselves.

In typological terms, utilitarian individualism embodies a *consequential* style of ethical evaluation. This means it is oriented toward the wants of agents to define what is good and to the empirical calculation and prediction of the consequences of given acts to determine which act is right. An act is right because it produces the greatest amount of good consequences. The moral question, "What should I do?" is posed in two parts. First, "What do I want?" and second, "Which act will yield the most of what I want?" The ensuing answer specifies the act that will be most efficient or effective in producing a desired result. The efficiency of agents in maximizing the satisfaction of their wants is the cardinal virtue of this ethic, not their obedience or rationality. The consequential style prescribes particular acts less specifically than any other ethical style, since it judges all acts not in themselves but by their effectiveness in producing desired consequences. Acts per se are merely instrumental procedures for utilitarianism. This gives the agent utter leeway in choosing the most useful act. Behind this choice lie the substantive moral questions of intrinsic value ("What is the nature of the good to be sought?") and justice ("Whose good is to be sought?"). Presuming general agreement about the goodness of consequences, the consequential style resolves disagreements about the rightness of a given act by rechecking the empirical evidence and calculations used to reckon that act's consequences. Failing resolution by rechecking the facts, it resorts to social-scientific explanation of why different persons perceive the facts differently.

To repeat, utilitarianism does not accept the deontological theory that certain acts are right in themselves, which biblical religion holds. Instead, it holds to a consequential or *teleological* theory of right action. This means that what makes an act right is the amount of good consequences it produces. It is by this logic that utilitarianism states that an act is right if and only if it will produce *at least as great a balance of good over bad consequences* as any available alternative act.

Utilitarian Morality and Society

What is the social genesis and what are the social implications of this consequential moral style? For utilitarianism, what an act *does* makes it right, not what an act *is*. In feudal society the duties and rights of men were defined by what they *were*—peasant, serf, lord—in relationship to the land. Among the new middle class, which was unlanded, social station was derived from what a person *did*, that is, the usefulness of his individual work and its contribution to society.[15] Status was to be earned instead of ascribed, and it was earned by individual achievement. Like radical Protestantism, the utilitarian viewpoint dismissed feudal social identities and exposed every individual to the same standards of judgment, likewise extending ethical universalism. All men are equal in both ethics. However, for Luther all men are equal by virtue of their relation to the highest authority, God. For Hobbes all men are equal by virtue of their relation to the most basic drive, self-preservation. Protestantism relates the individual to the absolute and personally unique judgments of God. Utilitarianism relates the individual to the constant end of his own self-preservation. It also relates him to the shifting, comparable (to objects as well as other persons) and impersonal judgments of the relative utility of means to the end of self-preservation. Every man has his price in this sense, just as every thing does.

An analogous separation of ends and means occurs in the economic sector. In a manorial economy production and consumption are performed by the same persons. They grow what they eat, make what they wear, and build what they live in. In a market economy these two processes become separated. Here one must calculate the consequences of different amounts and sorts of production on an uncertain market in order to sustain a given level of consumption from it. Now we must take our goods to market to find out what they are worth. Their value appears to inhere in their exchange, not in the goods themselves as a simple function of the labor, land, or materials that went into their production, nor of the needs they satisfy in their consumer.[16] In a market it is vital to calculate outcomes accurately in terms of self-interest and to coordinate means efficiently to maximize these outcomes. Conformity to fixed commands or rules preestablishing particular acts as right will not suffice. Nor will good intentions, no matter how faithful. In a market economy only results count.

Utilitarian individualism locates the end of human action in the subjective satisfaction of self-interest rather than in objectified obedience to God's will or compliance with rational principles. We ought not to injure others because in the long run it does not serve our own interest in self-preservation to do so, not because God forbids it or reason refutes it.[17] No authority or reason beyond the individual can make an act right.[18] "Right" acts have become "useful" acts—useful, that is, to their agent. As an agent's interests or an act's consequences vary, so does what constitutes the right act.[19] This consequential logic places utilitarianism at odds not only with biblical morality but with any ethical system that uses rules and direct commands to specify that a particular act is itself right or wrong. (For example, "Thou shalt not kill," or "It is wrong to kill.") Because doing the right act is a matter of choosing *whatever* means effect his desired end, utilitarianism does not direct the individual agent to do or not do any particular act in itself. Insofar as rules and commands prescribing acts and intentions in themselves do, in fact, form and transmit norms in social life, utilitarianism is disposed inherently toward moral normlessness. Its almost exclusive concern with outcomes makes for the breakdown of any autonomous regulatory structure.[20] Prescriptions follow entirely from factual consequences. Utility displaces duty. Note that utility *as a norm*, not merely self-interest, tends to undermine conformity to act-specific commands or moral rules for their own sake. A principled commitment to utility, which is itself moral, thereby tends to result in moral normlessness.

(Recognition of this difficulty and attempts to solve it *as a philosophical problem* have taken the form of *rule-utilitarian* moral theory, which acknowledges the central place of rules in morality, but argues that rules are determined and justified by the consequences of their recognition. Instead of asking which *act* will produce the greatest good consequences, this theory asks which *rule* will do so. Rule-utilitarianism still holds to the principle of utility and its consequential logic, but it uses them to evaluate rules instead of particular acts. It thereby tends to stabilize moral rules and give them more autonomy. It does so by requiring the agent, once she has assessed which complete set of rules produces by its recognition the greatest balance of good consequences for everyone, to act according to the relevant rule of that set in any particular case, even when a given act contrary to the rule would seem to yield better consequences in that particular case. While moral rules must be justified by their consequences in this view, an act violating a moral rule cannot itself be so justified. Acts can only be justified in the regular style, by whether or not they comply with the relevant rule.[21]

(Recognition of the difficulty of coordinating the actions of self-interested individuals in a market-oriented utilitarian society, and attempts to resolve this difficulty *as a social problem*, have taken the form of bureaucratic social organization. Indeed, bureaucratic organization provides the social structure of plausibility for rule-utilitarian moral thought. Bureaucracy, too, sets up procedural rules and justifies compliance with them as means to utilitarian ends, notably maximum productivity and profit.

Bureaucratic rules are justified by the consequences of their recognition, not by divine authority, dialectical reasoning, or first principles seen to reflect the fundamental nature of reality. Bureaucracy calls on each person to "go along to get along." The individual complies with collective rules, such as corporate regulations, in order to maximize her own benefits, such as salary and promotions, even when a given act contrary to the rules would seem to yield better consequences to the client or corporation in a particular case.)[22]

The plausibility of utilitarian culture's solutions to its moral problems relies on the social conditions in which it developed. First, in order to determine the right act in terms of its consequences, utilitarianism needs a method. It invokes a "calculus" or cost-benefit analysis to indicate which act will produce the *greatest amount* of good consequences on balance. Second, in order to fit the data of consequences to this calculus, utilitarianism needs a principle to standardize their goodness. It posits that what makes consequences good (for example, the intensity and duration of the pleasure they provide) is itself quantifiable and summable. This makes all consequences of every different sort of act comparable to one another, no matter what their particular form or quality may be. Utilitarian individualism then allows each person to pursue her own interests, based on her own wants. Wants are given and are not themselves subject to moral evaluation. This implies that there exist no common standards of moral evaluation applicable to individual wants; or, if there are, that they are less important than the right of each person to pursue her own interests. It also implies a belief in the basic empirical identity or harmony of individual self-interest among persons.[23]

Now it is more plausible under certain social conditions than others to treat what is good in terms of quantifiable consequences, to take human wants as unquestionably given, and to identify individuals' own interests with one another. First, when we experience different concrete ends to be essentially alike, then such ends can be comparably ordered, summed, and selected from without recourse to any moral standards for their qualitative differentiation and appraisal. Second, when one or several means can achieve a wide variety of concretely different ends, then these ends may be identified with one another and taken as givens without recourse to moral standards. Precisely these two conditions are provided by a market economy; first, in the form of a price or cost and, second, in the form of the all-purpose utilities of money and that technical knowledge which is equivalent to power. Alvin Gouldner makes the point,

> A large variety of concrete ends may be viewed as essentially alike when they are all for sale on the market and thus all have a price. And in a market economy there is a thing that permits the routine acquisition of a wide variety of concrete ends, namely, *money....* There is one other all-purpose utility in middle class society, and that is knowledge. In order to appraise consequences, one must know them; in order to control consequences one must employ technology and science.[24]

The consequential moral logic of utilitarianism relies on the conditions of a market economy for its plausibility. So does the Lockean assumption of a harmonious identity of individual interests. This in turn underlies the premise of the mutual advantage of exchange, which is used to advance the market economy as a model for social action in general. By this assumption the multiple interests of each utilitarian individual are correlated with one another, and the interests of one individual are correlated with those of every other individual, leaving each ideally free and able to maximize his own self-interest.

Utilitarian definition of individual action by its consequences for the agent extends to interaction among individuals and profoundly affects the idea of social relations. Utility becomes the principle governing social relationships, rather than duties (from which correlative rights derive) defined by revealed commandments, moral rules, and traditional social statuses. The claims an individual can make on others are seen to depend on the contributions he makes to those others. Conversely, the claims they can exert on him depend on the benefits he receives from them. Robert Bellah characterizes the connection between these sorts of social relationships, utilitarian moral logic, and its idea of the social order:

> The tradition of utilitarian individualism expressed no interest in shared values or ends since it considered the only significant end to be individual interest maximization, and individual ends are essentially random. Utilitarianism tended therefore to concentrate solely on the rationalization of means, on technical reason. As a result the rationalization of means became an end in itself. . . . Society like everything else was to be used instrumentally. The key term was organization, the instrumental use of social relationships. "Effective organization" was as much a hallmark of the American ethos as technological inventiveness.[25]

The ideal of the Christian community in which social relations manifest the *virtue* of charity gives way to a collectivity of individuals whose social relations manifest the *contingent fact* of reciprocity (not, strictly speaking, cupidity). One gives in order to get, or because one has already gotten. One does not give in order to give.[26]

Assessments of utility in terms of reciprocity as a contingent fact—give only if you get—affected relationships among persons, and also between persons and the society as a whole, which appears in utilitarian culture as the state.[27] The political loyalty of the person as citizen depends increasingly upon the state's contribution to her individual well-being. Public policy, like private action, is judged by reference to its consequences for the interests of individuals. The biblical holy community, dedicated to common ends and bound by objective moral judgments, has become entirely privatized. In the form of the state, society is itself demystified. It starts on the road, first, to laissez faire neutrality, in which its legitimacy derives from how far it permits its citizens to pursue their individual interests. Later it also develops in the direction of the welfare state, whose legitimacy derives from what it can do for the individual well-being of its citizens, not in what it obliges each of them to do for the general well-being and the moral good of the community.

To summarize the contrasts between biblical religion and utilitarian individualism, we note that biblical religion presupposes agreement on ends. In its society there is a recognized list of virtues, a fixed set of commandments and derivative rules, and an institutionalized connection between obedience to commandments, practice of virtues, and attainment of the society's ultimately religious ends. Social contract theorists in the eighteenth century and utilitarians in the nineteenth describe the moral order of a society already structured by individualism. The social order is no longer defined by a preexisting framework of common moral ends and rules within which each individual must live. Rather it is the sum of the individual wants and interests of all those individuals who collectively constitute it. Society is a collection of individuals. Divine commandments and moral rules are transformed via the principle of utility into instrumental strategies for gaining the ends of private satisfaction. Individuals seeking to maximize their own satisfaction within a neutral state happily end up creating public prosperity and social harmony, by the assumption of an inherently harmonious identity of their individual interests.[28]

The contrast between biblical religion and utilitarian individualism can be seen most clearly by juxtaposing the biblical covenant and the Hobbesian social contract.[29] In the biblical myth Adam and Eve begin innocently in a garden of paradise ruled by God's purpose and command (Genesis 2:15-17). They disobey, are cast out, and society begins. God then makes a covenant with an already existing society, which subjects its people to a preexisting law and moral judgment of divine origin in return for divine favor. In the contractarian myth individual men are alone in a "state of nature," where life is "solitary, poor, nasty, brutish, and short." Nature's fearful dangers drive them to constitute society, via the contract, out of self-interest. Society rests on each individual's "right of self-preservation," which requires of him no correlative duties to others. Nor does it oblige them to allow him to exercise this right. Society arises as a prudential alternative to the war of all against all that would otherwise ensue in this state of nature; it is thus the best means for each individual to preserve his own life (and liberty, and property). It is not a community bound by divine command or fixed moral law. No divine or natural law imposes on men fixed duties to one another and society, from which their rights derive.

By this construction utilitarian culture detached the meanings of *society* and of a human *right* from their earlier moral connotations. Biblical religion and classical ethics both had emphasized the primacy of *duties*, defined by divine commands or moral principles. They insisted that if a person failed to do his duty, he forfeited its correlative rights; and that one person's right entails the corresponding duty of others to respect it. Utilitarian culture separates individual rights from duties in both of these respects. It treats rights either as purely natural (Locke), as purely axiomatic (Rousseau), or as purely calculable (Bentham) from those human wants whose satisfaction would maximize good consequences.[30]

The actual historical relationship between biblical religion and utilitarian individualism is far more complex and ambiguous than the contrasts stressed in the foregoing typifications can suggest.[31] Puritan moralism, for example, had repressive social and psychological effects, from which utilitarian individualism represented a liberating release. However, utilitarianism by itself has not been able to rationalize or justify American social life, especially in those vital areas where general needs have required the sacrifice of self-interest by individuals. Faced with the need for justice, love, and heroism, utilitarian reason has had to go on appealing, however uneasily or vaguely, to the motifs and the prescriptions of biblical religion. Hobbes espoused an ethical egoism and what he took to be a radically empirical scientism, based on a determinist view of human nature and the premise that though God continued to exist, he had no practical effect on human affairs. Locke and his followers obscured the contrast between Hobbesian egoism and biblical religion. After Locke the social contract tradition advanced "natural rights" that apparently corresponded to the duties of biblical morality. On the other hand, biblical religion promised that virtue would be rewarded in this world, not only in the next. Both traditions held individual freedom to be a central value, even though, as we have seen, they meant quite different things by it—the freedom to obey God faithfully or to pursue self-interest efficiently. The increasingly utilitarian slant of this ambiguous central value of individual freedom, and the political egalitarianism it implies, has intensified concern with distributive justice in twentieth-century America, even as it has justified a slackening sense of personal moral obligation to others.

In general, American society continued to invoke the rhetoric and symbols of biblical religion even when it acted according to utilitarian values. But, writes Bellah,

> the most pervasive mechanism for the harmonization of the two traditions was the corruption of the biblical tradition by utilitarian individualism so that religion itself finally became for many a means for the maximization of self-interest with no effective link to virtue, charity, or community. A purely private pietism emphasizing only individual rewards that grew up in the 19th century and took many forms in the 20th, from Norman Vincent Peale to Reverend Ike, was the expression of that corruption.[32]

Intertwined with industrial, technological, and bureaucratic social conditions that have spread throughout a modernizing America, the "bottom line" of utilitarian values has lengthened until today they govern many areas of American life in practice if not in the rhetoric of "one nation under God." They have redrawn the contours of our culture, in the process straining the integrative powers of its civil religion to the point of crisis.

The counterculture of the 1960s rose up from the romantic tradition to repudiate these two conceptions of reality, biblical religion and utilitarian individualism. Its attack was aimed primarily at the latter, since most of the young discounted the biblical tradition as an empty shell already taken over by utilitarian individualism. Many counterculture rebels retained aspects of the utilitarian outlook in their own behavior and attitudes even as they were repudiating it in theory. Moreover, the counterculture itself comprised a wide range of views, some of them at odds with one another. Granting these two facts, I wish nonetheless to review the countercultural critique of the mainstream culture and its alternative views as a coherent if unsystematic set of meanings, norms, and social thought in opposition to utilitarian individualism.

AMERICAN MORAL CULTURE III: THE COUNTERCULTURE

The counterculture begins its conception of reality with the individual, not as an agent rationally pursuing her own self-interest, but as a personality that experiences, knows, and simply *is*.[33] Thus "The way to do is to be." Human nature for utilitarianism was mechanistically determined and primitive. Its psychology of association describes the personality as a largely unorganized collection of wants. Both ideas have become motivationally complex and developmentally fluid in the post-Freudian world. The spread of psychotherapeutic, pharmacological, mystical, and also literary-academic modes of introspection has given a highly reflexive quality to the counterculture's concept of the individual. Self-awareness is the touchstone, not self-preservation and all the achievements that follow from it.

Mixed meanings make up the world in which the counterculture's individual lives, and a mixed moral logic governs her actions in it. Conceptions of the divine, where they do exist, tend to be nontheistic or at least they describe a nonprophetic sort of god who issues no commandments. Nor is the countercultural universe a cosmos structured by natural law or philosophical principle in the usual Western sense. Instead, there is the fundamental assumption of an acosmic monism, that "all is one," pure energy or existence without any enduring structure or *logos*. This monism constitutes the fundamental difference in cognitive orientation between the counterculture and utilitarian culture, which is predicated on philosophical realism or dualism—the view that material objects exist externally to us and are independent of our experience. Utilitarianism begins with the indissoluble distinction between subject and object, self and other. It posits the post-

Cartesian self as a fixed entity over against the mathematical-mechanical universe which that self knows and uses as an object, mind versus matter. Countercultural monism also breaks with the pre-Cartesian dualism of biblical religion, which posits the existence of an objective God and a correlative individual soul. This break is reflected not only by the counterculture's rejection of the conventional Christian outlook but by its acceptance of a few mystical Christian writers (e.g., Meister Eckhart) as monistic exceptions to the dualistic rule.

The counterculture's monism permeates those few, rather diffuse moral rules included in its ethic: "Love your brothers and sisters," or just "Love!"; and "Don't hurt anybody." Universal love and noninjury as obligations do not emanate from God's biblically revealed will nor from the utilitarian's rational self-interest. They guide a way of living in accord with the monistic assumption that all life is united and all existence is one. Following the rules of love and noninjury is one way that the counterculture defines right action. A moral logic of rules, though little developed and never predominant in the counterculture's ethic, does perform a significant function in it.

What of the utilitarian's definition of right action by its good consequences? This consequential moral style also shows up in the counterculture. So does the definition of the goodness of consequences in terms of how effectively they satisfy individual wants or interests ("Do whatever turns you on. Do your own thing."), to some extent. Ideally, however, the counterculture uses the consequential style to prescribe concretely different acts than does utilitarian culture, because the counterculture defines what constitutes good consequences differently. We might say that the counterculture acts on the principle that "Everybody should always do that act which will produce the greatest amount of love and awareness for all beings—the most good vibes." Not the greatest amount of wealth, power, and technical knowledge—those all-purpose utilities with which each person can then satisfy her own privately given wants and interests. So there is a similarity between utilitarian culture and the counterculture in *how* good consequences determine right actions for both. And there is a crucial difference between them in answering the question of *what* consequences are good. It is on this point—the question of ends—that the counterculture differs most significantly from utilitarian culture, and we will return to it below.

Neither a logic of following rules nor one of maximizing consequences predominates in the counterculture's definition of right action. What does is the idea that everyone ought to act in any given situation and moment in a way that fully expresses himself, specifically his inner feelings and his experience of the situation. This situational and *expressive* approach, as I will call it, has two aspects. First, it is an ethic of impulse ("Do what you feel.") and *self*-expression ("Let it all hang out."). Second, it is an ethic of situational appropriateness ("Go with the flow. Different strokes for different folks."). Impulse and self-expression replace self-interest as the fundamental motives of human action. For its mode of knowledge the counterculture ethic relies on an intuitive, affectively centered self-awareness, an empathic feeling for others, and a relaxed, nonanalytical attention to the present situation. "Be here now," it exhorts, "Get in touch with yourself." By contrast, the utilitarian's maximizing calculus and his technical reason are always aimed toward calculating future consequences. Biblical commands and rules often look back to the past in prescribing, for example, that we keep the promises we have made. For both utilitarianism and the counterculture, *freedom* refers to external conditions of nonrestraint, but now it is freedom to "do your own thing" impulsively rather than to pursue your own interest efficiently. The counterculture's cardinal virtue is sensitivity of feeling, not utilitarian efficiency or biblical obedience.

In typological terms, the expressive style of ethical evaluation is mainly oriented toward the agent's feelings, the feelings of others around him, and to the particular situation in which they find themselves, as discerned by intuition. An act is right because "it feels right," most simply, or because it expresses the inner integrity of the agent and is most appropriate to the situation. The expressive style poses the moral question, "What should I do?" by asking, "What's happening?" and the ensuing answer specifies whatever act feels most fitting in response. Moral disagreement is resolved, if at all, by exchanging discrepant intuitions within the context of an ongoing social interaction, thereby reshaping the situation and the agents' states of consciousness as formed by the situation. The expressive style prescribes acts less specifically than does the regular or authoritative style of biblical religion, but more specifically than the consequential style of utilitarianism. Its prescriptions come from the intuited moral sense of the relevant group or community regarding the most appropriate feeling about a given situation and the most fitting action in response to it.

Several premises are necessary to support the expressive ethic and restrain its tendency to drift toward moral normlessness. These premises are sufficiently fragile (for many of its countercultural professors, at least) to permit its collapse into an image of the consequential style.[34] The hippie's almost exclusive concern with inner feelings, like the utilitarian's with outcomes, threatens to break down any autonomous structure of moral rules. If it does not, this is because the hippie holds the monistic view that one's own self is actually one with other persons' selves and with existence as a whole. This makes one's innermost feelings ultimately integral with those of others and with the transpersonal nature of the universe. Given this premise, the idea of appropriateness resonates not merely with social etiquette, but with the deepest level of religious meaning. There is also the related idea that each individual possesses what I will call a "true inner self" of impulse, feeling, and experience in need of intimate expression to others. One such self simply communicates with other congruent selves to create social relations that are harmonious and loving as well as spontaneous, honest, and "natural." This view assumes that human nature is basically good, in contrast to the biblical view of it as evil yet perfectible and the utilitarian view of it as a mutable mixture of good and evil. A similar basic goodness is attributed to the world of physical nature, which becomes a "gentle wilderness" to engage, instead of an antagonist to master technologically, or an array of neutral phenomena to analyze scientifically.

At first glance the antinomian character of the counterculture's expressive ethic seems to make it antithetical to moral evaluation of individual wants and goals. But given the premises described above, it can be experienced as just the opposite. If we assume that self and other are one, that human nature is good, and that the individual personality can fluently express a pure and true inner self, then we can reopen human ends to moral evaluation. They are needs instead of wants, subject to intuitively shared moral standards and evaluations. Stemming from love instead of self-preservation, these needs are thematized by social life instead of the solitary psyche. They are needs for love, first of all, self-awareness and self-expression; for intimacy, understanding, and friendship with others; for community; for a clean and green physical environment; for simplicity of life, and so on. The litany implies a list of moral and social virtues, however psychologized its formulation.

None of the foregoing assumptions satisfies the philosophical realist. He continues to ask what happens when the motivating feelings of one agent in a situation conflict with those of the others and their sense of the situation, as often seems to be the case in fact. If the communication of relevant intuitions has no effect on such disagreement, then there must be a sufficiently communal or cohesive social setting, and enough time and personal willingness for the agents to reform their feelings indirectly through ongoing interaction. This is their only recourse under the expressive style of ethical evaluation, since they can invoke no act-specific commandments, moral principles, or cost-benefit calculations to sway an individual against her own feelings. The heart has its reasons the mind can never know, and the expressive style always rests with them.

Counterculture Morality and Society

The counterculture assumes that all persons can know with certainty what is good by means of direct experience and intuition. They can simply look at and see their own feelings, whether on drugs, making love, or sitting alone in an empty room. And everyone has the same feelings, with the same moral implications to be drawn from them. This substantive and evaluative identity of feelings (in contrast to the utilitarian's instrumental and formal identity of interests) anchors the counterculture's conception of society. The good of the individual is to be aware—to experience and to know herself fully. In relation to others the good is likewise for her and them to experience and "encounter" each other, face to face. They are to do so without the mediation and fragmentation of social roles ("role playing"), striving after status and power ("power tripping"), or the distraction of impersonal and abstract communication ("head tripping"). One seeks to know the *person,* not *about* the person. Social relations are to be informed by the intimacy of gnostic and carnal knowledge rather than by conventional ideas of familiarity or acquaintance, cooperation or exchange. Persons are to *be* with each other, *à la* the "be-in," rather than doing anything in particular together. This ideal is expressed in its extreme form by the countercultural myth of fusion or mystical merger. It is enacted in psychedelic, musical, sexual, and meditative experiences of the individual's self merging and being one with others and all existence.

In this ideal society persons relate to each other as ends in themselves, not as reciprocal means to the satisfaction of their own individual ends. For all the individual impulse and expression it allows, this society is intensely communal. Indeed, individual self-expression is felt to cement such communal social relations. The social structure of the community is egalitarian. Decisions are reached and authority is exercised collegially. Where an individual leader appears, his authority is not a function of bureaucratic office or traditional station, but of an exemplary charisma that makes no demands on others and asserts no superiority over them. Like the guru or sage, such a figure simply does what everyone else does, yet he does it perfectly. Others respond freely to the manifestation of his extraordinary personality, entering of their own impulse into an intensely personal face-to-face relationship with him.

The counterculture's ideal society is exemplified by a small-scale, intimate, collegial, and relatively self-supporting commune. It contrasts with the large-scale, impersonal, hierarchical, and associational bureaucracy that organizes modern society in tandem with the nuclear family. The commune is collectively oriented and stresses interpersonal relatedness over individual achievement. Social roles are diffuse (rotating chores versus a fixed job), status is ascribed (friends, lovers, and mutual helpers versus co-workers), and relationships are highly affective (a warm embrace versus a brisk handshake). The bureaucracy is oriented toward the individual, roles are functionally specific, status is earned by achievement, and relationships are affectively neutral.

We have seen that the counterculture defines the ends of individual activity in terms of self-awareness, self-expression, self-realization, and the like. These categories have a developmental dimension in the counterculture's usage, and this fact has a crucial effect on its view of social affiliation. In seeking to realize oneself rather than maximize one's interests, achievement becomes an internal activity of the psychic or spiritual life, instead of an external activity of the social or economic life. Individuation occurs as a function of some proposed form of spiritual development, which in a monistic context aims at merger or fusion with the whole. Individual achievement in this context does not conflict with social affiliation, for the individual is not seeking to gain the world, at others' expense, but to lose himself. That is, he seeks to give himself to the world and to others. The enlightened personal identity that constitutes the goal of this process of self-realization implies the perfected capacity to enact interpersonally the psychic fact of one's realized unity with all existence. In the countercultural ideal, then, a person's individual achievement leads him toward greater, more intimate, and more sensitive affiliation with others, rather than coming at the expense of it.[35]

The counterculture challenged utilitarian culture at the most fundamental level. It asked what in life possessed intrinsic value, and to what ends ought we to act. Do ever more money and power add up to life's meaning, or do they obscure it? Does ever more efficient organization assure the quality of life, in social and ecological terms, or does it endanger it? The counterculture asked, in short, "What is good?" And it is precisely on this question of ends, in its conception of what has intrinsic value, that utilitarianism both as a philosophy and a way of life is weakest. Its idea of what is good in itself for human beings was found by sixties youth to be either irresolvably implicit (happiness), psychologically simpleminded (pleasure and the absence of pain), or jejune (self-preservation). Maximizing utility in the all-purpose forms of money, power, and technical knowledge no longer seemed the self-evidently right way to live, since the counterculture rejected as good consequences what these utilities are useful for. It rejected key elements of "the good life" of middle-class society as ends good in themselves. Instead it identified them as means that did not, in fact, enable one to experience what is intrinsically valuable—love, self-awareness, intimacy with others and nature.

To ask what has intrinsic value in life is to express concerns institutionalized in the religious sector of a society. During the 1960s the principal forms of that institutionalization in middle-class America began to wane. The mainline Protestant denominations and the Catholic church suffered declines in membership, church attendance, and influence, especially among the young.[36] The countercultural young saw such religion reiterating the verbalism, intellectualism, and lack of ecstatic experience they found in utilitarian culture, as well as its associational, bureaucratic organization. The authoritative and rule-oriented moralism of such religion was an additional if peculiarly biblical offense against the counterculture's sensibility. In general, the counterculture's primary thrust toward unmediated experience led it away from the rationalism of middle-class American religion. Its secondary thrust toward a receptive and monistic holism in conceiving of both the self and the world led it away from the cosmological and psychological dualism of Christianity expressed in distrust of nature and the impulse life.

The counterculture had little affinity for the spirit of asceticism that has shaped the mainstream of American Christianity;[37] even its espousal of the universal love ethic suggested a much greater affinity for the mystical mode and the monist point of view. In Eastern spirituality it found both. It drew on gnostic, mystical, and devotional features of Buddhism, Hinduism, Taoism, and Sufism to form an outlook that gave precedence to direct experience over abstract reasoning, to "being here now" over future-oriented achievement, to harmonizing with nature and others over utilizing them. With roots in America going back to Transcendentalism, Eastern spirituality—particularly in the form of Zen Buddhism—had been expanding its influence in the literary-artistic, bohemian, and psychotherapeutic subcultures since the end of World War II. In the process it developed an articulate familiarity with romantic, aesthetic, and psychological issues crucial to the counterculture.[38] This context was already established by the time Timothy Leary and Richard Alpert introduced psychedelic drugs to a mass American audience and interpreted the drug experience in terms of Eastern spirituality. Thereafter the connection between Eastern religion and the counterculture was explicit and popularly accessible.

ALTERNATIVE ATTITUDES TOWARD MODERN SOCIETY

If we ask why the counterculture emerged, we find answers on several different levels of analysis. On the cultural level there is a tendency toward normlessness, the incapacity to generate substantive values or justify prescriptive rules inherent in the consequential style of utilitarian morality.[39] Also on the cultural level of analysis there exists a deep-rooted tension in America between the way biblical religion or humanism conceives reality and the way utilitarian individualism does so, a tension unrelieved by the latter's growing predominance in practice. If we ask for the social-structural causes of the counterculture, our attention turns to the process of social modernization, the growth of technological economic production, and bureaucratic social organization. As Leary's exhortation to "turn on, tune in, drop out" reminds us, hippies themselves believed that by adopting countercultural views and taking psychedelic drugs they were rejecting not only the utilitarian outlook, but the industrial society and the middle-class way of life it rationalized. Yet hippies were, of course, the children of this class and its society. However prodigal and playful these children, however contradictory their ideas, they represented alternative values already existing *within* modern society, based on certain of its conditions, notably postindustrial work, and reflecting them in turn. Thus, while openness, creativity, and interpersonal sensitivity may interfere with the efficient production of uniform objects by industrial labor, innovative professional, technical, and managerial work requires precisely such expressive qualities to produce complex knowledge and services.[40]

Given this polarity let us recall the cultural patterns we have discussed up to now as styles of ethical evaluation and reexamine them as styles of life, alternative attitudes toward reality that both reflect and react to modern social conditions, that is, to the social institutional conditions attending technologically induced economic growth. We will thereby place the cultural conflict of the sixties within a social context, and establish a frame of reference which may later help us assess post-sixties religious movements. These alternative attitudes may be resolved into four related pairs: (1) ecstatic experience versus technical reason; (2) holism versus analytic discrimination; (3) acceptance versus problem-solving activism; (4) intuitive certainty versus pluralistic relativism.[41]

The *ecstatic, experiential, and expressive attitudes* of the counterculture run contrary to the operation of *technical reason* in conventional society. Instead of seeking to control the world, others, and oneself, the counterculture urges one to experience them fully. Instead of being implicitly machinelike and "uptight," people should be natural and "hang-loose." The looseness of hip dress, language, gesture, and gait all symbolized a "turned-on" personality ideal exactly counter to the efficient organization man neatly turned out in a gray flannel suit. The counterculture imbued sexual, drug, and musical experiences with sacramental significance inasmuch as these represented ecstatic avenues of release from the attitude of technical rationality toward everyday life.[42]

But technical reason is rooted in the nature of technological economic production, and it permeates bureaucratic social organization. To the extent a person participates in either, technical reason constrains her behavior and influences her state of mind. Most obviously, the technologized work process is mechanistic and sequentially organized, standardized and reproducible, unitized and measurable. Human beings are fitted into the archetypal assembly line by "human engineering" and more subtly adjusted by "the human relations approach" to industrial management. Persons become "human resources," arranged by technical reason as means to the end of efficient production.

Bureaucracy likewise relates persons according to their technical functions, not making things but "handling paper and money and people," in C. Wright Mills's phrase. Bureaucratic social relations are delimited by explicit boundaries of competency and jurisdiction for each office and its occupants. These are interconnected by avenues of referral and supervision, appeal and redress—all governed by fixed rules and standard operating procedures to insure consistent and predictable results. Personal intimacy has little place here. Reciprocity is limited formally by the principle of jurisdiction and informally by the splitting of intention between client and bureaucrat. While the client wants a certain action taken on her behalf, the bureaucrat often wants simply to get rid of the client.[43] The sort of active cooperation imposed on various persons by a common agricultural or manufacturing task, even building a car on an assembly line, is less evident in the bureaucratic world although it may reappear in the committees and research groups of postindustrial elites. Bureaucrats and white-collar workers are instead required to manage other persons in order to maximize outcomes essential to their own work as, for example, the salesman must motivate others to buy in order to increase his sales. To manage others and their impressions for profit, one must similarly manage his own feelings; that is, he must sell his personality as well as his time and energy. The engineering ethos extends to the inner life of the individual, adding his private feelings and interpersonal responses into its calculations of efficiency.

The monistic *holism* of the counterculture contrasts with the dualism of utilitarian culture. It also contrasts with the attitude of *analytic discrimination* that inheres in technology and bureaucracy as social institutions.[44] Their division of labor makes reality seem to consist of discretely separated components, analytically related by function and causation, like cogs in the proverbial machine of modernity. Persons, too, are reduced to their functional components. They are educated and employed to perform specific technical functions. The same criterion of technical utility stratifies modern society by occupation, and it influences the selective development of the individual's personality to fit his job. Whatever its social and economic effects, this selectivity produces personal and psychological effects that have become a familiar theme in modern literature and psychotherapy. Alvin Gouldner renders it as follows:

> Because of the exclusions and devaluations of self fostered by an industrial system oriented toward utility, many men develop a dim sense of loss, for the excluded self, although muffled, is not voiceless and makes its protest heard. They feel an intimation that something is being wasted, and this something may be nothing less than their lives.[45]

The counterculture's holistic impulse to put the pieces of modern social life back together also appears in psychotherapies of self-integration, the ecology movement's defense of "the whole earth," and alternative religion's mystical merger of self and other.[46] It takes social form in the ideal commune, where life lies in one coherent piece and all relationships are deeply and diffusely meaningful.

In the reality of modern society, by contrast, life lies in many pieces scattered across different social settings. Each setting contains diverse social relationships, most of them functionally circumscribed and personally superficial.[47] The individual must relate to a great variety of objects, persons, and abstractions at the same time. By creating separate jurisdictions and governing them by special procedures, bureaucracy orders these multiple relationships. It frames separate social existences as roles, each given a place and a person put into it. The individual moves back and forth among these roles while defending the integrity of his personal identity by keeping some distance from most of his roles and playing them "tongue in cheek."[48] Such self-defense relies on the dichotomy between public and private life in modern society.[49] Some professionals, like scientists and intellectuals, may identify themselves almost entirely with their vocations, throwing themselves into their work and bringing it home with them. But private life, in which the individual can let down and just be himself, usually goes on after hours, at home, and, to a degree, around the water cooler. It does not go on around the conference table or on the assembly line. The counterculture perceives this dichotomy as the hypocrisy of role playing and seeks to extend the self-expressive virtues of openness, honesty, and sincerity to all social relationships.[50]

The counterculture opposes two fundamental characteristics of modern social structure, the breaking down of society into many discrete parts and its reintegration *as a system* by the mechanisms of technology and bureaucratic taxonomy. The counterculture conceives society as an organism moved by the spontaneous confluence of feelings, intuitions, and wills. Countercultural ideals favor the relatively unstructured community over the structured society and social movements over established organizations. In this stance the counterculture is not anarchic but it is utopian. It assumes that what I have called a "true inner self" beyond modern social institutions will create and express itself through the communalistic institutions of an alternative social order to come.[51]

The *accepting* and *receptive* attitude of the counterculture toward reality, counseling that we "let it be," conflicts with the *problem-solving activism* of technology. For technology life is an ongoing problem-solving enterprise, where "progress is our most important product." Humans are continuously making the world over, putting it together. The counterculture asserts its contrary view most clearly in ecological terms. "You can't put it together," advises the *Whole Earth Catalogue* below a picture of the Earth. "It *is* together."[52] The sort of steady-state, no-growth economy associated with the communal ideal and backed by the ecological judgment that "small is beautiful" runs counter to the "bigger is better" judgment of modern progress, implicit even in the modernist maxim that "less is more." In the maximizing logic of utilitarianism, carried over into the engineering mentality of technology, "More is better." Better consequences are, by utilitarian definition, a greater amount of good consequences. When asked what he wants, the utilitarian, like Gompers, can simply assert, "More!" Ever-increasing economic growth is, in fact, a prerequisite for realizing the central political value of equality as it is construed in utilitarian culture. "Equality of opportunity" means the opportunity to get more, and unless the entire pie expands, those with small pieces can get more only at the expense of those with larger pieces.

Rejecting the problem-solving and progressive attitudes of modern society, countercultural acceptance also rejects the ethic of achievement. Seeking after status, wealth, and power by means of careerism, and the calculated life planning and deferred gratification it requires, no longer justifies the sacrifice of self-expression and fulfillment in the present. Professional and white-collar work, especially when it demands high commitment and personal identification, is rejected in favor of craft work, manual labor, amateur farming, and unskilled service jobs. This rejection takes place even as white-collar and professional work make up the ever-increasing bulk of a modern society's needs and markets for labor.

The counterculture seeks *intuitive certainty* via direct experience and self-fulfillment within an intimate community. This conflicts with the *pluralistic relativism* inherent in an urbanized, specialized society. Such a society consists of many different social worlds, defined and legitimated in discrepant ways.[53] The individual migrates through these worlds in the course of her daily life and over the course of her lifetime. As she passes from one to the next, she continually reorients herself to meanings that relativize one another by their discrepancy and cast doubt on the existence of any one ultimate meaning by their number. But modern social conditions have not put an end to the need for such meaning. We must still make sense out of the apparently ultimate difficulties of human life, that we suffer deprivation, sickness, old age, and death in a world that is not just. Modern society has given many of us a less miserable and more abundant life, but, as Peter Berger says, "it has not fundamentally changed the finitude, fragility, and mortality of the human condition. What it has accomplished is to seriously weaken those definitions of reality that previously made that human condition easier to bear."[54]

Under the relativizing pressure of our constant migration through discrepant social worlds, the cognitive and normative definitions of modern culture become abstracted and emptied of specific content in order to be flexible. Such emptying is performed by utilitarianism, psychologism, and mysticism, for example, though in quite different ways. Conversely, specific cultural definitions become insulated and defended from change by special social conditions, such as sectarianism. Utilitarian ethics deal with the need for flexibility by detaching intrinsic value from any particular activity and by setting each person at the center of her own universe of calculated consequences. The shortcoming of this strategy, as we have seen, amounts to the moral predicament of utilitarian culture. One ends up knowing the price of everything and the value of nothing.

CAUSES OF THE COUNTERCULTURE

As a crisis of meaning and morality, the counterculture's causes are themselves chiefly cultural. But they have a social-structural context, driven by its own dynamic. Technology has expanded according to its own inner logic of ever-increasing productivity and efficiency. Bureaucracy has expanded to keep pace with the increasing complexity and population of the world created by technological production.

As a result of technological advances two connected changes have occurred in the modern economy which have had important cultural side effects. First, the proportion of the labor force engaged in producing industrial and agricultural goods has declined, while that involved in white-collar and semiprofessional work, especially in services to other persons, has expanded sharply. Work becomes a game *between* persons instead of a game *by* persons against nature or its fabricated forms.[55] It is played face to face instead of side by side. These shifts in occupational structure have placed more people in bureaucratized relationship to one another, spreading the culturally problematic effects of managing others and oneself. Growth in innovative professional and technical work has also lent support to self-expression, self-development, and interpersonal sensitivity as instrumental values. Second, technological advances in production have expanded personal consumption and leisure. This is generally viewed as a great good, since private life is seen to hold compensations and even solutions for the discontents of public life in modern society. It does so, significantly enough, by espousing intrinsic values akin to the counterculture's. Psychologically and socially in the private sphere (1) feelings are to be expressed, not managed, and pleasures enjoyed, not denied; (2) personal identity is to be a diffuse, unique, and ultimate end, not an instrument geared to functional efficiency; (3) relationships are to be intimate and affective, encompass many different activities, and provide profound meaning and enjoyment. These relationships are limited in number and most of them are chosen voluntarily by the individual. Morally, the private sphere centered in the family calls for love and noninjury *as obligations,* for moral universalism ("Do unto others") *on deontological grounds,* and for charity and trust as virtues.[56] As a utilitarian morality of self-interest comes to govern public life in the society, authority and rule-oriented moralities recede into the family, like biblical religion itself. At the same time the private sphere as a whole sponsors an expressive ethic. There each individual is left free to find and fulfill herself however and with whomever she wishes.

The relationship of this private sphere to the rest of modern society is paradoxical. First, what is perceived to be the single greatest advantage of the private sphere—individual freedom and voluntarism derived from an absence of institutional definition—is also the source of its problems. Precisely because the individual is free to construct the order and meaning of her own private life, she experiences its meanings as unreliable and even artificial. They are only functions of inner preference, instead of reflections of the way the world really is "out there." Voluntary associations, from the ski club to the contemporary Christian denomination, have arisen or been modified to fill the institutional vacuum of private life in modern society. But as long as they retain the optional character of private life, their meaning remains unreliable, since it lacks the quality of necessity that belief requires.[57] We believe something because we think *that* something is true, not because we think we need to believe something.

A second paradox in the relation of the private sphere to modern society is that the intrinsic values of the private sphere—which are seen as the values that make life worth living—hold true only within its boundaries.

They are not generalizable beyond it. They respond to the discontents of modernity in the sense that they enable the individual to live with the discontents she feels, not in the sense that they enable her to resolve the social and cultural problems generating those discontents. If, however, the psychological and moral values of the private sphere are generalized to all of social life, what ensues is a position and an historical phenomenon similar to the counterculture of the 1960s.[58]

Why should such a generalization occur? There is evidence that the actual weight of work on our lives, which holds us daily in the public sphere, has lessened over the past fifty years, especially since World War II.[59] Most of us enter the labor force later, leave it earlier, and take more time off. On the job, in the office and kitchen as well as the factory, more education and more labor-saving technology combine to make many of us feel that the work we do does not fully engage our energies and capacities. Overeducated and underemployed workers don't simply grow bored with work more quickly. They look elsewhere more readily for a source of values and a sense of their own worth. They identify themselves more by what they are "into" off the job than by what they do on the job. Finally, on the higher rungs of the job ladder, where work remains demanding and absorbing, its character is growing more interpersonal and knowledge-oriented in ways that support expressive values based in private life. Such work often requires a person to direct his own efforts without close supervision, interact sensitively with diverse others, communicate precise or subtle information to them, and keep learning new skills to cope creatively with changing circumstances. Meeting these occupational needs for continuing flexibility and innovation can lead us toward a more personalistic sort of self-awareness, more concern with our own developing life course, more fluid relations with others, and less deference to authority.

Seeking to understand why the values of private life should become generalized to the public sphere leads us to consider how these values grew up in the first place, within the middle-class family.[60] The middle class produced a new world of childhood, located in the family after it became separated from economic activity by industrialization. Adults went out to work away from the home. The home became a refuge of intimacy and tenderness, love and duty, insulated from the outside economic world of self-interest. A new ethos infused childhood and then youth, via lengthening education, with personalistic psychological values and universalistic moral values based in the family. In particular this new ethos fostered the expectation that each individual would be treated as an end, with the respect and consideration due a uniquely valuable person. The stronger this expectation, the more antagonistic the confrontation between its youthful carriers and the impersonal and instrumental utilitarianism of the technological and bureaucratic world. Many of the upper-middle-class sixties youth whose families and educations most developed this new ethos rebelled not so much against their parents' values as against the larger society's failure to enact these values in its public policy or bureaucratic structure. They charged their parents with hypocrisy for failing to enact the values they espoused *in the home* once they went outside of it.[61]

The large-scale structural changes of social modernization set the scene for the much more specific cultural transformation of the 1960s, but they did not specifically cause it. The rise of the middle class and its new ethos of childhood occurred over several centuries, after all, not in 1960. It occurred throughout the industrializing West, not just in Scarsdale. Social modernization set the scene by enabling diverse, even contrary patterns of moral meaning to grow up in the American mainstream, along the lines we have already typified. Some of these meanings, like the ultimate value of love and self-awareness, the counterculture took from traditional romance, religion, and leisure, or from the emerging ethic of a relatively narrow post-industrial elite. Then it set these words to popular music, amplifying their message across the entire spectrum of social life.

To ask why the counterculture emerged leads to the more specific question of why it emerged when it did, in the 1960s. Its immediate social and economic context largely, if ironically, results from the relative success of the corporate liberal state in realizing the goals of modern industrial society and utilitarian culture in postwar America.[62] From 1945 into the 1960s immense economic growth was accompanied by an absence of wide-spread social conflict, giving rise to a better-educated and "affluent society."[63] The ensuing confidence that ongoing economic growth and increased education would eventually bring about a solution to all our social problems made it possible to look critically at what lay beyond the affluence, which was concentrated in the private sector and in the middle and upper social strata. Americans came to see the poverty and powerlessness of the excluded, especially those also oppressed by racism, no longer as regrettable necessities or as opportunities for charity, but as problems which the entire society was responsible for solving as soon as possible. The promises of liberalism were not completely fulfilled. This perception led to the Civil Rights movement, the New Frontier, and the Great Society. Their problems, in turn, made it clear that the liberal program itself would not suffice to fulfill the promises of liberalism. Racism persisted despite the law. Structural poverty persisted despite more money, education, public housing, and public works. The inability of liberalism to complete its own agenda led primarily to the political revolution of the counterculture's radical activist wing. Radicals saw liberalism's failure resulting from the concentration of effective political power in the hands of an elite unwilling to share it, an issue highlighted by black political militancy.

The cultural revolution of the counterculture's psychedelic wing arose from the postwar generation's experience of affluence not as a promise of panacean security in the future, but as a present fact whose advantages did not add up to happiness or fulfillment. The great goals of corporate liberalism and of the previous generation—material abundance, economic and social security, leisure opportunities, and relative political freedom—had become accomplished facts, and as such were taken for granted by their children. Sixties youth were too young to have experienced anything else, yet they were old enough and educated enough to be convinced that technological society had accomplished its goals at great personal, social, and ecological costs. Now they saw it unable to define convincing goals beyond utility and the comforts it could purchase. With the accomplishment of its economic objectives, what had been deferred for their sake reemerged: personal, cultural, and social goals gathered under the rubric of "the quality of life" and posed as the question of ends.

A second condition of the counterculture's emergence in the 1960s follows from youth as a stage of life genetically rooted in the ethos of middle-class childhood and presently characterized by institutional uninvolvement in work or the family. As a result, youth has a peculiarly free and detached relationship to the economic, political, and public sector of modern society. Its singular institutional tie, the college, can sharpen the attitude of criticality fostered by such detachment, insofar as education actually constitutes a process of coming to the use of one's own understanding.[64] The expansion and humanistic upgrading of higher education in the 1960s contributed to this effect, and to the belief that public policy should derive from expert knowledge and humane feeling instead of following from entrenched or clashing interests. The social effects of these inherent characteristics of modern youth, detachment and criticality, were magnified in the 1960s by the great increase in the sheer numbers of youth. This dramatic change of cohort size, an increase of about 50 percent in a single decade, resulted from the demographic bulge of the postwar baby boom reaching the stage of youth.[65] This increase in numbers made itself felt in the generation's expanded sense of the power and accuracy of their viewpoint, and their expanded sense of the possibility for enacting it in their own lives and in the society at large.

Finally, although the Vietnam War did not cause the counterculture to emerge nor the old order to lose its legitimacy, it catalyzed the conflict of the sixties. To be sure, rising draft calls threatened the young directly, but those youths who led in the protest against it were precisely the ones most assured of being protected by student deferments. For those already favoring radical political ideology it proved the United States to be a counterrevolutionary, neocolonial power. But these were not its principal effects. Most sixties youths saw the Vietnam War, in the force and ultimacy of its horror, as "an example of technical reason gone mad."[66] Destroying a village "in order to save it;" unleashing the largest bombing campaign in history on a relatively small and powerless country in order "to make the world safe for democracy;" killing great masses of civilians and forcing the resettlement of still more; defoliating and decimating the land: the disproportionate, ineffectual, and finally meaningless relation of means to ends raised questions of morality and then sanity that two administrations neither answered nor addressed.[67] Instead their highest officials systematically lied. For many of the young the government that waged this war forfeited its own credibility and legitimacy in a way that catalyzed their rejection of the social and cultural order which that government claimed to represent.

THE AFTERMATH

What can the causes of the counterculture tell us about its effects? Conditions peculiar to the 1960s undeniably played a part in ending the effervescent prime of the counterculture's life. The draft and then the War wound down. Liberalism's Great Society collapsed, and so did radical political hopes for revolution. Sixties youth grew older if not wiser in conventional terms, and the conventional constraints of adulthood—job, home, marriage, and family—loomed larger as they made their way through the seventies. "It's the difference," says one, "between being a kid and thinking of having one." The same demographic conditions that had earlier invigorated the counterculture now began to sap it. Sixties youth were now out of school, and their numbers contributed to the devaluation of their educational assets and to the overcrowding of a recessionary job market in an inflated economy. Such conditions shifted concern away from changing the world to surviving in it. The counterculture's own structural and moral fragility also contributed to its downfall. Because it relied on unregulated feelings to realize its values, it could not institutionalize them stably.

Beyond these factors, however, discovering how closely tied are the attitudes of utilitarian culture to the social conditions of modernity suggests the deeper limitations imposed on the counterculture's radical impulse. Its attempts to transform utilitarian culture outright or to ignore it completely were bound to fail—short of overthrowing technological and bureaucratic society per se, and uprooting its values from the rebels' own outlook. And these attempts at revolution or utopia did fail. Large-scale social change in the direction of the countercultural ideals of mysticism, communalism, and socialism did not occur, either by radical political transformation of the old order or by ever-expanding growth of the new psychedelic lifestyle.

But a profound change did occur as a result of the cultural conflict of the 1960s—the delegitimation of utilitarian culture, and with it the stripping away of moral authority from major American social institutions: government, law, business, religion, marriage and the family. The conflict between utilitarian culture and counterculture in the 1960s left *both* sides of the battlefield strewn with expired dreams and ideological wreckage. It resulted in the disillusioned withdrawal of young and old, hip and straight alike, away from active concern with public institutions and back into the refuge of private life. But this has been no simple return to normalcy. As the strength of our political parties and the active portion of our electorate have declined, single-issue voting and ideological lobbies have grown. In its drift from utilitarian values and liberal institutions toward self-fulfillment in a laissez faire landscape, this new mood marks a spreading of the counterculture's personalism along with reaction against it.[68] Now it is more privatized, restrained from its quest for community, and severed from its aim of overturning the established social order. But this personalism remains estranged from the established culture, as the religious right reminds us, and it marks ongoing changes in that culture, quickened in the sixties and as yet unresolved.[69] From the standpoint of our analysis this situation reflects both the underlying discontents generated by the social conditions of modernity, and the incapacity of utilitarian culture to make sense of these discontents.

In the atmosphere of disappointment and depression that followed the conflicts and failures of the sixties, many youths sought out alternative religious movements.[70] Disoriented by drugs, embittered by politics, disillusioned by the apparent worthlessness of work and the transiency of love, they have found a way back through these movements, a way to get along with conventional American society and to cope with the demands of their own maturing lives. For some youths the social and ideological stability of these movements has meant psychological and even physical survival. For many more, membership in alternative religious movements has meant moral survival and a sense of meaning and purpose recovered through recombining expressive ideals with moralities of authority, rules, and utility. On one hand, these movements have thereby adapted and reconciled their youthful adherents to the traditional order. On the other, they have meant moral survival precisely by sustaining countercultural themes, albeit in altered forms. Viewed negatively, especially if bathed in the macabre light of Jonestown and "brainwashing cults," this mediation appears to be an adaptation without full acceptance, an outer conformity based on an alternative rationale and often glossing actual deviancy. Viewed positively, though, these mediative successors to the conflicts of the sixties may be seeking to synthesize the most valuable elements of the counterculture with the most functionally necessary conditions of modern society. If so, we can inquire into them as experiments in the transformation of moral meaning. And, perhaps, we can learn from them something about our society as a whole, and ourselves, that we genuinely need to know.

COMMUNAL LOVE AND ORDER
The Authoritative Ethic of a Christian Sect

The Living Word Fellowship (LWF) is a "born-again, spirit-filled, revival church" of some 300 members, most of them lower-middle-class whites in their twenties. It is located in a modest suburb of San Francisco, adjoined by affluent communities and a prestigious university. The church occupies a large, well-maintained storefront in the old center of town, and its members live clustered in nearby neighborhoods. They meet twenty to forty hours weekly for services and Bible classes, meals and "fellowship," recreation, and householding activities. Members speak in tongues and "dance in the Spirit." They prophesy in the name of God and give testimonial witness to his daily working in their lives. The pastor lays hands on them, "filling them with the Holy Spirit" and "casting out demons." Pentecostal in its ritual, the LWF nonetheless requires members to study the Bible and obey its own rules with fundamentalist diligence. Although they do not proclaim millenarian beliefs to outsiders, LWF members are convinced that God will destroy urban America by firestorm in a few years and that he has commissioned them, "the chosen remnant among the last generation," to prepare for this end. Accordingly, they are building a $250,000 church, "The Ark," in a small town high in the Sierras where they have settled fifty members and plan to locate the remainder as soon as possible. They are also engaged in a process of "spiritual perfection" expected to climax in their ecstatic union with Jesus at the Second Coming and their theocratic rule over the world during the millennium to follow. Committed members of the LWF believe that their bodies are becoming "incorrupt" through this process of perfection and that they will not die a physical death.

The LWF has informal ties with other revival churches, but it recognizes no earthly authority above that of its founder and pastor, a sixty-year-old woman of great energy, faith, and forcefulness named Bobbi Morris.[1] Pastor Bobbi is second-generation Portuguese, born and raised in San Francisco's Mission District when it was largely Irish and Catholic. Orphaned in her early teens, she overcame language difficulties and ethnic ridicule at school to graduate a high school valedictorian with dreams of college which went unfulfilled. She went to work as a ballroom dancer in San Francisco in the late 1930s, where she came to know "money, travel, fine clothes," and much of men and love in the world. At twenty-nine she married a handsome sailor-turned-mason, who remains her loyal husband. Childless, she managed a small dress shop in the early years of their marriage.

At the age of thirty-six Pastor Bobbi repented her past life and was "saved." She joined a fundamentalist church, where "they forced me to wear gunny sacks and hide in a barrel," left soon afterward, and eventually settled in a more joyful Pentecostal church. She began working out her own religious viewpoint as a Bible class teacher, a role she filled with ever-increasing success for fifteen years. In 1968 she visited a Pentecostal congregation whose prophets predicted that she would found and lead a church of her own "to raise up an army of youth." She did not heed this prophecy at first, and became chronically ill and feverish as a result. Finally she suffered a massive heart attack during which, she says, she journeyed to "the valley of death," where God charged her with disobedience and threatened to take her life. She contested with him for her soul, and promised to obey if she should live. She awoke in the limbo of an intensive-care unit, alive but paralyzed and speechless. All of her hair fell out. Then, over the next months, Pastor Bobbi made a miraculous recovery. She began the LWF in 1970 from her sickbed with several dozen conservative Christian adults drawn from her Bible classes.[2]

A trickle of recruits to the LWF from among hip street kids and drug users, attracted at first by Pastor Bobbi's reputation as a witch and the church's ritual "weirdness," turned into a deluge after the conversion of several key rock musicians and drug dealers who had extended networks of friends, followers, and clients. Roughly 150 youths entered the LWF within one year. As they were assimilated, the LWF adapted to them in turn. The kids went off drugs, cut their hair, took conventional jobs, and began to marry. The church got electrified "clean" rock music, grew more intensely ecstatic in its ritual, and became decisively millenarian. In 1973, Pastor Bobbi had an apocalyptic vision that led to concrete action. The LWF purchased ten acres of land in Mountain Town to build "a church that will be a fortress," plans were drawn up and money was raised. Youths who once dreamed of "going up the country" as hippie communards now began to settle in the Sierras as millenarian Christians. The church began systematic food hoarding a year later, with pooled buying of freeze-dried foods and staples (including $18,000 of protein powder) to be stockpiled on the site of the future church. Construction got underway in 1975. By that time members of the LWF had purchased a dozen homes and eight small businesses in Mountain Town, including its newspaper, and one of them was running for a seat on the town council.

The LWF offers its members a picture of reality and a program for moral perfection merged with ecstatic rites and a loving community. These elements, which make up the LWF's "spiritual knowledge," holistically engage the ex-hippie's body, mind, and spirit, in contrast to the purely mental appeal of the "natural knowledge" offered by conventional society.

Ritual experience in the LWF centers around conversion and begins with *repentance*, which implies a moral commitment "to turn from sin and dedicate yourself to the amendment of your life" in accord with sect rules.[3] Reciting a short "Sinner's Prayer," the convert acknowledges his old identity as a sinner and then sheds it by taking Jesus as his personal savior. This is known as "getting saved." Next he "gets filled with the Holy Spirit," imparted by the pastor through laying on of hands and signaled by the convert's speaking in tongues, "a perfect prayer from a perfect soul to a perfect God." This effervescent experience surges through LWF services, as all its members speak aloud in tongues together, touching and swaying in unison, to lift "a sweet-smelling incense to God." Such "praising" inspires syntactical conversation between believers and God in the form of spontaneous public prayers offered by various sect intercessors and answered in the divine first person by specially chosen prophets. "We prophesy exactly the same unpremeditated way we speak in tongues—simply opening our mouths, and under God's anointing, allowing Him to use our mouths for His words." Through these means communal self-expression as heartfelt as a be-in's enters into Christian worship and revelation.

Two related rites, *deliverance* and *baptism*, enable the convert to press on toward moral perfection. When Pastor Bobbi lays hands on LWF members to deliver them from demons, they "go down under the power" in ways that resemble a faint, seizure, or orgasm and evoke reports of death and rebirth. In deliverance, "we are slain in the Spirit by the power of God, and when we rise up again in new life, Satan is gone." Baptism occurs by full immersion into "the grave of the waters," in which the convert "buries the sins of the flesh, our old man," and unites with Jesus in "resurrection life." The LWF teaches, "When we by faith begin to believe that we actually have this resurrection life, we will not die physically. Death had no more dominion over Christ and it has no more dominion over us. (Rom. 6:8-11)" The baptized convert is "born again as a child of God," his personality and feelings radically changed by means of "the circumcision of the heart" (Deut. 30:6). He passes from the sinful and mortal world system of the larger society into the eternal kingdom of God, represented on earth by the LWF. (See illustration on following page.) Thus conversion to the LWF makes up a physical and emotional transformation, not only a spiritual one: "In full salvation God first saves the spirit of man, then at water baptism He saves the heart, and lastly in perfection He is in the process of saving the body."

Through the LWF's ritual experience of "the Spirit" grows its conviction that there exists a personal God. "God is a real person. He is accessible. He actually walks among His people. He listens to them, talks to them, and affects their daily lives. God has a mind of His own. He has feelings, too, especially longing and grieving after union with a perfected people." Jesus is the perfect lover and savior, who feels, forgives, and heals all wrongs. He mediates between men and "Father God," the just lawgiver, judge, and millennial executor who promises immortality to the faithful, death to the sin-

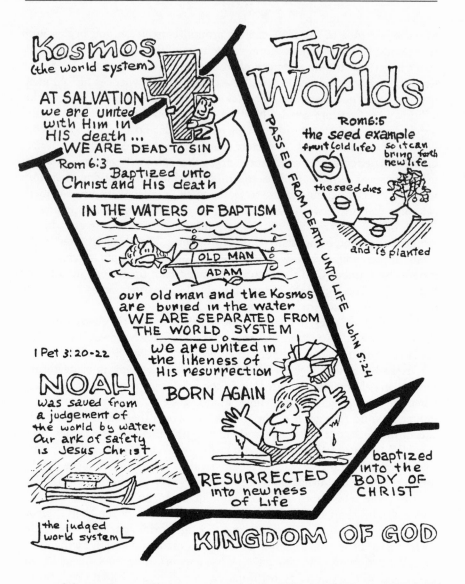

ner, and destruction to the present social order. The LWF believes that God acts providentially in history and in each person's daily life. He has a special millennial destiny for the LWF as a whole and a mission for each of its members in the present. Evil exists positively and personally in the form of Satan and various demons. "Demons are personalities and not just an influence. They cry and speak and have feelings. The world is dominated by the devil. He is the one we battle." These agents of evil also act on individuals and can possess the mind and senses, though not the soul, of any saved Christian who opens the door to them by choosing to sin.

The Bible is the literal will of God; "God and His Word are One."

Without error or contradiction, it is to be studied by traditional methods of "searching the Scriptures," thereby "proof-texting" the LWF's tenets and chartering its faith. "We believe in our heart what God has said in His Word —this is faith." At the same time, these ex-hippies stress, only direct experience of the Spirit can "quicken" the words of the Bible and make them come alive with personal meaning. Pastor Bobbi is God's prophet and the Bible's authoritative interpreter. She is "the shepherd who rules God's people, and leads them in His will. The voice of the shepherd is the voice of Christ," and the faithful are to obey it without question. For the LWF the relationship between God and man, and so among men, is first of all a moral relationship, defined by a covenant: "We are God's Covenant people, and He is a faithful God, Who keepeth Covenant and mercy with them that love Him and keep His Commandments."

The LWF is formally organized as a church of priests. Below Pastor Bobbi are six elders and more than 120 ministers, 90 percent of them males, hierarchically ranked in various stages of training. Prophets assign all sect members additional ministerial roles as apostles, pastors, prophets, evangels, or teachers (Eph. 4:11) and as exercisers of the charismatic gifts of healing, miracle working, discerning spirits, speaking and interpreting tongues, prophecy, faith, and the word of wisdom and knowledge (1 Cor. 12:4-10). Such organization is seen to follow from each person's direct relationship to God as one of a priesthood of all believers and from the LWF's status as an elite "nation of priests" preparing for millennial world governance. A clear-cut division of spiritual labor and a hierarchy of ministerial ranks orders the LWF as "God's Army," while brotherly love joins it in one intimate "forever family."

Like the counterculture, the LWF conceives itself set over against the larger society by its direct experience of the truth. It seeks to save ever more sinners from the world and to withdraw from the world's doctrinal and moral dangers in order to "perfect a people." "The Word of God tells us to keep sound doctrine," declares the pastor. "We *cannot* fellowship with those who do not believe in speaking in tongues or in water baptism and the circumcision of the heart." Against ecumenical calls to "Come together, no matter what you believe," Paul's admonition to separate saints from sinners is often quoted: "Do not be yoked with unbelievers. For what partnership have righteousness and iniquity? Or what fellowship has light with darkness?" (2 Cor. 6:14). The LWF's need for spiritual purity justifies its closed social organization. "Sure we're sectarian," acknowledges a deacon, "because God's sectarian." The LWF sets up sectarian boundaries between its members and outsiders in three ways. First, distinctive ethical and ritual requirements set LWF youths apart from others and limit interaction between them. These requirements include a ban on drinking, drugs, extramarital sex, "sensual music," long hair for men, and short dresses for women. Second, the obligation to proselytize all outsiders, adamantly and continuously, distances or ruptures relationships with those who are unreceptive. Third, the effort, time, and commitment needed to take part in the full round of LWF activities preclude much more than instrumental relationships with outsiders.

Roughly three-quarters of the LWF's members range in age from their early twenties to their midthirties, with an average age of twenty-eight. There are slightly more males than females (the ratio is about fifteen to fourteen). Most of these youths come from working-class and lower-middle-class family backgrounds, and their present social status remains much like that of their parents. They usually finished high school or dropped out during the first year of junior college. The men typically work at blue-collar jobs, ranging from laborer and gas station attendant through delivery driver and electronics technician to machinist, mechanic, and carpenter.[4] Until they marry, the women work as waitresses, sales clerks, electronics assemblers, secretaries, and licensed practical nurses.

Almost all LWF youths took an active part in the sixties' counterculture, particularly its hip wing marked by psychedelic drugs and rock music. Drug use typically began early in high school and quickly turned regular and heavy. It was no intermittent assist in the pursuit of meaning or recreation but a central focus of life, which shaped their experience of school, work, politics, and personal relationships. Virtually every sect youth smoked marijuana ("grass," "weed," "doobies") steadily, if not daily. More than 80 percent took LSD ("acid"), some of them hundreds of times. Shaken by psychedelic "bad trips," many switched to amphetamines ("speed"), barbiturates ("downs"), and alcohol, often becoming addicted to these drugs or to heroin. A dozen LWF males were deeply involved in dealing drugs and have arrest records to show for it. Youths of both sexes used drugs in groups of their peers and identified themselves as "heads, dopers, freaks, hippies: whatever you want to call it, we weren't surfers or greasers." Those still in high school during the later sixties lived at home but spent much of their time hanging out on the streets. Older youths lived in communal houses or "crash pads," some in the Haight-Ashbury, or moved about nomadically "drifting and doping." They worked on and off at unskilled jobs, dealt drugs, or "hustled" to support themselves, sometimes receiving help from home. More than twenty males aspired to careers as rock musicians, but only half that many ever worked as such; four were full-time professionals.

Few LWF youths deeply committed themselves to radical political activity or organizations, and none was ever arrested in this connection. Almost a third of them, however, took part in demonstrations of political protest at least once. "I went to marches, but mostly just to hear the bands and get stoned," says one. "My motto was, 'Doobies first, then the Revolution.'" Most of these hip youths nonetheless sympathized with political activism, because they saw its ends—and its enemies—resembling their own.

Youths in the LWF were commonly involved in preconversion sexual relationships beginning in mid-adolescence. These ranged from casual and promiscuous one-night stands through girlfriend-boyfriend relationships lasting several months to "having an old lady or an old man" and cohabiting for a year or more. Also common were long-term friendships and cliques, which began in high school and were cemented by drug use. Recruited by one another through social networks woven out of such ties, youths typically entered the LWF unmarried, became engaged after six months or so, and married twelve to eighteen months later. About 150 of the LWF's 230 young persons are now married, 16 are engaged, and the remainder are single. Virtually no couples married in the sect have yet divorced.

A minority of sect youths, some 15 percent, came from upper-middle-class or upper-class family backgrounds and elite colleges, after exhausting careers as hip or bohemian dropouts. The core of this group grew up in politically conservative families of inherited wealth, and several of them share in sizable family fortunes. These youths have left previous spouses or lovers and are now married to other sect members, with the men steadily employed in blue-collar jobs. By religious background this upper-class minority includes Episcopalians, Presbyterians, Congregationalists, a few Catholics, and the LWF's only two Jews. Evangelical and conservative Protestant affiliation predominates in the lower-middle-class majority, but only barely over Catholicism, usually associated with Irish and Italian ethnicity. Few youths were specifically religious rebels, however. Their families' religious ties were rarely strong, and they drifted away from conventional religious institutions more than they broke off from them.[5] They encountered spiritual disciplines and neo-Oriental religions such as TM, yoga, and Krishna Consciousness usually only at second hand, filtered through the drug subculture.

HIP TRIPS: EARLIER MORAL VIEWS OF LWF YOUTH

In describing their earlier moral views, young members of the LWF express mixed feelings and intentions that, when explored, reveal a sense of puzzlement and anguish. Looking back at their own past, and at the society around them now, they see a world of moral ambiguity and relativism whose tolerance masks either egoism or normlessness. "In the Word of God we've got a rock to stand on," says one youth. "There's a center. In the world there's nothing enduring or stable. It's all sorts of things that look alike—counterfeits, false religions. There's no black and white. It's all gray." These youths had committed themselves to the expressive ethic of the hip counterculture, experienced its inner contradictions and the antagonism of mainstream culture, and concluded that living it out was impossible:

> One person tells you to do one thing, and the next person says to do the opposite. "Get a job, get a haircut." Or "Turn on, tune in, drop out." Or "Support the President," and someone else says,

"Impeach Nixon" or "Stop the War," or whatever it is, you
know. It makes you crazy. What do you do? It's typical of the
world. You're in confusion. In the Lord the Word shows you
what to do, and you can rest in it. You don't have to be gray.

In contrast to the larger society, the LWF stands for an unambiguous black-
and-white moral order that is objectively fixed, internally coherent, and
exclusively true.

An authoritative ethic figures more prominently in the histories of
LWF members from working- and lower-middle-class backgrounds than in
other groups in this study. Asked how his parents dealt with issues of right
and wrong, one such youth replies:

My folks laid down the law to us kids, "Do this, don't do that."
My dad had this old belt he used to use on us.

*When you were supposed to do something, did you ever ask,
"Why should I?" What was your folks' answer?*

"Because I said so!" That was it most of the time.

What happened later, when you got out on your own more?

When I got into high school I started wandering away from my
parents and what they had to say. You get away from obedience,
because they don't set a real example or goal for you. They can't,
if they don't really believe. I started looking around for myself
out on the street. That was a time—'67, '68, '69—when there was
a lot of different places to be at, and it didn't take me very long
to figure out there was more to life than what the old man said,
just going out and getting a job.

Sect youths criticize their parents for rigidly "trying to lay their trip on me,"
but also for not actually practicing the beliefs and norms they espoused.
Parents were "hypocrites, phonies, people with façades":

In the type of family I grew up in there were never any ideals or
strong type of morals people really lived. There was hypocrisy. I
was told, like, such and such was bad, but then I would see my
parents doing it with my eyes.

I guess I don't really respect them because of the way they treated
each other. My dad would come home from work and yell and
scream at my mom and get violent. But they've got such a front,
it's unbelievable. Finally I just said, "Forget it. That's phony,"
and did what I felt like.

Many of these families were disorganized by such ills as alcoholism, chronic unemployment, and physical abuse. More than half were split by divorce.[6] But perceptions of parental hypocrisy also reflect a gap between the children's hip standards and their parents' conventional ones, for example, in the degree of affectionate behavior deemed necessary to indicate genuine love.

Further, such perceptions of hypocrisy reflect contrary moral stances held by their parents, who were themselves raised with the relatively authoritative morality of conservative Christians and who later moved toward the more privatized, secular outlook of utilitarian culture.[7] Under the pressure of conflict with their hip children, these parents tended to regress to an authoritative defense of conventional norms. But they had diluted or abandoned the traditional biblical beliefs and commitments that anchored this ethic. They did so in pursuit of middle-class economic and social status during the postwar boom years, yet most of them found only marginal rewards for their efforts. In joining the LWF, their children returned to the sectarian idealism that marked their parents' own early backgrounds, espousing it with a vengeance aimed both at their parents and their society. "Pastor is more of a mother to me than my own mother ever was," one woman declares.

> I'm not saying our parents, many of them, didn't love us. The reason is that we know God is the answer, and our parents have rejected God. Even the ones that still go to church, it's more a socially enjoyable type atmosphere, like the Presbyterian Church, where you go for an hour and then come on home and relax. They aren't looking for a relationship with God that takes over your whole life. The very thing that for us life is about, our parents deny it.

A generation gap still divides LWF youth and their parents, but now its lines have shifted ground.

Before converting to the LWF, its youths held to the expressive ethic of the hip counterculture. They grounded its assumptions in their benign experience of themselves and other persons while using drugs:

> From the way that I felt when I was on acid, I thought that everyone else would feel like that, too. So if we all felt like that, how could there be any violence or evil? Because when I was on acid, I didn't feel like being hassled. All I wanted to do was sit and rap or just think about something. Just sit down between the stereo speakers and put on Janis [Joplin] singing "Summertime" and just watch the fish swim in the aquarium. That was the most mellow state I could be in.

So experiencing one's own "true inner self" leads to the conviction that others feel likewise. If these selves are expressed to one another, a loving communion ensues. This is all that the good life and the good society require to be realized. One of a large circle of drug-using friends who converted en masse to the LWF describes the wordless yet complete communication that flowed among them:

> There were a bunch of us in the world that were like a family. We hung around together—a lot of us didn't have fathers—and we did dope together. We would get down and talk about our feelings, and we could really get into each other. We were getting so far gone, we didn't even have to talk, the vibes were so heavy. We'd just look at each other, and we'd know what was happening. We knew what each other was like. It was a bond of love. The world can't really know what love is, but we had something.

Drug-assisted self-revelation builds a sense of mutual interpenetration and knowledge that generates a fictive family of like-minded friends. This doper's *koinonia* resembles the sect's, both of them formed by communicants sharing a sacramental meal and a "bond of love."[8] Like the sect, the drug-using circle linked its communion to the prospect of millennial world unification, but it faced special difficulties in trying to sustain its experience of mystical merger:

> A group of us would do our acid, and talk and talk—about God and what it all meant. We figured out that if I could communicate with you, then we would have a flow of communication, a oneness. Then we gotta get someone that could communicate with you over there and with me. So then we would have a three-in-oneness. Then it would go to another triangle and expand until everything was one.
>
> That was the closest we got to this oneness in the world, beyond words, but we couldn't experience that all the time, because games would come in. After you came down, things would get lost.
>
> Also, what we didn't count on was that everybody's personality was changing, because of drugs, while this was going on. So you would start off knowing you all understand each other, then you start wondering if maybe you just *think* you know that person, and he just thinks he knows you and you know him, but it's just in your head. It's not real.

Heightened awareness on drugs led to the social communion of brotherly love, which began rather philosophically and proceeded beyond words to the silence of mystical union. Eventually, however, it broke down, according to a sort of psychedelic indeterminacy principle, into suspicions of drug-induced solipsism and the evanescence of state-dependent insight.

The loving content of the hip ethic was at odds with conditions both inside and beyond the counterculture. The flower child's love wilted in the heat of disorienting bad trips, the ravages of hard drug use, drifting and doping itineracy, and the no-holds-barred economy of drug dealing. "Speed and heroin came in and started burning people out," remembers a Haight-Ashbury veteran. "Guns hit the streets, because you needed them to pull jobs to buy hard drugs, and then there was a lot of ripping off in the drug business. People started to find out, 'Hey, this is not all peace and love and flowers, like we thought it was.'" Straight society's antagonism toward hip ways of life and conflicts between the established political order and the radical wing of the counterculture also hardened the hippie's loving heart.

The expressive *style* of the hip ethic, which holds that an act is right if it expresses the agent's feelings and responds to the situation, runs counter to its rulelike expectations that persons ought to love and not injure one another, whenever the individual actually does feel like behaving otherwise in response to a given situation. "I always tried to go by what I felt," a young woman recalls, "only sometimes I felt out of it. It's like the speed freak who says, 'Screw you!' and it's supposed to be OK, because that's how he really feels. The idea is that you can do anything you want to as long as you're being 'sincere,' you know." Tales of injury, betrayal, and cruel indifference among fellow hippies are commonplace in LWF testimony,[9] but one youth suggests a subtler side of the problem in recollecting his hip moral views:

> I felt like life was just a matter of live and let live. Do what you want as long as you don't bum out someone else's trip. What I did with my own life was my business. So when people got on my case for smoking or drugs I'd just tell them, "It's my life, so don't bother me about it." But I wanted to be really mellow, too, you know, like George Harrison—peace and love and laying good vibes on people. He was like a spiritual example, and after I started drugs I never did get violent with guys, when before if they hassled me I'd try to chop them in half.

The conflict between freedom of individual impulse and the need for non-injury and universal love recalls the tension in mainstream culture between a Christian personality ideal and biblical moral obligations on one side and a utilitarian principle of negative liberty on the other. Hip individuals, each doing their own thing, often did hurt one another, not to mention themselves; and ineffable states of consciousness, "good vibes," sometimes proved beyond access or transmission of any kind. Thus the hip ethic of nonjudgmental tolerance based on one's own intuited feelings and the presumption of sympathetic response from others tended to unravel. The youth goes on:

I figured, "If it feels right, it's all right to do. Do it." I never forced anything on anybody, so I thought I was considerate of the next person. If she didn't want to do it, or he didn't want to talk about it, that was OK. It's funny. I thought I was free and easy, but actually I was hard a lot of the time, because I cut people off. I didn't show my real feelings to them when they didn't feel the same way.

Freedom to "do your own thing" and follow your own feelings led away from self-expression, warm interpersonal relations, and intimate community, when those feelings did not fit with the feelings of others.

In sum, LWF youths felt strongly ambivalent toward the authoritative ethic of their parents, which clashed with the parents' own growing individualism and with the counterculture's personalism, yet at the same time anticipated part of the LWF's ethic. Neither the ethic of rules proclaimed by conventional society nor its counterpart minimally implied by their own hip viewpoint seemed very comprehensible to them. Conventional rules, often represented by laws banning drugs, appeared unjustifiably authoritarian to sect youth. A former drug user and dealer remarks:

Most of my time was spent in the drug world and with other kids. The older people I met were cops, probation officers, prison people. They always represented the authority I blamed for putting me down and putting me in jail. I hated them. I always thought, here's these people with their world, but how do they know that what I'm doing is *really* wrong? How do they know that? Who invented this law they say I'm breaking? I always thought they were upholding something that was a lie, that wasn't real.

From this viewpoint the law stands for the commands of an unreasoning authority. Its after-the-fact rationalizations are unmasked by the user's immediate, positive experience of drugs. The principles of love and non-injury implicit in the hip ethic, in contrast to the law, seem to arise directly from experience, not from reason, authority, or cost-benefit calculation. When sincere hippies nonetheless injure each other and themselves, this is taken as an unaccountable failure of a given person's feelings, not of the counterculture's style of evaluation. Scant notice goes to the fact that the hip ethic of situational response and self-expression tends to collapse into the instrumental pursuit of individual want-satisfaction. The consequential style of utilitarian individualism is associated only with members of conventional society, who are condemned for cheating each other and striving after money and power.

THE ETHIC OF A CHRISTIAN SECT

The Living Word Fellowship holds to a predominantly authoritative style of evaluation. God commands which acts are right or wrong in themselves. Reinforced by calculation of millennial consequences and surrounded by sectarian boundaries, this ethic of commands creates a reliably clear, controlled, and binding moral order. As such, it appears to clear up the confusing over-choice of the expressive ethic ("I can do whatever I feel like, but why should I do this or that?") and resolve the conflicts of the consequential ethic ("Which costs outweigh which benefits, and for whom?") by replacing them with an entirely new outlook. But the LWF carries over the message of love from the counterculture's ethic into its own, so that the Christian youth feels himself, at last, to be living out the counterculture's highest ideals while being saved from its actual contradictions.

Central to the LWF's ethic is the "Greatest Commandment," to love God and others (Mt. 22:36-40), focused by the moral example of Jesus as the perfect lover. Here the obligation to obey God out of duty translates into the aspiration to imitate Jesus out of love. "Love God and do what you will," a minister declares, as did Augustine. Then he adds, "Of course, if you love God, you will keep His Commandments." Thus loving intention, the axis of the expressive ethic, is stabilized by alignment with act-specific commands and examples. Through ecstatic ritual and intimate community, the Christian sect calls forth the trusting love its authority steadies and protects, a love that the counterculture idealized but could not sustain in the individualistic atmosphere of an associational society. Let us look at the way sixties youth have recovered God's will and love from the biblical tradition, recombined them with hip ideals, and applied them in the present to their inner experience and social relations, their work and politics.

A Cosmos of Commands: Do God's Will and Be Saved

For the LWF norms come as commands from God through holy scripture or directly through a prophetic leader. Objective and universal, they apply ultimately to all persons, whether or not they choose to obey or acknowledge them. "God's Word holds for all cultures, and beyond all cultures," the LWF teaches. From the commandments of the Decalogue to the comprehensive casuistic rules set by the pastor, norms prescribe and forbid specific acts: "Thou shalt not kill. Thou shalt not commit adultery. Thou shalt not steal" (Ex. 20:13-15). All activities, feelings, and thoughts are either good or evil according to sect rules, which are sufficiently specific to enjoin against drinking and listening to sensual music, to prohibit a single man and woman from riding alone in a car after dark and a married couple from french kissing, and to require a tithe equal to 10 percent of one's gross rather than net income. Faithful obedience to specific commands and rules defines moral virtue in the LWF. A good person is one who obeys God. A young deacon points out how radically this authoritative ethic differs from conventional American morality:

> In the world people relate by man-made philosophies. All the way through school it seemed like the main idea they were trying to impart to me was that I was an individual, that I had the ability to choose right and wrong, that I had to decide what is right and wrong and why I was alive and what I was living for, and pursue those goals. That kind of philosophy completely motivates modern America. Now, because of science and atheistic philosophers, people don't believe in God. They don't believe in the authority of His will. They're looking for answers, because they know their lives aren't satisfying. So they're looking for different ways to have governments, to raise their kids, to replace marriage. Everything's questioning and searching. No answers, no security, no stable pattern. It's actually a way of going insane.
>
> A Christian is just the reverse. He doesn't have to decide what's right or wrong. He just has to decide to *do* right or wrong. He already knows. That's the worst thing to do to a man—make him decide everything himself, because he can't. It's a Satanic trap, an ego thing, wanting to be independent, when you can't be. As if you can just treat other people however *you* want to treat them. It's amazing. I see it in people my age and younger kids, and now I see it in adults, too. People who lived their life the old way before, giving up now and believing in independence and self-will. Even my own mother. . . .

God's will is fixed, explicit, and knowable through revelation. No formal place remains in the LWF, therefore, for ongoing moral inquiry by means of dialectical reasoning, cost-benefit calculation, or intuition. The utilitarian individualism of the larger society is identified as a moral egoism coincident with loss of faith not only in God but in the commonweal.

Divinely revealed commands chart a different moral logic as well as a different course of action for sixties youth who converted to the LWF. In the expressive ethic they espoused earlier, the right act was defined by one's feelings in response to a given situation. In the consequential ethic to which the hippie often reverted, the right act was defined by its good consequences. These in turn were defined by what satisfied one's own wants or interests. Here the great moral problem was trying to know what you wanted, as one young woman recounts:

> Life was a downer for me in the world. I didn't enjoy it at all and, boy, I sure tried hard. Nobody tried harder. I didn't know what I

wanted. No, I wanted happiness, but I didn't know what it was. I thought it was being high twenty-four hours a day, and I couldn't get it. Now I know it's being contented. In the world that's impossible—there's always something wrong with you— but the Lord takes you just the way you are and if you've got something wrong in your heart, He'll deliver you from it. All you have to do is obey His Word.

The utilitarian individual acts to maximize satisfaction of her wants. But what, ultimately, does she want? If happiness, then what is its content? Pleasurable sensation is one answer, given distinctive form by the drug subculture, but this leaves open the question of whether one can, in fact, reach the end of happiness directly through empirical means. LWF youth finally found that happiness was as inaccessible through drugs as it was through the conventional utilities of money, status, and power. "There's always something wrong with you" in the utilitarian sense that wants continue as long as life does. Life is defined as a matter of acting in order to satisfy wants. As long as it goes on, wants never get satisfied once and for all.[10] The LWF ends the hip search for an ever-elusive inner good through probing one's wants and feelings, and instead sets its moral sights by reference to externally fixed commands defining which acts are right. The individual does the right act, because God wills it, and as an aftereffect she feels good. "When I do God's will," a youth testifies, "I'm on the path of perfection. *That's* when I feel happy."

In an authoritative ethic the definition of right acts occurs prior to the definition of good consequences. An act can be identified as right or wrong apart from calculating its consequences, by reference to divine commands. A deacon spells out these changed moral meanings:

What does it mean when we say some act is right *or something is* good? *Has that meaning changed for you since the Lord?*

I used to have a real loose idea of that. Before, *good* just had to do with people, what they wanted and how they felt. Now the Lord has set down a particular guideline or rule in every area of our life. Whatever goes with God's plan and fits Bible pattern, that's what's right and good. What it says in the Book is right.

Did you ever think what's right is relative to how people see it or feel about it?

I did, before I got involved with God. Now I can say maybe some people have different *ideas* about what's right, but that's not the same as different things *being* right. In the end, at the Judgment, man, it's gonna all be straightened out, and the hand of God is gonna fall. The world says, "It all depends, it's all situational, right?" Wrong! There *are* absolutes. It's that way because God says it's that way, regardless of whether we understand it or not. God put the tree in the Garden and told Adam, "Don't eat of it." God didn't give him a bunch of reasons to satisfy his curiosity. God just said, "Don't eat of it! And if you do eat of it, you're gonna die." It's that absolute.

It's His will, not my will. The situation doesn't make it right or wrong. For example, if I answered just one question differently on the unemployment form, I'd get ninety dollars a month more. But I won't do it, because it's a lie, and the Lord tells me not to lie.

Good persons and things are those that conform to the divine commands of right action recognized by the LWF as an orthodox unit. Relativism is rejected. However powerful the diverse feelings and conflicting wants of individuals may prove in exploding the harmony of an expressive ethic, they cannot disrupt the integrity of this fixed definition of right acts.

The ethic of the LWF, like the regular ethic, sees acts as inherently good or evil, and it obliges its adherents to perform particular acts, which it conceives as duties. But the sect's authoritative ethic echoes the counterculture's expressive style in rejecting discursive reasoning as a means to moral knowledge and in stressing the individual's need to know by direct experience. Unlike either regular or expressive ethics, however, the LWF goes on to emphasize the need to know God the "Ruler and King" as the source of its rules, and the need to obey God as the end of complying with the rules:

Rebellion from God is the greatest sin, not beating your brother up or committing adultery with his wife. Disobedience is the greatest sin, not what you do to disobey. That's why, if you don't know God, even if you do good things, they're dead works, because you can't obey God if you don't know Him. *Good* is whatever God is doing, whatever that is. So the key to doing the right thing is getting saved. If you're not saved, no matter what your moral judgments are, God will judge against you.

Religious faith is a necessary condition of moral virtue, because doing the right act is ultimately a matter of obeying God. Without faith, ritually reborn by "getting saved and filled" in the LWF, right action is relegated to the status of "dead works" without ultimate value. "Dead works are things which a person does that do not have spiritual life," the LWF teaches, "because they are not done in faith or direct service to God. Everything that an unbeliever does is dead works." To serve God one must know him. To know him, one must experience him directly.

Salvation, Self-Interest, and Purity of Heart

The authoritative style of evaluation predominates in the LWF's ethic, but it does not stand unalloyed. LWF doctrine lists three conditions that make acts right: "If what a believer does centers around striving for righteousness, standing on and striving for full salvation; if all that is done is backed up by the Word; and if what we do is to encourage and increase the Body of Christ and the Body ministry, then our works will be the works of God." Here the right-making characteristic of following God's word is joined by the need for intentions of righteousness and sanctity, and by the good consequences of advancing the LWF's collective spiritual welfare. Sect members, especially ex-Catholics, sometimes refer to natural-law arguments in explaining the nature of God's commands: "There are laws in life. If you play with fire, you get burned. If you go in water, you get wet. And God's Word shows you what the laws are."

The consequential style of evaluation finds its way into the LWF's ethic in justifying adherence to the sect's rules, rather than commission of particular acts, as the best means to realizing collective goals that are themselves formulated in religious terms.[11] One ex-hippie remarks,

A lot of people say, "Do your own thing." But now I realize you have to have rules in your life if you want to grow and mature. There has to be a balance and goals. And to attain certain goals, you have to obey the rules. Like football, if you want to score a goal, you have to play by the rules. So I respect the rules.

Before I always based success on two things, what I wanted to do, and what other people feel is right. Like if I succeed on a job, it's what the boss thinks about the job, no matter how I did it. Now it's totally different. It's the *how* that is important, obeying God's Word. Then God will take care of the results, because He's in control.

What's the end result?

To be like Jesus.

Then what?

[Hesitating] Well, if we become perfected as a people, then we'll dwell in the Kingdom forever and come into God's [millennial] promises.

Impulse and self-interest, tied to meeting others' moral expectations insofar as this advanced one's own interests, made up an earlier frame of reference for evaluating action in terms of success. After conversion, divinely revealed law becomes the reference that defines what one does and does not do. The shift from impulse to fixed rules reflects the adult need for more reliably ordered behavior than the youth's expressive ethic can insure. Thus rule compliance can be justified consequentially for satisfying the social interests of persons who want to grow and mature, but it also satisfies the spiritual interests of Christians who want to get saved, in contrast to hippies who want to get high.

The convert sees this transformation of moral meaning as a shift from blind impulse or calculated self-interest to the regulated "how" of behavior prescribed by divine authority and to the altruistic example set by Jesus.[12] Even from a consequential viewpoint, he holds that the Christian's rewards, like the hippie's, do not derive from conventional utilities: "The peace that God gives is not like the peace that the world gives. It doesn't depend on circumstances like what you have or who you know." Moreover, LWF doctrine contends that the Christian's knowledge of what is good, and thus his criterion for calculating rewards, is not continuous with the unbeliever's knowledge:

Life, truth, and love: this makes man. None of these can be known in perfection in this earthly realm (here truth is mingled with error, life with death, and love with hate) but only when we go to the source of life, truth, and love, which is Jesus Christ. We can go to the very source, into His very presence by being obedient to his word.

By this account, obedience to God is itself a precondition of knowing the good for what it is. Obedient acts, therefore, cannot be chosen simply as means calculated to effect good consequences, since the good cannot actually be known before one obeys God. The Christian's moral insight replaces the hippie's gnostic illumination, while likewise claiming direct access to "the source of life, truth, and love."

From the viewpoint of the authoritative ethic itself, calculating the outcomes of divine reward and punishment, or the social benefits of rule compliance, merely reinforces morality. It does not constitute or explain it. Asked to explain why he obeys God, a youth pauses at the strange question, whose answer seems so self-evident. Then he replies, "Really obeying God is like being in a faithful marriage where the husband gives everything he can for the wife because he loves her, and the wife does everything she can for him because she loves him." The committed member of the LWF obeys God because God is good—God created, sustains, and loves him—and ultimately "because God is God. You don't need any other reason." Similarly, he imitates the example of Jesus because "Jesus loves me and I love Him, so I want to be like Him. It's that simple." To be like Jesus is an end in itself, not just a means to the end of millennial or mundane rewards.

An essential part of the LWF's ethic, like that of the counterculture, insists that certain intentions, motives, and feelings are necessary. "It's not just what you do but why you do it," declares the pastor. "We have to do God's will with a pure heart. If you do it just to get a reward, you're gonna get a surprise instead, because you can't fool God. He sees into your heart." But it takes more than a psychedelic experience or a sober act of will by the agent himself to purify his motives. This change of heart takes place in conversion to the LWF, as each new member undergoes a ritual transformation of his moral motives and knowledge. "Our old mind desires the old ways of the world system," explains sect doctrine.

> As the Jews were marked with a physical circumcision, we are marked with a circumcision of the heart [in baptism]. God cuts away the old mind and gives us a new mind, free of old ways! This new mind can then do God's word and love God with its entirety because it is no longer an enemy to God. We *desire* to do God's will and LOVE HIM! See Matt. 22:37-40 and Deut. 30:19. . . . This circumcision of our mind is the seal of the New Covenant we have with God. He can now write his laws on our new hearts of flesh.

Conversion to the LWF endows the individual with a place among God's people, and this carries with it a new moral outlook. Once saved and baptized, the saint seeks to be like Jesus out of love, humility, and the unconditional conviction that this is how he *ought* to be:

> In the Lord, Jesus is the perfect example. He is the perfect lover, the perfect man. The world says to do your own thing. Use people, get what you want. Self is on the throne in the world. Jesus dethroned self. He lived and died to save others, for the glory of God. This is love.

Thus the "circumcision" of the hippie's loving heart seals the convert's covenant with God. The example of Jesus as perfect lover anchors a Christian morality of aspiration that intertwines with the biblical morality of obligation anchored by "Father God" as the absolute authority who issues commandments to men and makes a covenant with them.

The Covenant: Relationship by Obligations and Rights

For the LWF the relationship between God and man, and so among men, consists of mutually balanced obligations that create corresponding rights. The commandments of God are unqualified in their demands and man's accountability to them, yet by his obedience man enters into a special sort of contractual relationship with God. The faithful become God's

"Covenant People," bound by his commands and therefore entitled to his rewards. The LWF teaches:

> A COVENANT is the giving forth of God's Will to man. It is God's plan and purpose to have certain things come to pass—and they surely shall with or without us—so then, we need only come into OBEDIENCE and be partakers (I Samuel 15:22,23). These covenants are always vertical agreements: of God's Word from Heaven disposed *down* to man; from the superior to the inferior. Man's contracts are horizontal agreements between two persons on a mutual basis or similar plane.

Because the covenant exists "vertically" between God and man, it cannot be conceived as an ordinary contract or "horizontal agreement." (See chapter 1.) The covenant states God's will, to which man accedes; and it assures God's "inheritance" to the obedient man. A youth explains,

> The Covenant isn't a tit-for-tat business deal between IBM and Xerox, where they get together and set the terms to go in a certain direction. No, God's already going in His direction. We agree to walk with *Him*. The terms are already set down in the Bible. If God says it's sin, you say it's sin. If God says it's right, then you say it's right.

> *OK. You have the duty to obey God with no ifs, ands, or buts. Do you have any rights?*

> I guess you could say we have rights, but there's nothing *we've* done to earn what God is giving us. It comes from God's love.

The covenant cannot be collapsed into a "tit-for-tat" exchange between self-interested utilitarians. Instead the ex-hippie still looks to love as the source of morality, and now finds in God's love a balanced moral order he could never make out in the flux of his own feelings. From God's love come the corresponding obligations and rights that exist on both sides of the covenant, a moral balance ritually enacted in the sect by intercessory prayer, on one hand, and the prophetic jeremiad, on the other. Both practices go back to God's covenant with Abraham (see Genesis 22), according to LWF doctrine. Abraham was so willing to obey God because he "bore the seal of the covenant in his body. He knew that everything he had was God's, even his son, and everything that was God's was his." Conversely, "because of this covenant, he could arbitrate with God. He said to God, 'Will not the God of this earth do right?' He established a precedent of intercession that has stood throughout the ages."

In intercessory prayer sect members publicly intercede with God to carry out his obligations toward his chosen people. In the following example, the LWF is seeking to evict the U.S. Forestry Service from a warehouse on their mountain property. The Forestry Service holds a legally valid long-term lease, yet the sect needs to use the warehouse to store food against the premillennial cataclysm, as required by God's plan:

Our gracious Heavenly Father, Thou did promise, Lord, the land of Canaan unto the children of Israel. But yet there were Canaanites and there were Hittites and Amarites, O Lord, in the land. And Thou did tell them to go in and possess the land. Heavenly Father, this is our property! And we command Thee this night to move the Canaanites out of our building. To move them out, out of our building, O Lord! It is needed. In the name of Jesus we come against powers and principalities, that would hold up the work of God. Father, by Thy name and by the power of the Lord Jesus Christ, we bind Satan. Lucifer, thou art bound in the name of Jesus! We cast out all spiritual power, in the name of Jesus. And we command you to loose your hold now upon these people, upon this building, O Lord. It is ours, we do need it. Therefore we shall go in to possess this land. And that we do need this building, Heavenly Father, to perform the work of the Lord, and to take care of the ministry Thou has sent us there to do, O Lord. . . . Halleluia, Father, we thank You. . . . Thank you, Lord. . . . Thank you. . . .

God is obliged to keep his promises and assist his people in all activities conforming to the divine plan. Thus assured, the LWF's intercessors "come boldly before the throne of God," pleading and arguing their claims in litigious fashion. They make demands and *command* God to aid their actions with a sense of moral certainty they could never feel before their hip companions. Prayer becomes prophetic action binding demonic forces, to which the problem is ultimately attributed, and then thanksgiving to God for having resolved it.

On the other hand, the LWF's status as chosen people, their chosenness, depends on their moral and ritual rectitude, specifically their commitment to the sect's perfectionist program. Only if members satisfy the progressive demands of this program will they come into the rewards offered by the covenant—physical immortality, union with Jesus at the second coming, and millennial world governance. Periods of confidence regarding these prospects are broken by waves of doubt which follow on such setbacks as a veteran member's defection. Then admonitory preaching and prophetic jeremiads excoriate the people for their sins and threaten divine punishment:

For I would say unto thee, hearken unto the word of the Lord. For I have spoken even this night, and I have revealed the thoughts and the intents of thy heart. Why would thou not repent before me? Why would thou not cry out unto me? That I may forgive thee thy sins, that thou mayest be cleansed. [gently] For my wrath shall surely come upon this area, and I shall even poison the water, saith the Lord. [vehemently] So that the people that do drink will become sick in mind and sick in body, saith the Lord. But my people that will hearken unto my word shall not partake of this disease that I am about ready to give unto this land, saith the Lord. Therefore I call unto thee, repent before me. Humble thyselves. Humble thyselves before me that I may forgive thy sin.

For do you not know that in a matter of time I will open the earth and swallow you up, saith the Lord. [angrily, roaring] Repent before me, saith the Lord, and cry out for forgiveness, for I do see thee, saith the Lord. And I do see thy sin before me, and I do know thy secret thoughts of idolatry and fornication, saith the Lord. [disgustedly] For thou hast other gods in thy life, and thou hast held onto them. But I would say unto thee, saith the Lord, Separate thyselves! Separate thyselves, saith the Lord. Separate thyselves . . . [the prophet's cries lower and trail off to join the moaning and sobbing of his listeners].

The entranced prophet speaks in the divine first person, and God is heard speaking through him, calling his Covenant People to account. God sees their sins, secret thoughts as well as deeds, which stand in the way of perfection. He demands repentance, lest the chosen people lose their status as victors in the apocalypse and join the worldly among its victims.[13] If God threatens sinners with his wrath in the jeremiad, he also promises the repentant his forgiveness, commanding sectarian separation from other gods and their followers as the road to righteousness. Hippies could neither ask moral responsibility of one another nor promise it. These Covenant People can do both. They can also find in their own misdeeds the moral meaning, however fearful, of troubled times, and in their God the moral strength to amend their lives and so set right the world.

The Moral Dynamic of Conversion

While the conversion of sixties youth to authoritative religious groups can be seen as a regressive escape from adult responsibility, it also represents an attempt to face the pressures of adulthood by resorting to fixed moral rules firmly backed by a cohesive community and exemplified by its leader. One young mother comments,

When I first came to the church, I saw all the rules and I thought, "How come freedom is bondage?" To me being free was not having anything pressing me. I had the wrong idea of freedom. That's why I was always unhappy, because there was always some pressure, and I had no way to handle it. Now I see it's being able to exist with the pressure, because you have truths and rules to go by. Before I thought it meant not having pressures. Now I still have the same pressures but I can handle them. Marriage, kids, friends, the future, the world. God's given me a way to organize my life and be part of a unified people who glorify him.

As one approaches the end of youth, the pressures of adulthood appear ever less escapable, and the negative idea of freedom from restraint an ever less accessible goal. A morality of authoritative rules within a strong community offers an organizing framework better suited to these conditions than does an expressive or consequential ethic based on impulse and aimed at protean experiment rather than the reliable shouldering of life's burdens.

LWF youth emerged scarred from the moral over-choice and conflict of the sixties, overlaid on an earlier moral authoritarianism. Faced with the burdens and limits of adulthood, they found the moral certainty and security of the LWF strongly appealing, worth the difficulty of restriction. Along with changes in their moral feelings and ideas, situational factors helped make the sect's authoritative ethic acceptable to them. A young woman remembers,

I really felt trapped after I first came to the Lord, because I really liked to do my own thing. I was twenty-six years old, I'd been married, I'd shot dope, I'd lived in the city and up the country. And I didn't like other people telling me what to do. So that was a problem.

In the world you're brought up to be on your own, to stand on your own feet. You're not together unless you do it yourself, and don't depend on anyone else. Don't let anyone run you or rule you. At first I thought I was being a coward, an inferior-type person, letting the Church run me, like a trained seal, with a rule for everything, having to go to church all the time, having to get permission from an elder if you want to go anywhere, even for a two-day trip.

I didn't want to be here. But I was too scared to leave. I knew there was nothing in the world, because I'd experienced so much and seen it was all vanity. If I left, I knew it would be ten times worse. I'd been there and hadn't made it, and then on top of that was the wrath of God coming down on me for leaving. I knew God wanted me here. Whenever I tried to walk my own way, I was miserable. Whenever I submitted to the Lord, he would just shower me with blessings. That's really what made me come around.

The high value attached to individual independence and discretion in American culture makes it difficult to accept an authority that enforces obligations and rules. Such rules, however, promise order to youth fed up with the predicament of "doing your own thing" without knowing why, and being injured by others doing likewise. The failure of the countercultural dream and of an unregulated life within it motivates the rebellious convert to stay on. So does the fear of turning back for one who has already begun to burn her bridges behind her and to accept the threats of damnation aimed by sect doctrine at the defector. Positive motivation is provided by the sect's blessings for compliance with its norms. These blessings include: (1) an inner experience of personal efficacy, purpose, and meaning unified with an external moral authority; (2) social relations offering acceptance and love, friends and a spouse, within an intimate and stable community; (3) secure intrasect status and status superiority in relation to the larger society, both based on moral rectitude; (4) reconciliation to low-status work in the world and a sacred career to compensate for it; (5) millennial political power. Let us recount these blessings as facets of an applied ethic created by recombining the counterculture's expressive ideals with biblical authority and Christian love.

I. THE EXPERIENTIAL BASES OF AUTHORITY: GETTING HIGH ON JESUS

In the LWF one looks to recognized authorities in order to find out which is the right way to live, but how does one come to recognize these authorities as true? This question remains at the root of the sect's moral style. The sect claims to enjoy a special relationship to God and to represent God's will; these claims become realities for its youthful members in two forms—ecstatic ritual experiences and communal relationships. These two forms resemble sect youths' earlier experience of psychedelic drugs and hippie communalism, yet each differs from its countercultural predecessor in telling ways.

The language of drug use colors testimonies by LWF youths of "getting high on Jesus" in Pentecostal rites. Conversely, they see their psychedelic experience, however faulted and deceptive, as somehow religious. "Acid seemed to open up a spiritual realm," avows one youth. "I can remember closing my eyes and flashing on white light, and feeling 'Oh God, I'm here,' you know. I had no conception of what Jesus Christ was. I just knew there was a God but I didn't know how to get in contact with him." Experience with drugs convinced the user of the existence of a divine or cosmic being that was essentially immanent and knowable through union or merger, rather than essentially transcendent and inaccessible. The relatively formless and ephemeral content of the psychedelic experience gave rise to concern for elaborating a ritual and doctrinal framework to make contact with the divine. Although the psychedelic experience was usually nonpersonal— for example, a "white light"—the mystical merger it triggered took place among fellow users who shared the hippie love ethic. This context left psychedelic ecstasy open to the personalization of devotional religion, whether the divine lover turned out to be the Pentecostal Jesus or the bhaktic Krishna.

The Christian's self-surrender to religious experience and then to authority recalls the drug user's self-surrender to psychedelic experience. Drug ideology counsels letting go of oneself completely in unmediated experience without concern for the consequences. So interpreted, the life of the senses is not mere hedonism. It has a self-transcendent character. Drugs flood the senses rather than simply gratifying them; this results in a blurring of and release from the categories of subject and object and a glimpse of monist truth. One woman compares this bohemian ethos with her parents' classic-become-conventional ideal of moderation in all things:

> I remember one thing I learned as a kid, from my family maybe, to do all things in moderation. [laughing] So I just figured I'd turn it upside down. That you'd be an acid head for awhile, a speed freak for awhile, an alcoholic. *The ultimate of every trip is when that trip controls you.* If you want to really understand any trip, you have to fall into it headfirst. [italics added]

The ultimate aim of life thus conceived is not to preserve or fortify the self, but to lose it, so that the drug "does" the doer, just as in Pentecostal glossolalia the tongues "speak" the speaker, or in Zen meditation the breathing "breathes" the breather. The counterculture's drug ideology and its ecstatic or mystical religious successors similarly value self-surrender. The latter, however, insist more strongly on the related need for commitment to the object and practice of one's surrender, and from this experience they construct some form of cosmic and social authority.

Psychedelic drug use fostered an epistemology of its own. It altered the mode of knowing as well as the object known in ways compatible with ecstatic and mystical religion. A veteran of several hundred LSD trips ponders the nature of psychedelic knowledge:

> Acid enabled you to sit down and stop reacting to things and just perceive where you are and what you're doing. That's why people are so spacy on acid, because they can concentrate and focus all their attention on just one thing. You can see things in reality, look at a person and see where they're really at. Then when you come down you're not in such an intense place, but the truth is still there. And you know it, even though you may not be able to explain it to other people.

Perception without reaction, observation without evaluation, *seeing* reality directly without thinking about it, knowledge that does not entail the capacity to verbalize or to explain: such an epistemology, sprouted from psyche- .

delic stock, can grow consistently into the experiential epistemology of Pentecostal Christianity, *est's* mysticized psychologism, or neo-Oriental meditation.

These religious successors sustained the intuitive certainty of psychedelic knowledge while informing its expressive subjectivity with the moral order of rules. Our speaker explores the labyrinths of this subjectivity:

> Acid expands your thinking. You can look at many different angles at the same time and get an overall picture of something. ...I started writing a book called *In Same*. It was automatic writing. I would write a word as I heard it, and pretty soon it wasn't English any more, but it made sense! Friends started reading it. It freaked them out. So I changed it to *Sin Same*. The idea was, where is the break from reality to insanity? Where is the break?

> I went from reality, what I thought it was, to insanity, and I could not tell any difference. It was just a difference in the *form* of communication. Then, when I changed it to *Sin Same*, it was the idea that we're all in sin, and also that there's no difference between being good and sin.

> I've noticed when we talk in tongues, it's words like I was writing. I didn't know if it was a kind of double-tongues or what, until years later I got a revelation from the Lord, and Pastor confirmed it, that Satan has a counterfeit of what God has, that even the elect might be deceived.

Here LSD is invested with powers of omniscience, but their effect is to create a separate world of supra-meaning that blurs the boundaries between significance and absurdity, right and wrong. Drug experience begins by affirming the reality of inner experience and fusing it with the outside world in utter clarity. Yet by erasing this discrimination, and with it the discriminations of syntactical language, psychedelic experience results in a disorientingly "insame" world that becomes "sinsame." The parallels between this phenomenon and that of tongue speaking alert us to differences between the two that enable sect ritual to reintegrate the ecstasy that drugs first unleashed. The chief difference is the integrity of the sect's ritual experience with its cosmological beliefs, authoritative ethic, and stable social organization.

Speaking in Tongues

Tongue-speaking makes a deep experiential impact, complete with extraordinary body sensations, on youths schooled through drugs to be

connoisseurs of experience. One of them testifies about his introduction
to tongues:

> It wasn't a head trip. It was a thing that really happened to me.
> My tongue began making these sounds without my mind telling
> it to. I had this wonderful light, warm feeling in my body coming
> up from here [pointing to his solar plexus]. Later Pastor showed
> me the scripture where it says, "Out of your belly shall flow riv-
> ers of living water" (John 7:38). That's where the Spirit is.
>
> It's a flow that goes through you. You just open your mouth and
> put your voice to it. It doesn't originate in your mind, because I
> could never have created those sounds myself. It's a supernatural
> intervention by the mind of the Holy Spirit.
>
> Another reason I know it didn't come out of my own mind is be-
> cause I have a lot of pride and I don't like to do anything stupid
> or silly. And tongues sounds stupid to the natural mind, like
> babbling. I'd even laugh at it myself at first, but it was neat, too.
> I felt so young. I was laughing out of relief and sheer joy, too.
> This was a sign that God had really accepted me.

What begins as an experience, not a "head trip," becomes evidence for
tenets that make religious sense of the experience. Peculiar body sensations
become signs of the Holy Spirit's presence, peculiar sounds become expressions of the Holy Spirit's "mind." Behavior that in most settings would be
considered embarrassingly childish becomes in the tongue-speaking sect an
occasion of acceptance by fellow believers as well as by God. Neotony and
intimacy go hand in hand, as even worldly lovers will attest, and attributing
the effects of tongue-speaking to God makes way for the faithful to engage
him in devotional relationships of great personal immediacy. "Tongues is
like being in a relationship," says one young woman, "where sometimes
you just laugh around and play, and other times it's a real serious, intimate
voicing of your love for each other. It's so fulfilling, the way the Lord
always meets you there."

For many LWF youths "getting high was like our control, our standard." It became an experiential frame of reference for their daily lives,
making the intensity and continuity of such altered states crucial to them.
But the drug user must inevitably come down from intense highs to struggle
with the everyday world of school, work, and personal relationships with
nonusers. One ex-dealer reflects on tongue-speaking in light of these
problems:

> When I began to speak in tongues I remember thinking it was a
> kind of Nirvana. [laughing] I was as high as I'd ever been on
> drugs, but it was a different kind of high, from a power outside
> myself, with a clearness and direction I'd never had before. The

reality of it was what was most beautiful. It was the reality of meeting God. I'd found something that was actually gonna take care of me and govern my life. It was something I could hold onto forever. It wasn't just a passing experience on a magical weekend.

With the Lord now, I have control of it. Whenever I want to speak to Him, I can. When I did drugs, I had a carefree feeling. I didn't worry about anything. It's the same way with God, that's how He wants us to be, only in a more real, responsible way. Don't worry about your job or where you're gonna eat. But God also says don't be lazy or just sit around, which is all I ever did before.

The carefree ecstasy of tongue-speaking compares with the hippie's psychedelic highs, Nirvana and all. But its divine agency, ritual control, and congregational context impart moral purpose and order to the convert's experience. If he follows this order, then his religious faith and community in turn reinforce the uplifting effects of the rite itself.

Ethicizing Ecstasy

Psychedelic bad trips produced a peculiar kind of *ekstasis*, one filled with solitary terror and self-disintegration: "I saw my skin come off in my hands. I saw the wall melting like candles." This, too, led sixties youth to appreciate the dualistic cosmology and regulated community of the LWF. Repeated bad trips instilled in those who took them a sense of life without meaning and a world preyed on by evil as a positive agency. The wife of a rock musician attests:

I got so I hated drugs. I remember once we were all on acid, and I had left my baby sleeping in a loft. All the muscles in my legs gave out. I heard my baby crying. He was hungry and I was supposed to nurse him. But I couldn't stand up or move. Then I began to think about nursing him with this drug inside of me, and it petrified me. I began to think drugs were something really evil, even though I didn't really understand what evil meant then.

Drug use leads to a sense of oneself liable to being labeled a sinner. This is the necessary precondition to repentance, and as such it is the first step of Christian conversion. "Call yourself what you are—a sinner!" cries Pastor Bobbi. "Then you can change." Even where overt dysfunctions related to drugs (illness, job loss, narcotic addiction) are absent and conversion is not clearly a "gutter-rebound" rescue, LWF youths claim, "If I had never become a hippie, I would never have realized I was a sinner. If you told my parents, 'You're sinners. You kill and cheat and steal and lie,' they'd just laugh and say you're crazy. But drugs showed us the bottom, the dregs." Drug use per se and adoption of the drug ideology gave the hippie a self-image as something of an outlaw and deviant, even if she did not act out these roles publicly or incur formal sanctions for doing so. Psychedelic drug experience often gave hallucinatory reality to various alternative or possible self-conceptions, some of them malevolent, perverse, and self-destructive. Thus one could experience herself as a murderer, thief, or suicide without actually intending or performing any such acts.

Psychedelic drugs motivated their own kind of perfectionism. Its gnostic dimensions are relatively familiar under the rubric of "expanding your consciousness" and lead more clearly to the appeals of religious mysticism and the human potential movement than to Christian sectarianism. But there is also a moral dimension to the perfectionism of the drug subculture. A sect youth describes his first bad acid trip:

> Scenes started flashing in my head, bummers. A knife going into my stomach and coming out, and pulling all my insides out. I began experiencing fears and bad things from all my life up to then. And I became convinced that I had to work on all the bad things, the weak spots, in my life. I was experiencing them, and I had to go through it and work on these areas, so they wouldn't be bad.

Psychedelic drugs can reveal moral faults and provide a means to work on them analogous to Pentecostal ritual and prayer in the LWF, which operate within the doctrinal traditions stemming from Methodist perfectionism.

Drugs also made it more plausible to judge the world as evil and doomed. Bad trips and fatal or near-fatal overdoses on hard drugs brought youths the experience of death coming without warning into the midst of life. This focused vaguer dispositions toward the counterculture's apocalyptic beliefs and later the sect's. A young woman involved with professional rock musicians, some of them drug fatalities, and herself a heroin addict for several years, comments:

> I feel real sorry for this generation in the world. We're living in an age where any day it's over [snaps fingers] just like that! Whether it's the atom bomb or an OD. We're living on the edge, edge city. In the world there's nothing to look forward to. While in the Lord it's a lucky time to live, because then you have everything to look forward to. We're the generation chosen to break the appointment of death.

Deaths on drugs and their psychic simulacra sharpened the apocalyptic edge of life for sixties youth raised with ideas of the atomic apocalypse. The present-oriented, out-of-time quality of much psychedelic experience smoothed their acceptance of the LWF's premillennial diagnosis of the present as an "end time" unlike any other, in which uniquely awful events like Vietnam and Watergate occur. Drug use drove home the disorienting impact of the social conflict of the 1960s, the cultural crisis underlying it, and the background fact that when social change quickens, the present does seem ever less like the past and the future seems ever less knowable.[14]

The LWF explains the disorienting effects of drug use in terms of demon possession, and "heals" the drug user by rites of demon expulsion that demonstrate to her the reality of cosmic agents of good and evil. A young woman describes her experience of demonic evil:

A couple of months after I got saved I was talking with Pastor. She began explaining thoughts and your thought life to me, and I started sharing with her thoughts I had from drugs and other thoughts I had had all my life. Bad thoughts, thoughts that didn't originate from God. She began to pray for me right there, and I actually doubled over—this is without ever having seen a deliverance or knowing anything about screaming demons, none of that. I began feeling something coming up through my body from my stomach and into my mouth. It was like water all stopped up with a cork, and every time the cork moves, you can feel a tug. It was a horrible thing. After a while the demon actually used my voice. It came all the way from the bottom of my gut, this terrible voice. [mimicking a raspy, groaning voice] It named itself, literally, which totally blew my mind. I couldn't believe it was me. What I'd thought was just part of myself became something else. My body went berserk. It was fighting and trying to knock off the ministers who were holding me down. It was the demon fighting back, because it was being threatened. Then there was a feeling like something physically being torn out of my mind. I was exhausted and weak after it was over, but I felt really clean.

Can you say what Pastor did?

We were sitting in her kitchen. She laid me down on the table and laid hands on me. On my face and head, on my shoulders, my stomach. She began to call on the Lord. "The Blood of Jesus," she said that over and over again. Then she began to talk to the demonic spirit—and it talked back. It actually verbalized and talked back. It was the strangest thing. My mind was split into two forces. One of them was resisting her, and it was really awful and full of rage. Then there was me, and I was like crouched in a little corner off to the side. It was like I didn't have much to do with it. All I had to do was be willing to let it go and not interfere. I didn't, and it definitely came out. I vomited and everything. It was frightening, but it was tremendous, too. Because I never even dreamed something like this could happen. It made me realize that the mind is our greatest problem.

Experiences familiar from using psychedelic drugs emerge here in a new setting: the receptive, passive quality of the conscious self; intrapsychic events attributed to or caused by an external agency; the dissociative splitting of the mind and a consequent multiplication of conflicting selves, some of them radically evil. Ritual expulsion of alien or alternative selves can also be seen as the moral reunification of the divided will which had been seduced into evil acts. This view is borne out by LWF interpretations of the rite as empowering unswervingly right choices regarding such acts as drug taking in the future.

The LWF ethicizes ecstasy by integrating it, via ritual, with a set of beliefs and moral rules that regiment the interaction of sect members within a community that affords prospects for work, study, romance, and symbolic political power. Effective drug therapy occurs within this context. So does the consolidation of ecstatic experience and moral value in the mind of the member. Says a young deacon:

> You always come down when you're on drugs. But if you're keeping your life right in the Lord, and confessing your faults and forsaking them, then you don't ever come down. You don't get sick because you had a heavy service the night before. [laughing] The movement is real.

Pentecostal ritual makes ecstasy collective and controllable in a way that psychedelic drugs cannot. It generates psychological and behavorial movement that continues beyond the evanescent leaps of intuition launched by drugs. It yields a continuous sense of oneself engaged in a process of change construable as moral perfection. A youth recalls his baptism:

> When I was baptized I panicked and started fighting up out of the waters, because I thought I was dying, like all the times in the world on drugs when I thought I was dying. It was exactly what they were telling me. They were drowning my old self and burying him and raising up a new self.

> When I came out of the waters I felt different. But I didn't really know how different until as each day went on for me, the love of the church grew in me, and some love in myself that I didn't know was there began to rise up in me.

The experience of psychic death on drugs is integrated into the death and rebirth scenario of baptism, which the convert experiences in doctrinal terms. The drug experience is at once traded on to realize the ritual experience, and that realization redeems the drug experience to a normative and a happy ending: ritual rebirth, self-definition as a morally good person, and loving relationships with others. The LWF does not merely switch mechanisms for inducing ecstatic experience. It makes over the meaning of such experience. "Our joy is not motivated by seeking," says a deacon. "It's spontaneous, because it's always already there." The sect frees experience from hip cultivation and conventional consumerism by locating it within a ritual and communal order governed by an objective moral authority. Although the feelings of its individual adherents vary, this authority and their responsibility to it remain relatively constant.

Prophetic Authority

What kind of authority does Pastor Bobbi represent? How does that authority differ from the conventional authority rejected by her young followers? The contrast between the pastor's prophetic authority and bureaucratic forms of authority in the larger society involves an ethical distinction. Sect youth indict American social institutions for failing to uphold deontological moral principles such as telling the truth. Says one,

> In the world I didn't have any respect for anyone in authority. None of them measured up to the ideals I believed in. I saw them abuse their power and act like hypocrites. I just don't believe what they say, from my parents to the President. That's what it came down to.

Biblical and humanist ideals of social authority in America still rely on a moral logic of rights and obligations, by which sect youths are judging it, not by the utilitarian logic of cost-benefit calculation which actually permeates bureaucratic decision making. Judged in the former terms, those vested with authority in American society, particularly during the Johnson and Nixon administrations, appeared hypocritically immoral to LWF youth, who implicitly rejected bureaucratic authority per se, at least insofar as it identified itself with a consequential moral style in which the good is merely some conception of social welfare.

The legitimacy of Pastor Bobbi's authority is marked by several characteristics. First, her history shows signs of divine selection: prophetic "anointment," an ecstatic journey to the edge of death, and a miraculous recovery.[15] The LWF accordingly teaches, "A shepherd must be called of God." Second, she exercises extraordinary shamanistic powers of trance induction, healing, and psychological insight, along with prophetic powers of interpretation and judgment. Thus "a shepherd tends and rules his sheep." Third, her behavior appears consistent with the textual authority of the Bible. A youth contrasts this consistency with the unconstitutional exercise of power by government leaders:

> Pastor has the authority of God because she *submits* to God. I trust her with my life, but you have to look beyond a person, even Pastor, and ask, "Do I respect what they stand for?" You

don't get your submission just from Pastor's charisma as a speaker or a figurehead. It's what she's saying, it's Bible principle. What she says is not true by her authority. It's true by God's authority, because she's using the Bible to back it up. Leaders outside, supposedly they're going by the Constitution, but that's not true. What they're saying doesn't fit with it. They're just going by their own ideas. So I don't really believe what people in government say, even though I obey it.

Fourth, Pastor Bobbi is a moral example of the sect's rules. "I don't ask you to do one thing I don't do myself," she declares. "Not one thing, and you know that." The pastor enacts the LWF's ideal of selfless love, just as "a shepherd gives his life for his sheep." She is a paragon of virtue whose entire life, complete with weeping public confessions of weakness, is exposed to the congregation. "In the church you have to have a clean life to lead," a youth remarks, "because here, man, people have moral microscopes. That's the trouble with politics in the world. You can't look at the guy's life. You never really see the guy, at least not until it's too late." Fifth, Pastor Bobbi knows each of her followers intimately, just as "a shepherd knows his sheep by name." Face to face she expresses her love for them and her moral judgment of them.

Moral Authority and Responsibility

The LWF's moral order rests on commitment to sect authority as the embodiment of divine law. One youth puts it simply, "Now that my life is governed by God's law, I go by what the Bible and Pastor and the elders say." The LWF teaches that responsibility is the ideal attitude toward moral authority. By this it means that the individual should be willing to subject and submit himself to those elders having authority over him in "God's Army," to accept discipline and chastening from them, and to assume authority for those under himself. Responsibility in the LWF also takes on a communal and egalitarian quality, since "here we *are* our brother's keeper." Each person has responsibility for his "brethren" as equals in God's "forever family," as well as responsibility to those who are "older in the Lord" and over those who are younger.

The shift from a negative to a positive conception of liberty is crucial to the responsible acceptance of sect authority by youths who rejected conventional authority. Freedom *from* restraint, integral to a utilitarian society where the good remains as varied and obscure as individual desires, becomes freedom *to* do the right act in a sectarian community where God is all-good and reveals precisely which acts are right. A youth contrasts the two concepts:

I came out of a rebellious generation in the world. We didn't listen to anybody. We just—[gives a Bronx cheer]. Freedom to me was not being tied down by rules, not being hassled by laws or cops. The less rules, the more freedom you have. You can do whatever you feel like.

The ultimate freedom the world promises is that you don't have to owe anybody anything. You don't have to rely on anybody, and they don't rely on you. That's what a lot of people are after. They're looking to get out of responsibility. They want to retire at forty-five. They don't want too many kids. They don't want to stick out their marriages.

Most people look at the Bible and see a book of do's and don'ts. But it's a law of liberty. Even though there's laws and things are set, the more you obey these laws, the more freedom in the Spirit you get. The more you obey, the more you *want* to do the right thing, the easier it is to do what you really want to. Man is only free when he is bound to Christ with a chain of love.

Negative liberty's promise that "you can do whatever you feel like" suits rebellious youth out on their own, but it offers little basis for living in a community of adults. Positive liberty, by contrast, rests on biblical rules requiring obedience to God and cooperation with others, yet it appeals to the "real" desires of a true self whose assumption echoes the counterculture. The heretofore baffling problem of knowing *what* will make one feel good is now answered by the reliable insight that knowing *how* to live—by God's laws—is the way one becomes good.

Changes of moral feeling accompany the shift from a negative to a positive idea of liberty. Former hip hedonists who once defined as right whatever act they anticipated would give them pleasure now report that they find pleasure in doing the right act, that is, the act commanded by God:

We're free! We can do anything we want. I smoke as much dope as I want right now, which is absolutely none. I don't want it. My desires are changed, by the Word of God.... And sometimes, when I have done something wrong, things that used to make me feel good don't even feel good for a moment now.

Do you mean the actual, physical feeling has changed? Like smoking dope, you don't get high any more?

No, you can still get high, but it doesn't feel good. The physical feeling hasn't changed. It's the way the feeling *feels* that's different.

Because the moral value of action now inheres in the act instead of being consequentially assigned to it from one's own wants, the rightness of acts determines the pleasure one feels, not vice versa. The anticipation of pleasure is replaced by the pleasure of anticipating doing the right act, as the hedonic calculus or the tides of impulse give way to the Decalogue.

A second change of feeling is a new sense of God-given purpose and meaning that embraces the whole of one's life. "The morning after I got saved," testifies a young woman, "I was really happy when I woke up, because I had a reason to get up. Before that, for as long as I could remember, I just didn't want to get out of bed. There was no *reason* to. Now it just came into my mind, I could serve the Lord. I've found God, and I know who I can serve now." Compliance with LWF norms establishes the convert's newfound capacity for impulse deflection, evidenced by recovery from chronic illness or ill feeling, and dramatically broken habits such as smoking, alcohol and drug use, masturbation, and sexual promiscuity. Surrendering individual discretion to an objectified moral authority yields a new feeling of personal agency, and a capacity to control one's moods and thoughts and turn them to God. This is particularly valued by heavy drug users, who describe it as a recovery of their senses:

Just thinking. To me it was normal to have about nine conversations going on in my brain at once, like a crazy cocktail party in your head. It tormented me. My mind felt like I had burned out parts of it, crystallized them with drugs. It was really terrible, that panicky weightless feeling, that you were incoherent and not making any sense at all.

The Lord had to heal my mind. The instant I came up out of the water [at baptism] I felt totally changed, like I was in the Lord's arms. He spoke to me in prophecy and said that the past was gone and like Mary [Magdalene] of old I was cleansed and forgiven.

Psychological self-control is initiated by rites of demon expulsion and baptism, aided by the mind-calming effects of tongue-speaking and private prayer, and understood in terms of forgiveness by divine authority and obedience to it.

Finally, after entry into a perfectionist community defined by a covenant, one experiences confession, discipline, and chastening as means of restitution essential to the community's ongoing intimacy and one's own sense of personal identity, not as retribution. A youth contrasts this moral feeling with her earlier attitudes, suggesting the rediscovery of a guilty conscience:

In the world when I did something wrong, I treated it like a mistake. It wasn't really my fault. It was the circumstances, the situation. I'd just try to forget about it, cover it over, and do the best I could. That's the end of it.

Now it's like I've made a promise to God, and then I broke it. It means more to me than before. I've offended someone who is all-good and powerful. And I've gone against my brothers and sisters, who love me. I need to express my grief and accept chastening in order to recover the fellowship. The hardest thing to overcome is pride and holding back from communication when you do something wrong.

By confessing and being judged in public the individual regains acceptance within the sect and recovers her own sense of self based on continuing compliance with an ethic of duty and a community of love.

Resolving Moral Disagreements

The obligation to love presses each sect member to open herself emotionally to others. These affective ties, in turn, help hold members in agreement over the content of God's will and the pastor's authority to interpret it. Interdependence between the LWF's loving community and its authoritative ethic is evident in the way sect members resolve ethical disagreements. A young deacon sketches an answer to the question:

How do you work it out when two people disagree about what's right?

In the Lord you just go to the scriptures.

What if they have different ideas about the same scripture?

Then you go to Pastor, because she's a mediator and a judge.

This strategy simply seems to follow the authoritative style of evaluation. Its dependence on the LWF's communalism becomes explicit by comparison to disagreements with outsiders:

What if you disagree with someone in the world?

I don't negotiate or compromise. I don't really debate or argue with people. I witness to them about my experience and how it's changed my life, and how I see things. You have to agree on a common source if you're gonna talk about the facts. It's like one person quoting AP and UPI for facts, and the other person says they're just not true sources. Well, God has touched me and quickened His Word in me. Man is not able, with his level of reasoning, to determine what is good or bad, and I can quote scripture to back that. But the other person has to have that experience for himself.

Intellectuals and people are always saying you gotta have an open mind and be objective and not push your beliefs. While they're always trying to push theirs on me. Because that's a doctrine, too. It is. To be objective you have to not just listen, but come to church and see the people of God, and let God touch you. Until you're really in it, you can't know what it's about.

The key issue here is how a person comes to accept sect authority as a true source of moral commands. The LWF asserts the absolute truth of scriptural and sect authority, yet acknowledges the need for a shared religious experience to generate acceptance of such authority. "The Bible is just another book before you get saved," says a youth. "Afterwards it's your survival manual. It's food."

Witnessing, the proselytizer's affirmation of his exemplary conversion experience, is distinguished from moral argument or rational persuasion. Ethical values are not derived from philosophical systems by reason, but from revelation validated, in the sense of being "quickened" or vitalized, by personal experience. "Facts" depend on consensual agreement regarding their authoritative source. This agreement itself depends on ritual experience induced by the communal group. The communal group, then, induces the ritual experience that proves the authority that validates the facts that evidence the values that maintain the group. This causal circle joins the LWF's fundamentalist emphasis on biblical revelation as the source of religious knowledge and its Pentecostal emphasis on the adherent's direct experience of the Spirit. Both revelation and ritual experience are beyond falsification, unlike rational argument or cost-benefit calculation. Their intersubjective "proof" is accessible to the outsider only by his deciding to expose himself to the sect's community and cultus. This begins the process of getting saved, which brings about vivid changes in the convert's moral life. These changes, too, are effects that become causes, since they, too, prove God's existence. "*We're* the proof of the Resurrection," proclaims a youth. "We know Christ rose by our own lives. If you look at what He drew us out of, you know nothing could have delivered us except the very power of God." Such is the proof that witnessing adduces. It aims to lead its listeners to their own "decision for Christ," which will enable God to change their lives, like the speaker's, into living proof of his glory.

II. COMMUNAL RELATIONSHIPS: SECT VERSUS SOCIETY

The communal relationships of the classic Christian sect stand counterposed to the associational relationships of modern society. The sect is intimate, private, exclusive, affective, undifferentiated, and collectively oriented. Modern society is detached, public, open, affectively neutral, differentiated, and self-oriented. the LWF follows the pattern of the classic Christian sect, and it also fulfills the communal expectations established by the counterculture in such forms as the dopers' *koinonia*. A young woman testifies:

> I used to think Indian tribes were real neat, and I wanted to be part of an Indian tribe. Communities like that, I wanted that. And here it was, just handed to me. A community of love and order. Made with God's laws. People can't do it. He had created it, so it was secure. I knew nothing could come against that. And it didn't depend on us or human government.

This is certainly the first generation of sectarian Christians for whom their church is like "an Indian tribe," yet the LWF has maintained its traditional integrity as a Christian sect. "It's all Bible pattern," says a deacon. "Whosoever is born of God loveth his brother."

Its members refer to the LWF as "the Body," explaining that "we are many members of one body, the Body of Christ, working in perfect harmony." This corporate image, found among early Christians (see I Cor. 12:12) as well as among acid heads, is worked out in ethical terms:

> If Jesus Christ is the head of the body of Christ, then we are the body, we are the Christ. If you hurt someone, you are hurting Jesus. We cannot get along without each other because we are making each other grow in grace.... When you are in trouble you make the rest of the body sick. When you are going against the Word you are making the rest of the body sick.

Since every member of the LWF's body is identified with its divine whole, for one to injure another is to offend God directly. For one to withdraw from another is to disrupt their collective effort of moral perfection. God has "cut covenant" with the LWF, commingling his son's blood with their own and morally binding them into one family. "We are blood brothers to Jesus and to one another by choice. Our relationship, fellowship, and obligations to one another are more binding and sacred than that of brothers born to the same family." These organic moral ties are symbolized by the body of Christ and ritually enacted in the sacrament of the Eucharist, whose sharing requires face-to-face confession between sect members "who have aught against their brother."

Both counterculture and sect criticize conventional society for its instrumental individualism, and both attribute their own superior status to experiential insight, moral virtuosity, and close-knit personal relationships, not to wealth, work, or power. Asked to compare relationships in the LWF to relationships outside it, a youth replies:

In the world people are looking out for number one. They're trying to just save their own skin. If they burn somebody else, they don't care. But in the church we're trying to love one another. Like a sister calls during dinner and needs a ride to the doctor. What are you gonna do? God has called us to a life of self-sacrifice. He loved us so much that He gave Himself for us, so that we can give our lives for each other. We want to give back what we've been given. We want to help each other, instead of looking the other way. There's a drawing even closer together when we see each other's weakness, instead of being repulsed and drawing back like in the world.

Self-interest and self-preservation appear to motivate relationships in society. In the LWF, relationships appear motivated by charity, an exemplary virtue that takes on obligatory weight in the biblical call to "lay down your lives for one another."

Acts of charity call forth similar acts from their recipient in response. Sect norms, too, call for each member to reciprocate the love of his fellows spontaneously and warmly, and to expose himself emotionally in both formal rites and informal fellowshipping. "People in the world don't really show themselves," observes a youth. "But in the Lord people get together and everything comes out in the open. Not just to do it, but because of perfection. We keep after each other. We want to make sure you're doing OK. Open up to us. What's going on? Let's share." Those who seek to hold back from such invitations meet a battery of ritual and pastoral sanctions, including demon expulsion and unremitting social pressure. "Satan will take hold of you when you're living in that city called 'me,'" warns the pastor. A Christian youth discusses his difficulties in fulfilling the obligation to love:

> There's a love for your brothers and sisters that surpasses all other emotions. It's a deep appreciation of each other, that God has brought each one of them there for a purpose, for your perfection. You're supposed to love each one, as if they're part of your body. People at Living Word showed that to me, and I felt it for them a lot.

> If you're having a problem in your walk and you're keeping it back, it's torment to go to church and be around the brethren. When you grow cold, it's a real drag. Something's holding you back from expressing yourself to them the way they deserve. Pastor revealed that to me. That I was satisfying my own self too much, and not laying down my life for my brothers when I could. So then a turning away was growing deeper in me. I was shunning opportunities to give willingly. She said there was a void in my life, because I joked with people too much and never let them know my real feelings and let them into me. In my heart

I knew she was right—I'm very sensitive and I cover it with joking.

That night some of the brothers stayed and laid hands on me, and prayed to God to help me. They were holding onto me, and I started feeling the love they had for me, and the love God had for me through them. It overwhelmed me. I started crying with joy, and grief that I'd let it happen. It was a beautiful thing.

At Pastor Bobbi's request, the speaker later confessed his reticence as a sin before the entire congregation. He admitted the fear underlying it, and thanked them for their forgiveness and love. Thus the emotional fabric of the LWF is woven of love but reinforced by beliefs and norms coupled with powerful ritual mechanisms, an authority who counsels individuals and directs their interaction, and the basic need to accept others because one cannot escape them short of leaving the sect. Christian perfectionism carries on the countercultural impulse to strip away hypocrisy and expose one's true and loving self to others. This self-expressive effort entails questions of moral order. Precisely who or what is one's true self, and how is it to act in a given situation? The LWF's authoritative ethic answers these questions more conclusively for its members than did the counterculture, thereby sustaining a more viable community of love.

The Moral Community

Like members of the counterculture, members of the LWF see relationships in the larger society as "game playing," in part because of their associational variety and instrumental focus. "Relating to people in the world, everything was a game," says one woman.

You have to put up fronts, a different front for each different person. Whereas in the church you just act like you want to act. People laugh when they want to laugh. I'm myself, completely. Where before I didn't even know who I was or what my real personality was. I put up so many fronts with different people, I didn't know which one was the real me. Then I started finding out what my true personality was—like the gurus talk about finding what your true self is. Well, I did it when I came to the Lord.

The experience of being known as the person one really is grows from the LWF's prescription of precisely what to do and how to do it, and from its explicit examples of a good person, set by its elders and the figure of Jesus. "Live like Christ and serve the Lord in all things," exhorts a preacher. "Whether it's ministry, family, or job, everything you do in different facets of life, do unto the Lord." This ethical ideal of the godly or Christlike person underpins a master social role centered around the sect member's calling to the ministry. As a communal social organization, the LWF seeks to regather and integrate social roles fragmented across the various sectors of an associational society: work, school, clubs, government, recreation, the marketplace. All these activities go on within the LWF. Its members interact as coworshippers, coworkers, counselors and advisees, healers and patients, teachers and students, athletes and fans, musicians and audience, and so on. In this way multiple roles become de-differentiated, giving social form to an all-encompassing definition of personhood that is essentially ethical.

The LWF criticizes relationships in the larger society for their inconstancy as the fortunes and feelings of individuals change. It attempts to transform both the structural stratification of conventional society and the affective inconstancy of countercultural society. A young deacon remarks:

> In the world people get together nine times out of ten because there's a profit in it. People are friends because they're using each other. Like when you're dealing, everybody's your friend, because you got money or good dope. But in the church people are still your friends, if you're broke or rich. Everybody is the same. There's no difference. They're not changing all the time, like people in the world. One morning they wake up feeling different, so they're gonna act different all day. In the church when you're down, people are still your friends. But in the world people are just fair-weather friends.

Conventional social acceptance hinges on status—tied to money, job, and schooling. This makes it vulnerable to unpredictable changes of circumstance and the all-too-predictable constraints of social-structural position. The LWF rejects stratification itself, insisting with millennial urgency on the universality of love and the absolute value of the individual soul before God:

> "Every valley shall be filled": Those who are the depressed and underprivileged shall be brought up. "Every mountain and hill shall be brought low": the overprivileged, the self-exalted shall be brought down (Luke 3:4-6).

> No matter who you are or what you are, no matter what problems, defeats, or circumstances, if you want to see the Lord, you will be a people who are equal, who are unified, who are one; of one accord, of one mind. Everything shall be coming up to the same level making the way of the Lord straight for His coming.

High and low standing in the larger society will be leveled by the Second Coming, and to prepare for this event the LWF pledges itself to utter social equality and unity in the present. But the sect does not simply reject conventional social status. It also shifts the bases of status from economic, educational, and political success to moral and spiritual perfection. In so doing it makes social acceptance invulnerable to circumstantial reverses or social-structural barriers. Ideally, it frees acceptance from the external forces of the society and the internal forces of impulse altogether, tying it solely to the individual's will to decide for Jesus and comply with authoritatively fixed rules. Thus the individual can find dignity, and a reliable community of friends can attain stability in the otherwise shifting wasteland of low-status associates or impulsive lovers.[16]

The sect separates itself from the society by commitment to a special doctrine, ethic, and organization. Few members are marginal, and few disagreements last long. "It's too uncomfortable to sit on the fence at the Living Word," says one youth. "It's too sharp and narrow. We all believe the same thing. If someone doesn't agree, we don't compromise. Either they come under subjection to Pastor, or they leave." The LWF's boundaries define a separate ideological generation, as it were, which is nonetheless integral with the larger society in two respects. First, the sect represents youth's re-entry into an age-integrated society, after adolescent exodus from their natural families and countercultural antagonism toward their elders, as expressed in the hip maxim, "You can't trust anybody over thirty." A young leader of prayer meetings reflects on his movement away from such sentiments:

> Before I really felt the generation gap. It wasn't just not trusting people over thirty, you didn't hang around with older people, you didn't know any of them. It was one of the things that really astounded me here, the unity of all ages. When I came in I began to have friends, really good friends, fifteen years older than me and people my parents' age. I'd never had that before. The inhibitions that I'd had before were gone. It was different here. It's a family, because we all have the same thing in common, the Lord.

The sect's single ideological generation spans age barriers, reconciling sixties youth to the generation of their parents, if not to the parents themselves, in a process of symbolic reparenting. Thus "Pastor is more of a mother to me than my own mother ever was," as sect youth testify. Rejecting age prejudice and hip self-righteousness has helped them communicate, work, and get along with their elders in the larger society, enabling them to function in the established order without surrendering their alienation from it. Sixties youth turned sectarian Christians have given their own special meaning to the Christian's traditional status of living "in but not of the world."

The second respect in which the sectarian out-group is integral with the established social order is its espousal *and* enactment of biblical morality, especially the ethic of universal love, insofar as that morality constitutes an important part of the rhetorical reality of American society.

One youth, who once belonged to a motorcycle gang, makes the point:

> In the world people run in groups. Society groups, rich people, poor people. Everybody finds a group. But what I found out from running with all different kinds of groups is everybody's cheating everybody else. But when I came to the Lord, all these people have shown me is love and trust—what you've been looking for all your life. People say, well, it's just because they're Christians. No, it's because they love the Lord, and believe in Him. The only thing I've ever seen hold up is Christians through their lives. I mean the real Christians, who are always following the Lord, not just on Sundays. *They live the way society says the perfect man should live.* They're always striving to do right, while in the world people just strive for money and power. They think they can buy a perfect life. But what it is is the love and trust the Lord gives each one of us. [italics added]

The LWF's rigorous authoritative ethic provides leverage for the sectarian's moral indictment of the society at large, and generates the compensatory status of his own moral superiority to it. But it also reintegrates him to the society. It redeems the biblical ideal itself, and the America of the mind for which it stands, by showing that the ideal can be lived out and that it can create a loving and ordered community when it is lived out.

Sex Roles, Courtship, and Marriage

When sixties youth entered the LWF, they found themselves within a familistic "marrying church" that strikingly altered their sexual attitudes and behavior. Especially for the working-class males, earlier sexual relationships were casual or exploitative and marked by a double standard of fidelity and great fear of commitment: "In the world a girl was just something to see how much you could get from. I never stayed with any woman. I spent my time with different women. They were my old ladies." The countercultural pattern of benevolent, personalistic, yet temporary serial relationships prevailed among women and lower-middle-class males:

> Girls, I loved girls, you know, and I had a lot of good times with a lot of different ones. Most of the time I respected what they wanted, and they got whatever they wanted.

> I believed in God, I guess, but I just didn't think He cared one way or the other about this kind of stuff that I was doing. So I slept with girls, if I liked them and they liked me. It was the culture, I guess. If everybody agrees and there's harmony, and it's fun, you just do it and go on your way. I just lived each day without thinking of the future. Later I saw people getting hurt.

Sexual behavior before conversion was a matter of mutual consent and enjoyment, apparently without moral value or obligation, but paradoxically with injury done. Usually it was done to women. "I got hurt by people I thought loved me," says one, "and from then on, I decided to play it hard."

Sexual abuse or romantic disappointment, lovers lost and time passed with no one left to hold onto led youths toward the LWF's highly regulated and protective sexual environment. Along the way came disenchantment with the counterculture's cult of unmediated and unjudged experience. A woman remembers,

> After three years I broke up with the man I'd been living with. At that point I was really bitter about guys. I was afraid of getting involved, because I didn't want to get burnt anymore. I partied a lot and went out with two or three guys at once. I found myself getting disgusted and frustrated with people.

> When you're a little child, you think about growing up and being Cinderella—marry the prince and going off to the castle. Then you grow up, and you find out it's not like that. You grow up and you see all different groups of people. I always wanted to know them all. I wanted to be the kind of person who could say I'd been everywhere, seen everything, done everything. That was a kind of driving force to get me to doing all these things—things I actually didn't want to do, but I made myself do. Because I didn't want to be narrow-minded, like my parents. I wanted to know.

Attempting to experience "everything" in a highly pluralistic society is bound to make for intense confusion. Doing so with hip assumptions of universal good will and a lack of street-bred savvy make for victimization. The hippie's weariness with experience represents more than battle fatigue from combat in the erogenous zone. It is weariness with a struggle, bohemian in its appetite and liberal in its tolerance, to release oneself and the world from the "narrow-minded" confines of ignorance and injustice. Failure to achieve these ends by any available means turns the seeker's concern toward regular certainty, even if it requires rigidity. Having been burnt herself, the hip seeker is prepared to accept Pastor Bobbi's indictment of the expressive ethic: "The world with its permissiveness of free love is an abomination unto God. They think they're 'expressing' themselves—huh!—but all they're expressing is sin and destruction." Communal love comes to be realized, by contrast, in the context of a community vested with powers of regulation and exclusion, like the LWF's.

All romantic behavior in the sect immediately implies serious courtship headed toward marriage, which is a commitment irreversible for the rest of one's sectarian lifetime. Compare the hippie's earlier description of his carefree affairs with that of his Christian engagement:

It's a kind of inner conviction I have that she's the one God set apart for me from a long time ago, that I should cherish and value. I know sometime we will have a family together.

Satan tempts your mind sexually, but you can say no to it. Where before it wasn't even a temptation. It was just there, like drinking when you're thirsty. Saying no is strengthening for us. There's a real depth that wasn't there before. We can see through each other.

The sect rationalizes courtship by a notion of romantic predestination, encourages interpersonal gratification as it unfolds, and withholds sexual gratification until marriage.

The aura of erotic as well as agapistic love surrounds the sect's devotionalism, which in turn fuels the fires of courtship. "Even before I knew any guys in the church," remarks a young woman, "I would dress up to be beautiful and glorifying to the Lord." Courting a divine lover has its earthly side effects, sensitizing the devout to one another's love and calling for extraordinarily tight yet finely adjusted controls on the development of that love. A courting couple is never to be alone together. Only light kissing on the lips, hugs, and handholding are allowed. Such rules hold down overt competition for partners and minimize breakups and reversals between them; they press romantically attracted persons to stabilize their relationship quickly, either to be or not to be a couple in public, and in the former event to become officially engaged. This encourages great care in initiating courtship. "You better be careful who you look at around here," jokes a young man, "or before you know it you'll wind up married to them." Caution in courting also arises because of the impossibility of hiding rejection or later avoiding the object of one's unreciprocated love. When his romantic attentions are reciprocated, the male then declares his intentions, not to the woman but to the pastor privately. She may approve or disapprove the relation, or control its probationary development by specifying where and how often the pair may court.

The restriction of sexual activity to marriage has allowed young sect members, especially women, to interact warmly with members of the other sex without fear of being misunderstood or entangled sexually as a result. One woman explains:

When I came to the Lord I didn't know how to relate to men as brothers, because there's always that fear and possibility of "Where's this gonna lead?" Always, with anybody you even talk to. Right away it's a big physical thing, then afterward you start to know them as a person—for better or worse. It's terrible, because it means there's no other kind of relationship possible. To have brothers, you have to learn and think how to relate to them. It's wonderful to have that freedom, from knowing exactly what the rules are.

Conventional categories dominating heterosexual relationships are those of potential, present, or discarded lover, or rejected candidate. By restricting sexual behavior, the LWF's positive liberty opens up the categories of "brother" and "sister," the fictive kin of heterosexual friendship, thereby cementing and stabilizing heterosexual relationships outside as well as within paired couples. In this way courtship in the LWF facilitates not only marriage but the kind of social network (dyads embedded in strong heterosexual cliques multiply articulated with one another) that gives the sect its tremendous solidarity and intimacy.

The Holy Family

The LWF holds up marriage as a necessary condition of adulthood. Getting married represents commitment to living as an adult, to "settling down and getting established." "It is time for us to stop being immature children and grow up in Jesus," exhorts Pastor Bobbi. Sixties youth entered the sect at the threshold of adulthood yet at odds with its values. Ideologically and circumstantially the LWF ushers them onward into a social world ideally composed of spouses and their families, regardless of all its young single members. In this world casual heterosexual relationships and extramarital sexual experience are categorically unavailable, and the meaning of being a man or a woman—working and loving—can only be realized in marriage. "When you're in the world," concludes a young man, "you're just running around all over the place with different girlfriends. Now you're settled down into a church, and it's just one family. So it's natural to get married." Once involved in a familistic movement and committed to its values, the youth "naturally" marries.

Monogamous marriage appears to sect members as the ideal human relation, since it corresponds to the biblical relation between God and elect. "It's just right to have that one person I belong to and he belongs to me," says one. "The Bible is full of that—God and His people. He talks about His relationship to man as a marriage. He puts it all on a sexual level." The marital ideal is also embodied in the LWF itself. Its social world revolves around the equation of familistic sect and sacralized family. "Your family is the most basic church, and Christ is its head. The church is one forever family. It's the bride of Christ." Both sect and family are hierarchical authority structures, in which power, grace, and wisdom are transmitted and mediated downward from the divine through human ranks. Explains a deacon,

> There is a definite order in God. A man doesn't lose his manhood, no, he learns his place and duties. He can rest in that. He doesn't have to be more than he is. God's on the throne, not man. He doesn't have to build himself up and get trapped in

pride and self-seeking. God is our head. Christ mediates between man and God. Man mediates between Christ and woman. A woman looks up to her husband as a man looks to Christ. She mediates between the man and the children, and they fall into place. It's a man's duty to be the spiritual head of his household. He's actually the priest and prophet of the household.

The husband is less lord of his own castle than priest transmitting God's will, revealed through the pastor, to his family. The husband's priestly role grants him work in his home more important than his work in the world of a blue-collar jobholder. It affords him the security of drawing on the external moral authority of the sect and its closed community for his own authority, instead of trying to assert his own will on a world unresponsive to the resources he can marshal.[17]

A woman submits to her husband as and if he submits to the authority and rules of the sect. If he does not, she is obligated to resist his wishes. "Pastor says to put the Lord before your husband," a young married woman comments. "As long as we put the Lord first, nothing can go wrong in our marriage. In the world, as soon as you don't please each other, it's all over." As "a woman of God" directly related to divine and sect authority, the woman acquires an ethical independence that gives her fixed rights as well as obligations. At the same time, the sect's moral authority stabilizes her marriage in a way that simple contractual parity with her husband could not. Young women commonly report increased self-respect based on their integrity as moral agents. Says one, "I'd try to come up to the guy's standards in the world, but I'd feel rebellion, because they were just his own. Now I know where I stand, and I can submit, too, because they're God's standards."

In addition to ethical independence for women, two other major changes in sex roles occur in the LWF. First, women are reconciled to the traditional (lower-) middle-class role of wife, homemaker, and mother idealized as active and ordained by God. The LWF stresses mastery of such household skills as cooking, sewing, and child care, and it calls for industry in their exercise. This differs sharply from the counterculture's ideal of a "free and natural woman," blue-jeaned and braless, who in fact lacked the job skills and education needed to make her own way in the world of work. Linked to impressive biblical figures (e.g. Deborah, Esther, and the "noble wife" of Proverbs 31) and embodied by Pastor Bobbi herself, the sect's ideal woman contrasts with the Women's Liberation ideal, whom sect youth brand as "competitive and selfish." The LWF's traditional activism suits upper-middle- and upper-class women without careers, "raised on permissiveness and Dr. Spock," who must now face the demands of keeping house and raising families on budgets cut back by their downward mobility as countercultural dropouts.

Second, the LWF brings about complementary changes in the emotionality and "strength" evinced by male and female. The LWF calls for men to expose and express themselves emotionally, to "break down and weep before God," and to respond to the emotional, psychic, and sexual needs of women. "If a man is really strong," says the pastor, "he will follow when the Lord leads him to be tender and humble." If it is acceptable for men to act weak in this sense, then it is all right for women to show a complementary and traditional sort of strength by mothering their men. "A man's wife takes care of him," explains one young husband. "He can cry on her shoulder." LWF youth criticize the conventional male role in tones that echo the counterculture: "What American society says a man should be is so limited. A man who cries is not manly. The only thing you're allowed to feel is an orgasm." By exemplary contrast the sect offers an image of the gentle and compassionate Jesus as perfect lover. "We have real needs," says a woman, "and the man is supposed to take care of them. He's supposed to be a provider, just like Jesus for the Church. Spiritually as well as physically. Not just putting food on the table." The conventional division of sexual labor, where men achieve and women feel, is rejected. The idea of *providing* is expanded from economic to emotional support and nurturance, which the male role of priest to the household accommodates. Women may seem to revert to traditionally subordinate roles in the LWF. But through the complementary changes just described, at least some of the interaction between the sexes in the LWF is more consonant with the empathic ideals of the counterculture than with the deferential conventions of the mainstream.[18]

III. WORK AND STATUS: REDEEMING SUCCESS

The LWF justifies low-status work and compensates for it with the sacred careers of sect ministers. Work histories of sect youth reveal the frustration of conventional professional ambitions and then of countercultural ambitions. "When I hit music, my dream was to be a rock star," says one. "Before that I wanted to be an architect, or maybe a forest ranger, but the only thing I learned how to do in high school was roll joints." Ill-equipped by social position and education to realize their early conventional aims, lower-class youths were also deflected by hip values and drug use. Most dropped out of high school or junior college, and some took up countercultural careers like drug dealing or rock music.[19] These proved competitively difficult, legally precarious or just plain dangerous, especially when one depended on them for long-term support after leaving home. Nonetheless a taste of the easy money and countercultural prestige that went with such careers made the eventual necessity of routine work all the harder to face. "You feel, well, why should I work eight hours a day," recalls an ex-dealer. "They should be giving me money, honey." Few upper-class youths directed their higher education toward conventional careers, even among those who finished college. They rejected such work on the countercultural grounds that it was simply not worth doing, in a society not worth working for. Eventually they gave up the search for alternative careers in music, arts and crafts, rural and communal living, and professional helping. "My dad was a doctor," says one. "He'd leave at seven-thirty in the morning and come home at seven-thirty at night. I mean, to me, that's not living." After an unsteady career and crushed dreams as a rock musician, the doctor's son now works as a hospital orderly, exemplifying the downward occupational mobility triggered by the hip work ethic and later rerationalized by the sect for upper-class youths.

The LWF reconciles its youth to low-status work by portraying it as divinely ordained and ultimately just. The believer is to work steadfastly in order to obey and glorify God, and to perfect himself morally, first of all; and then to provide for his family, gain resources to prepare for the millennium, aid other sect members in need, and demonstrate his own competency and manliness.[20] Work is presented as a necessity of life in the world after Adam's fall from a life of preternatural leisure in the Garden. There are many different kinds of work in the world today, some apparently more desirable than others, but God has ordained all of them, high and low, and thus we should accept as divinely given whatever it is we are doing. An elder, himself a machinist's helper for ten years, observes:

> Sure, we'd all like jobs that suit our fancy. But very few of us really have jobs like that. In the mornings we'd just as soon stay in bed sometimes. But the point is, the Lord wants us to be where we are. And our job is to do His will. He's our boss, and He's just. You go to work and you work as unto the Lord. You give your boss an honest day's work. A Christian who doesn't work is a sinner.

Socially unrewarding work is nonetheless divinely ordained. The sect undercuts both conventional careerism and the dropout alternative by transforming the different contents of secular work into the single religious category of "doing God's will." The immediate injustices of social superiors and stratification itself are outshone by the ultimate justice of God, who has made a millennial promise to the LWF to turn the existing order upside-down and place them at the top.

Upper-middle-class and upper-class youth are the most adamant in stressing the exclusively religious content of work. Most of them have dropped down to unskilled service jobs in contrast to the skilled blue-collar or clerical positions taken by many youths from lower-class backgrounds. The estranged heir of a wealthy family, who graduated from an elite college and is now pumping gas, explains his attitude toward work:

It took me a long time to realize I didn't know how to work in the world. I couldn't follow orders. I did things the way *I* wanted to. I didn't want to take any responsibility. God brought me to a place where I *could* take responsibility and where I could be totally satisfied with whatever job I got. Because He's given it to me, and I should be blessing Him for it. There's a reason for it. I don't need to think about it. I should just do it and enjoy it.

It's like Paul, who made tents. Wherever he went, he took nothing. He worked. I should be prepared to do that, too. Jesus was a carpenter, and work is necessary. It's a school of the spirit.

Such downwardly mobile youths embrace a work ethic that adaptively prescribes following orders without question or ambition instead of careerist creativity or self-advancement. The counterculture questioned the possibility of prestige or intrinsic interest in conventional work. The LWF justifies a contrasting dedication to conventional work, significantly enough, without positing either its intrinsic interest or attendant prestige. "Work can be a drudgery, it can be," says a warehouseman. "But if you seek the Lord in it, your work will praise God." This ethic, honed within a working-class tradition, suited youths who had rejected the middle-class rationale for work, who lacked the education or motive to enact it, and who found no long-term alternatives to routine occupations. The LWF enabled them to accept such work without selling out their sense of critical superiority toward the conventional society employing them.

Simultaneously, the LWF's work ethic permitted lower-middle-class youths to act on their desire for vocational competency and modest advancement, for example, from carpenter to construction crew foreman. A young baker observes,

When I was on drugs I was slow and messed up at work. I didn't like to work. Now I'm more refined in my work, and I get satisfaction from that. I've kinda worked my way up.

If I was on drugs now, I'd probably be on welfare, the type of guy who would just loaf off the government as much as I could. But now I wouldn't do it. I think I'm kind of into this Protestant worth ethic, with Horatio Alger and stuff like that. I take pride in that.

Indeed a version of the "Protestant worth ethic" can be detected in these youths, but it is neither the sort that justified the exertions of Weber's classical capitalist nor his latter-day American successor, the worldly striver laying up his consumer's kingdom on earth. The LWF encourages dependable low-status work as a condition of social respectability in the present, and as a means to support millenarian efforts whose future rewards look less like the economic striver's individual ascent to higher status than the political revolutionary's collective ascent to power.

Ministry as a Vocation

Sect ministries redeem work in several ways. They replace occupational ambitions unrealized in conventional or countercultural society with equivalent ones—teacher, musician, healer, counselor, and the like—realizable within its own boundaries. The sect translates past educational and occupational failures into preparatory steps leading to ministerial success. This prospect and the genuine personal acceptance the sect gives its young members offer them a new lease on learning. "We must respect the weakest member when they start to minister," writes the pastor. "This we prove by our response. We exercise their faith and our patience, thus a wonderful growth in all occurs because we are all learning." A young carpenter, who dreamed of going to law school before he dropped out of high school on drugs, compares his conventional and religious educations:

> In school I felt like they were forcing me to learn stuff I had no interest in. It didn't make any difference to my life. But in the church there was a spiritual experience that went along with learning that gave me the desire to know more about it. That's why I started reading the Bible, where I'd never read anything in school. The more that I knew, the better with the Lord I'd be, the better minister I'd be, just like the better lawyer knows more about the law than the other guy.

Ritual gives experiential impact to LWF doctrine and makes it worth thinking about. Practical, on-the-job training before a responsive audience brings alive the minister's career and makes it possible to pursue, as the lawyer's career never was.

Ministries make use of skills involved in members' present jobs, as in the construction trades turned to "the great work of building God's temple on the mountain." Ministries also redeem youths' preconversion experience as "trips guide," drug dealer, artist, musician, and hip ideologue. "Every bit of music I've picked up in fifteen years in the world has been used in the Lord," remarks a youth. "My old music just showed man's problems. This music answers them." Suits and ties, briefcases embossed with "Living Word Fellowship" in gold, scholarly reference works on the Bible, and medical terminology abound in the LWF. The trappings of social power and knowledge, however, are accompanied by a measure of their responsibility, substance, and results. These range from psychosomatic medical cures to business takeovers, all on a modest scale yet characterized by communal coparticipation in place of the conventional relationship between professional or technical specialist and a client-consumer.

Like the conventional professional, the LWF minister identifies himself in terms of his vocation. A young Bible teacher explains,

> You can expect your eyes to be opened to understand things, if your ministry is given to be a teacher. If it is to show mercy, you can expect your heart to change and become merciful. When we minister now, it's our lives that are affected and changed and perfected. And there's gonna be a time when our lives are so totally given over to the Lord, that whenever our lives go forth, our ministries will be expressed. They won't be separated. Your ministry should be so woven in and become a part of your life so much that when you're a teacher, you're a teacher all the time.

A ministerial vocation transforms one's personal life. The personality assimilates the peculiar requirements of a vocation, so that vocational ends are served just in the process of everyday life. In a society of secular specialists the sect reaffirms the vocation of the specifically religious virtuoso and, in contrast to the hip counterculture, it stresses the discipline needed to fill this role.

A sect ministry is considered a fulltime job. For the present this means, "We don't have time for our problems and troubles. We are drawn out and given a job to praise and honor the Lord, and He is obligated to take care of the circumstances." In return for commitment to the sect and subordination of worldly work to it, the LWF fulfills a divine promise to care for its members' material needs by means of an informal welfare system that provides groceries, rent checks, and help with medical bills and job hunting. For the future, a full-time ministry means that all sect members will be released from routine work shortly before the premillennial cataclysm, in order to announce the glad and terrifying tidings throughout the world. Asked how he feels about his job as a carpenter, a youth concludes, "I definitely won't be swinging a hammer the rest of my life. I'll be doing something that's better, building my house in the Kingdom." The millenarian accepts unacceptable work, recognizing that it is necessary for the time being yet believing that that time will be short. This belief also justifies his failure to pursue a conventional education or career, since "it's too much of a future-type thing, and that future is not gonna be there."

The Cultural Bases of Sect Status

The LWF rejects conventional status and the economic bases on which it rests. It relocates the values of success and failure from an economic to a religious context. "What I want to be successful at is spiritual work," testifies a young laborer. "That's the one thing that's really important." It follows, then, that "you can lose everything in the world but in no way is it a failure. The only failure is failing to serve God." The LWF defines status in terms of symbolic kinship, which is not earned by what one does but bestowed by God because of who one is, namely "a child of God." A young sect member sings spontaneously,

> Each one of ye shall be called sons of the most high King
> He has stretched forth His Hands and called ye unto Himself,
> And cleansed thee and made you to sit in heavenly places,
> Wherefore ye are no longer servants.
> Ye are sons of God, and therefore heirs to all His promises
> And the riches He has laid up for you.

This theme is taught to children in the LWF by adapting the story of "The Prince and the Pauper." It portrays the convert as the pauper discovered to possess "the same seed and blood" as the prince, Jesus Christ. He is brought to the palace, where, after a (baptismal) bath and "the finest schools and food and clothing," he comes into his father's inheritance. Such status is ascriptive. Like inherited wealth or kingship, it derives from the acts of others operating along kin lines. But it has social-structural effects. Though such status comes through no achievement or power of one's own, it results in one's acquisition of power and wealth. Since "God is King," his offspring are princes who gain a rich and powerful inheritance, to be wielded at the millennial dawn. In fact, symbolic kinship must be earned by the ritual and moral effort of "perfection." Viewed as an organization, then, the LWF functions like any other, making status contingent upon compliance with its rules, commitment of time and energy to its goals, and loyalty to its authorities.

Why have the youth of the LWF sought this kind of status in this kind of organization? Most of them come from class backgrounds with relatively little money, education, power, or career prospects. Denied social-structural access to conventional status, they turned first to the counterculture and then to the LWF in attempts to attain alternative sorts of status. One side of our evidence bears out this sort of social-structural explanation. It gives short shrift to the cultural as well as subjective meaning of these youths' conversion, however, and it leaves us baffled by the presence of upper-class youth in the LWF.

To fill out the picture we should note that many sect youths, while apparently failing in school and conventional careers during the sixties, nonetheless enjoyed relatively high status within a communal peer group. The hip counterculture valued their ecstatic experience and gnosis, their interpersonal and sexual precocity. "There were times on acid," recalls an ex-user of LSD, "when I'd come onto people loaded on booze, and I'd think they were this high [putting his hand at his waist]. They were inferior. I thought at the time I was having every answer to every question there could be." The hippie's superior status had a wider, more strongly legitimated appeal than that of the deviant "rebel without a cause" of previous generations of American youth. For some of the sect's youth it was reinforced by the very real prestige and pay of being a musician or drug dealer. Sixties youth found coherent ideological justification as self-perceived standard-bearers of the Age of Aquarius. It was circulated not only by their local peers but by national media. It was associated with a vanguard of upper-middle-class youth, and it was bolstered by ties with seriously posed political and cultural criticism of the larger social order and the meaning of work within it. Popular and serious justification of the counterculture's position was more strongly developed in the San Francisco Bay Area than perhaps any other region of the country. The upshot of these conditions is that sect youth had come to identify themselves with a separate and superior social status derived from distinctive cultural values, not from job, school, or income, well before they entered the LWF. Earlier countercultural forms of such status were continuous with its sectarian forms in many respects, giving way to them at the end of the counterculture's effervescence and its members' youth.

IV. POLITICAL PROTEST: FROM RADICAL TO MILLENARIAN

Almost a third of the LWF's youth joined in radical political protest. The rest were strongly aware of it, and most sympathized with it.[21] Still, lower-middle-class youth in the sect usually engaged in political activity because they identified themselves as hippies and "heads," not as radicals per se. One of them makes the distinction:

I was a rebel. Not a rebel like the radicals, though— people who were just being down on pigs and going to marches. I went to marches, but mostly just to hear the bands and get stoned. I had that antisociety attitude, but not like where I was getting militant about it.

How did you relate to the radicals?

Oh, they were my friends, because they got stoned. Like "Country Joe and the Fish" [a politicized rock music group] playing in Civic Center and Joe yelling up at the mayor in his window, "You punk!" I was on Country Joe's side, of course, because those people don't dig drugs and they aren't into our trip. See, people that took drugs had something in common through these kind of experiences that *made* them together. You figured that somebody else that did drugs, as naive or as stupid as they could be, has to go through the same things that you do. So you both know where it's at, and you're equal and together on that level.

When people came on to you about Vietnam or the government, how did you relate to it?

When people put out anything that detracted me from drugs, forget it. My motto was "Doobies [marijuana] first, then the Revolution." I thought drugs were therapy for everybody and everything. My parents should be on drugs. The President should smoke weed, the Vietnamese, the blacks. If everybody did it, the world would be perfect. That was my politics and my religion.

The lines of battle here are psychic and cultural, not social-structural. They divide "straight" from "hip" more than they divide oppressor from oppressed, rich from poor, hawk from dove, or even old from young. Expanding one's own consciousness and "turning on" others, not political conflict, are the ways to bring about a new future in which peace and love prevail. This psychedelic strategy is paralleled by that of the proselytizing sect dedicated to self-perfection and to the world's millennial transformation, though, to be sure, by different means. Both criticize the society on spiritual grounds, from which they draw their own political power.

The hip subculture in its prime had a strongly millennial thrust aimed at a utopian "Age of Aquarius" already underway. The blunting of this thrust left many hippies disappointed, angry, and tending toward their own psychedelic version of the apocalypse. Unwilling to follow the increasingly violent or theoretical course of hard-core political radicals, they were nonetheless plagued by questions about the need for coercive force and the limits of love in society. A sect youth who once led a band of itinerant drug users in a "psychedelic church" traces the evolution of his political views:

I was in the flower child generation. "Put a flower in a gun barrel." I believed what Allen Ginsberg said in *The Oracle* [an underground newspaper published during the heyday of the Haight-Ashbury] that if we did that then the cities and skyscrapers and machines would all return to nature.

But then I looked at the realities. All political changes in history come through technology and power and who controls the police. I realized the kids couldn't push out the power structure just by love. I saw the kids didn't get how strong the power was, how established the establishment was.

I thought we needed a different political system in this country. Reform and liberalism was just patchwork. We needed some other kind of government with a real order, whether it was military or religious or political, because this system was over with.

Early hopes for ending the existing order and its war by flower power, and for a romantic new age given birth by psychedelics went unfulfilled, leaving the hippie pondering the sort of ideas and forces needed to bring down one social order and establish another. The LWF's millenarism offered a picture of God and history equal to the task.

Through encounters with older activists at demonstrations or in radical campaigns to organize local high-school students and street people, some lower-class youths in the LWF developed explicitly political commitments themselves and joined activist groups around nearby Western University and several junior colleges. One such activist looks back on her political career:

I started going to political meetings and demonstrations at Western University. I began studying stuff they put me onto. The more I understood, the more there seemed to be something behind it all. Before everything had seemed so disconnected. For the first time I met people who could tie it in, and I thought I was beginning to see things fit together. Poverty, the War, the blacks. It wasn't just this or that particular problem. It was imperialism and capitalism. At least that's what I thought it was then. Now I know that isn't true, but it *is* all one thing. Like we were reading in The [LWF] Notes last night about the "mystery of iniquity": underneath all that was a diabolical power and intelligence that was causing all the injustice and chaos to come about. I saw it before in a real childlike way, like "through a glass darkly."

When I felt really good was during a sit-in, when there was a drawing together, a unity. . . . The marches I went on, they made me feel like I was doing something. When I saw it wasn't going anywhere, it started turning me off. All I was doing was stretching my legs. People would yell and shake their fist, and the government would once in a while come out and throw them a bone or push them around, then pass them off.

Meanwhile I'd see all these mouths moving, everybody arguing about the way things were. They were part of it, too, everybody angry and frustrated. People in La Raza, the blacks, white radicals against the War. It started to look like a terrible mess with no answer, like you might as well give up. I got really embittered against political people and intellectuals, people who thought they had the answers for everybody. They didn't even have the answers for themselves, while personally a lot of them were pretty hardened from hatred.

It's like I had a big hole in my heart, a big ache. If you have a searching heart in the world, or some kind of confusion, then the devil is there, using all kinds of circumstances to take advantage of it. That's what politics and drugs were. It was like I was falling into that hole in my own heart.

Initially vague, piecemeal impressions of social wrongs and one's obligation to right them were sharpened by contact with activists. They fitted a wide range of political events into a relatively integrated causal explanation, which indicted American society as a capitalist and imperialist *system*. This imputation of the causal integrity of evil is continuous with the LWF's analysis of the "mystery of iniquity," although demonism replaces capitalism as the root of all evil. As an unjust system, American society can be set right only by revolutionary transformation, not by the patchwork of liberal reform. This resembles the LWF's millennial diagnosis of the present world system as entirely corrupted by Satan and therefore savable only by God. Commitment to radical political protest, measured by great expectations of societal change, gave way to the disappointed conclusion that the political movement lacked the power needed to overturn the established order. The Revolution would not come. Increasingly striferidden, frustrated, and confused as it strained against its own sense of failure, the political movement also failed to nurture an alternative society of harmony, love, and equality within its own boundaries. Thus the true believer lost faith in the answers proposed by radical politics, but she still carries with her the charges it pointed at American society as well as the personal need, "that hole in my own heart," that the political movement promised for a time to fill. The LWF fills this personal need with an intimate countercommunity, and it subsumes the radical critique within a symbolic politics aimed at the millennial transformation of the society as a whole.

Political Disillusionment and Religious Rebirth

The political views of sect youth underwent a series of progressive disillusionments with the justice of the established society, and the power of radical or psychedelic politics to change it or to embody an alternative to it. The political outlook of the LWF is predicated upon and supports these disillusionments. The sect goes along in charging that American society is systematically wrong, positing a unified cause of this wrong, and requiring a total societal transformation in response to it. Radicals misattributed the cause of these social wrongs to mundane social-structural and political conditions instead of to supernatural agencies and their mundane moral (not political) agents. The LWF reformulates the two principal causes in the radical political analysis. Class-defined self-interest becomes man's spiritually flawed "sin nature." The forces of social determinism become those of cosmic determinism.[22] This reattribution of cause decisively explains the self-apparent failure of sixties radicals to transform the established order. "They were trying to change things men can't change. Only God can." Radicals failed to attack the real cause of the problem—demonically engendered moral evil. They lost, in short, because God was not on their side. And they couldn't do it by themselves, since only God's power can prevail against Satan's.

What emerges, then, is a neat symbolic explanation for the self-perceived failure of sixties radicals to "make the Revolution." Like much of the hip subculture, sect youths drew a deeper inference from the activists' failure than the need for a broader-based movement. Trying to change the world seemed pointless, so "you'd better change your mind instead," in the Beatles' phrase. The real locus of change lies within the self, not outside in the world. Only by changing oneself will the world be changed. "What's the best thing you can do for this country?" asks a youth. "Live like Jesus, that's what, because God's the ruler of America. Fulfill His plan, and He'll take care of the political system." Faced with their own powerlessness on the one hand and the need to change society on the other, these sixties youth adopted a program of self-transformation aimed at contractually enlisting God on their side to work the millennial transformation of society.

The LWF's present effectiveness as an exemplary alternative community of love and order, in contrast to the political or hip movement, and its power to alter accordingly the individual lives of its born-again converts are taken as proof of the powerful truth of its millenarian vision. The change from radical to millenarian political protest involves a redefinition of social power and the needs it meets. A young heiress assesses the evolution of her political involvement in terms of power:

How do your past political ideas look to you now?

I saw things then that I didn't like or that seemed unfair, and I wanted to change them. In a group of people you have, you think you have power. And that's really what the pitch is, "Power to the People." That's what's given to you, the power to change things. I remember when we were demonstrating, "*You* have the power. *You're* responsible." That's why we came together. And I had hope in it then. Afterwards I began to see we couldn't do anything by ourselves.

I feel like I have much more power now than I did then. Power to change people's lives, to make them happy. That's really what all that was about, because people are needy. Back then we didn't understand how and *why* people were needy. The Lord is the provider, of physical things, too, not just spiritual. He provides you with self-respect. That's what the movements in the sixties were partly about—people standing up and saying, "You can't walk on me." But their self-respect depends on what other people think of them. In the Lord you're delivered from that, because God's people are persecuted and trodden down. In the early church and even now, in different countries, they're starved to death and killed. They suffer as much as anybody that's oppressed. But they have a freedom that's genuine, because it's not dependent on earthly things, so nobody can take it away.

Political activists sought changes from the larger society in the distribution of social rewards and rights for certain groups, in large measure failed to get them, and so were left without self-respect. The sect renounces this "earthly" effort, generates its own internal status system instead, and lays claim to the undeniable freedom that religious renunciation provides. the LWF claims the power to effect born-again personal change, self-acceptance, and contentment, thereby addressing the root causes of human neediness. It promises its members ultimate physical and spiritual benefits from God, including millennial power and justice, and it actually looks after their day-to-day welfare in the present. Thus the LWF responds to the powerlessness of the failed political radical, elided with the more traditional powerlessness of the lower middle class. It sustains the radicals' alienation and ambition in symbolic forms that trade on and overcome their sense of past failure, while practically reconciling them to the society in which they must live until the millennial day arrives.

A Sectarian Vision of American Society

Following the biblical model, the LWF sees itself as standing outside of and prophetically indicting a society gone bad: "A nation that forsakes the Lord will ultimately be destroyed—and this nation has done that." America began as God's new Israel and is still to be loved as such. It has been brought to its present conflict and confusion by its own misdeeds, which God is punishing. How did American society reach these straits? In the following discussion two LWF deacons, an ex-drug dealer, now a retail clerk, and a baker majoring in political science at a local junior college, address this question:

How did we get to where we are now politically?

There's two ways to look at what's been happening in the government and the country. Either it's an accident, or it's been a well-planned conspiracy. Almost everybody believes in the accidental idea, but we're on the conspiracy side.

Our forefathers founded this country on the Word of God. Everything is based on the Word of God, and you can't separate it out. That's why I'm in love with this country....

How did it go wrong then?

Power corrupts. It's true. Now the people in government have always had money, but in the beginning they were God-fearing, too. They had principles. Once they moved away from God, it was just money and power. You do me a favor, and I'll do you one. Bribery, blackmail, corruption. It's still going on. People get away from the Lord, and all of a sudden the Constitution starts to change, until now they're trying to take all our rights away, like trying to get rid of guns, for example.

Is it due to individual corruption, then?

That's how it started, but then the times changed. One individual or a small group can have tremendous power. Look at Rockefeller. They change the Constitution, the media, and everything changes, so people change. It happened when people started dropping the Word of God. Instead of being concerned about other people and real needs in life, they're getting into selfish desires. There's no satisfaction, just apathy. People don't know anymore what reality is. It's confusion.

First there was radio and television, then drugs. The more that stuff was introduced into this society to fill your mind, the more the Bible got pushed out. A long time ago you could write your name in the Bible for being married and having kids, and that made it legal. That was the center. People used to gather around the Bible, and the father would read it. People were God-fearing. They prayed every day. All that stuff people don't pay any attention to now: "That's stupid." People are just concerned about themselves now, that's why there's more suicide and mental torment. Everybody's on downs, tranks, pain pills. It's easy to get them, I've done it. "Feed 'em drugs, feed 'em booze, feed 'em perversion. Keep 'em distracted and half-satisfied, while we take over the country."

Who's "we"?

First, the sect posits that American society began as a pristine ideal at one with the pristine ideal of true and original Christianity that the LWF sees itself embodying. Movement away from an authoritative ethic of Christian conduct led to a consequential morality based on money and power as the utilities that amount to the good. Thus has American society been corrupted. Separation of religion from the political, legal, and educational sectors of social life accompanied a shift from family-based communalism to an individualistic mass society. The Bible-reading family was replaced by the TV-watching individual. A sensate ideal of reality replaced an ethical ideal. Released from any ethic of obligation, persons in authority turn from law to exploitative self-aggrandizement while others drift into apathy and distracted consumption.

Who are the agents of the demonic in the world? The answer describes a power elite of every ideological stripe, centered on the liberal establishment but ranging from the big-business right to the radical and Communist left.

Who's "we"?

Actually, it's been a whole plan, started in 1776 by Adam Weintraub and a secret society of occultists, the Illuminati, to control the world through financial influence. So what's happening today is that the whole world is in the hands of a small, growing elite that's like the richest and most influential people in politics, big business, the mass media, the jet set, and the churches, and the U.N. If they want to corrupt the youth, they pump money in to do that. Or if they want to start a war, they pump money in to start it. Like there's documented proof that the Ford Foundation pumps money into the Black Panthers to get underground revolutionary and black-market stuff going to corrupt the youth.

Where is it all headed?

It isn't gonna be Communism at all, even though most people think that's what the conspiracy is all about. But the Communists are just being used by the ruling elite to bring forth one world government. So the big question of capitalism or socialism really doesn't matter. The capitalists *want* a supersocialist country. Because that means the government owns everything, government control, and this ruling elite *is* the government. That means they own everything!

How does the LWF relate to all this?

This conspiracy is what the Bible calls the false church. There's a false church, the Antichrist, and a true church. This elite is the Antichrist. It has the highest religious leaders, too—the World Council of Churches. They've got definite people, like George McGovern, who are in with this conspiracy that sit on the board of the Council. So, on the one hand, there's this false church rising up, and people are gonna start bowing down at this one-world government. On the other hand, there is rising up a remnant that God has selected to fight the Antichrist. Like the Bible says, "One of this church, even the weakest of them, shall put to flight 10,000; and two, 100,000."

Those sound like pretty good odds.

They are.

Through this symbolic history, echoing C. Wright Mills as well as Robert Welch,[23] parade the figures of post-Christian modernity, ranging from representatives of eighteenth-century enlightenment and nineteenth-century progress to the liberal-radical axis of the 1960s. The pluralistic, transideological character of this ruling elite represents a compromising and inclusive universalism, like that of the World Council of Churches, which draws the specially pointed attack of the cosmologically dualistic sect.[24] Peace and ecumenical unity constitute the greatest and most dangerous of delusions from this viewpoint, because they obscure the conflict between God and Satan the sect sees as essential to reality, and they accept the present social order it is dedicated to inverting.

The LWF lumps together Communist and capitalist, Black Panther and the World Council of Churches. Then it reduces this would-be political and cultural synthesis to one side of an apocalyptic conflict that mirrors its cosmology. One-world government is transformed into the this-worldly church of the Antichrist, locked in mortal conflict with its adversary, the LWF itself. In working out the details of this struggle, a vision of two diametric adversaries—one all-good and the other all-evil—has woven into it the paired motifs of totalitarianism and anarchy:

> *How does the Christ and Antichrist vision fit into the way things are now?*

> The way things are right now, there are so many problems that people just don't believe in the government anymore. They have revolution and rebellion toward it, and it's coming to the point where the whole society is gonna be uncontrollable, especially the youth. When people in the government and people in the street start hating each other so much, and start hating the police so much that they're bombing and killing them, then it's getting toward government overthrow. It's gonna turn more and more into a police state, until it's Nazi. It's just gonna be dictated. Everything, "This is the way it's gonna be."

> When the shooting starts in this country, it won't be just two sides. It'll be more like Vietnam, with about five different sides, all fighting each other. The hippies, the blacks, the cops, big business, the government.

> When people are completely freaking out and killing each other, fighting over scraps of food in riots—like it's headed right now— then there will be a people of saviors that can say, "Come with us. We'll show you the way. What is wrong and how to fix it." Zachariah talks about this. We're gonna be powerful. We're gonna have a real impact on the world system. The manifested sons of God. Just like Jesus was manifested on earth, He's gonna manifest this people that are without sin.

The end of the established social order will arrive with a Vietnam War brought home, an American individualism broken down to the war of all against all. This manmade firefight will climax in the destruction of urban America by a divinely ordained firestorm. Armed with this vision, sect members face the crises of the society and their own lives with a trepidation lit by excitement and anticipation, much like sixties radicals welcoming George Wallace as a reactionary speeding up the dialectic. Catastrophe is cause for millenarian optimism.

Sect members engage in a program of moral perfection to prepare for their role as world saviors, avoiding present political entanglements as pointless: "We're an army in training for the Kingdom. There's nothing we can do for this world system. It's predestined to doom, and there's no saving it from the inside." On one hand, the LWF is an intimate countercommunity that represents a refuge from the larger society, a withdrawal in response to the disappointment of high expectations formed in the sixties. Says one woman, "The whole heart of the hippie movement was peace and love. Well, the world isn't peace and love. It's death and violence. The world is ugly, and I'm glad I've been taken out of it. I'm sheltered now, and I'm thankful that we're in the world, but not of it." On the other hand, the sect represents a millennial lever of societal change:

God is preparing us to do something tremendous, that the world has never seen before. *This* is what I've been called for, not just to die and be raptured away to heaven. God is gonna use us to perform a great thing on the earth. We're going for the big one. We're going all the way. I've always wanted to help people, but I've never been able to do that on my own. I've never found a way—until now.

This essentially political vocation is framed by a promise of societal transformation in keeping with the grandest ambitions of sixties political radicals. Frustrated in more direct enactment, this political impulse has entered a symbolic dimension in the LWF comparable to the triangulated course of revolutionary theorizing or terrorism taken by other youths.

The LWF is presently enacting its political vocation via the sort of "briarpatch" communalism—pooling resources to buy land and businesses, creating one's own employment and social services—that characterizes contemporary developments among more moderate political, hip, and alternative religious groups that have emerged from the sixties counterculture nationwide and especially in the San Francisco Bay Area.[25] Thus the LWF's settlement in the Sierras sets a social example that harks back to communal ideals of the counterculture. But to these it adds entrepreneurial ideals of the lower middle class, and religious ideals of sectarian Christianity which reach back to the Puritans. The mountains are "God's wilderness," unscarred by the ecological pollution of industry and the moral pollution of godless men. Mountain Town itself appears as an embryonic holy community in LWF testimonies, which merge the myths of the hippie commune, the all-American small town, and Winthrop's godly "City upon a Hill." It is a face-to-face community of persons who are at once neighbors, coworkers, and friends. Economically they are their own masters—independent farm-

ers, craftsmen, and shopowners. Yet they all cooperate socially, and they
are all governed by one religious authority.

Both the LWF's millennial vision and its communal practices give clear
evidence that disenchantment with full-scale political struggle has led sixties
youth not simply to abandon it but to elaborate it symbolically and, in fact,
to create alternative political institutions on a more modest scale. For all its
generational specificity, the LWF expresses a political morality that resonates through much of America's lower middle class and through much of
its Pentecostal, Fundamentalist, and Evangelical religious traditions. In this
sense the Living Word Fellowship represents one of three major strands of a
new antiliberal consensus presently growing in American culture, this one
rooted in conservative Christianity and its authoritative ethic.

ANTINOMIAN RULES
The Ethical Outlook of American Zen Students

3

Pacific Zen Center* is a "spiritual center" engaged in "finding a way to transplant and develop this ancient Oriental tradition of withdrawal and return, of spiritual centering for modern America."[1] Its members practice Zen Buddhism by "sitting still" in Zen meditation, encountering a Zen master and following his example, living communally and following a monastic regimen. Zen Center numbers some 300 full-time "students," most of them unmarried upper-middle-class whites in their twenties and thirties, who practice daily in six locations. Seventy live in a large dormitory-style residence located between a black ghetto and the downtown section of a major Bay Area city, with as many others in nearby apartments. Fifty live in a monastic retreat secluded in coastal mountains several hours away. Another fifty live on an exurban farm, which they work according to ecological principles. Committed members move back and forth among these three communities and three smaller affiliated centers, staying anywhere from a few months to years at any one. One hundred of these students have been with Zen Center more than six years, another hundred more than three.[2] Several hundred other persons in the area meditate less often or simply come to lectures at these centers. Measured by its members and assets, Pacific Zen Center is among the largest Zen Buddhist organizations outside of Japan. Its leadership enjoys strong informal ties with leaders in government, the ecology movement, the artistic and psychotherapeutic subcultures, and a number of religious, educational, and charitable institutions located primarily in the area but ranging across the country as well.

Pacific Zen Center coalesced around a Japanese Zen master, a *roshi* who brought to the Bay Area his long experience as a priest and scholar, an intuitive feeling for Americans and their culture, and an uncanny power to inspire them. He arrived in 1958, at the age of fifty-three, to assist at a traditional Buddhist church serving the local Japanese-American community. Within a few months, a handful of Caucasians were joining him there in daily meditation. Aesthetic, therapeutic, and intellectual interests in Zen had led them to practice it informally in lay "householder's" fashion while they went on with relatively conventional jobs and lifestyles. Mostly

*A composite of Zen groups in the San Francisco Bay Area.

middle-aged at first, this group came to include younger members who were more committed to the specifically religious side of Zen and more akin to the cultural radicals of the Beat movement than to traditional bohemians. These younger students saw in Zen Buddhism the promise of intense spiritual discipline and, later on, an all-encompassing way of life. To this end they worked to expand Zen Center toward a more monastic form of religious practice and social organization. The master led more frequent, prolonged, and disciplined meditation. He began to delegate ritual and administrative tasks to the group's members as if they were more his fellow monks than his lay parishioners.

Incorporated in 1961, Zen Center grew modestly over the next few years around a stable nucleus of a dozen committed students.[3] In 1966 the rising tide of the counterculture began to carry increasing numbers of a new, youthful generation of members into Zen Center. Its regular attendance of twenty-five in 1965 doubled in the following year. It soared into the hundreds in the later sixties, as the ranks of hip youth swelled and many of them turned their personal aspirations toward religious expression. Then, too, Zen Center began to publicize and raise funds to open a secluded monastic retreat, which became a highly visible and attractive symbol for the aspirations of sixties youth. A trickle of middle-aged adults, tied down by steady jobs and families, who wanted to join a meditation group turned into a flood of sixties youths, burdened by little more than their backpacks, who wanted to enter Zen as a total way of life.[4]

Backed by a constituency of sixties youth and led by a handful of older students contemporary with the Beat generation, Zen Center developed its informal, nonresidential householder's practice of the early 1960s into its more rigorous, routinized, and residential monastic practice of today. Between periods of monastic retreat, students live communally in and around Zen Center's urban headquarters, working at unskilled service jobs, living on several hundred dollars per month, and saving money to return to the monastery or farm community. Students employed outside and in Zen Center's own enterprises (a bakery, print shop, restaurant, vegetable farm, grocery store, sewing shop, carpentry and housepainting crews, operation of a conference facility and a summer retreat-resort) make Zen Center financially self-sufficient in its operation, with donations going for mortgage and interest payments on its plant.[5] Zen Center's income and frugality have enabled some fifty students, most of them ordained as priests, to "go on scholarship," living and working within the center.[6] The Zen Buddhist tradition plays down doctrinal understanding in favor of actually experiencing meditation, encountering a master, and living monastically. Through these three avenues sketched below, it claims a "special transmission outside the scriptures" of Buddhist orthodoxy.[7]The student does Zen-style meditation, called *zazen*, by sitting upright with his buttocks on a low, firm cushion and both his knees on the floor. This tilts the pelvis forward and straightens the back, which sets the spine in a gentle curve and allows the muscles above the waist to relax. It lowers the chest cage and pushes the lower abdomen forward, where the body's gravity becomes centered. These conditions give the posture great stability and, more importantly, they encourage diaphragmatic or abdominal breathing. The student places his hands together in his lap, palms upward and thumbs lightly touching. (See illustrations on following pages.)[8] The head is held erect along the line of the spine, leaving the face tilted downward slightly and the chin in. The eyes are half-opened and unfocused, fixed about a yard forward on a bare wall or floor. The mouth is closed, the tongue lightly touching the palate just behind the front teeth. The beginning student is told to count silently "one" as he inhales naturally through his nose, and "two" as he exhales slowly and fully. He counts up to ten and then begins over again. If a thought comes to mind or he feels a sensation, the student is directed neither to follow it out nor to push it away, but to let it come and go without moving or losing count of his breathing. Eventually the student may simply follow his breathing without counting, work on a *koan*,[9] or "just sit."[10] Thus the student meditates without meditating *on* any conceptually defined object.

The student practices zazen in this manner for periods of forty minutes. At least three or four such periods are scheduled in each of Zen Center's residential communities in a normal day, and the rest of the day's activities are designed around zazen. The most demanding schedule, kept at the monastery, runs as follows:

3:45 A.M.	wake-up bell
4:00	zazen
4:40	kinhin (walking meditation)
4:50	zazen
5:30	service (bowing and chanting sutras)
6:00	silent study
7:00	breakfast
7:40	break
8:00	work
11:10	zazen
11:50	service
12:00 P.M.	lunch
1:00	work
4:40	bath
5:30	service
5:45	dinner
6:30	break
7:30	zazen
8:10	kinhin
8:20	zazen
9:10	zazen ends
9:30	lights out

ZAZEN POSTURE*

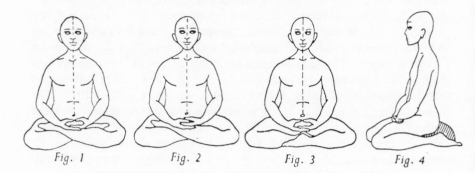

Fig. 1   Fig. 2   Fig. 3   Fig. 4

1. The full-lotus position.
2. The half-lotus position.
3. A modified Burmese posture.
4. A posture in which the legs are directed backward and placed on either side of the cushion.

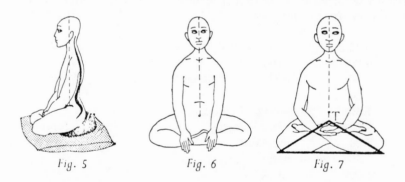

Fig. 5   Fig. 6   Fig. 7

5. The configuration of the spinal cord in a correct posture. Note that the spine is not held in a straight line.
6. This figure illustrates the method of relaxing and lowering the shoulders by placing the hands on the legs and exhaling deeply. In a correct posture a vertical line can be drawn through the center of the forehead, nose, chin, throat, and navel.
7. In a correct zazen posture the buttocks and knees form a triangle that acts as a base for the body. The weight of the body is concentrated in the lower abdomen, with the center of stress at (T). The trunk is perfectly vertical.

*From Katsuki Sekida, *Zen Training.*

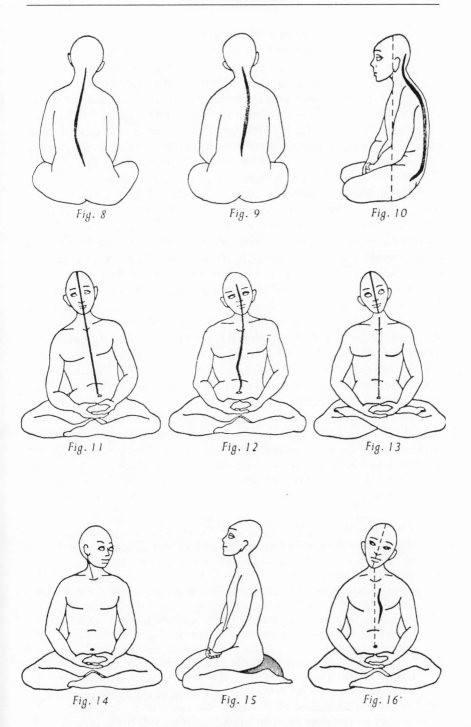

Figs. 8-16. Faulty zazen postures.

Meals are eaten in the meditation hall (*zendo*) in *oryoki*, a ritual similar to the tea ceremony. Leisure time is limited to a one-hour break after dinner.[11] Otherwise students usually go about their scheduled activities in silence. The erect posture of sitting and walking in the zendo is carried over into the rest of the day, as are the steady breathing and attention practiced in zazen. This ritual carryover provides a behavioral inner reference for Zen Center's emphasis on how everyday activities and tasks are entered into, while their external performance is defined by comprehensive procedural rules rooted in Zen's monastic tradition. By these means almost all of Zen Center's monastic life is ritualized as well as regimented.

The master lives with his students, watching them meditate, work, and interact. He lives out an example for them to follow in each of these respects. "The example of a Zen master is followed because his whole life manifests this teaching and he communicates it in every way," explains a Zen Center spokesman. "Although he works, eats, and practices under the same conditions as the students, there is some difference. And the students, perceiving this difference, are led to an examination of their own lives."[12] The devotional aspect of Buddhism, never dominant in Zen, shows up in chanting, bowing, and incense offering that take place before altars and statues of the Buddha at Zen Center. But the Buddha tends to be seen as a reminder of "the unconditioned nature of ourselves" realized by Zen practice, not as a savior or divinity.[13] Students' trust or faith in Zen is less evident in their relation to the Buddha than in their relation to the master and the practice of zazen itself.

Practice includes all activity at Zen Center, but it consists paradigmatically of doing zazen as a way "for us to experience ourselves before we think or act." *Za* means sitting and *Zen* means "that concentration or absorption in which you are one with everything, in which there is no subject-object distinction."[14] A spokesman describes this experience in characteristic terms:

> Although Zen practice begins with the simplest things, breathing, or how to sit most awakely on a chair or cushion, it brings us (you) to an experience of totality, a realization and an assurance about who and what we are which eludes verbal definition, but allows us to act with an equilibrium and deep sense of meaningfulness. We find the world not different from the possibilities within us. This does not mean that the definition of the world is limited to ourselves, but rather we experience and expand that definition to include the mutality of ourselves and the world.... Sitting still without any definite plan, we begin to experience more than we know, more than the limitations of our plan or what we have thought in the past. We observe the comings and goings and formation of thoughts. We begin to experience the sources and springs of action just by sitting still for a regular length of time every day. Not learned patterns, but the basic

functioning and natural order of body and mind are the guides of practice and ground of everyday experience. Our experience of ourselves begins to approach the totality of what we are.[15]

Zen practice "begins with the simplest things," sitting and breathing, but it seeks to realize the deepest meaning of human identity. By direct experience and self-observation, it aims to bring out the phenomenal qualities of physical posture and location, breathing, and states of mind that together make up "an assurance about who and what we are."

Zen's "conceptual teaching is aimed solely at freedom from concepts and limitations and even from Buddhism itself."[16] At the same time, the felt effects of Zen practice suggest certain conceptions of reality and find interpretation by them. From an experience of "human totality" come definitions of self and world that stress their transiency, mutuality, and monistic identity. In this ever-changing world one cannot grasp anything, not even herself. But she can find her balance, moment by moment, in "that emptiness that includes form and emptiness." (See "The Heart Sutra.") Becoming free of learned patterns, the ideal Zen student engages the expressive immediacy of "who we are at each moment and place." She also comes to recognize and be guided by certain natural regularities, "the basic functioning and natural order of body and mind." The student sits without any definite plan in mind, but she sits for a regular length of time every day, at a regular time and in a highly regularized fashion. From this regularity of practice more than from doctrine—that is, from an orthopraxy more than an orthodoxy— the recognizable shape of the Zen student's understanding emerges.

This understanding is formulated in predominantly epistemological, not cosmological terms. But it implies an ontology nonetheless, that of acosmic monism. Zen Center's spokesman goes on:

> Buddhism does not assert what is the Truth. It directs people to understand and explore their own mind and feelings, for in trying to understand Reality it is more important to know the awareness itself through which we know everything, rather than to know only what the mind knows about. This Awareness includes knowing our mind, feelings, emotions, and the conditions of our physiology. It is sometimes called Big Mind. And when we experience the root-source of our thoughts, feelings-emotions without a particular object of thought or emotion, we discover in ourselves that the essential expression of this pure-awareness is a love-compassion-gratefulness-awe for the people and things of this world. Such an expression is independent of and underlies whether we like or dislike, approve or disapprove, accept or reject.[17]

Epistemological study of "the awareness itself through which we know everything" becomes ontological realization of the Awareness called Big

Mind. Zen teaches that study of one's own awareness through practicing Zen reveals that awareness itself has no particular object, source, or referent. It is not related to anything. It includes everything. The mind that includes everything is the ultimate monist reality of Big Mind—universal and unitary consciousness. The mind that is related to something, and thus is distinct from something, is the dualist phenomenon of "small mind"—individual consciousness. Zen practice aims to break down what it takes to be the artificial dichotomy between subject and object. It "awakens" and "enlightens" the person to the conviction that in the totality of experience there is no experiencing subject or experienced object. There is only experiencing. That is, there is only Big Mind.[18] Zen disclaims any fixed cosmological "Truth" to its revelation, like that asserted by the Bible, but it does claim to change a person's existential perceptions of particular situations and his behavior in them, as described in Zen's voluminous anecdotal literature.[19]

Zen's realization of monist pure awareness engenders an attitude or disposition of character at the heart of its ethic: "a love-compassion-gratefulness-awe for the people and things of this world." Independent of like or dislike, of subjective wants or interests, this attitude of compassion, I will argue, amounts to a cardinal moral virtue that gives rise to behavior in accord with Buddhism's moral precepts. Pacific Zen Center states these as follows:

> First, no killing life
> Second, no stealing
> Third, no attaching to fulfillment
> Fourth, no illusory words
> Fifth, no selling the wine of delusion
> Sixth, no dwelling on past mistakes
> Seventh, no praise or blame
> Eighth, no hoarding materials or teachings
> Ninth, no being angry
> Tenth, no abusing the Three Treasures [of Buddhism's teaching, Buddha, and community][20]

Little discussed or directly enforced, these precepts are nonetheless recognized as describing appropriate action and underlying Zen Center's regimen.

Zen Center defines itself as a *Sangha* or Buddhist practice community, to which one belongs through religious practice rather than belief or residence. If you stop practicing meditation, you leave. Zen Center's formal organization revolves around the master. He is its abbot and chief priest and as such its administrative head. In this role he is assisted by appointed officers and a board of directors elected by a majority of Zen Center's active members. Each of Zen Center's residential communities is run routinely by another group of officers: a director, a leader of zendo activity, a work leader, guest manager, head cook, and a financial manager and purchasing agent. These and a full complement of supporting positions are distinctly titled and arranged according to a model adapted from Japanese Zen monasteries. In general, the longer a student remains at Zen Center and the greater his diligence at zazen and his competence in less responsible jobs, the more responsible the job he receives. At the same time, however, all but a few senior leaders are rotated among jobs, often in a contrapuntal fashion aimed at loosening their identification with the authority and expertise acquired in a given position.

Full-time members of Pacific Zen Center are typically college-educated young adults from upper-middle-class backgrounds.[21] Some 95 percent are Caucasian.[22] They include more single than married persons; and more men than women, in a 3 to 2 ratio that is reversed among the few students over forty.[23] Some two-thirds of those who live and practice daily in Zen Center's communities come from the generation of sixties youth. The ten students formally interviewed for this study average 30.6 years of age; all except one were between twenty-five and thirty-four. They have been involved in Zen Center for an average of 6.3 years, coming in at age twenty-four.[24] They are, then, roughly the same age as the upper-class elite in the Christian sect, but older than the Christian group as a whole. Coming from upper-middle-class backgrounds, Zen students enjoyed a longer period of education and youth than did most sect members, but they likewise entered alternative religious movements at the same point in their life cycles, toward the end of their schooling and their youth, as they came face to face with problems of long-term work, relationships, and political posture posed by the adult world.

Students at Zen Center usually grew up in affluent suburbs of major American cities, their fathers employed as professionals or business executives, and their mothers holding college degrees. There was little divorce or personal disorganization in these families compared to those of LWF youths, but there was misunderstanding and sometimes stormy generation-gap conflict. These sixties youths apparently rejected the successful professional careers and settled family lives their parents prized. Conversely, most Zen students see religion having little meaning in their parents' lives, either being ignored or confined to minimal participation in a middle-class denomination.[25] Almost all Zen students—85 to 90 percent—had some college education, often at prestigious schools. More than half have B.A. degrees and a fifth have advanced degrees, disproportionately in the humanities and arts.[26] Many reported great interest, even passion, in their studies, but few of them directed their higher education toward the professional or white-collar careers of their parents. Disillusioned with such work on countercultural grounds, these youths left college to take up the pattern of unskilled part-time or temporary labor and service work that now predominates among Zen students, although Zen Center has transformed the meaning and context of such work. They work as handymen, cabdrivers, gardeners, messengers, busboys, dishwashers, hotel and hospital help. Others, especially women, clean houses, babysit, read to the blind, keep house for the aged, and fill in as office temporaries.[27] Some men do skilled blue-collar work, as carpenters, mechanics, housepainters, and bakers. A handful of Zen students work as artists or artisans, or teach school, music, or art. Measured by conventional occupational status and income, sixties youth practicing Zen have undergone marked downward mobility in relation to their upper-middle-class parents.

Youthful Zen students formerly moved in the hip stream of the counterculture, but they were not submerged in it as were LWF youth. Older and better educated, Zen students participated in the counterculture in ways mediated more by literary-intellectual ties to the bohemian and humanist traditions and less by the popular media or a close-knit, ongoing group of peers. They characteristically used drugs as seekers after a gnostically expanded consciousness, not as "dopers" trying to "blow their minds." Before coming to Zen Center, more than three-quarters of these sixties youth used psychedelic drugs, some of them steadily over several years, but relatively few were hospitalized, arrested, or subsequently addicted to hard drugs.

The long-term friendships and cliques common among working-class youth in the LWF rarely show up among Zen students from upper-middle-class backgrounds. They spent more time studying in high school and less time hanging around outside of it. They left behind hometown friends to go to college, and parted from classmates in turn when they finished school. In some cases hip friends, college classmates, or relatives introduced one another to Zen Center by example and low-key invitations to "try out sitting on a cushion." But often individuals first recruited themselves to Zen through its literature, then came from around the country to seek out Zen Center, where on arrival they knew no one. Zen Center welcomes visitors, guests, and prospective students, but it does not engage in systematic institutional or network recruiting of new members, unlike the Christian sect and Erhard Seminars Training. Compared to LWF youth, Zen students entered sexual relationships later in adolescence, did so less casually, and had more serious thoughts of marriage before coming to Zen Center later in their twenties. They typically arrive uncoupled, and single students are more likely than couples to stay. Fewer marriages occur at Zen Center than in the Christian sect, and they come about more slowly. Roughly one-third of all sixties youths at Zen Center have married, usually after three or four years of familiarity, first as fellow students and then as steady lovers. Some of these marriages have ended in divorce, and many other serious couples end in separation instead of marriage. Partners who have split typically return to single life within the community rather than leaving it or quickly switching mates.[28]

One out of five sixties youth practicing Zen had prior ties to some social-activist or radical political organization, often while they were college students.[29] Most such organizations, like the War Resisters League, were nonviolent and aimed at opposing the Vietnam War, although their ranks extended from SDS, CORE, and the Free Speech Movement to VISTA and the American Friends Service Committee. With a half-dozen exceptions, no Zen students took leadership roles or were ever arrested for their activities connected with these organizations, yet 50 to 60 percent of them took some part in political protest, mainly by joining anti-Vietnam War demonstrations. Pacific Zen Center students were more politically involved than members of either the LWF, Erhard Seminars Training, or most other Eastern religious groups.[30] But they tended to be nonrevolutionary in strategy and consciously nonviolent in tactics. Their involvement in political protest peaked before they entered Zen Center and sharply declined afterward.

A disproportionate number of young Zen students, about half, come from Jewish backgrounds, a fact students acknowledge by joking reference to "Zen Judaism."[31] Catholic backgrounds are also overrepresented, though less so, accounting for about a quarter of the membership. Families with ties to liberal Protestant denominations or with no church ties at all yield the remaining students, leaving Evangelical and conservative Christianity barely represented. Prior to Zen perhaps a quarter of these sixties youth had some experience of conventional psychotherapy, and they were generally critical of it.[32] Yet almost all of them came to Zen with largely psychological categories to interpret it. Few had tried other alternative religions, forms of meditation, or human-potential disciplines beforehand, although students who give up Zen often go on to such alternatives.

RULES AND FEELINGS: EARLIER MORAL VIEWS

Many younger Zen students look back on their earlier moral views as an amalgam of ideas and feelings that were often ambiguous in themselves and at odds with one another. They express uneasiness or puzzlement about this, along with the belief that it was part of what led them to practice Zen. They see Zen not so much as a neat solution to earlier ethical problems but as an experiential and interpretive dissolution of them. More modestly, it appears to them as a practical way to live truly in the middle of a morally problematic world.

Zen students attribute their early sense of moral obligation to their families. "My parents had a very definite idea of how you treat people," says one, "although they didn't base it on any formal religion. It was just a fundamental respect for other human beings. You don't hurt people. You don't lie." Few of their families were devoutly or even explicitly religious, but many of them held ideals of a good person and a good society drawn from the biblical and liberal-humanist traditions. These ideals were set in terms of prescriptive principles and rules, toward which their children became increasingly ambivalent as they grew older and entered the youth culture of the 1960s. On one hand, they perceived a morality of obligation expressing the true nature of life, and they saw this definition being threatened by self-interest. One student recalls,

What did right and wrong mean to you before the sixties?

When I was a kid I used to caddy for some wealthy business executives. One of them was the descendant of a famous American philosopher. He always used to tee his ball up in the rough. Being a kid, I felt like the rules of the game were the rules of the game. A rule was something that you agreed to keep. To find out that grownups actually cheated instead of playing by the rules made the whole game senseless. They were playing to get pleasure out of it, but they were manipulating the feedback of the situation. They weren't getting any real feedback. That seemed scary, to be growing up in a world where very few people seemed to respect their own word or the reality of what they were doing.

Here keeping rules is no simple matter of individual choice consequentially pegged to pleasure. Rather, rules define the game itself, whether of golf or life, and the reality of one's actions and their feedback within it. To live meaningfully, then, one must abide by moral rules.

On the other hand, Zen students also felt tensions between moralities of apparently inflexible rules and those of self-interest or situational response. This tension is explored by a second student, somewhat older and more active politically than most but otherwise representative, as he seeks to unfold the complexity of his ethical history before beginning Zen practice:

What did you go by before you began to do Zen? What was right?

I had a real feeling of justice, of what was fair. Right meant what was fair and just, or helpful to other people. Wrong was what was hurtful, destructive, dishonest. But it's just not that simple at all. . . .

Where did that sense of fairness come from?

Mostly from my family. There was real love and acceptance there, but along with it came a lot of strings attached that were really hard to take. "Be loyal, no matter what. Make people happy. You *should* love everybody. You *should* be honest. You *should* be a good person." My parents were always talking about human nature like it was something you had to live up to. . . . When I was a kid I couldn't tell the difference between how I actually felt relating to people, and all the things I "should" feel.

How did that feeling of fairness come out in what you did?

Politically that was pretty obvious. I got into the Civil Rights movement and things at Berkeley afterwards. I went to Mississippi in 1965. My feelings of right and wrong and that kind of obligation I had for other human beings became absolute then. What was happening to other human beings was wrong. It was very, very wrong. It was very clear and very simple, and I knew where I stood. I didn't even have to think about it. What was needed at that time was people to act and to do what was right, and so I did.

In personal relationships I tried to do what was fair, but my own distortions clouded my actions. I was running all the time on what I wanted.

How did that fit with what was fair?

Well, it didn't. Politics were clear-cut. People shouldn't get ripped off. But in my personal life I was basically going by expediency, even though I had ideals and scruples, and I judged other people by what I thought I should be doing. My main ideal was treating other people as ends in themselves. Not using other people as means, not manipulating other people. Not manipulating yourself. In theory that tied everything together. But I didn't mind being dishonest or short-tempered or selfish when I felt like it. I could never work it out. It was that problem between me having legitimate needs and other people having them, too, and not being able to know where to draw the line. . . . The problem came from my feeling of being special and feeling the other person as being *other*, instead of our being together in a situation.

An ethic of rules and principles, a consequential ethic of self-interest, and the unattained ideal of an expressive ethic all coexist uneasily in this account. A sense of principled obligation, bred in the family, applies forcefully to political issues of distributive justice and equality, civil rights and liberties. When applied to the realm of personal behavior and relationships, however, such an ethic of obligation is felt, first, to be uncomfortably constraining and unrealistic in relation to the actual operation of self-interest, which is itself thought not quite justifiable. Second, an ethic of obligation is felt to suffocate expressive ideals of personal behavior.

Interpersonal relationships, especially those in the sphere of private life, ideally conform to an expressive ethic, but in practice they often fall to self-interested expediency. Zen students also report that a consequential ethic of self-interest tended to govern their earlier choices regarding school and work, attributing its encouragement to their relatively secularized, achievement-oriented upper-middle-class families. One student remarks,

Before the sixties I guess what I was most interested in was following the traditional path to conventional success, being a good
student and then a professional. Sure, I would have agreed with
all the usual moralism. Do unto others, the greatest good for the
greatest number, even the Ten Commandments. I was bound by
beliefs about right and wrong, mostly from my parents, about
going by the rules and not dumping on other people. But at the
same time it never occurred to me that it was good to have loving relations with as many people as you could, to pay real attention to other people. So the sixties kind of turned me upside-
down at first with its whole thing on love.

I was raised to be pretty selfish, although I don't think that was
my parents' overt intention. I got the idea that the model person
was someone who enjoyed a lot of external success and acted to
get that. It was someone who was kind and thoughtful of others,
too, but that was secondary. You weren't supposed to be
grouchy at the dinner table, but it was OK—as long as you got
A's in school. I felt pulled between ambitions to succeed and
meet certain intellectual and cultural standards besides, and to
be able to get along with people and be decent.

Here the heavy stress placed by the family on individual achievement and
success, applied specifically to getting ahead in school and work, propels its
consequential ethical style into general conflict with a regular ethic forbid-
ding injury and with an expressive ethic extolling spontaneous love.

In sum, Zen students looking back on their earlier moral views see
themselves little influenced by an authoritative ethical style, far less than
LWF youths. Zen students do not simply dismiss a regular ethic as authoritarian or untrue to experience, as did LWF youths. Instead they see conventional rule-oriented morality in a deeply ambiguous light. It justifies social
order and political ideals, yet it is dangerously inflexible and personally
unrealistic in its reliance on intellectual reason and its canon of consistency.
The humanistic meaning of life depends on keeping moral rules, yet in their
conventional form such rules seem neither imbued with deep inner feelings
nor fully enacted in the everyday world of work and relationships. In the
relatively rationalized, secularized background these youths knew, moral
rules had been loosened from their roots in symbolic and ritual experience,
the grounds on which countercultural personalism challenged them, and
bent to the ends of utilitarian success.

Zen students see the consequential style of utilitarianism, with its cost-
benefit calculation of want-satisfaction, as omnipresent yet associated with
expediency and manipulation. Says one, "Just going by what I wanted was
an easy thing for me to fall into, and I still do. But it's destructive, because
then you don't live life at all. You don't touch it. You just deal with it." An
expressive ethic is the one primarily associated with experiencing life both

as it is and ought to be. Zen students usually adopted this ethical style according to the countercultural pattern described above (see chapter 1), sometimes beginning with their prior exposure to bohemian views: "I remember reading stuff like Miller's *Tropic of Cancer*, where there's a certain clarity that feels right through all the shit, and that's what you go by," says one. "But it's just not as easy as that. You do something that feels right at the moment, and then afterwards it doesn't feel right anymore, and you feel bad about it." Too often feelings can't be trusted because they are biased, and so the expressive ideal breaks down into egoism. Caught in this bind, recalls a student, "I began to think that human values should last if they really come from inside us. You should know how you're supposed to be. That's why I've trusted Zen, because it does last." Seen from the standpoint of such moral histories, Zen appeals to sixties youth because it seems to create a reliable and lasting moral order immediately out of inner experience.

ZEN AND ETHICS

Like the counterculture, American Zen Buddhist morality takes in three styles of ethical evaluation—regular, consequential, and expressive—but it differs significantly in its handling of these three styles. Instead of the counterculture's largely implicit obligations of love and noninjury, these and other moral obligations are formalized in Zen by explicit rules. A set of general precepts forbids killing, stealing, lying, sexual immorality, and the use of intoxicants. Numerous "rules of order" and ad hoc regulations govern monastic life. These rules are justified, first, as instrumental means to releasing the adherent from desire and thus from suffering.[33] Second, and more basically, the rules are justified as a true expression of the nature of existence. In this respect Zen Buddhism holds a morality of rules and obligations similar to the natural-law tradition in Christianity. This is coupled with an antinomian ethical style similar to the counterculture's expressive ethic, but now the intuitions and feelings motivating the agent are shaped directly by the practice of meditation and the regimen of Zen monastic or communal life. An ethic of spontaneous, direct self-expression and situational responsiveness predominates in both the counterculture and American Zen Buddhism, but in Zen you "express your Big Self" through a meditational orthopraxy, a daily regimen, and moral rules, instead of simply "doing your own thing."

Felt Realization of Situational and Expressive Ideals

The major moral effect of Zen practice felt by its young students has been to enable them to enact the expressive ethic idealized but unattained in the counterculture. They attribute this realization primarily to the practice of Zen meditation itself and secondarily to the way of life generated within the *sangha,* the community of fellow Zen students. The expressive ethic rests on the assumption that persons have feelings that lead spontaneously to appropriate action. Zen students perceive themselves as often having failed to have such feelings in the past, or having failed to act on them. They now see themselves able to do both more reliably.

A student earlier frustrated by the vulnerability of expressive ideals to collapse into self-interest under the weight of egoistically biased feelings now reaffirms these ideals over against concepts of right based on fairness or helpfulness to others:

What do you go by now? What do right and wrong mean:

There's something to go by, but it's not any idea of right or wrong.

What is it? How do you know it?

You know it by your heart. There's a kind of acceptance and trust of myself not as a proclaimer of right and wrong but as a human being in relation to another human being.

So how do you know what to do?

I don't.

How does whatever happens happen?

Something happens. The situation *is* there, and you are in that situation. Sometimes I feel like I am a medium through which the situation is happening. The situation is there, it's happening, and it's happening through me and the other people who are there. And it's *me* who's there in the situation. It's *my* karma. So something comes out of that, too, in a way I don't even understand.

Wasn't that feeling of being one with the situation something you were looking for before? Why now and not then?

Now I'm more able to feel the situation from a place that allows for the different persons to be there without it breaking the situation down into myself and other. The difference between myself and other people isn't so clear anymore. I'm beginning to accept the feeling of separateness that I've always had, actually, and seeing that that feeling doesn't mean the condition of truly *being* separate. That feeling is just there, and it *can* be there now, without it meaning that the universe is really you against me.

Here moral knowledge is identified as the intuition of action appropriate to a given situation, which consists of persons in direct relationship. This contrasts with conceptually proclaiming right and wrong as an authority, rule maker, or cost-benefit calculator. Such intuition renders agents one with the situation itself, which appears to elicit their action simply in the process of its own happening. The individual feels himself becoming a medium of the situation. At the same time his "karmic" self, defined by the totality of his history rather than any rational choice, spontaneously expresses itself in response to the situation.

By this account the crucial transformation of feelings from a dualistic to a monistic standpoint consists, paradoxically, in accepting feelings of separateness from others, feelings that previously led to egoistic action. If the feeling of separateness between self and other is taken to validate a dualistic standpoint, then the expressive ethic gives way to displacement by another ethical style, as the agent on his own seeks guidance in rules, authority, or a calculus. To the observer, Zen's transformation of moral feeling appears to be a monistic transformation of the *interpretation* of feelings such as separateness that remain constant as feelings. The Zen student, in reply, affirms his experience of some feeling of underlying unity, attributed to meditation and monastic life. Comparison with the sixties counterculture, which also held monistic beliefs yet found itself relatively unable to realize expressive ideals, suggests how important such ritual enactment is to this realization. No less important, I will argue, are the reciprocal roles of Zen's monistic beliefs and practical rules in defining its rites.

Synthesis of the Expressive and Regular Ethical Styles: A Theory of Virtue and Obligation

The feeling that realizes the expressive ethic implies a sense of one's unity with the situation and others in it that nevertheless allows for feelings of separateness. It also conveys the interdependence of one's individual identity in relation to others. What further characteristics describe this feeling and the responses it motivates? Are they, for example, marked by consistency and generalizability in the rational philosophical sense associated with a regular ethic? "No," a student answers,

It's certainly not a matter of consistency. That's exactly what it's not. Because everything changes all the time. Each situation is itself.

Do you have some idea or maxim in your mind when you respond to a situation, like "Don't hurt anyone"?

It's more a clear, empty mind-state where you simply respond. When a situation arises, you just respond to it. You don't think

ahead of time of what you might do, because that's just hypoth-
esizing about an infinity of possible situations.... If the building's on fire, you grab everyone you can, yell "Fire!" and run
out. If you see someone drowning and you can swim, you go in
after them. Those are simple situations. When things get more
complicated, you just look at it carefully, without holding onto
any particular idea or desire about it, and you'll naturally feel
what the right thing is to do.

The expressive ethic assigns no fixed values to acts in themselves, unlike the
authoritative and regular ethical styles, so it sees no point in the latter's kind
of consistency or generalizability. However, it does imply a consistent or
constant state of mind from which appropriate acts "naturally" arise
according to the situation's conditions.

Does such a state of mind bear any resemblance to the Western idea of
moral character or virtue? If so, it appears closer to the Aristotelian ideal of
the person who knows, feels, and does the right act integrally and naturally
than it does to the Kantian ideal, who self-consciously acts from duty as distinct from personal inclination. The conversation begun above proceeds to
this question:

*So this natural feeling or clear mind-state has something to do
with what's fitting. Is there any other way to point to it? How
would you describe the kind of person who acts appropriately?*

Compassion is one side of it. Right action comes out of compassion as a feeling, not as a concept. The real work that a person
needs to be doing may take many different forms—loving people, being alone, social work, seeking truth, science. But in some
way you feel compassion and respond to what's really important
through it all as you go along....

What we're talking about is actually the Bodhisattva's way. It's a
lot to swallow. It's bigger than life. The vows are like a koan:

Sentient being are numberless, I vow to save them;
Desires are inexhaustible, I vow to put an end to them;
The dharmas are boundless, I vow to master them;
The Buddha's way is unsurpassable, I vow to attain it.

I can relate to the endlessness of it. Endless compassion and giving without any thought or condition. Without any attachment.

*What's that mean? Zen talks about "non-attachment" pretty
often. What's that mean to you?*

Non-attachment is to die.

Does it mean giving up ties to other people?

No. It's total attachment, too. Total acceptance. Being attached to our own small selves means not relating to other people or the world. It's the holding back from relating. It's the part of our mind that always wants to know, "What's in it for me?" *That's* the attachment, and the suffering comes when you don't get what you're looking for. You can't really experience what's there, because you're always looking out for yourself.

Attachment *is* compassion, and we never leave it as long as we live in the world. True compassion is attachment to everything, instead of to some particular idea of ourselves that we have. Part of the Bodhisattva's practice is to look at what you're attached to and let go of it. Letting go of it means returning to the basic state of total attachment that Buddhism calls non-attachment or no-self. This is our true nature, which we really never leave, except in some different feeling in our body-mind.

Compassion is identified as a feeling or attitude characterizing persons who act rightly. It is embodied by the Bodhisattva, a moral exemplar and personality ideal in the Mahayana Buddhist tradition, whose explicitly impossible aims the adherent vows to keep. Emulating the Bodhisattva by acting from compassion entails a certain state of consciousness described as non-attachment to one's individual self and a total acceptance of all existence. This amounts to the felt realization of acosmic monism. Consequently, the Zen student rejects comparison of non-attachment with either self-denial or altruism. He sees it instead as a monistic transcendence of the dualistic categories of egoism or altruism, of self-regarding or other-regarding moral motives. By such definition the traditional Zen Buddhist doctrine of non-attachment emerges not as a principle of ascetic self-denial or other-worldly quietism, but as that attitude of unselfish and unqualified relating to other persons essential to appropriate action. Unattached to considerations of self-interest or even perceptions of his own specialness, the Bodhisattva is free to experience the situation as it is and respond in a way that is both honestly self-expressive and truly compassionate.

American Zen students have found a cardinal moral virtue, a personality ideal, and an ideal state of consciousness all deeply rooted in the Buddhist tradition to open an avenue toward realizing the expressive ethic. Their attainment, in turn, requires diligently meditating and practicing Zen according to its rules. The Four Noble Truths of Buddhist doctrine promise that such practice will release the adherent from the suffering of life.[34] As our conversation continues, we seek to unravel this consequential argument from the regular idea of doing Zen practice for its own sake, in order to uncover the relationship these two ethical styles bear to each other and to the expressive style in Zen's moral discourse and experience:

How does non-attachment come about?

Zazen practice [Zen meditation] is the precise expression of no-self. It returns you to your own self-expression, to your own simple feeling of what's good.

How?

Well, it clarifies your perception. It gives you a chance to wake up and look around. You can see how your mind works, how desire works. You become sensitive, not in a moral sense, but like finding a certain [zazen] posture, finding out how to sit up straight from actually doing it, from practicing it.

It gives you a way to accept your own pain. "To keep paying attention even when you don't feel so good," like Roshi says. To some extent maybe you could say it enables you to act against your own desires, but it's really letting go of desires. Then the desires change form in a way. I'm not so interested in sugar anymore. That means being a little more able to do what's right, and that makes it easier to see what's right, because we're all fairly weak, so we like to tell ourselves what's in our favor is what's right, and to ignore what's likely to go the other way.

Is release from suffering the basic reason for practicing Zen? If someone looks at the Four Noble Truths it seems like Buddhists are people who feel they're suffering and they want to get out of it. What's the difference between that and doing anything else because I want to feel pleasure or not feel pain?

That's true in a way. My own feeling of suffering is what brought me to practice. If I didn't suffer at all and others did, I really wonder if I would keep practicing. Still, it feels like it's not true, too.

The Four Noble Truths say, "Life is suffering. Suffering comes from desire. So, end desire, and your suffering ends. You end desire by following Buddha's Eightfold Path: right meditation, right livelihood, and the rest. . . ." The Four Noble Truths are a brilliant exposition of human psychology about the nature of desire and point of view. When an idea of self enters our life, then it becomes very confusing. "Am I alone? Why do I feel lonely?" And we suffer. That's the function of zazen, that's the problem that non-thinking faces, to release us from that suffering. "No path, no cognition, no origination. . . ."[35] That feeling of "no" is the only way I can relate to karma, the phenomena of life as suffering.

But life *is* suffering. If we're really trying to get rid of suffering, we're not practicing Zen. We're trying to end our life. Death is the only way out of it. Zen is a way of *relating* to that suffering, moment by moment, that ends the cycle of death and rebirth that comes with the idea of self. I started Zen to get something for myself, to stop suffering, to get enlightened. Whatever it was, I was doing it for myself. I had hold of myself and I was reaching for something. Then to do it, I found out I had to give up that hold on myself. Now it has hold of me, whatever "it" is.

Our individual, conditional point of view is that everything's for me, where it's actually that everything is happening all at once and each of us is in the middle of that. Each of us is gonna have some difficulty, and each of us is gonna die after a while. And everything keeps going on. From the point of view of everything, that's OK. The world doesn't get upset just because you have some difficulty. It just keeps going on.

The world doesn't care about me individually like I want it to. Life doesn't *mean* the way we want it to. Zen practice is finally about *that* kind of suffering. It's about accepting the actual meaning of life and expressing it. So I still want things I don't get, and I still suffer. But when I don't get them, it's not like the world is all wrong and senseless. It has some meaningless meaning now that is its actual meaning.

The gist of this discussion for our purposes is that the mind-state of non-attachment, realized in the diligent performance of Zen practice, *is* a viewpoint reflecting the nature of existence. As such it *has* certain positive effects on the suffering a person feels. Suffering is caused by desire. Desire is caused not by living itself but by the dualistic delusion that I constitute a separate self for whose benefit the world and others exist. Consequently, release from suffering results from release from desire. This results from release from delusion—that is, from the enlightened awareness of the unity of existence. Release from suffering is the consequential reason the student begins to practice Zen. In the process of doing so, she reports a felt shift from the viewpoint of self-interested dualism to nonattached monism. The latter viewpoint reveals a second justification of Zen practice as a true reflection or expression of existence. The student sees this latter justification to be more fundamental.

The Four Noble Truths justify following Buddhist precepts and monastic regulations in the consequential style of egoism. Certain kinds of actions are justified by reference to the good consequences they confer on their doer. By this logic the Zen student's behavior changes not because his self-interested desires have ceased but because their content has changed. Like the millenarian Christian, the Zen student now understands different actions to be in his self-interest, and therefore he acts differently. By way of reply, the student likewise affirms a felt shift of viewpoint away from egoism and the consequential style of evaluation occurring at the crux of Zen's moral outlook. Release from suffering as the good consequence that makes acts right is translated into release from delusion (non-attachment, awareness, enlightenment) as the good state of consciousness that arises from acting rightly, that is, meditating, working, and living together on the Eightfold Path defined by regular principles in accord with reality.

Antinomian Rules

Formally, then, Buddhism obliges its adherents to follow moral rules that to Western eyes resemble natural laws or the Ten Commandments. Despite their formal importance to the Buddhist tradition, however, moral precepts and monastic regulations are hardly mentioned in Western literature on Zen. More to the point, most young Americans practicing Zen, even those in monastic and communal settings whose observed behavior conforms with the precepts and regulations, report themselves relatively unconcerned with the rules. "I don't think much about that stuff," says one. "I probably couldn't even tell you what all the precepts are offhand." Such as it is, Zen students' conscious concern with the precepts emphasizes their descriptive as opposed to prescriptive nature. One student stresses,

> The precepts express the life that we practice, not ideally but actually. They're not moral rules or commandments. They don't have that kind of [prescriptive] weight. The precepts aren't there to order us around. They're there because they *are* there in reality. They're part of truth. If you really understand your relationship with everything, there's no such thing as stealing. There's no such thing as killing. It's just a "not."

The premise of monism is necessary to make sense of this purely descriptive view of rules. A priest explains,

> The precepts come out of the inconceivable, like all of Zen. The inconceivable is the realm in which we are completely at one with each other. At that level you can't have any rules, because rules are thoughts; and as soon as we begin to think, we're separate. The precepts you can read about are just an externalized description of someone's actions who lives in the inconceivable.

For the Zen student the "inconceivable" unity of all existence is axiomatic. Its conscious realization by a given individual is conditional. Therefore, the Buddhist precepts are seen to describe unconditionally the nature of existence. And they describe the "natural" actions of a given individual, as he himself understands them, *if* that individual has realized the monistic nature of existence in his own attitudes and behavior.

Given Zen's monist premise, the precepts and rules of Buddhism merely offer an ex post facto description of compassionate behavior flowing spontaneously from the non-attached yet all-accepting state of consciousness idealized by the Bodhisattva. "The precepts are the beauty of human nature," affirms a student. Understood in this sense, these rules describe the dynamic of the expressive ethic. The student experiences this ethic and its requisite state of consciousness as the reality of moral action, generated directly from her practice of meditation. Consequently, the precepts can be seen simply as manifestations of zazen: "It's just as accurate not to talk about the form of the precepts, and just say, 'The precepts are zazen.' It's not necessary to name the parts of a flower for it to bloom. It just blooms."

Nonetheless, the observer notes that the precepts and monastic regulations externally govern meditation and define related activities. Listen, for example, to how a master interprets one of the precepts:

> The first precept, "do not kill," means do not interfere with what you cannot repair or replace (including this moment). For example, it would extend to minimizing the use of non-renewable resources—try not to use so much gasoline, propane and so forth; try to use replaceable fuels such as wood or wind. In the Sangha this is expressed through physical activity, attitudes, and rules. When Dogen-roshi, one of the greatest Zen masters of Japan, used water from a running stream to wash his clothes, he put the water that was left over back into the stream. In a Zen monastery when you pour out waste water, you should pour it towards yourself. You will treat the water very carefully. In this way you will be aware and careful with everything, treating everything as yourself, even waste.[36]

"Do not kill" broadens into a principle of not interfering with what you cannot replace. This draws on the transient, reciprocally related view of world and self in Buddhism's picture of reality, and it extends to conserving resources in ecological fashion. Note how the precept is translated into concrete monastic rules and examples, with a prescriptive as well as ritual weight: You *should* pour waste water toward yourself. Following these rules generates a certain experience and attitude of carefully "treating everything as yourself," which expresses the self and responds to the situation as conceived by Buddhist monism. Prescriptive rules are themselves embedded, indeed fused, into the descriptively given details of monastic life. "A community needs a wise, wide, intentional, philosophical, and practical base," writes a master, "that is expressed not so much by rules or philosophy itself as by the nature, details, and trivia of the daily physical activity, attitudes, and way of life."[37] Precepts and rules come down to how you actually pour out the waste water. Their recognition vanishes into an immediate response to a given situation.

For all this, norms explicitly cast in the regular style of ethical evaluation remain necessary for the unenlightened person whose practical view-point remains that of the philosophical realist or dualist. An older student underscores the point, and with it the ambiguous status of rules in American Zen:

What's the relation between following the rules and just acting appropriately?

They say the enlightened man doesn't follow the precepts. He just does what's in front of him. The precepts say that if you haven't realized your enlightenment yet—or if you don't know what you're doing and you can cop to that—then here is some guide for your behavior. If you follow it, you'll end your self-deception. For example, "Don't steal," because it's not possible to steal. If you steal, you perpetuate your dualistic misunderstanding of reality. You think, "I'm taking this from *him.*" You're reinforcing that deception, so that it strengthens itself from what you do. When we hurt someone, we cut off our own hand. When we lie, everything turns into lies. "A poppy seed swallows the Universe." The precepts say that if you behave according to them, in the world that emerges, there will be right reflection from your actions, so you'll be able to see yourself clearly and to practice.

What it comes down to is that if you don't know what's going on, you'd better observe the rules. And if you do know what's going on, you'll observe the rules anyway, without even noticing them. So you might as well observe the rules.

How are the precepts related to Zen practice itself?

The precepts are given to us as reminders of what we already know from our practice in sitting [meditation] and in everyday life. If you pay attention to whatever it is you're doing, your relationship with other people, as part of your practice, then you'll see what needs doing and how to do it. We live from moment to moment. Dogen says, "The sound that issues from the striking of emptiness is an endless and a wondrous voice that resounds before and after the fall of the hammer."[38] You listen to that resonating in your life, and you give it expression. Then periodically you check in and see how you're doing. You feel remorse or whatever. You notice your shortcomings and let go of them. Then put some effort into the next moment.

The precepts and rules dissolve into the "emptiness" of the enlightened person's monistic consciousness, merely yielding a retrospective description of the appropriate behavior that arises from it. At the same time, they retain their prescriptive form and weight for the unenlightened, who do not intuitively know what they're doing or who do not enact it spontaneously. "The Precepts are boundaries that only exist when they are crossed," as a master puts it.[39] These moral rules serve as reminders or reference points for behavior that is more continuously and experientially shaped by the flow of meditational and monastic activity.

Both Absolute and Relative

The nature of Zen's synthesis of the regular and expressive ethical styles shows up clearly in its adherents' answers to questions of ethical absolutism or relativism. Are acts right or wrong in themselves, or does their moral value vary systematically with their evaluator? Youthful members of the Christian sect have repudiated the relativistic strains of the counter-culture ethic for a thoroughgoing fundamentalist moral absolutism. Zen students typically seek to encompass both sides of the issue:

Is what's right and wrong relative to how a given person sees it or feels about it?

I'm beginning to feel clear about relative and absolute, that both are true. It's strange now to talk with people who want one or the other. Sometimes I even feel like Roshi talks out of both sides of his mouth. He does, but that's OK. Because sometimes it's appropriate to say one thing out of one side of your mouth, and sometimes it's appropriate to say something else out of the other side. It's just when *I'm* talking with him and I want some kind of set answer that I don't like it. [laughing]

So are you in a different place, then, from the person who says either it's all relative or there are moral absolutes?

That's right. He's saying, "It's relative, so there's no absolute. There's no truth. There's no right or wrong. Therefore, I get to do anything I want." Well, that's not so. You can even say "Everything is relative," and that's so. But the conclusion that, therefore, you can do anything you want to is not so. Because the opposite is also true. There are absolutely so's. You can't relinquish responsibility for what you do just because you say everything is relative. The very fact that you say it that way is automatically a recognition that you're about to do something that, absolutely, is wrong.

The Zen student rejects the extreme position of popular relativism: "If nothing is absolutely right, then it follows that absolutely nothing is wrong." Both the existence and the human need for norms formulated in the regular style are acknowledged, even while the appropriateness of an act as self-expression and situational response is held to be its ultimate right-making characteristic.

An older student succinctly summarizes Zen's synthesis of the regular and expressive ethical styles:

> The teaching is to get *beyond* right and wrong. Not to get *out* of right and wrong. Sometimes it may not just be laying your opinion on a situation to say, "That's right."

> *When is that?*

> When it's actually right. [laughing]

> *When is that?*

> When, according to circumstances, you're harmonizing body and mind with the situation. When how you are and what you're doing is actually the way things are.

> *How do you know that? Do the rules show you?*

> They can give you the idea. To get the feeling you have to wake up.

Zen's ethic follows the expressive style in positing unfailing intuition and spontaneous performance of whatever act fits a given situation at a given moment. It invites the agent to practice zazen, and then to act however he will—on the premise that the nonattached and all-accepting consciousness ideally accompanying meditation practice will lead him to harmonize with any situation a monistic world may offer. From a certain state of consciousness, then, right acts are seen to flow spontaneously, without any reference to moral rules that nevertheless describe them. Like Augustine's counsel to "Love God and do what you will," this appears to reverse the usual notion of rule-moralities that a good state of consciousness or character results from the commission of right acts and omission of wrong ones, which the rules define. But the meditational and monastic practices by which the Zen student develops the ideal state of consciousness are in their own way right acts defined by the rules, which make up more of an orthopraxy than an orthodoxy in Zen. Thus moral rules find their way back into an expressive ethic, sustaining the counterculture ideal by regularly reinforcing the otherwise uncertain attitudes and states of consciousness necessary to enact it reliably.

Now let us see how American Zen makes moral sense of the inner experience and social relations, the work and politics of sixties youth who practice it.

I. ZAZEN AND VIRTUE: FROM PSYCHEDELIC ECSTASY TO MEDITATIONAL ENSTASY

How does the experience of Zen meditation generate the non-attached state of mind and compassionate character that originate right action in Zen's ethic? What connection, if any, exists between the *enstatic* experience of Zen meditation and the ecstatic experience of psychedelic drugs?[40] To approach these two questions let us listen to the experiences youthful Zen students report on psychedelic drugs and then in meditation.

Positive experiences on psychedelic drugs, which evanesced as soon as the trip ended, marked a wished-for state of consciousness for some sixties youth, who sought in Zen a route to its permanent realization. "The last [mescaline] trip I ever took," recalls a beginning student, "really got me into Zen.":

> We went on this long walk, and it was amazing because every step of our walk was a new experience and every moment was completely full.... I really didn't know what Zen was or what meditation was, and so I really went into it blind, but I had an intuition that it was what I wanted, that Zen was a way to stay high like I had been on mescaline that day. From that day on I did zazen daily.[41]

In such cases drugs introduce the youth to a state of consciousness they themselves prove unable to sustain, and he seeks in Zen an alternative means to doing so. This simple ends-means model of the connection between drugs and Zen cannot be dismissed, but neither can it stand alone.

For one thing, many Zen students experienced a turnabout, familiar from the LWF, from initially wonderful ecstasies and insights to the terrors, confusion, and "death" of bad trips on drugs. "My last trip on acid I lived through my own death," remembers one. "I couldn't stop it. I needed thorazine to get off the trip. It terrified me. Knowing that was there and that I had to do something about it pushed me toward Zen." Zen stresses the transiency of life and the presence of death, and it presents Zen practice as a way to face "the great matter of life and death." If we consider ritual action, among its other functions, as coming to terms with indeterminable questions of human existence by symbolically enacting them, then the non-moving, noninteracting, nonthinking activity of zazen offers a living facsimile of death. From this ritual experience of death-in-life can some sense of life-in-death be made? A master explains,

> Before we were born we had no feeling; we were one with the universe. This is called "mind-only," or "essence of mind," or "big mind." After we are separated by birth from this oneness, as

the water falling from the waterfall is separated by the wind and
the rocks, then we have feeling. You have difficulty because you
have feeling. You attach to the feeling you have without knowing just how this kind of feeling is created. When you do not
realize that you are one with the river, or one with the universe,
you have fear. Whether it is separated into drops or not, water is
water. Our life and death are the same thing. When we realize
this fact we have no fear of death anymore, and we have no
actual difficulty in our life.[42]

In zazen the student ideally lets go of the feelings that evidence his separate
individuality and cause his fear of death.[43] He senses himself "becoming
unborn" and rejoining the original oneness of acosmic monism, like water
falling to its original river. Thus death no longer threatens to end our existence but offers in Nirvana the perfect composure of our original nature.

A Zen student with a long drug history touches on some of the other
ties between psychedelic and zazen experience:

Drugs come out of the technological confidence that's part of this
society. You're disillusioned with the culture, so you look for the
answer in a substance, a medicine. The obvious thing for a medicine culture, an alcohol culture. But then acid led us into new ter-
ritory, the shamanistic vision. It allowed us an experience we'd
never had before. White light, the One: the God experience,
where before all we ever had was the god idea. It gave us the
experience of being our bodies and not just having bodies. So
we're ambivalent, because we want to survive in our present
form and, besides, we don't really have a method to change how
we're living.

What about a theory?

That, too. America just didn't deliver on its basic reality description. It didn't tell us that reality is always changing, that it is un-
graspable. It pretended that everything was solid and reasonable.
All you had to do was grab hold and you'd get what you wanted
and be somebody. Which is total delusion. Acid shows you that
delusion, but it doesn't show you any way out of it.

The more you deal with the world where everything changes, the
more you ask, "How do I find a measure for my actions?" You
begin to look for what lasts. When you start that search, the only
thing you can find is to sit still, to maintain a posture. Sitting still
in itself becomes a way of searching for what lasts. In practice we
have the experience of everything always changing and our
being able to accept that.

Psychedelic drugs are seen to widen conflicts of values already present in American culture, not to cause them. Utilitarian use of drugs to manipulate moods and mental states ironically leads to shamanistic visions that undercut the mechanically reasonable premises of utilitarian culture, not merely in favor of its bohemian counterpart but in favor of mystical religion. There the student finds a surer sense of monistic truth and a lasting moral measure which drugs cannot provide.

The effects of psychedelic drugs in altering perception of self and other became clearest to LWF youths in the context of a small group, first cementing then solipsizing interpersonal relations among drug-using friends. Among Zen students, where this group context is much weaker and self-consciousness more articulated, the emphasis falls on the paradoxical changes drugs work on self-perception. Drug experience is portrayed as more exclusively gnostic, without the devotional dimension added by the intimate group. "Most of the time people are stuck in their own minds," observes a student, "with the rest of the world being an obstacle or a background to their mental drama. Drugs unstick you. The world becomes more palpable than your ideas about it." Do drugs, then, enable the individual to know herself and the world as they are? No, says the student. "Drugs don't exactly mirror reality. They set it shimmering."

One effect of drugs, however, does strike the Zen student as more real than the conditions of ordinary consciousness. Drugs dissolve the relatively rational, reified sense of self maintained by the conscious mind: "Drugs take the lid off who you think you are. You have to let go of that little number, because they tear down the conscious apparatus of your mind, which I'd never trusted much anyway. I'd really smelled a rat there!" Here the rationalist's identity becomes a coverup, a "lid" or theatrical "number" concealing an underlying reality. The conventional virtue of keeping your wits about you is inverted to that of letting go of them, in order to discover who you "really" are underneath.

Who is that? The psychedelic answer is ambiguous and practically problematic. A student reports,

> You go up and down on drugs. You have feelings of great beatitude, insight, and power. Other times you feel like a rotten, miserable dog. You're totally paranoid. Dope opens you up, for sure, but it also spaces you out. It can devastate you in your everyday functioning and your relationships, because you don't have anything to keep your act together. You know it's an act, and you can't do it anymore.

Psychedelic surrender of the rational self raises problems of how to grasp and reintegrate the nonrational self that emerges. Fundamentalist Christianity responds by reunifying the self as God's creature and partitioning the cosmos between God and Satan, while the human potential movement partitions the individual psyche in a neutral world. Zen, by contrast, seeks to dissolve the self as an entity, replacing the cosmological soul and psychological dynamics with an epistemological *no-self*. A student testifies:

> Before I started sitting I had some idea of who I was, and I took that seriously. Drugs gave me more ideas, only now they weren't reasonable ones, whereas Zen has freed me from my ideas more than anything else. Zen practice is a mystery to me. I don't *know* anything about it or about myself from doing it. We're here and we're not. We are and we aren't. The mind, which is the normal tool we know things with, is really a sixth sense. Impressions come in and go out. All we can do actually is let them come and go.
>
> In sitting you can *feel* your breathing. It feels like any other phenomenon you experience. The quality of the experience is the same. My breathing is as close as I can get to the core of my being, right? So what is it that's experiencing the breathing? I don't know. Some kind of nothing. And this breathing *is*. It's breathing me. I don't have to wonder about it anymore. The doubt of "What's this? What's that? Who am I?"—that doubt explodes. It's all one absolutely continuous fabric of existence. You can't separate out anything.

The functionally rational self of utilitarian culture is reenchanted by psychedelic drugs and "set shimmering." The irrational self that problematically ensues is resolved radically into Zen's no-self. This resolution takes place through the experience of practicing zazen—for example, through the experience of one's own breathing as establishing neither the identity of a subject nor that of any object distinct from a subject.[44]

How Zazen Alters Selfhood

How does zazen bring the student to feel and act as if released from attachment to particular ideas and desires, especially the idea that his own individual self is an enduring entity?[45] Like taking psychedelic drugs, doing zazen is "not so logical. It's more physio-logical," observes a student.

> It's like there's a big heart beating everywhere through Zen. Practice is something you work on for a long time, fifteen or twenty years, say, because there has to be an organic, physical penetration of the teaching. That's because the body—and this is something we found out on acid—will recapitulate the mind's habits. Even while you may see through your delusion in that

[psychedelic] moment of openness and clarity, when you come down, it all comes back. You find yourself in the same old situations, setting up the same emotional conflicts.

This suggests that zazen is a psychosomatic (de)conditioning process that alters the student's thoughts, feelings, and behavior by influencing the causal links between his physical and mental state, and the external situation in which he finds himself. How does zazen do this?

Immobility is the most obvious characteristic of zazen posture. Put simply, stillness of body stills the mind.[46] Zazen posture is unmoving, upright, with eyes unfocused and limbs pulled in. This posture and the abdominal breathing it induces serve to diminish stimuli reaching the brain and cortical activity in itself. In particular, they result in a softening or loss of the body's *conceptual* image, position, and location, without causing the subject to fall asleep or go numb.[47] These neurophysiological effects correspond closely to the philosophical teachings of Zen Buddhism, especially its interpretation of the individual ego as a succession of physical and mental events that momentarily appear and pass away. "Because each existence is in constant change, there is no abiding self," a master states. "In fact, the self-nature of each existence is nothing but change itself, the self-nature of all existence."[48] Zazen alters the meditator's body sense accordingly. The discrete self at once dissolves into no-self and joins with everything else. "Instead of your skin being the barrier between yourself and the world," attests a priest, "it becomes the connective tissue that joins them. Usually your body touches an 'other' at just a few points: your hands, your eyes, your sex organs. In zazen you touch the world at every point of your body. You *join* it." In zazen, then, posture changes breathing, which changes state of mind. Thus a master can say, "To take this posture itself is the purpose of our practice. When you have this posture, you have the right state of mind."[49]

Like immobile posture, quiet breathing quiets the mind. In breathing during zazen, only the muscles of the abdomen and the diaphragm are active. Other muscles, notably those of the chest, are either relaxed or in a state of constant, moderate tension. Continually retensing the abdominal respiratory muscles in opposition to the diaphragm, without moving any other parts of the body, inhibits thinking yet sustains wakefulness.[50] As when staring fixedly while holding one's breath for a minute, the subject can continue to sense things without having ideas or associations about these sensations. Immediate sensation goes on, but emotion and thought fall off. This "falling-off of body and mind," discussed in Zen teaching, corresponds to behaviorally induced changes in neurological activity, indicated on an electroencephalograph by the appearance of alpha waves, their increasing amplitude and then decreasing frequency, and finally the development of a theta rhythm.[51] The subject experiences this falling-off of body and mind with the easing of circumstantial stimuli, then of reflective self-consciousness, and finally of space, time, and causation, the categories of consciousness itself. This condition, traditionally called *samadhi*, is retrospectively reported as a kind of "emptiness" or "pure awareness" or "Big Mind" that transforms conscious activity in its wake.[52] Observes a master,

> When we sit we are nothing, we do not even realize what we are; we just sit. But when we stand up, we are there! That is the first step in creation. When you are there, everything else is there; everything is created all at once. When we emerge from nothing, when everything emerges from nothing, we see it all as a fresh new creation. This is non-attachment.[53]

Experiencing "nothing" in zazen introduces the experience of everything as created fresh and new, undulled by association or distraction. Interrupting ordinary perception in this way dehabituates it and thus renews it.[54] This renewed state of recognition *after* zazen, called *kensho* in its most vivid form, corresponds more closely to the psychedelic experience than does the *samadhi* state of sensation without recognition *during* zazen.

Ritual Practice and Moral Virtue

What does such experience in zazen imply for moral behavior? Relatively undistracted by background stimuli and uncompelled by her own thoughts and preconceptions, desires and fantasies, the ideal Zen student can be fully "there" in the situation at hand, and so she can see it truly and respond to it appropriately. Zazen demands continuous, active attention of a peculiar sort to count, follow one's breath, and "just sit." Because it is nonevaluative, such attention may seem to have little moral relevance. But repeatedly performing such activities, detached from the immediate payoffs of both utilitarian and psychic self-maintenance, requires attention not based on thinking, feeling, or judging in relation to the self. Because it is not self-interested in such a radical sense, such attention appears to provide an intuitively unbiased key to unlocking the expressive ethic.

Unlike the counterculture, Zen holds that one's capacity for unselfish attention can be realized only through disciplined practice. In zazen it offers precise forms to develop this capacity. These forms, as opposed to drugs or tongue-speaking, can be mastered and yield results only with persistent effort of will by the subject. Indeed, their results include convoluting and changing the will through this effort. While focused on breath counting, working on a koan, or just sitting, the meditator is not to follow out or suppress other objects of attention. When thoughts, feelings, and images enter her mind, she is instructed to "let them come and go. Take note of them and then let them go. Hold on to nothing." This turns out to be difficult to do, and difficult in a baffling way. "You start out trying to *do* zazen like you do other things," reflects a student. "But then you find out you can't. You can't make it happen. You can't make yourself do it. The harder you try, the more frustrated you get. You have to *be* it to do it. but how do you do that? How do you give up trying to do it, and keep on doing it?" The conscious mind cannot by itself diminish its own activity of perception and cognition. It seems instead to resist this. But it can choose to persist in a posture and a mode of breathing that gradually cause such diminution.

Physically, even ideal zazen posture exerts ongoing pressure on the muscles and joints of the legs, which eventually brings pain to even experienced students. Discouraged from moving or abandoning the posture, the beginning student tends to squirm, to quicken or force his breathing by using his chest muscles to do it, and to tense these muscles against the leg pain. He discovers that these responses intensify the pain. Through practice he learns to maintain his posture, continue breathing abdominally, and relax his muscles "through" the pain. By thus relaxing into the pain and becoming one with it, the student feels it lessen. He thereby demonstrates to himself the practical truth of Zen's monistic teaching. As long as the student holds onto and struggles against leg pain as if it were a dualistic object separable from himself, the leg pain comes and intensifies to the point of numbness. Once he accepts and monistically merges with it, leg pain comes and goes with a bearable, wavelike constancy. When he is "just sitting" and doing nothing else, the pain seems to disappear utterly.

This physical dynamic operates along with a mental one. Denied physical movement, social interaction, or any directed mental activity save breath counting, the student becomes acutely aware of his own undirected mental activity in zazen. A captive audience of one, he can freely observe but not manipulate otherwise unconscious, repressed, or rationalized associations, thoughts, desires, and fears as they come up and go through his mind.[55] If he begins to follow them out or fight them off, he is distracted from his own posture, breathing, and muscle relaxation, thereby inviting his leg pains to intensify. This occurs even when the associations themselves seem pleasurable. He discovers that pleasurable associations tie in to painful ones. He also discovers that mental events in themselves, unaccompanied by their external causes or conditions, trigger physical discomfort marked by quickened breathing, increased muscle tension, and leg pains. A master draws the monist moral of this discovery:

> Many sensations come, many thoughts or images arise, but they are just waves of your own mind. Nothing comes from outside your mind.... You yourself make the waves in your mind. If you leave your mind as it is, it will become calm. This mind is called big mind.[56]

The student learns to leave his mind as it is, to let it alone, by continually returning his attention from its "waves" of thought and feeling to his breathing, koan, or just sitting. By repeating this effort the ideal student gradually becomes more able (1) to focus his conscious attention without reference to any particular object, notably himself; (2) to see and accept otherwise unconscious associations passing through his mind without being distracted from the present situation or biasing his responses to it; and (3) to maintain a relaxed, wakeful physiological state relatively uninfluenced by the passage of unsettling external stimuli or internal associations. He comes to experience and exercise these three abilities as one and the same.

Insofar as these abilities of a person generate moral motives, knowledge, and choice that are not self-interested, they lead to right action. The counterculture usually claimed that knowledge of what is right is a sufficient condition of doing what is right. This recalls Plato's position, although for the counterculture moral knowledge is by nature intuitive and affective, not rational. Some Zen students take this view, for example, in diagnosing the breakdown of the expressive ethic as due to a failure of feeling alone. Others attribute right action at least in part to what Westerners usually call strength of will, a category developed in Aristotle's moral philosophy. Zen practice itself appears quite Aristotelian, if it is considered as a form of moral education.[57] Regularized repeated enactment of right acts, even when performed without the appropriate emotions breeds a virtuous character, which subsequently feels such emotions and naturally does the right act. Doing zazen with a regularly prescribed posture, breathing, and mental focus ideally leads to intuitive moral knowledge, feelings, and choice free of self-clinging and ambivalence toward others.[58] Zazen breeds virtue, in effect. Strength or weakness of will is not a category in the discourse of American Zen students, but *willingness* is. Zazen reportedly involves massive doses of frustration and convolutes individual volition. It calls at once for the individual to surrender his willfulness and exercise his willingness in persistently doing nothing in the face of discomfort and doubt. The transformation of moral viewpoint that Zen practice involves is not exclusively gnostic. It includes volitional change as well.

Zen's conception of the moral agent stresses his willingness and his strength to be vulnerable. This sense of self seems continuous with the counterculture and its receptive, all-accepting, even passive quality—being instead of doing. But Zen stresses being as a continuous doing, as a ground or medium of action, not simply a state of being. The focal question in koan practice, for example, is not, "What's the answer to the koan?" but "How do I express the answer to my teacher?" The continuously attentive self practicing Zen differs sharply from the psychedelic self immersed in its own visions and separated by them from the active world around it. A student suggests this difference as he complains about vainly trying to live out such visions in "the regular normal world": "I had this new fleeting understanding of the depth of my life, but I couldn't figure out how to change my practice. See, I didn't even have the word practice in my vocabulary."[59] Psychedelic ecstasies, soaring to heights outside of ordinary experience, distort perception and impair judgment. Meditational enstasy comes down to a sort of ground-level experience, which includes everyday life and focuses perception of its nature. Comments a student,

> Drugs turn the world around inside your head, but it's still out there the other way around. That makes a problem for you. Zen turns your head around and lets you see the world like it is, and you feel that's all right. Like roshi says, "The world is its own magic." Your life feels totally different than before, but it's totally ordinary. It's the way it's actually always been.

Drugs set up a separate intrapsychic world whose felt certainties jar against the world outside. The intuitive certainty of zazen encompasses the world of ordinary perception and behavior, and this world, in fact, becomes identified as Zen practice. "After you do this practice for a while," affirms a student, "you find out that, strictly speaking, there is no other way to live."

Compared to drugs, zazen experience can be better integrated with daily life because of its inherently enstatic character, but also because the ritual means of its induction (like the Christian's tongue-speaking) are integrated with Zen Center's beliefs, ethic, and social organization. Thus the experience of non-attachment takes exemplary form in the compassionate Bodhisattva, whose spontaneous actions comply with fixed moral precepts and fit the monastic regimen. The monastery embodies the identity of Zen practice and everyday life by effectively guiding its members' behavior through a shared daily round led by a master.

Master, Student, and Authority

The student makes Zen's moral viewpoint her own by meditating but also by engaging the master. What is the nature of this relationship between master and student? How does it combine with zazen practice in moral education? A long-time student writes in tribute to her master:

> A roshi is a person who has actualized that perfect freedom which is the potentiality for all human beings. He exists freely in the fullness of his whole being. The flow of his consciousness is not the fixed repetitive patterns of our usual self-centered consciousness, but rather arises spontaneously and naturally from the actual circumstances of the present. The results of this in terms of the quality of his life are extraordinary—buoyancy, vigor, straightforwardness, simplicity, humility, serenity, joyousness, uncanny perspicacity and unfathomable compassion. His whole being testifies to what it means to live in the reality of the present. Without anything said or done, just the impact of meeting a personality so developed can be enough to change

another's whole way of life. But in the end it is not the extraordinariness of the teacher which perplexes, intrigues, and deepens the student, it is the teacher's utter ordinariness. Because he is just himself, he is a mirror for his students. When we are with him we feel our own strengths and shortcomings without any sense of praise or criticism from him. In his presence we see our original face, and the extraordinariness we see is only our own true nature. When we learn to let our own nature free, the boundaries between master and student disappear in a deep flow of being and joy in the unfolding of Buddha mind.[60]

In this description something very like the cardinal virtue of the expressive ethic—a flow of consciousness that "arises spontaneously and naturally from the actual circumstances of the present"—catalyzes all the other characteristics that make up the master's exemplary personality. Simply by being who and how he is, the master transforms what is possible in the student's life. To do so, he need *do* nothing in particular, let alone hold any ritual or bureaucratic office. His extraordinary yet utterly ordinary identity as a human being, realized and enacted in some absolute sense, mirrors the "original face" of the student's own identity.[61]

This encounter, significantly enough, opens up an evaluative insight for the student into her own "strengths and shortcomings" without transmitting "any sense of praise or criticism" from the master. The moral character of the agent is illuminated without being colored by any subjective approval or disapproval. Here emerges the experience that at once frames Zen's formal ethic of natural laws and makes it vanish into "the empty mirror" of awareness shining in the antinomian consciousness of the nonattached meditator. As the ideal student deepens her own practice of meditation, she enters more deeply into the master's state of mind, until it becomes identical with an absolute and universal consciousness ("Buddha mind") that fuses with her own. "What the teacher really offers the student," writes a master, "is literally the living proof that all this talk and seemingly impossible goals can be realized in this lifetime."[62] Adds a student, "If you ask someone why they practice, maybe the simplest answer is, 'Well, I want to be like Roshi.'" The master embodies the ideal person of Zen's Bodhisattva and the fulfillment of its practice.

As the picture above suggests, Zen students do not perceive their master primarily in ethical terms comparable to those describing the moral authority of the Christian sect's pastor. But the master's gnostic status as a fully realized human being able to see and reflect life as it truly is makes him an ideal observer of moral phenomena and thus a perfect moral judge. Affirms a student,

> I know he's gonna be right on moral questions, because he doesn't have any particular bias. Just about everybody I've known looks at things in terms of what's gonna be the best for

them. Roshi's different. He's an enlightener, you know. He's there to open your eyes, wise you up. That's not like telling you the right thing to do, but the right thing comes out of it.

From true moral intuition, however antinomian, comes right action in this view. Impartially at one with the situation, the master unerringly acts in appropriate response to it and he enables the student to do likewise.

Face to face with a master, the student comes on her own to recognize his authority. Although it is charismatic in shape, this authority derives from the extraordinarily ordinary human being attuned to the moment, not the biblical prophet ordained by God. A student testifies:

Here was someone who was simply practicing his life in a certain way. I just responded. I thought, "I have to practice my life in this way, too," because I was suffering. Roshi's magic was that he was just living, all the time, moment after moment. He had no excuses. I couldn't deny that. It was a reality instead of an icon.

Students usually object to the use of the ideas of authority and accepting authority to interpret their relationship to this exemplary figure. Counters one, "To me the word *authority* means that power and inequality are being expressed. Roshi isn't an authority figure. He *acts* authoritatively. He goes out and does it, that's all." Another adds,

Most of our generation have a problem with authority, being against it. Roshi's a perfect teacher, because with him there's nothing there to push against. He keeps returning your projection of authority back to you, until you see it's just yourself.

When I first really met him it was in *dokusan* [a formal interview preceded by the student's ritual bowing]. I didn't know how to bow, so I just stood there. So he gets up and does a full prostration, with his forehead down on the floor in front of me, to show me how to bow. It was so moving. That kind of sincerity expressing itself cuts through all the lies in your life.

Thus the student finds himself transcending the dualistic problem of either submitting to or rebelling against authority. Instead, through paradox and reversal, he comes to respect and identify with the master: "He is you, but you are not him." This relationship is actually just two persons engaging each other with a "Hi, how are you?" explains a master, but it uses monastic rules "to give us some distance between teacher and disciple. So because of the distance, student may have some freedom in his activity and teacher will find out how to help him."[63] Monastic rules, such as those defining bowing, free the student to experience his own needs and to recognize the master's response to them as so fitting as to be exemplary.

The charismatic authority enacted by the master in meditating, teaching, and living with students is accompanied by ritual and bureaucratic forms of authority, renewing their value for sixties youth. Each master is the "dharma heir" of *his* master, a status based on his own enlightenment but formally recognized by rites of "dharma transmission" which mark a lineage traced back for centuries in fact, and for eons in liturgy, to Gautama Buddha himself. Zen Center's master is also its abbot and chief priest, surrounded by the institutional demands and resources of a monastic organization. How do young Zen students perceive the relation between these charismatic and bureaucratic forms of authority? The master's personal authority is seen creating and legitimating the institution's authority. "This whole institution grew up around Roshi," says one. "It's an offshoot of the quality he's continually manifesting in his life." Adds a priest, "Zen is not a church. It's a person-church. It's an institution that should have one person's stamp."

The protobureaucratic authority exercised in a monastery at times troubles some younger Zen students in a way that the master's personal authority does not. A student distinguishes between them:

> Sometimes at Zen Center I have the feeling of my life being run by committee, and I don't like that at all. With Roshi it's different. I trust him with my life. I might not always want to do some particular thing, but I want to do what he asks me to. I'm not willing to give the committee that kind of power over my life.

Surrendering individual discretion to bureaucratic forms of authority, a familiar issue of counterculture complaint, remains an unresolved problem for some students, though eased by the master's personal authority. Such students have gravitated toward Zen Center's periphery or left altogether since the late 1960s, as Pacific Zen Center has grown in size and developed further along monastic lines, making the master less accessible and the organization more complex. Other students have adjusted, however, crediting Zen Center's bureaucratic development with important benefits no commune could deliver. One observes astutely,

> Unless it's real small, the hang-loose feeling of most communes makes it hard to organize people to do things, especially if they're complicated. There's the problem of "Who's the boss here? What's your job and what's mine?" The monastic system takes care of that. There's someone at the top, there are different positions marked out, and there's a way to do things. Size has created its own problems, but it's given us a freedom to practic* that we wouldn't have had any other way.

Free of families and established careers, sixties youth have been more able than older students to use Zen Center's increased size and complexity to live and work together under conditions tailored to meditation practice. In the process they have undergone the greatest change in attitude toward its bureaucratic organization, particularly as they come to administer it. "After a while you find yourself in some position of authority," says one, "which makes you relate to other people and things with a sort of overall view. Seeing how the monastic system works is part of practice, because it shows you that your own practice includes everyone else's."

Sixties youth, then, have accepted bureaucracy at Zen Center for several reasons. It has aided them in pursuing their religious vocations. It has been rejustified by the monist tenet that apparently separate persons are interdependent and united. And its forms have been re-merged with those of charismatic and traditional authority, as a priest points out:

> We haven't let ourselves get any bigger than where all the students know one another and each one knows the teacher. In fact, that's one way they know each other, through all knowing one person and being known by one person. The community itself becomes an expression of the master's life.

> The outer form of the organization is based on seniority and staff structure. But the staff isn't a leadership elite. It's more a changing cross-section of the community that only goes ahead with something when everyone agrees on it.

> We come to trust each other in the form of committees for the same reason we accept the roshi: we trust that they both really care for us and our practice, even when it runs counter to the organization's welfare. Again and again you'll see someone get taken off a job that needs to be done so he can sit [zazen] or so he can do something else that *he* needs to do.

A scale that still permits face-to-face relations, a permeable leadership that makes decisions by consensus, and a policy that gives religious goals priority over organizational ones: such characteristics help a relatively large and bureaucratic institution, headed by a central authority, to function in ways that resemble the expressive dynamic of a smaller communal group.[64]

Religious interpretation of administrative functions is aided by understanding everyday activities as rites to be performed as much as jobs to be done. The procedural rules and inner attitudes that shape them are simply there, in the situation and oneself, rather than coming from some external authority. Directives at Zen Center are usually expressed as descriptions ("This is how we do the dishes"), suggestions ("Maybe we can all do it this way"), mild exhortations ("Let's all do it this way") and conditional constructions ("If we could do it this way, it would be best"), instead of as imperatives ("Do it this way"). They take the passive rather than active voice ("The dishes should be washed like this").[65] These formulations mute individual self-assertion. More importantly, they translate the descriptive "is" into the prescriptive "ought" through ritual forms and implicit natural law conceptions, not through the commands of authority figures or the merely instrumental rules of a bureaucracy. Like custom, the rules of Zen Center's regimen are largely unwritten, even unspoken, but everywhere followed. After twenty minutes' instruction in zazen posture and zendo protocol, with a glance at the daily schedule, the newcomer is left to learn her way by observing and imitating others. It takes some doing. "Monastic training is like growing up all over again," remembers a student. "At first all your energy goes into just getting around. How to sit, how to walk, how to eat zendo meals: no matter how hard you try, you're making one mistake after another." Following rules that carry both procedural and ritual force is necessary in order to enter the community's daily round, engage its older members, and be recognized by them. Furthermore, Zen teaching defines attention to detail and nuance in everyday life as a key indicator of spiritual awareness. Although effort is emphasized over actual success in performing tasks and rites at Zen Center, the new student tends to see her status depending on the latter and jeopardized by her mistakes.

The omnipresence of monastic rules at Zen Center bears out its ethical assumption that human beings continually face obligatory moral choices: "There's always something you should be doing," observes a student, "even when you're trying to ignore it or get out of it. When the bell rings in the morning, just say Yes! and get up. Don't even think about it. Wanting to do it or not wanting to doesn't make any difference. Practice means just doing what you have to do." Neither authority nor individual want-satisfaction in their usual form justify Zen Center's rules. The beginning student may believe on the master's authority that following the rules will facilitate that state of enlightened awareness she seeks. The older student comes to feel that it expresses that awareness in itself.

The student at Zen Center has voluntarily entered a semimonastic situation, and he likewise chooses to stay in it. Engaging this situation by following the example of older students, he appropriates the rules that govern it. They become almost invisibly his own, leaving only the intuitive familiarity of the situation itself and the smoothly meshing interaction of its participants. Zen Center's monastic social control rehearses its meditational self-control. The meditator lets mental images come and go without approving or rejecting them. Instead he concentrates on posture and breathing, the orthopractical forms of zazen. By doing so he develops an intuitive familiarity with zazen as the situation of his life. Reportedly he does not stop his thinking—he lets it stop by itself. In this way he obtains a characteristic calmness of mind, not by rejecting certain mental activity and adopting rules to calm his mind directly. Self-control or concentration is not the purpose of zazen, observes a master: "The true purpose is to see things as they are, to observe things as they are, and to let everything go as it goes. This is to put everything under control in its widest sense."⁶⁶ Social control operates similarly at Zen Center through its rule-governed monastic situation. The master offers a metaphor:

> Even though you try to put people under some control, it is impossible. You cannot do it. The best way to control people is to encourage them to be mischievous. Then they will be in control in its wider sense. To give your sheep or cow a large, spacious meadow is the way to control him. So it is with people: first let them do what they want and watch them. This is the best policy.⁶⁷

In the institutionally enclosed "meadow" of a monastery, free-roaming sixties youth come to experience Zen Center's daily regimen and meditational orthopraxy as the basis of their own positive liberty to express themselves and to feel at home in the situation of their maturing lives.

Moral Responsibility and Freedom

Zen's synthesis of expressive and regular ethical styles in defining authority, virtue, and duty has been accompanied by striking changes in the ideas of moral responsibility and freedom held by younger Zen students. Most obviously, there has been a shift from a negative to a positive conception of liberty, usually tied to the experience of doing Zen meditation with others in a regularized monastic setting. One student describes this change:

> *Has the meaning of freedom changed for you?*
>
> Yeah. It used to mean just, "I get to do what I want to do," in a very simple way. That's still functioning now, even though it's subtler. I still have a tendency to do things, to practice, to learn or to get better. That really ties me down.
>
> But I know now that it's within the restrictions that we can really be who we are and feel free. It's in those limits, those forms, that I'm really able to express myself the most. Roshi talks about how when we all adopt the same posture in the zendo, we don't do that to all be alike. It's so that we eliminate the distractions of choice—what do our small, petty minds want to do?—so we can express ourselves most fully. When everybody is sitting still in the same posture, then you can see their individuality. When everybody is sitting in their own way, their individuality is obscured.

Such experience of positive liberty in zazen extends to the recognition that rules and principles in general can enable creativity, expressiveness, and freedom in the deepest sense, even as they overtly constrain an individual's behavior. Conversely, self-interest can be felt as a self-limiting motive of action.

Zen students are sensitive to the fact that their idea of freedom within restriction may seem odd or threatening to outsiders, and they seek to distinguish between its social and psychological meanings. Asked, "How do you respond to someone who sees how structured life is at Zen Center and feels concerned about personal freedom?" a student replies:

> On the surface you can point out that this is a totally voluntary community. There's no proselytizing, no coercion. People come and stay here because they want to, and they're free to leave at any time.

> More deeply, the idea of freedom is a real kicker. Most of people's thinking is censored dreaming. We're not free to think whatever we want to think, because we can't accept ourselves thinking it. That's the deeper sort of freedom that begins to appear in practice. It allows your dreams to push up into your sitting [zazen]. You can't censor them there, but you can begin to feel OK with them by facing them wide awake. This kind of discipline gives you freedom from compulsive behavior, conditioned responses.

> Everybody has the freedom to move, but what about the freedom to sit still? What looks like freedom—I can do it if I want to—is actually slavery, because you're not free not to do it, not to want it. Practice gives you freedom to do or not to do, so you can do either. You have real freedom of choice, because you've consciously faced the full inventory of human choice, including your dreams, hatred, anger, fear. Once you know all of that, then you really can choose freely. So in Zen we have the freedom to think about anything we want, where our culture doesn't have that freedom. It's taboo, forbidden.

To reassure the liberal concerned about political freedom and authoritarianism, the student cites Zen Center's status as a purely voluntary community. But for him the deeper issue is freedom from desire, usually overlooked by the liberal American. Seen as Hobbesian men, driven by our desires, we are free only to seek their satisfaction, not release from them. Our outer freedom masks an inner compulsion, from which Zen promises release. Like the romantic bohemian and the hippie, the young Zen student sees freedom primarily in psychic and cultural terms, but his vision of it implies religious self-discipline instead of self-indulgence, and a monastic social order instead of anarchy or utopia.

The Zen student's adoption of positive liberty resembles the Christian sectarian's, but there are important differences, too. The sect's morality is rigidly authoritative in form, though softened by the felt spontaneity of its love, the intimacy of its social relations, and the ecstasy of its ritual life. The Zen community's ritual and monastic life is strictly regimented, and like the sect, "Zen Center gives a kind of focus to your life. In the world there are too many choices, really, where at Zen Center you just have to choose to be there, and then follow the schedule." But otherwise the student's orientation toward the rules is left largely to himself. His attitude of moral responsibility both reflects the counterculture's ambiguity in this regard and reconciles its two facets.

The Zen student recognizes the community's rules as applying to his behavior in the breach as well as the observance. He also sees the rules themselves as an object of the ideal attitude of non-attachment. One student discusses this bifocal view:

When you do something you know is wrong, has your feeling changed since starting to do Zen?

I accept now that I did it. I don't try to cover it over anymore. Sometimes I break the precepts. Now I just watch myself do it. Before it was like invisible to me. . . . But I don't beat myself up about it either. I used to go through the whole "I should, I should" routine. The tyranny of the "should." Now I just accept that I did whatever I did. If doubt comes up or self-judgment, I'm much gentler in handling myself. I make myself suffer less because of doing something wrong, and because of fighting against feeling guilty about it, too.

So there's guilt about what's wrong, but less heat and more light with it. How do you feel when you do what's right?

There's less charge there, too, because you just experience those things happening, instead of yourself being the cause of it all. Instead of getting off on it, I'm aware now of being uncomfortable with that feeling of being righteous.

This sort of attitude toward moral rules has several implications. For one, it consolidates elements of the regular and expressive styles into a moral psychology that admits feelings of responsibility for complying with moral rules, yet fosters a therapeutic form of self-acceptance in the absence of traditional Judaeo-Christian expiatory rites or pastoral relationships. One student, raised a Catholic, observes, "Zazen is like self-absolution," comparing the effects of meditation to those of the sacrament of penance (although Zen's relativizing the individual self and its guilt qualifies the parallel).

Second, this attitude of moral responsibility, by espousing non-attachment to feelings of righteousness as well as to guilt, implies acceptance of others in a morally pluralistic culture, and acceptance of the social world itself as a morally imperfect place. In the latter connection, ideas of *karma* can come to bear on explaining the inevitability of evil. Says one student,

> My old sense of responsibility was a misunderstood sense of guilt. I think we should try to minimize hurt to others and ourselves, but at times it's unavoidable. There's some basic flaw or karma, and all I can do about that is practice. We're all interconnected, and compassion expresses that. But it's also true that we can't take care of everything for people. Some suffering is just inevitable.

While the danger of withdrawal from social concern inheres in this attitude, the Zen student sees it enabling him to reject normlessness and act on moral concerns without being pushed by feelings of self-righteousness and anger into the sort of confrontations that characterized sixties conflicts. Whether the observer judges such personal or social conflict as necessary and beneficial or gratuitously destructive, the experience of its difficulties by sixties youth helps to account for their attraction to attitudes of acceptance found in Zen.

Resolving Moral Disagreements

The question of what to do about social conflict and injustice is answered in part by Zen students' ideas of how to resolve moral disagreements. Although it may actually involve recourse to rules and moral argument, they perceive such resolution taking place by the sort of ongoing and diffuse interaction the expressive ethic indicates:

> *What do you do when you disagree with someone about how things are and what you should do?*

> Even after a real disagreement with someone, being angry and everything, you come back to the situation clear. It happened. That's the way you felt. You've gone away and done other things, then you come back and meet the other person again, and something else is happening. There is that person, and it's new. That relation keeps renewing itself. So the argument you had before is not carried into the next meeting. It may come up again, and you may argue and get angry again. But then the same thing happens again. It just goes away.

> *Is there anything about Zen Center that makes disagreements work like this?*

Zazen itself absorbs a lot of problems and conflicts, so they don't keep carrying over. Everyone here is in the process of changing all the time, through practice. They're aware of being in that process. You don't have to push on a disagreement right then, because you know they'll change. So will you. So eventually you'll come to an agreement.

What about its being a community?

Well, if you disagree with someone here, you know they can't go away. That allows you to be openly angry, instead of holding it in. Your disagreement has a lot of room to come out, because you can't really alienate them.

This sort of resolution process is facilitated by certain attitudes tied to Zen practice: (1) a present-oriented, moment-by-moment sense of time; (2) non-attachment toward one's feelings, judgments, and states of mind, and the intent to let go of them instead of defining and elaborating them; and (3) the consciously shared aim of religious self-transformation. It also relies on a communal setting. Here one relates to others in many different ways, some of them requiring cooperation in order to perform housekeeping tasks vitally necessary to all involved. As in family and marriage relationships, the diffuse and ongoing nature of such communal cooperation makes it easier not to let a disagreement harden, and the commune's need for house-keeping cooperation implies severe practical penalties for doing so.

The resolution of any disagreement, like the integrity of any culture, relies on a common reservoir of shared experiences and implicit meanings and norms, but this is especially the case where formal argument and reason giving are depreciated as means to such resolution, as they are in an expressive ethic. The experiential coherence of the Zen Center community plays a crucial part in resolving disagreements under this rubric:

Is there any difference in what happens when you disagree with someone in the sangha and an outsider?

One of the difficulties of being with people who don't do this kind of practice is all the words you run into. Where in the sangha there are certain understandings that people develop in common in experience. Everybody does that, but here it's clearer. Usually there are too many things happening to see what's actually going on. But here our lives have been simplified and cut down, so we can cut through the intellectual part of it.

Speed is real important. Slowing down is part of practicing. It helps to be with other people who are also aware of that. Then if you feel hassled and you just want to stop for a few moments and breathe, you can. This way you can go back to feeling OK, so you can expand from there.

The shared experience of meditation and the monastic extension of its associated states of feeling into daily interaction help to resolve conflicts situationally. So does the inherently normative focus of a monastery, where rules more clearly and comprehensively pattern daily activity, enabling the participant to feel the moral order of that activity without conscious reference to the rules.[68]

Such an orientation to moral disagreement sees it as a conflicted encounter between persons, to be harmonized, rather than the engagement of various positions on an issue, to be thrashed out. This represents the intersection of several different views that share considerable respect for the nonrational aspect of human behavior. The first is the stance of mystical and also postcritical religion away from dogmatic belief and toward experiential constants open to varying interpretations. The second is a psychologically based view of the importance of unconscious motives in interpersonal behavior. The third is a positivistic view of moral judgments as a function of subjective likes and dislikes rather than objective reasons and values. The fourth view, stressed by sixties radicals, sees class-specific interests and powers predominating over reason and moral values in political debate. Generalized beyond the small group to society as a whole, at least some of these views can lead toward tolerance of diverse opinions and acceptance of diverse others in a pluralistic society. By depreciating moral argument, however, they may also slow exposure of injustice and excuse the absence of action in response to it. Or, on the contrary, they may speed entry into overt conflict decided by power alone.

II. MONASTIC COMMUNITY AND MASS SOCIETY

Zen Center's communalism, like the counterculture's, contrasts with the larger society's associational relationships. It is collectively oriented, exclusive, private, and relatively undifferentiated. But, unlike the hippie commune or the Christian sect, this monastic community mutes interpersonal affect and intimacy. Instead it creates a transpersonal intimacy based on shared belief and effort in a demanding religious discipline, meditating together and sharing a daily schedule. As a group, Zen students sit side by side, cloaked in monks' robes and rules, more than they stand face to face, exposing each other in communal encounters or Christian confessions. "We are here in a common disguise," remarks the master. "That's how we recognize each other." Zen Center, like other monastic communities and unlike the hippie commune, possesses a highly rationalized organization, although its nonutilitarian aim is to foster certain values of compassion and awareness in its members, not to maximize productivity.[69]

As do members of the Christian sect, Zen students mark themselves off from the society by commitment to special rites, teachings, and social organization, reinforced by distinctive physical location, appearance, and scheduling of the daily round. The sect's aggressive self-justification, branding society for its sinful egoism and extolling its own altruistic virtue, has no visible equivalent at Zen Center. Neither does the sect's angry millenarism. Zen teaching does analyze ordinary, self-oriented consciousness as fundamentally delusive, however, and this critique of the human condition fits with countercultural criticism of individualistic American society. All beings are Bodhisattvas from Zen's nondiscriminating viewpoint. But it is also true, a master suggests rather whimsically yet seriously, too, that "most people you meet are crazy," in terms of their conditioned behavior. Zen Center sees itself presenting "an unconditioned response to a conditioned world."[70] The outward movement of conventional American social life appears to reflect its inner confusion, posing ecological, economic, and political problems to which Zen Center's distinctive practice and community offer answers. "After all," says a student, "you wouldn't be at Zen Center if you didn't think this was the best way for you to live, just like you wouldn't be studying with Roshi if you didn't think he was the best teacher you could have." Zen Center leaders see such social criticism running through the monastic Buddhist tradition, not singling out contemporary America. "Implicit in the idea and practice of Sangha is that the prevailing society of every period of history will be to some degree corrupt, misguided, or chaotic," writes a master; "and that the antidote to this, the fundamental social action, the only hope, is the maintenance of a tradition that produces realized, enlightened, radically sane individuals."[71] Thus do religious claims underlie social criticism.

Although Zen Center stands outside the mainstream society, it reduces some tensions its young members feel between mainstream culture and the counterculture. Like the Christian sect, Zen Center makes up a relatively age-integrated society, whose minority of older members provide aging sixties youth with models of stabler alternative lifestyles than the counterculture's. "Some of the best students at Zen Center are the older people," admires a youth. "Seeing them makes me feel better about getting older myself. I feel I can go on practicing. I don't have to give it up when I hit forty." Older students have often forgone or left behind conventional careers and family life for bohemian or religious alternatives, yet they have sustained themselves as adults in the interstices of conventional society.

Zen Center does not justify itself by invoking the rhetorical reality of America as one nation under a biblical God, as does the Christian sect. But it does represent a mystical, monist view of reality spreading through the popular culture of the urban middle class. *Zen* is a cultural symbol and catchword that circulates meaningfully and commands respect beyond the counterculture's old boundaries, and Zen Center draws vigor and legitimacy from this changing climate of opinion. Zen Center has established its own position as a kind of "high church" among alternative religious sects, cults, disciplines, and human potential movements. This position, evident in Zen Center's growing material resources, organizational stability, and explicitly religious institutional appearance, has made its committed members acceptable to an audience beyond their countercultural peers. These sixties youths are no longer dropouts. They are monks and priests, teachers, administrators, and institution builders within a recognizable religious tradition. This also changes the way they see themselves. They now belong to a tradition that spans generations, indeed millennia, making them feel less isolated as a generation and less frustrated about changing the society all at once. They now belong to a community, making them feel less isolated as individuals, and less driven to strive for individual success or rebel against it.

Zen practice itself has worked changes in its young adherents that have helped smooth their relations with the larger society. "After some point in practice even middle-class folks are Buddhas, too," smiles a student. Nowhere is such acceptance stronger for students than in relation to their own parents. "I feel closer to them now," says one. "I can accept their feelings better now. They're suffering, too, you know." He adds,

> I'm more able to see them, and allow my feelings of love, and anger, to come up. At first I felt I had to be very kind to them all the time, and it practically killed me. Now I see that my feelings of annoyance or anger actually arise *because* I love them. I can see that that's all they really ever cared about or ever wanted— my love. They still hope I'll get married and, sure, they'd rather I was a doctor. But my succeeding wasn't really that important. That's clear to me, and they're coming to acknowledge it, too.

Conventional parental concerns have not vanished, but counterculture youths have now come to reinterpret them more gently, even when they have not entirely satisfied them. Pain, difficulty, and conflict with others are to be accepted as part of practice, just like the mental difficulties and leg pains of zazen.[72] Instead of struggling against others, blaming them, or withdrawing from them, the student accepts and becomes one with them. Cued to see that "they're suffering, too" by Buddhism's premise that life is suffering, the young Zen student seeks to respond to his parents compassionately instead of self-righteously opposing them. The passage of time, distance, and financial independence provide circumstantial aid to him in doing so.

The Koan of Self and Other

Zen students' earlier relationships with their peers were less settled in local neighborhoods, schools, and long-lived cliques than those of lower-class sect youths. The connection between individual identity and relatedness to others is often a conscious problem for them. Remembers one student,

I grew up pretty much a self-contained person. I had friends, and boyfriends, but I felt like I wasn't so dependent on them. I could see over their shoulder, beyond them. I was content relating to people in that way for a long time, but that changed as I got older. Part of what I was looking for with Zen was to get to the bottom of my own aloneness. From practice I've been able to see how, no matter how independent you feel, you're completely connected with everybody and everything that's alive, in your ultimate being and in that rough part of yourself that comes out in what you do every day.

Another adds,

For years I kept a journal, where I'd write about the experiences I had. When things got really heavy in a relationship, I could feel myself wanting to get off by myself, so I could figure it out and write it down.

Well, the night before I left for the monastery, I took out my notebooks, maybe fifteen of them, and put them in the garbage can. . . . From sitting I've been able to accept the gut feelings that were underneath the intellectual relationships I used to have. Doing zazen and not being able to control it has made it easier to be with other people and accept that I can't control what goes on with them either.

Though hardly solitaries, Zen students report a high degree of conscious self-involvement in their earlier lives. Affect tends to be held under cognitive scrutiny if not control, and self-study is freighted with ambivalent feelings of self-criticism and self-importance. "Unless you're really pure and simple," remarks a student, "you have to be pretty willful and stubborn to go for this kind of practice. Roshi said once that it was learning how to be kind to yourself. That's a whole other thing from being attached to yourself and hard on yourself, too, which is how we feel most of the time." The strength of such ambivalence may reflect upper-middle-class families that gave relatively great individual attention and love to their children, yet exerted high demands for performance on them, and placed a premium on their capacity for critical self-explanation.

Interpersonal relationships at Zen Center develop on several grounds. First, all students meditate for several hours daily, indirectly supporting one another's efforts by persisting in their own beside them. Second, students live and work together in a precisely orchestrated household, on a tight budget and time schedule. Third, students develop personal relationships based on mutual interest and attraction. These are reinforced by their shared experience within Zen Center and the circumstantial limits it places on outside relationships. Any one student's close personal relationships are usually small in number and slow in developing, characteristically growing up after he has spent months gaining a foothold in the meditation practice, demonstrating his institutional commitment to Zen Center, and absorbing its values. A longtime student observes,

> There are a lot of people I know at Zen Center, that I have a good feeling for, but just a few people I'm really close to. Zen Center forces you to be in close proximity with all kinds of people, including people you would avoid on the outside. When you live next to them all the time, you work with them, you sit next to them in the zendo, you *have* to accept them. You find a different way of relating to them instead of whether you like them or not. Outside, it's whether a person shares the same interests with you, whether you hit it off, how attractive they are. At Zen Center it's more that we're all trying to do something, to do the same thing, to practice. There's that sameness.
>
> At Zen Center you get away from judging people's actions. It's just "Accept, accept, accept." I criticize people less now. I don't know God's will and neither do they, so why discriminate? You find out they're just like you. They've all got their own mind trips going on.

Continually living, working, and meditating next to diverse other persons enforces an acceptance of them not based on judging their individual personalities. One's own evaluative judgments are undercut by meditational experience of how changeable and passing they are and by an ideology that relativizes individual identity itself. "Thinking you're right," says a student, "is a way of thinking you know who *you* are. But actually we don't know who we are like that. Roshi says, 'Your skin doesn't make you separate from me. I am inside your skin. You are inside my skin.'" A self-enclosed social environment also requires accepting others simply because you have to go on living with them. Zen Center features a highly regulated and rationalized social setting, with an extraordinary level of conformity to its rules and consensus over its goals. This de-differentiates its social life, enabling it to proceed on the basis of collective sameness instead of individuals hitting it off.[73] Such consensus holds the Zen community together over time and personnel changes with a stability that neither friendship nor romantic love can offer the typical commune.

Zen Center's understanding of interpersonal encounter is enacted by a "bow and gassho." As one student meets another, he brings his hands up palm to palm before his chin, drops his eyes, and bows slightly from the waist, slowing but not stopping to do so, then passing on. The gesture signals mutual acknowledgment, consideration, and deference between monks quietly passing in work or ritual. A longtime student comments,

> Bowing to someone is so beautiful. It says, "Yes, you're here; I'm
> here," without having to add anything more. You don't have to
> define these relationships or compare them. Bowing, you start to
> have a very pure, simple feeling about people, instead of think-
> ing about what's going on between you and them.

The dedicated student experiences the silence, downcast eyes, uniform
robes, and other muted conditions of monastic life as release from the
hippie's endless odyssey of emotion and from the utilitarian's relationships
of calculated exchange. Other observers interpret Zen Center's interpersonal environment less favorably, however, seeing in it a disturbing form of
emotional self-denial. "My subjective feeling when I go into Zen Center is
the same feeling that I get when I go into a library or a hospital," writes one
newcomer. "Four people could be facing the door and none of them would
look up at the person who entered the room. . . . Many of the Zen students
—perhaps half, in my judgment—are, in part, motivated out of a fear of
intimacy with other people."[74] Such interpersonal muting bears more
directly on newcomers and marginal members than on older students dedicated to Zen practice and Zen Center. Personal recognition and status in the
community are categorically denied on other bases. This serves to stabilize
the long-term membership against those who come and go. It also reinforces
the newcomer in determined efforts to establish his meditation practice and
commitment to Zen Center and its values. The new student who persists in
seeking acceptance on interpersonal grounds will be repeatedly put off and
frustrated. The one who concentrates on meditation and work becomes an
older student himself, usually after a stint in the monastery. He thereby
gains access to a circle of personal friends, prospective lovers, and a highly
developed network of gossip that transmits interpersonal information and
feelings among older students. A priest comments on this arrangement,
"Insofar as your interest in Zen Center is in becoming part of the community, there's a separation between new and older students. Insofar as it's
in practicing Zen, there's no separation at all."

Zen Center's communalism sustains countercultural social ideals even
as it tempers them with a stable interpersonal order of its own. This offers
sixties youth side-by-side acceptance and intimacy as an answer to their
earlier self-involvement. To them the regular design of this order implies
moral criticism of utilitarian individualism in the larger society, yet its
autonomy moderates their own felt tension toward that society.

Gender Roles, Courtship, and Marriage

Sixties youth typically arrive at Zen Center uncoupled, and single students are more likely than couples to stay and become committed members.

Though sexually experienced, few of these youths were married when they arrived, and fewer still were divorced. Their earlier sexual relationships were marked by the same self-consciousness and concern for independence that characterized their earlier social relations generally. "My relationships with lovers were an inward sort of experience," remembers a young man, "like you might have with drugs or with the small kind of zazen experience that explodes just inside your head. I was involved, but it was most real *inside* myself." A young woman stresses the theme of independence:

> I never really wanted to commit myself to the kind of loving that had consequences, like marriage-kids-family consequences. I balked at having unreal relationships, where you just close your eyes and screw, but the only real ones I saw were like suffocating for my own being. I didn't want to give up responsibility for myself and my own adequacy just to get acceptance and security, or even love.

Such attitudes among upper-middle-class youths in their twenties, out of school but not embarked on careers and not at ease with the idea of conventional adulthood, added up to an unwillingness to make lasting commitments to stay coupled, marry, or raise children.

Compared to the Christian sect, Zen Center says little about sexual identity or conduct and exerts little direct control over its members' sexual behavior, which varies widely. "There are really only two Zen Center rules in principle," says a priest. "You don't hurt others and you don't deceive them. Any relationship that doesn't hurt or deceive, we have nothing to say about it." These two commonsense rules nonetheless delimit sexual relationships at Zen Center, which can be grouped into several categories. Serious incoming students during their first six months of residence at Zen Center are not to start a sexual relationship with another student, although sex with outsiders is permitted. "This is not a rule about sex," says a priest. "It's a rule about practice. To protect the new student's opportunity to practice, without it being colored by some intense relationship." The rule also helps protect the community from newcomers enacting their earlier values or desires for sex, status, or personal comfort at the community's expense. Novices find few chances to do so, moreover, since they must face the demands of beginning to meditate and follow a regimen that affords little chance for personal interaction within the daily round and little access to the social network of older students. Monastic celibacy is not an institutional norm, but some older students may choose to maintain celibacy for months or as long as several years with the counsel of the master, and other students respect their doing so.

Casual or promiscuous relationships among older students are formally proscribed as hurting or deceiving others. They are also discouraged by Zen Center's communalism. "Responding and responsibility are so close in Zen. You can't respond to another person without being responsible for them," a student remarks. "I feel part of a family with other students. And anything you do, it will get around to the other members of the family. It will have some effect on the house in which you live. You don't want to mess up your own bed." Within the community sexual relationships among older students begin cautiously, almost invisibly, based on long-term familiarity and friendship. They proceed in the privacy of students' own rooms, along the edges and in the gaps of the monastic schedule. Once they have begun, the monastic community, like the sect, encourages couples to stabilize rapidly—either to split or become publicly recognized. Then the partners may live together within Zen Center and move together between its monastery, farm, and urban center. Such coupling is serious and personal, lasting for months or years, but it ends as often with the partners separating as marrying.

Marriage is supported in serious relationships at Zen Center, though not at the expense of single life. Those ordained as priests or considering it must receive the master's permission to marry, while other serious students usually consult with him before doing so. Perhaps one of three sixties youths at Zen Center has married or definitely intends to do so, another third report no such intention, and the rest are undecided.[75] Although it is neither familist nor natalist, Zen Center treats weddings, and births, as joyful occasions, and it celebrates them in serious rites. "Marriage is practice, too," remarks a student. "When you get married it's a sort of ordination." Some members see the high rate of breakups among established couples, like the divorce of married members, as problematic. "We'd like people to stay together once they've chosen that," says a priest. "But we can't make them." What Zen Center has done is to lend support to young couples and families by giving them extra time, space, and privacy to live together, setting up a day-care center for the kids, and arranging some staff jobs around parenting.

Nonetheless, Zen Center's primary commitment to rigorous meditation within a basically monastic setting puts pressure on married life. An older student considers the question:

What's it like being in a couple or having a family at Zen Center? Are there any special problems with it?

There are couples here, and children. But, still, Zen Center doesn't elevate the family to the point where it obscures the individual in relation to practice. It's much more like Jesus saying "I am sent to set husband against wife." And, in fact, it does set husband against wife.

How?

By pressing each person to express himself fully and stand on his own ground. It puts pressure on you not to be satisfied with role playing. You can't ever find a permanent refuge from yourself and the problem you have. You can't get away and go stand on being a husband or being a father.

Couples come together and come apart here. Maybe you think, "Oh, it shouldn't be that way." On the other hand, maybe it's good to have a community that can take care of couples changing like that, since that's what's happening.

Why is it happening here? Why do couples break up?

I think there are different reasons. Practice is one. It makes heavy energy demands on you, without any letup, and so does a relationship or a family. Usually one person in a couple that splits up will be getting more involved in practice. That person will feel like the other one is getting in the way of their practice, and the other one will feel cut adrift.

Maybe another reason is that Zen Center itself is a kind of family, so the real family *can* be looser, because there's more to fall back on, where outside there's nothing. . . . You'll hear married people, even the priests, say their family is not so important to them. They're just like all the other people around. There's no extra care put into family relationships. . . . Outside, you're either married or not. In Zen Center there's a much wider range of living together, living together with kids but not as sexual partners, or parenting without living together.

The monastic role takes precedence over marital and parental roles, and it can take time and energy away from them. Meditation raises the problem of one's own consciousness and life in paradoxical terms (the "genjo koan") that require continued meditation to resolve. Monastic communalism permits the individual to loosen or sever marital ties, and still remain within a reliable network of friends and associates. It obliges him to follow out his parental and family responsibilities, yet it offers him alternative arrangements for doing so. Thus Zen Center accommodates the increasing fluidity of marital ties characteristic of the larger society, especially the urban upper-middle-class milieu its youth come from, with an uncharacteristically resilient religious community. Unlike the familistic Christian sect, it enables sixties youth to support themselves into adulthood without settling down into conventional jobs or careers, the occupational anchor of marital commitment.[76] With work still unsettled, marriage is more likely to seem an unsettling prospect and to turn out to be an unsteady tie.[77]

Male and Female

At first glance Zen Center's ethic elaborates no personality ideals along sexual dimensions. "The Buddhist standard is that there is no special sexual identity," a priest points out. "The aim for a man *as a man* is to become unattached to his idea of himself as a man. The same for a woman." Sexual relationships at Zen Center are influenced by an ethic, however elastic and implicit, of personal responsibility and friendship. The priest continues,

> After some time you begin to see people as friends. You respect their capacity, not to be a woman and handle a woman's problems, but to be a person and stand her own ground. You don't find yourself noticing something about a person as a man or woman. You notice, "Is this person still manipulative or not? Is he greedy? What's he clear of?"

A woman adds, "In between being lovers and not being lovers, there's a widening space for friendship. I could kiss the ground for that! Somehow 'friend' has more room in it than 'boyfriend' or 'girlfriend.' Friends last longer, too. From 'friend' you can decide what kind of friend you want to be." Here, as with the Christian sect and as opposed to the hip counterculture, more regulated, slower-moving sexual relationships lead to greater positive liberty and permanence in friendships between members of an ongoing community.

Zen students hold a strongly egalitarian view of gender roles. Accordingly, Zen Center has ordained women as "priests," not as Japanese-style nuns, and it has consciously included them in its hierarchy. There are proportionately fewer women than men ordained (a 5:8 ratio among sixties youth) and in positions of authority, however, and women have grown firmer in calling this situation into question over the past several years. "The change in how women look at their lives has touched Zen Center," acknowledges a priest. "They're saying, 'I want to choose my own life, and not just fit in.'" Zen students report convergent changes in their understanding of themselves as men and women, notably a growing sense of independence and competency among women and emotional "softening" among men. "I think of myself as a person, like almost all of the women at Zen Center," says one. "There's total equality in the practice itself. It puts you on your own. *You* have to do it. No one else can sit for you." Another adds,

> I guess as a woman I feel much more comfortable with my own aggression and strength. Yesterday, for example, someone was trying to help with dinner, but he was in the way. I could just say, "You're in the way," without worrying about it. I can take on more in work. I feel stronger and more at home in my body from sitting.

Equality, independence, unstrident since unworried self-assertion ("selfless self-assertion" one woman called it), active competency in work, and physical ease: these sound familiar as feminist goals. A male student suggests the other side of the issue:

> You see a few people get into the samurai role, strutting around like "Macho Roshi," but basically Zen practice softens up the idea we have of ourselves, whatever it is.... I was never very hard or tough as a man. Zen didn't change that so much as make it more OK for me to be the way I was.

Independence and activism for women are bred by zazen and monastic work instead of the Christian sect's fixed rules and housework. Meditational instead of devotional ritual softens male emotions. Although they differ in genesis, form, and statement, changes in gender roles among youthful Zen students have occurred in the same convergent directions as those among members of the Christian sect.

III. EDUCATION, WORK, AND STATUS: PERSONAL LEARNING

Sixties youth practicing Zen hold personalistic ideas of education, which figure critically in their reasons for leaving behind conventional school and work to enter Zen. These youths typically come from upper-middle-class families that possessed a high level of education, valued it, and raised their children to do likewise. Most of them finished college and many had postgraduate schooling. More significant than the amount of education they received was the high quality and intensity of their academic careers, even among those who dropped out, and their subsequent disillusionment with such study as a means to personal awareness. For these youths saw education (mostly in the arts, humanities, and social sciences) as a means of seeking after meaning, fulfillment, and self-expression in life, not as a means of making a living. Career goals, where they were defined, centered on artistic, intellectual, and academic careers (writer, painter, professor, clinical psychologist) that were marked off from the bourgeois business of making a living and, in the case of the arts, from the academy itself.

A woman with an M.F.A. degree who taught painting in elementary school for several years before coming to Zen Center looks back on her own education:

> School is geared toward learning to make a living. The whole socializing process is horrendous. It was just functioning for what they thought I should be doing when I went to college, got married, had two children, and the rest of it. But I wasn't interested in that! I wanted to be an artist.

What did that mean for you?

Art for me was like a taste of [Zen] practice beforehand. When I finally decided in college that I was gonna do what I really wanted to do, learning became an explosion. Everywhere I turned, I was with my love. Practice is like that: it's what you finally, finally admit you want most of all to do. Then you learn. *Everything* is relevant. Every little bit comes together into one thing. You have to make an effort, but it's all around you. You're living and breathing it. School is almost never like that.

Did you see painting as a way to make a living?

For me painting was a way of looking at the world and expressing it. I was never totally dedicated to technique or turning out a product. What I was getting out of art personally was more important.

Why did you go from painting to Zen?

Painting brings everything together in the world of "form is form," where your mind is always working on something. Zazen-mind I like better, because it's freer. It takes in "form is emptiness," too.[78]

Art is espoused in tones familiar from the romantic and bohemian tradition, chosen in place of a bourgeois career and defined as a way of life. Artistic technique and finished product take second place to the process of creation seen as a discovery of meaning that unifies oneself and the world. This parallels the ritual process of Zen strikingly enough to suggest the line of continuity between pursuing art as a religion and the religious life itself. Aestheticism carried many youths away from professional or business careers while they were still in school, yet it later led few of them to economically viable careers as artists.

Other Zen students left the path to conventional careers under the direct influence of psychedelic drugs and the hip ideology. "Acid made my work and my life appear unconnected," recalls a youth in his early thirties who abandoned "the professor-professional syndrome" of a psychology doctoral program to become a priest at Zen Center. "It made me see that I was getting a Ph.D. primarily to get a Ph.D., and that I was following a dream that I had seen didn't work."[79] Another ordained priest came from a high-powered doctoral program in comparative literature, through a countercultural excursus, to Zen practice. He contrasts the different types of learning he experienced along the way:

In college learning was a matter of accumulating information. That meant accumulating power, because information is power.

It's what you use to define your position and defend yourself. You become identified with what you know. If you don't know something, you feel incomplete and at a loss. You're constantly being driven to know enough, but there never *is* enough. You never have enough time.

I was pretty compulsive, like a lot of grad students and professors. There's a grasping, driven quality to the work that tightens you up. I felt it in my face and jaw, my shoulders. Actually I didn't feel it then. You don't even notice it. But now, when I'm reading, I'm aware that it's hard for me to breathe evenly.

I conceived of being a scholar as being a seeker, really, but keeping up and doing well usually has to come before wanting to know. I identified with being a professor and leading an academic life, although I never felt entirely easy with it.

Why did you leave the university?

Because I felt like I was manipulating myself. I was making myself into a tool in order to do the work. If you're a good scholar, you're supposed to be satisfied with that and muffle the pain you feel about your own life. I couldn't do that, so I left.

Rimbaud said, "By the spirit one goes to God, heart-tearing misfortune." We *can* experience some enlightenment in our spirit or mind, but on the surface of wrinkled reality that just makes life all the more painful. I felt like I had to get outside my mind and learn something else, like Dogen saying, "To study Buddhism is to study the self. To study the self is to forget the self." That's how I wanted to learn.

What did you learn in the counterculture? How was it different from school?

In school I was accumulating facts and theories. First it was Henry James and T. S. Eliot. When I became politicized it was Noam Chomsky. Later, with drugs and Gestalt, it was getting to know yourself by accumulating experiences, "peak experiences."

So the content changes, but the process of accumulation stays the same?

Right.

What about Zen?

When I started sitting, and I'd have some experience, I'd label it an "enlightenment experience," because I'd heard about enlightenment, and I'd try to hold onto it, which I couldn't do. Now sitting is just being in whatever presents itself. There's nothing to bank.

Are you learning anything in Zen?

I don't know. The irony is, when I was in school, I felt sometimes like I had to know everything there was to know. Actually what I needed to know was how to breathe, the one thing I'd been doing all my life. That's more like what I'm learning now, how to breathe.

In school I would be swayed back and forth by whatever I was studying. But I was very inflexible, too, because I was struggling to validate my position against someone else's. Now I'm more willing to be who I am and rest in my ignorance, which is a kind of openness, too. I'm beginning to listen to other people and get a feeling of them, not just some data or a projection of myself. I'm willing to be changed by them. Dogen says, "If you are moved by things, you will move them." That's my feeling of learning now. To know someone is not to be able to characterize them verbally. It's being able to respond to them in the appropriate way at the appropriate time.

Technical knowledge, a cornerstone of utilitarian culture, is here cast aside in favor of a conception of knowledge that is by turns more philosophical, romantic, and religious. Academic study undertaken as a search for meaning leads away from a production-oriented academic career towards a meditational, religious one. This aims at a psychosomatic sort of self-consciousness and an engaging openness to others that realizes the counterculture's situational and expressive ideals while devaluing the university's instrumental demands.

Zen's apparent anti-intellectualism has a peculiar appeal for intellectuals. Why so? "Because it doesn't tell you to believe in anything," retorts a former law student. "That's fine with most intellectuals, who think they're skeptics. Actually they're people who have a lot of fancy ideas in their heads, but they can't shit straight. Zen practice can straighten out your life without handing you any more ideas." Zen's doctrinal focus is critical and epistemological, not constructive and cosmological. It is presented as a practical interpretive framework that follows on the experience of meditation, and remains secondary to it. The ex-law student continues,

I've always been drawn to look at things intellectually and conceptualize them. Zazen practice is really a slap in the face to that desire. It can make you think you feel suffocated sometimes, but then you realize you have never been clearer than when there's nothing going on in your mind, when there's nothing to be worried about.

Buddhism offered me a direct experience. That's what I wanted, absolute dumb existence, not any more information or abstraction. I already had plenty of that.

The skeptic in me wants to pierce through the practice, but you can't figure out where it starts or stops. When I asked Roshi whether I really was understanding any of this stuff, he said, "You know, it's not important what you understand. The thing is to act it out. That's how you change." So then you think you're not supposed to think when you practice Zen. Then Roshi says, "You think the problem is that you think. It's that you don't think."

To act comes first in Zen, but it doesn't exclude understanding, and the complexity of Zen Buddhist doctrine can rival that of any other religious tradition. Doctrinal study has grown in importance at Zen Center since the early 1970s, and it has taken on increasingly scholarly forms. In 1973 a Study Center began offering preregistered courses in Buddhist thought and history, as well as associated arts like tea ceremony, some taught by university faculty and awarded university extension credits. Zen Center has sent several of its younger leaders back to school to study classical Buddhist doctrine, canonical languages, and history. More importantly, Zen Center has drawn on the university and the considerable university experience of its American members (who have, after all, spent little time in traditional monasteries) as implicit models to help it appropriate an explicitly monastic model of institutional life. Zen Center's members are Zen students rather than Zen monks not only in name but in the institutional process of their self-identification. They have chosen to study Zen for reasons learned in the counterculture, to be sure, but also in the course of an elite liberal education itself partly at odds with utilitarian society.

Work as Monastic Practice

Upper-middle-class youths now practicing Zen were raised and schooled to achievement. Many report professional ambitions, such as "becoming an international lawyer," which go back to childhood. Creative, expressive, and scholarly impulses began early, too, and carried into their college years. Swayed by humanistic, bohemian, and countercultural critiques, many youths rejected conventional careers for an artist's or dropout's life. Before coming to Zen Center, these ex-students usually met their living expenses by working in low-status, relatively unskilled labor or service jobs, often on a part-time or temporary basis. Says one, "For as long as I can remember, until Zen, all I wanted to do was write. That covered a multitude of sins about work. I did jobs like drive cab just to get along, without ever finding anything I really liked." Seen as worthless in itself, such work was merely a means of making enough money to live on for the present, without being saddled with conventional occupational responsibilities. Except for those relatively few youths who have become "scholarship students" employed as Zen Center staff or who have learned trades or professions, Zen students still do unskilled labor or service work. But they do so now with a different understanding of its meaning and as part of a different plan of life.

For Zen students work has become "practice." A Center spokesman writes, "Working is an intrinsic part of the practice—integrating meditation and every-day life."[80] Regardless of its content or its circumstances, work is to be done with the same diligent, careful, quiet effort, unattached to outcome yet attentive to process, that the Zen student should bring to zazen and every other activity. And work is to be done for the same purpose: to fulfill one's own life, serve others, and express their interdependent unity. A Center publication explains:

> [We are] supporting ourselves . . . through the Buddhist practice of right livelihood, work activity consistent with meditation practice, based on a moral life, a sense of ethics beyond fixed values. That kind of work is based not on growth, but on the idea of balance, just enough. Our practice of right livelihood is having just enough to sustain our life together.[81]

Monastic labor at Zen Center, especially when performed in its mountain monastery and exurban farming communities, carries on the spirit of meditation—and the ideals of the hip and ecological counterculture. It is careful housekeeping, craft work, organic farming, and construction done in a natural setting to support the community's daily life in simplicity.

Buddhist monasticism began in India as contemplative activity supported by the gifts of laymen, for whom the monks performed ritual and teaching services. In China, Ch'an monasteries developed a work ethic best known in the maxim of Hyakujo, an eighth-century master, that "A day without working is a day without eating." Zen Center calls on financial donors beyond its students but within a circle who know them. Inside the student community one finds long hours, diligent work, and a low-consumption lifestyle. This seems to offer an example of ascetic labor replaced within its classic religious context, the monastery, and divorced from the contemporary American ethic of working for the sake of leisure and consumption, or for prestige and accomplishment in themselves. Zen Center's ethic stresses activity and effort, but it is couched in an overall view more mystical than ascetic, which calls for an attitude of non-attachment to the outcome of one's activity. Some Zen Center leaders and staff (for example, cooks) put in twelve-hour work days. But most of its members work six to eight hours, with the rest of their eighteen-hour days going to meditation and other specifically monastic activity. The Zen student works seeking to integrate meditation and life as an expression of monist awareness rather than to achieve worldly success as a sign of dualist salvation. Care in work is a mode of self-expression more than success in work is a measure of self-worth.

A Zen student who dropped out of an elite college and now works as a carpenter explains his experience of work in terms of Zen's ethic:

> I feel like my work is a complete expression of my practice. It's not a part of life. It's life itself. Before I was always hung up in thinking, so I could never get my ass in gear. It's really been a good experience, having to actually physically do this and that.
>
> After I'd been in the monastery, I wanted to find as close a parallel to it in my daily life, because I knew what that wonderful monastic thing does, and I wanted to keep it going. When the bell rings you go to work and just do it. Then it rings again and you put the tools down and let go of it. Don't be attached to it or getting it done.
>
> *What are you working for? Who are you working for? Yourself?*
>
> Well, you have to work to support your life. "A day of no working is a day of no eating." But work extends to other people. The economy thwarts that with the idea of having customers so you can make a profit. But really work is a pure expression of mutual aid. It's serving people without worrying about the economics.

As with the LWF, the differential contents of worldly work are emptied into a single religious category, that of "practice," similar to the LWF's "doing God's will." The idea of work is thus severed from economic profit and social status. Instead it is tied to the immediate necessity of minimal self-support within a communal context that makes each person's labor a form of aid to others, not a means of advancing himself ahead of them. This notion of mutual aid, reminiscent of Kropotkin's,[82] sets work in social perspective for the Zen student. It is cooperative instead of competitive.

Zen's emphasis on ritual enactment in meditation, not doctrinal thought, is echoed by its emphasis on work as active self-expression, not intellectual or hip self-contemplation. Zen Center puts the dropout back to work, with attention and diligence on the job. But it does not put him back in the rat race of competitive work aimed at maximizing production, profit, and advancement. How things are done outweighs how much is done. Traditional Buddhist norms of right livelihood forbid work that injures or exploits others. The idea of work as practice, moreover, makes the kind of activity, attitudes, and mind states represented by zazen and monastic labor into the criteria for desirable outside occupations as well. For sixties youth, the category of practice not only empties work of its differential conventional contents. It also implies an alternative scale for evaluating and selecting jobs.

A "good job" becomes one that offers a good opportunity for practice.[83] This means, first, that its performance does not clash with the attitudes and relationships that characterize monastic life. Second, it means a job that allows a student to take off anywhere from a day to more than a year to devote herself to monastic Zen practice, which it helps to defray. A college-educated student explains why she has cleaned houses for several years:

> Housecleaning allows me flexibility, so I can go to training period, or take a week off for sesshin, or just be around the center when I need to.

What about the work itself?

> It's fine. It's quiet, it needs to be done, and it's right there in front of you. When you do it, it's done. There's nothing left over.

Zen students tend to do relatively simple work with things, like housecleaning, which doesn't lay emphasis on the success or failure of the final product. (Some do skilled trades or artisan's work, where production is more complex but is judged by craft and aesthetic standards, not industrial ones.) Or they do relatively quiet service work with people—for example, caring for the aged or handicapped—which doesn't call for verbal self-assertion or polished self-presentation. They also avoid work that requires a high level of abstraction or difficult problem solving. Serious students repeatedly withdraw from all outside commitments to engage in full-time monastic training for periods ranging from three months to several years at a time. This makes it impossible for them to hold down conventional jobs, except those that can be left and reentered easily because they require little investment in training or experience. Such jobs are usually passed back and forth among Zen students as they move between city and monastery. Their neat appearance and care in performing such work make employers agreeable to such exchanges.

These working conditions exclude nearly all Zen students from white-collar and professional work, keeping them off the upper rungs of the job ladder. Downward occupational mobility characterizes sixties youth practicing Zen full time, as measured against the trajectory of their upper-middle-class parents and earlier education. Many dropped out originally into the bohemian or hip counterculture. When they came to Zen Center they went back to work, but they did not drop back in to resume their earlier career path, as did some converts to more permeable, nonmonastic alternative religious groups like Meher Baba.[84] Instead Zen students refocused their energies on Zen practice itself. The monk works primarily on himself.

The Monk in the World

Few students, even those working regularly as teachers or craftsmen, mention occupational careers in discussing their goals. Instead they aim to "deepen my practice" or "keep studying with Roshi" and continue living communally with other students. Like the sacred career of being an LWF minister, the modified monastic career of being a Zen student replaces conventional careers and translates all work into its own terms.[85] What does it mean to pursue such a career? A priest replies,

> First of all, you have some idea of what it means to be a good student: sitting, following the schedule, doing your work. When you start out, you look around and find out how difficult that is, how far away you are from it. It surprises you. In some ways you feel like you can't do the simplest, most rudimentary things. And yet at some point, after a while, you feel so free. It's so wonderful to do all those simple, simple things, one at a time. I was just overjoyed every single day.
>
> Then you run into a stone wall at fifty miles an hour. You see, if you want to be completely devoted to this, it means sacrifices. I wasn't sure I could give up my other lives for good just for this one. I was really scared. Then you actually have to commit yourself to doing it. You have to jump. There's no turning back.
>
> *Is one of those other lives having a career?*
>
> It could be. My calling is to be a monk. Actually that can be pretty much formless, but on the surface it means freeing your time to sit and be with people at Zen Center, and do whatever needs doing here. On that level being a monk maybe means not taking up some other career.

The Zen student begins his or her career by learning how to meditate and keep the schedule of monastic life in elementary fashion. As he begins to master this surprisingly difficult regimen, a tremendous sense of positive liberty arises in the student. It comes from having made his own an externally set way, time, and place to perform each daily activity (rising, bathing, eating, working, resting, studying) built around the practice of meditation, and predictably coordinated with the uniform activities of others. The monk's career is total in the sense that almost all his daily activities are institutionally defined, regulated, and ritualized. It is also "formless" or "nothing special," since these are the ordinary activities of the quotidian. The monk's career is total in a second sense, in that it excludes or at least subordinates other occupations. The dynamic of renunciation and commitment, familiar from religious and utopian communities in every age, is at work here.[86]

For sixties youth the avenue to renouncing other careers was cleared by the counterculture's criticism of conventional work as worthless and its idealization of communal self-support, to which Zen Center's monasticism gives an organizational structure and a religious rationale. An older student analyzes the issue accordingly:

How does practicing Zen compare with working a straight job?

The straight world sets up a tradeoff situation: take the stress, drive yourself, wear your body down. Then you can go out and enjoy yourself. You get a job and pretty soon you're doing things that don't really make you feel so good, but you do them because there's the tradeoff. You can go home to your nice house, have a drink, and listen to the stereo. That's where the hippies came in. They wanted to enjoy the tradeoff without feeling bad to get it, but it doesn't work that way.

Is there a tradeoff in Zen?

No, in sitting there isn't any relief. There's only the determination to get to the root of the problem of living. You have to take your own ground and relinquish everything.

What does that mean?

You have to express yourself fully, without relying on anything outside of yourself, and you have to hold it all together day by day. Monastic training is not interested in any end product, except whether you can live out the self the way it is.

Conventional work is interpreted as purely instrumental. It is empty of intrinsic value. It is identified by the product it turns out and justified by the enjoyment its performance can buy in the form of leisure consumption and status. The Zen student's career, by contrast, is seen to be noninstrumental. It is intrinsically valuable, because it expresses the true nature of the monistic self even as it cuts off the material and social substantiation of the individual self.

Some sixties youths, common among the Center's leadership, came directly to life as Zen students from demanding schooling and professional jobs, which they criticize from their experience of Zen practice. Says one,

Zen practice is probably the first serious thing that I've come into that I've really believed and felt was of objective importance to the world and to me. That it matters whether I sit in the morning every day, whether I go to sesshin—and not only to me. Learning how to love something like zazen, really deeply, has made it all the more apparent to me that I never liked professional school or work.

I wasn't so able to practice in my work. It always came from a place that's higher than my hara [lower belly]. It's a more intellectual or egoistic level that just doesn't feel right somehow.

The value believed to be inherent in Zen practice and the love experienced for it discredit a professional career. The psychosomatic form of self-consciousness bred by zazen experientially grounds criticism of the tension-producing head work performed by the professional.

For sixties youth who brought blue-collar or craft skills to Zen Center or have since acquired them, the relationship between outside work and a monastic career has been relatively smooth. For those who left the path to intellectual and professional careers and have since neither mastered manual skills nor joined Zen Center's administration, the relationship between working inside and outside Zen Center has its difficulties. One of the latter students comments, "It seems easier if you're a carpenter and you practice Zen, because you can do them side by side. Having been an intellectual and no longer doing that, I'm kind of at a loss in that regard.... I've cleaned houses and been a baker. Now I'm washing dishes in a restaurant."

How have Zen students adapted to downward occupational mobility? Working and living cheaply and simply within Zen Center as part of practice constitute the crux of this adaptation. Remaining unmarried and, more importantly, childless often accompanies not working a steadily paying job. A larger proportion of Zen students with steady jobs outside or on scholarships inside Zen Center have married.[87] Conversely, many of the small flow of students who leave Zen Center after extended stays do so to return to school, pursue careers, or begin families. A just-married Zen student now working steadily as a schoolteacher acknowledges, "For our parents wanting to be secure and have an income was a big thing. It's not for me, but I still feel twinges of it, particularly since I've gotten married and we're thinking of having a child."

Leaving Zen Center after a long stay to return to the world of conventional work and social institutions can be a disorienting transition. A student considers it:

I spent eight or nine years at Zen Center, thinking it was for a lifetime, and now I find myself not doing that anymore. I'm going to at least try the career route [in deaf-blind education]. I suppose I feel more pressure about work now. It's partly being away from the structure of Zen Center and being older, with things still up in the air.

The monastic career exerts a continuing influence on those who eventually leave it and Zen Center. A priest comments,

We've learned a lot just going through the process of letting go and giving up our idea of securing a place [in conventional society]. You can get anxious again and come to the place where you want to be a nurse or go back to school. Some people who dropped out are dropping back in. But they're different now. It's more that they're working to learn and practice. They're not learning just to work and get a payoff.

This qualitative carryover is borne out by the fact that most older students who leave Zen Center continue to meditate, if less frequently, and gravitate toward either helping professions like teaching and nursing or toward skilled labor and crafts like carpentry and pottery.

As individuals, these aging sixties youths now ask themselves whether living and working as a full-time Zen student will be a temporary or permanent social identity. As an institution, Zen Center faces a similar question: whether it will be a temporary or permanent home to its members. "For most members," its published answer states, "Zen Center is not a lifetime residential community. But, since it usually takes as much as ten years to understand Zen, and longer to become a Zen teacher, a residential community has developed."[88] Over the past several years, as more of its younger students have married and begun families, the idea of Zen Center as a long-term residential community, not only a monastic training community, has grown stronger. So have Zen Center's efforts to create income-producing jobs for its members, to make more personal time and living space for its couples, and to arrange schooling for their children.

Zen Center's monastic role offers sixties youth a definite alternative to bourgeois adulthood for the time being, with the possibility of working out a permanent alternative compounded of Zen's monastic and lay householder traditions, and countercultural motifs. This long-range ideal, which I will call *the monk in the world*, describes a figure who works quietly and calmly to take care of things or other people in some simple, direct occupation (farming, baking, carpentry, crafts, practical nursing), earning just enough to support his daily needs. He lives communally with other Zen students, often in the country, maintaining close relationships to a master and to nature. Conspicuously absent from this vision are the nuclear family, suburban home, and white-collar or professional career: in short, the hallmarks of middle-class life. The Zen student is a monk *in* the world, relatively uninsulated by the celibacy or cloister of the classic Christian contemplative. But his attitude toward the world in which he moves is mystically undriven, unattached yet all-accepting. The Puritan's this-worldly asceticism has given way to the Zen Buddhist's this-worldly mysticism.[89] This attitude and its monk-in-the-world ideal usually remain with students who leave Zen Center. It also seems to have spread among Zen Center's lay friends, and perhaps beyond them, to others in the urban upper middle class. Few of these laypersons have dropped out, yet their understanding of what it means to stay in and do the world's work may be changing in ways related to Zen's mediation of countercultural values.

Status: Seniority, Commitment, and Courage

Zen Center both empties social stratification of meaning, and it transforms that meaning. Monistic denial of the individual self as an independent entity undercuts the idea of better or worse selves, higher or lower status individuals. Conventional measures of social status—income, wealth, occupation, education, professional-intellectual-artistic achievement—are themselves devalued (more to less devalued, perhaps, in the order listed). Are they replaced by indices of spiritual awareness? The answer is ambiguous. A master explains,

> Although we all have the same fundamental practice which we carry out in the same way, some may attain enlightenment and some may not . . . even if we have no experience of enlightenment, if we sit in the proper way with the right attitude and understanding of practice, then that is Zen.[90]

Enlightened and unenlightened persons are likewise practicing Zen. At the same time, more or less proper practice with more or less the right attitude and understanding of Zen Center activity distinguishes serious or committed students from not-so-committed ones. "A Sangha-community is organized and defined in a way that does not produce winners and losers," says a master summing up the issue. "Status is determined primarily by seniority, commitment, kindness, flexibility, receptivity, and similar attitudes."[91] An attitude of "courage"—unconditionally dedicated and persistent effort—toward Zen practice itself is the essential qualification of the good student. Commitment to the community is the second most important qualification. "There's status in practice and status in the community," observes a priest. "Real status is entirely related to practice. Courage in sitting is what counts." Given this essence, several indicators of status appear at Zen Center. There is seniority, for one, and ability in the visible performance of meditation, especially its posture; and, to a lesser degree, ability in related ritual behavior such as chanting and bowing. Students watch their relationship to the master, who acknowledges the student's effort and attitude, thereby "pointing to your status but not giving it to you." Finally, status attaches to diligence in work and a willingness to do whatever task one is given, especially if it appears menial, like cleaning toilets or dumping garbage. Less paradoxically, status also attaches to manual and managerial skills that fit Zen Center's needs.

Gracefully enacting the correct posture for zazen meditation implies that state of consciousness which Zen Buddhism seeks to realize. Shared experience of meditation reportedly gives rise to a shared ability to recognize "how your body and physical actions reflect your state of mind," according to older students. A largely intuitive standard of what I will call "yogic competency" allows the external performance of meditation to be read as a kind of spiritual body language. This leads not to ranked comparisons between individual students but rather to their gradual inclusion into the group of older students and their arrangement into a loose continuum there. Perceptions of more or less mastery of ritual activity extend to bowing, chanting, walking, and eating in the zendo, all of which are defined in ways that overlap religious rite, artistic performance, and social etiquette.

The number of years the student has practiced at Zen Center bears on his standing there, although seniority does not approach the importance it carries traditionally in Japanese monasteries. There arrival a day or even an hour earlier gives one monk formal precedence over another. After three or four years of regular practice at Zen Center, students become "ordained laymen" in a ceremony that grants each of them a *raksu*, a biblike garment resembling that worn by priests, and a place up front during services.[92] After six months' training as novices, all students wear standardized robes sewn at Zen Center. These in turn give way to formal robes, tailored in Japan, for students ordained as priests, usually after completing some six years of training in exemplary fashion.[93]

Labor at Zen Center is neatly divided, with clear-cut areas of jurisdiction and lines of supervision. Given its extensive physical plant and building program, coupled with its aims of self-support, Zen Center has a special need for students with manual, craft, and trade skills. They are likely to gain job responsibility more rapidly than others, stay longer in jobs fitted to their skills, and be subjected a little less stringently to the routine religious demands of the Zen Center schedule. "This is an obvious tendency," concedes a priest; "and we consciously hedge against it." Eventually, even the best carpenters are switched to administrative or priestly positions, and the best managers go back to work as laborers. A student comments,

> Jobs at Zen Center get traded around. You can't sign up for life as the cook, even though you may be a very good cook. There's a recognition that wherever we get comfortable, we want to stay there. The pressure to move is not to cut you off but it's a teaching about how to be comfortable wherever you are, and

how to accept changes. Most of the work is pretty simple in itself, but it's complicated because relationships and interdependency with other people are part of it as practice.

Contrapuntal rotation of jobs among committed older students occurs along with their ascent to positions of increasing responsibility. This develops a sense of self and relationships with others dissociated from any given occupation. It also creates a core group of leaders and supporting functionaries, whose members all combine religious, administrative, and technical experience without permanently controlling specific areas of authority and expertise. Authority and decision making at Zen Center rest on the consensus of this core group, which is stratified by seniority as well as ability. Consensus and seniority protect the community from competition and takeover fueled by individual drive or talent. "Leadership by talent alone develops leaders and followers but not leaders who develop," observes a master.[94] Like the Christian sect, Zen Center seeks to shift the grounds of status from an individual's skills in winning external success to his will in making a religious commitment.

A Place at Society's Edge

The millenarian sect sees itself standing above and opposed to the larger society, which mocks or persecutes it. Zen Center sees itself standing at the edge of the larger society, which either admires it or doesn't know what to make of it. A student describes the larger society and status within it:

> America focuses on money. There's something exciting about it, the passion to acquire and accumulate. And there are these examples of people who've made it. But we're such an open society; if you really look around, these people don't look so good actually. You find out alcohol supports them. There's suicide, anxiety, and all the other negative reflections of success. There's hardly anybody around who's really at peace.

> The culture tells you to define yourself in duality, not to try to transcend it. You have to do. There's no permission not to do. Succeed. Don't fail. Make your own way. You can't really be a citizen without having your property thing together.

As a Buddhist monastery, Zen Center faces beyond the society's dualist distinctions toward "the other shore" of acosmic monism realized in everyday experience. Physically it is located in the interstices of the larger society. Its city center stands between a ghetto and a downtown area, its farm between a national park and a posh exurb. Its monastery is an inholding in a national forest. Economically its students work either in its own small businesses or along the edges of unionized labor and bureaucracy. Yet those around Zen Center see it as a vanguard and model for a new society in the making. Those at its center refer more cautiously to its power of example: "We're trying to find out how to work, live, and practice as a community in one place. That naturally means rethinking the usual way our society does things."

Based on the quality of his own life and state of mind, the youthful Zen student perceives his status differing from that of the conventional member of the upper middle class as the bohemian artist differs from the bourgeois philistine or the hippie differs from the straight. This difference extends to the sort of work the Zen student does, inverting the usual relation between head work and hand work. A student elaborates,

> *How would you compare your place in the world as a Zen student to someone who never dropped out or got involved in Zen?*
>
> I don't really think of myself as having a place in the world like that.
>
> *OK. Can you say how you see it compared to how that other person might see it?*
>
> By the time I was a teenager I knew I didn't want to grow up to be like other people. I wanted to be a writer. That feeling stayed with me even afterward, when what I wanted to do was practice Zen.
>
> The businessman just assumes it's better to be a businessman or a lawyer than it is to be a carpenter or a janitor. It's a good thing to be a lawyer, just by itself, even without all the money. Well, I don't agree with that. Maybe it's not better. Maybe it's worse. I mean, do you really want to argue with people for the rest of your life? Do you really want to have to be nice to them to sell them something? In terms of practicing zazen in your daily life, it's really difficult to do that kind of stuff.
>
> At least as a carpenter I feel like I can practice, and that's why I chose it. Being a lawyer or selling stock is actually doing the dirty work. You don't get your hands dirty. You get your head dirty.

The experience of zazen and monastic life grounds a sense of what is good that devalues white-collar and professional careers since they require emotional management of oneself and others, which is seen as mental or psychic "dirty work." Furthermore, the student sees the exemplary activity of Zen

Center and its members to be serving the society in ways more vital to it than any conventional work. "Face it," says a student, "right now the world needs Zen priests a lot more than it needs doctors or college professors. We know a lot about surgery and physics, but we don't know much at all about our own nature." True self-understanding and social life in accord with it come before further increments in abstract or applied technical knowledge.

Zen Center makes high demands for active accomplishment and inner discipline on sixties youth earlier socialized to both. Yet Zen Center also seeks to detach such accomplishment from individual competition and differential rewards, instead turning it to the service of spiritual development and self-fulfillment in a cooperative community. Similar ideals were espoused by the counterculture, which also contraposed them to conventional competition between "winners" and "losers" striving to establish their individual worth. In the professional and managerial world of upper-middle-class adulthood, these sixties youths faced the duality of individual success or failure. Here, "You have to do. There's no permission not to do. Succeed. Don't fail." They shied away from this ultimatum, as much from fear of success as failure. Pulled by the aesthetic and contemplative sides of their experience both as elite college students and bohemian or hip dropouts, they have found in Zen Center the possibility of transcending the predicament of these conflicting life plans. This solution involves giving up their place in the upper-middle-class mainstream and diligently creating another one in the margins of skilled labor, small business, and institutional religion itself.

IV. SOCIAL RESPONSIBILITY: POLITICS BY EXAMPLE

Zen students generally disapprove of what they take to be the confrontational style and antagonistic spirit of radical politics in the sixties. They nonetheless see themselves as persons with a sense of social architecture, who shared with radicals a deep concern for American society and its need for change. "Radical politics makes sense intellectually," one student comments; "it's just that a lot of people who came to that intellectual conclusion hadn't cracked the emotional nut of their own anger and hatred." Zen students' sense of social responsibility begins with the necessity of a compassionate rather than antagonistic spirit, and a style of exemplary service rather than aggressive confrontation. This social stance calls to mind the moral example of the Bodhisattva. It is predicated on the monistic assumption that the society is one interdependent whole and that social change, so far as it is possible, begins with self-transformation and spreads outward harmoniously.

In explaining why they held back from full participation in sixties political protest, Zen students cite reasons that suggest why Zen Center stands as a viable alternative to it. Most of their criticism aims at violent conflict associated with political radicalism. Says one,

> Radicals threatened people, who resisted, of course. So before you know it you have people hating one another. The radicals gave off the same arrogance that the Establishment did. *They* were the best and the brightest. Everyone else was inferior. The Establishment position was so reprehensible it made you gag, but you can't fight violence with violence. Yelling "Fuck Nixon" is like yelling "Kill the Cong." It has the same inner feeling. It's a commitment to be angry and hate that's exactly the opposite of the commitment to practice [Zen], which means letting go of those feelings.

> Even if society is at fault, you have to deal with opening up yourself in order to open it up. Politics can't solve its problems as long as it looks for them being outside of ourselves. You can't end manipulation by trying to manipulate it back. You have to seek some way out of your own greed-hatred-delusion.

Zen students little involved organizationally in sixties politics reported themselves personally involved with the issues of Vietnam, civil rights, and social justice. But they shied away from the tactics, rhetoric, revolutionary theory, and aggressive attitudes of radicals organized around such issues. Instead they devoted their energies to "opening up our personal horizons and experience," whether through drugs, art, or intellectual study.

Significantly, the minority of students who were organizationally involved in politics emphasize the exemplary personal and social character of such involvement in itself, not its wider consequences, and they trace their disappointment with the political movement to its loss of this character. A student remembers his summer in Mississippi,

> It was a very wonderful thing with people. The relating that was going on was really careful and trusting and appreciative of other people being with you, because it was dangerous. You really looked at that other human being, like a reflection of yourself, and you wanted to know what was in him. I loved people there very quickly, and I felt safe with them.

Another student looks back on civil disobedience against the Vietnam war and time spent in jail with other pacifists:

> For months afterward I remember feeling, "Here's a community of people who feel like I do." Here was a place where ends and means were the same, where you acted out of the love you felt

in your heart, not some policy. You could live your life in peace and understanding, and that would come out in the world. At least that's how it seemed at first.

Good politics consists of an exemplary way of life and community that are good in themselves, because they are appropriate to the human situation and reflect its natural regularities. Politics is not an instrumental organizational activity, aggressive or manipulative in itself, that produces putatively good social and structural changes. Utopian ends do not justify utilitarian political means.

One Zen student, more hippie than radical in the sixties but involved in antiwar demonstrations, considers the society and his responsibility for it at present:

> *Has practicing Zen changed the way you see politics or social problems now as compared to the sixties?*
>
> Let me tell you a story. One day, during the Vietnam war, someone asked Roshi, "What is war?" He said it was like a bamboo mat when two people want to sit on it. They both want to smooth out their side so there aren't any wrinkles. Then there are a bunch of wrinkles in the center, which nobody quite knows what to do with. That's war.
>
> A lot of people picked up on this and kept asking about war and pacifism, pressing the point, 'What does he really think, is he against war or isn't he? What about this big peace demonstration next week? Should we go to it or not? What should we do? Why doesn't he take a definite stand?"
>
> Finally, all at once, Roshi jumped up. He took the nearest older student and started hitting him with the stick, again and again. Roaring, "Dreamer! Dreamer! What are you dreaming about?" Then he went back and sat down, totally livid—his face was white—and he said very quietly, "I'm not angry."
>
> Everybody just sat there stunned, because he was such a gentle person. Looking back later I could see—here we were against the Vietnam war but our minds were in the same state that produces war in the first place. So what were we talking about? It was all a dream. We were thinking of something out there that was the big problem, when the problem was identical to what we were expressing at that very moment. It wasn't that he was for or against war but that he was dealing with the reality of the people who were right in front of him.
>
> That was a big event for me, because it shifted my awareness of where the real problem was from something outside me to some-

thing not outside or inside, something that doesn't exclude myself or any other individual person.

When you look at the society now, what do you see? Do you see any problems?

I used to think everything in the society was a problem. Now it's still that way and exactly the opposite. Social problems are our own problems of what we can do about society. Each of us has that problem. So instead of being outside us, society is just part of that wilderness of mind that we are, that we have to deal with.

What can you do about your problem of society?

The answer for me lies in somehow being able to practice and extend zazen practice. In very basic mundane terms of being able to sit every day in the zendo at five in the morning. To actually get there and sit and establish that beginning for my life that day. Only through that, through being that person who does that, can I get anything done with other people.... It's like Milarepa, who was sitting alone in his cave to liberate the rest of the world. Sitting zazen enlightens the whole world. That's very hard to understand, but it has to be true.... Roshi has said that we're remaking society by sitting zazen, because we're formed by social ideas. In practice we're asking ourselves, "Who forms form?" We're beginning to release the source of our ideas of how to live.

How do other people come into it?

Practicing with your brothers and sisters in the sangha, the oneness of everything comes out in a feeling of human solidarity. It's really a true and real feeling that expresses how things are, not just some idea of altruism. That feeling is the opposite of the whole thing of "It's a dog-eat-dog world." Usually people focus on the institutions, instead of the person's actual feeling or perception. But that's how practice comes into the world, and how it changes things.

There's some big angry frustration in the world. It's clear that we're all stumbling around. God isn't doing what he should be doing. Buddhism isn't. So what do we do? We practice. Roshi said once, "The pure practice of a monk like Han Shan is like a drop of water that evaporates before it ever hits the ground." The only thing I can do is practice and practice together in the sangha.

Roshi's feeling of the sangha is not just existing as a small group, but actually being everything, everyone. Not facing inward but

acting outward through the whole society. Being a kind of mandala for it and extending our practice to it and including it.

Everything is interconnected. So if people change, then institutions will change. I think people will change through Zen practice, so institutions will change. That doesn't mean it will trigger
a cultural revolution. I don't think problems are necessarily soluble, or that they're even here to be solved. They're here to be
worked on, and that's what we're doing here, working something out. . . . Besides, Zen's such a pain in the ass, you know,
that it's always going to have just a few people doing it. And it's
confusing. Other people make great claims for it, and it has an
important position in the counterculture candy store, but it
doesn't make those kind of claims for itself. So most people look
at it and decide, "It's not for me." It will never be a mass movement. But it can be a kind of model of how to take care of life
and how to live together.

In this account human change occurs from the inside out, from the consciousness of the individual meditator, through the face-to-face community
of his fellow Zen students, to the institutions of the society at large. This
idea takes radical religious form in the assertion that "sitting zazen enlightens the whole world." It is elaborated into the "who forms form?" paradox
that social ideas originate within individual consciousness as well as form it.
Therefore society can be transformed by transforming consciousness. Yet
social problems are seen as not necessarily soluble, a paraphrase of the new
politics of monist conservatism. Under monist interpretation the social
world tends to merge with the inner world of consciousness, to reunite with
"the wilderness of mind." War in Vietnam is not separable from one's own
contentiousness, here and now. The political activist might well characterize this shift as a dangerous regression toward self-absorption and the acceptance of social ills. But it is worth noting that the Zen student rejects Social
Darwinism and the reciprocal use of others to one's own self-interest in no
uncertain terms. Against these "dog-eat-dog" principles of utilitarian society he opposes the communal solidarity of the sangha, in which Zen's compassionate state of mind is seen to take social form.

The condition of the larger society, then, continues to appear problematic to the Zen student in a way familiar from the counterculture. But he
does not diagnose this condition as susceptible to direct, dramatic change,
whether political or psychedelic, and he rejects either such role for Zen Center. Still, the religious community is perceived to be an exemplar for the
society. Like a mandala, it embodies an ideal or principle of universal order.
Its members seek by their everyday activity to extend this order harmoniously into the society as a whole, holding out some promise, however
hedged, of institutional change to come.

The point of view reflects developments in the lives of its proponents
and in American society since the sixties. Youthful expectations of dramatic

social change by radical political means have faded along with psychedelic hopes for similar changes of consciousness. A student admits,

> In college I thought you could take ideas backed up by power and use them like tools to change the world. I don't feel that way any more. The radicals and the people at the top of the big bureaucracies are as bamboozled as everybody else. . . . What we do have is the power of community. That doesn't come from money and influence. It comes from accepting your life and giving up everything to live it out together.

Following in the wake of revolutionary disappointments, postsixties support for slower, more evolutionary social changes anchored in the daily activity of work and householding has been reinforced by the longer-term, more conservative projects and concerns intrinsic to adulthood as a stage of life in comparison to youth. Moreover, the social issues that dominated the sixties—Vietnam, civil rights, social inequality, political power and its corruption—emphasized the two-sided conflict of sharply opposed interest groups—black and white, rich and poor, military and draftee, powerful and powerless. The ecological and economic issues perceived to dominate the 1970s and eighties imply social conflict, to be sure, but they lend themselves to more monistic interpretations of the social world. They appear to be problems arising more directly from the mode and style of life pursued by the society as a whole, oriented toward material consumption and production, toward individualistic competition for goods, status, and power. To analyze such problems the Zen student looks neither to Marx nor liberalism but to the "Buddhist economics" set out by thinkers like E. F. Schumacher, who writes,

> The Buddhist sees the essence of civilization not in multiplication of wants but in the purification of human character . . . since consumption is merely a means to human well-being, the aim should be to obtain the maximum of well-being with the minimum of consumption.[95]

The solution of social problems, then, lies in purifying character through cutting consumption to simple needs, and communally reordering work and social life to nurture cooperation, compassion, and artistic creativity. It does not lie in increasing the standard of living by maximizing consumption through the most efficient pattern of productive effort. Nor does it lie in redistributing goods to consume and the power to produce them.

Ecotopia: Re-Creating Society

Ecology, in particular, has offered a monistic interpretation of societal conditions that is powerfully convincing to Zen students and congruent

with their religious vision. The millennialism implicit in Zen Center's understanding of itself as an exemplary community comes to light most clearly in
an ecological context. One student comments,

> There's no more time to keep on going like we have. The envi-
> ronment can't take it. The cornucopia is running out. The truth
> is that we need everything else that's alive in order to survive.
> It's all interdependent. That's straight Buddhism! While we've
> been acting like we can go tramping over every other species and
> dominate and control everything, we can't. We have to learn to
> appreciate the earth and take care of it like it is, before it's too
> late.

Another adds,

> The ideas of Buddhism are beginning to coalesce with practical
> political decisions that have to be made now, whether we're
> going to take an ecological or exploitative approach to natural
> resources. I doubt if that's because more people are studying
> Schumacher and Lao Tzu now. As much as anything, it's just
> the reality that we're running out. Buddhism isn't all that special.
> It's just a more accurate working out of what people already
> know and can express when things come down to it in a crisis.

In a world that may be headed toward eco-catastrophe Zen students see
themselves exemplifying needed personal attitudes and interpersonal behavior. Furthermore, their ideal communities exemplify the cooperative lifestyle, social structure, and economy needed by the larger society—communities that feature small-scale, low-consumption and no-waste econo-
mies, which are labor-intensive and based on farming, trades, and crafts
occupations aimed at self-support. They are localized, long-term communities with coresidential core groups, whose organization combines communal intimacy with monastic self-control. Ascetic labor in its monastic
form gives rigor to the economic activity of self-support and the spiritual
activity of self-realization. The social ethic of Zen Center assumes its greatest political and institutional definition within this vision of "Ecotopia."[96]
Even at this extreme it is an exemplary ethic, not an aggressively activistic
one. It consistently sees institutional change as arising from self-transformation. The Zen student may transform himself by practicing within a specially structured community, but that community is itself taken to be the
creation of the master's and his disciples' state of consciousness.

How does Zen Center's community compare to those envisioned by
the political and hip wings of the counterculture? Monastic withdrawal,
especially when robed in Japanese cultural forms, can answer the hip call to
drop out of American society. Longtime students acknowledge this, but

they report Zen Center and their own lives growing more integrated with the larger society over the past several years. Says one,

> When I first came to Zen Center I felt that I'd gotten out of the old society, I'd escaped. I stopped reading the newspapers. I didn't pay any attention to what was happening outside, because that was *samsara* [illusion], right, and we're working on ourselves. Conflict [with others] cooled off because Zen Center's super-organized and, besides, you've got all this conflict going on inside your own head. It's unreal because "you do not understand the oneness of the universe."

> But, you know, the Bodhisattva's path leads back into everything. Practice goes on in the middle of conflict and the rest of everyday life. It feels like Zen Center is less insulated now. Working in the neighborhood has made a big difference. We haven't done so much really, but now there's a social dimension *in* Zen Center. When I go out the front door, I don't feel as scared on the street. I'm more at home. When you're trying to change things, you don't have to feel bad about the way they are. . . . Zen Center itself seems less Japanesey. Like five years ago everyone was wearing straw sandals from Japantown. Now it's these rubber surfer sandals, "Beachcomber Bills."

The aging of sixties youth, Zen Center's institutional stabilization, and changes in the larger society have all contributed to a sense of self and society reconverging. So has the dynamic of Zen monastic training itself, as expressed in the ideal of the Bodhisattva, who withdraws to meditate and returns to realize his enlightenment by acting it out with others in everyday life. Promises a student, "Once you become your practice, you can do it anywhere." Like Zen Center itself, once a sixties youth has stably internalized Zen practice and his own identity as a Zen student, he need not maintain them by defining himself so strongly through separation from the larger society or opposition to it.

Zen Center's stability as an institution and its well-placed supporters also distinguish it from the radical political wing of the counterculture. A priest explains:

> *How do you see Zen Center in relation to the counterculture's political ideals?*

> I think it's still harmonious with those ideals. In a way maybe the core spirit of the counterculture is contained in Zen Center. But it hasn't just criticized power in the society. It's figured out something about it. It ties in with a wide circle of younger artists and intellectuals, and politicians, with a pretty broad and influential base. We're all interested in shifting power in the culture, but

we've learned that the whole culture is caught up in this process. The *counter*-culture negation, by itself, is too one-sided. It's not good guys against bad guys.

Instead of fighting to change society, like the radicals, we're trying to *create* society. The point is you have to do something with some limitations. We're not individually capable of changing the society by ourselves all at once. We should all do something, *and* we should be able to carry it all along day by day, and take care of our lives. You can live broadly in that way only when you accept some limitation. Zen Center has been able to transmit that point existentially: we have to accept the limits of our own reality right now. Can you actually transform somebody right now? Can you convert them? You want to pour out love and truth on everybody, but they don't respond. By taking some limitation in monastic training, you can see these experiences from different viewpoints.

That's why we stay in one place, with one practice, in one community. By being committed to ourselves together and not to the *idea* of community, we can take care of the community and not be swept away by its failures. By taking care of our own lives like this we can change what's possible for the people around us. Look around. The neighborhood's changed since we've come here. It's cleaner and quieter. There's the park now, the store, a community garden. We're rehabbing buildings, and working with kids and neighborhood groups. It's taken money and connections, but the real reason we've had some success is that people know we live here, too, and we're committed to staying. The reason we stay together is the satisfaction of zazen and the gratefulness we feel to help other people to practice.[97]

Zen Center's political thrust is grounded in its cultural and experiential integrity, and backed by its institutional stability and vigor in caring for its own members. Criticism of conventional social structures has been implicit, while attempts to construct alternatives to them have been explicit and well publicized. In this sense Zen Center tries to "create society" instead of change it. These attempts have drawn on connections well placed in the larger society, but the commitment of sixties youth to the instituional limitation of monastic training has been the key to Zen Center's success.

A student summarizes the contrast between Zen's social ethic and that of sixties activism by reference to the figures of Buddha and Moses, a contrast that can be generalized to their respective traditions:

How does Zen practice relate to the society, compared to political radicalism in the sixties?

There you were trying to transform the external social thing, and that's going to transform individuals. Here we work on ourselves, and in some way the world changes. That's very much the difference between Moses and Buddha. Buddha was a prince, and what puts him on the path is seeing sickness, old age, and death—and the way to salvation. Desire is the big problem. What starts Moses off is seeing a Hebrew slave being beaten by an Egyptian. What he discovers in his *samadhi* [state of awareness] is that you have to get in there and right social wrongs, create some social situation where there's justice. Well, they were both enlightened. It's a matter of how it expresses itself in history. Maybe Buddha is more formless than Moses, but, who knows, maybe at some time Zen practice will take form like that. When I first began sitting I felt more like socialism wasn't where it was at, and Zen was. Now it's like Zen doesn't exclude anything.

The activist prophet identifies himself with an oppressed people and seeks to alter their social situation to fulfill their ultimate destiny. The exemplary prophet identifies himself with the unalterable predicament of humankind and seeks to alter his own consciousness to transcend it. (He does so, significantly enough, in a politically precarious era undergoing disjointed social and cultural change.) The Zen student espouses a notion of social responsibility based on a radically epistemological critique of human existence that proposes an exemplary *mode* of personal and social activity in daily life, not a social program with some specific content.

For all this, the daily life of the youthful resident at Pacific Zen Center has an implicit social content that gives some bite to his exemplary ethic. A communal lifestyle, social structure, and form of property ownership, in effect, predominate over the autonomous household or individual. Families and children are accommodated but kept subordinate to the requisites of a modified monastic life. Communal businesses are in operation, some of them vertically integrated. Bureaucratic and professional work in the larger society has typically been left behind. Ascetic labor has been divorced from the ethic of individual success and consumption. Many youths from upper-middle-class backgrounds have apparently accepted the consequences of downward occupational mobility. Time, energy, and money have gone into organizing and improving the ghetto neighborhood Zen students have made their urban home. The Zen Center community sees itself as giving rise to a more satisfying kind of awareness, work, and relationship than its members found in the larger society, and doing so in ways that may become ecologically necessary for others in the future. Moral ideals and social arrangements consonant with the counterculture of the sixties have been discovered within the doctrinal tradition and the monastic social structure of Zen Buddhism. This discovery has enabled sixties youth to live with American society into the 1980s even as they seek to live out an alternative to it.

EST AND ETHICS
Rule-Egoism in
Middle-Class Culture

4

Erhard Seminars Training (*est*) describes itself as an educational corporation that trains its clients "to transform your ability to experience living
so that the situations you have been trying to change or have been putting
up with clear up just in the process of life itself."[1] The standard training program takes over sixty hours spread across four days on two consecutive
weekends. A single trainer delivers it in a hotel ballroom to groups of 200-
250 persons who are mostly urban, middle-class young adults, at a cost of
$400 per person. "Graduates" of this program are encouraged to attend on-
going graduate seminars, occupationally specialized workshops, and mass
special events in order to enhance the training's effects.

Werner Erhard gave the first *est* training in a friend's borrowed apartment in 1971. Ten years later the *est* organization is a model bureaucracy,
molded by a former Harvard Business School professor and Coca-Cola
executive, which coordinates the efforts of some 300 paid employees and
25,000 volunteers in twenty-nine cities. At a rate peaking above 6,000 per
month, *est* trained roughly 270,000 persons through 1980, a third of whom
are concentrated in California. In the San Francisco Bay Area, where *est* is
based, one out of every nine college-educated young adults has taken the
training. *est* grossed $25 million in 1980, its revenues sheltered by a network
of trusts, foundations, and licensing arrangements that stretches to Switzerland.[2]

Werner Erhard was born in 1935 in Philadelphia as John Paul (Jack)
Rosenberg, grandson of an immigrant tailor and son of a small-restaurant
manager who left Judaism for a Baptist mission before joining his wife in the
Episcopal Church. Erhard married and went into sales work after finishing
high school. In 1960 he disappeared from his family, changed his name, and
moved west, eventually remarrying. From 1961 to 1971 he managed and
trained door-to-door salesmen of encyclopedias. To this task he applied
more than a decade's eclectic study of self-help and psychic disciplines like
positive thinking and hypnosis, Scientology and Mind Dynamics, psychol-
ogies like Gestalt, and eastern religions like Zen. At the end of this period,
says Erhard, he had a sudden experience "outside of space and time" of "getting it" while driving along the freeway, and he began *est* shortly afterward
to serve others by enabling them to share this enlightening experience.[3]

The *est* training consists alternately of three sorts of activity. Participants listen to the trainer present the "data" of *est*'s view of reality and interact with him by questioning this material and responding to it. They do "processes," in which the trainer instructs them to close their eyes and mentally "create" or visualize various experiences: opening a space in different parts of their bodies, relaxing at the beach, reliving past incidents associated with unwanted emotions and psychosomatic symptoms, feeling terrified of the person next to them, confronting their parents, intuiting the personality of a stranger. Finally, participants "share" their experience of the processes with the group as a whole.

Participants sit theatre-style facing the trainer on a low stage throughout most of the training, except for a few hours of processes done standing or lying on the floor. They are not allowed to touch or talk to each other, take notes, smoke, leave their chairs, or address the group without the trainer's recognition. Participants are encouraged but not required to talk in front of the group and to the trainer. At least a quarter of them never do. A smaller proportion of the group does most of the talking, acknowledged by the compulsory applause of the rest, who report coming to identify with the talkers. Each day usually lasts sixteen or more hours, punctuated by one meal break and two or three brief water and bathroom breaks. Almost all participants report physical tension, fatigue, and mental strain in the course of the training, which they attribute to its long hours and circumstantial restrictions (*est* has been called "the no-piss training"), and to the upsetting character of the trainer's behavior, the data and processes, and others' sharing.

What goes on in the *est* training? *est* informs participants beforehand that they need not figure out, remember, or believe in the training for it to work. They need only be present, follow instructions, and experience whatever comes up. "You have the opportunity to replace believing with experiencing," says *est*. What they will experience is "what is really so for you . . . your natural ability . . . the part of [you] that is truly able, and perfect."[4] Comparing records of several trainings shows the uniform appearance of a few central tenets and techniques in all of them, redundancy in each in developing these tenets, and variation between trainings in the detailed discussion and argument of these tenets and their demonstration by psychological and dramatic enactment. What follows is a quick summary of the few hours' conceptual script from which each trainer improvises sixty hours of psycho-theatre.[5]

On the training's first day its procedural rules are announced, and the trainees are instructed to agree to them by sitting still. "Your lives don't work, assholes. Otherwise you wouldn't be here," the trainer begins irrefutably. Instead of feeling alive, people believe they are right. Instead of "accepting, observing, realizing, sharing, and sourcing" their experience at its cause, people are at its effect in "hoping, deciding, helping, and being reasonable" about their experience. Their received and psychologically conditioned beliefs of how life could or should be block their experience of how it actually is in the present and preclude their effective response to it. In this sense each person is the *total cause* of all his own problems, a fact that he must acknowledge in order to take responsibility for his life, give up his "act," and clear up his problems. After hours of restriction and felt attack as this message is driven home, trainees usually have aching muscles and heads. These aches are "experienced out"—progressively relaxed and caused to disappear—by directing nonevaluative, visualized attention at them in several "body processes" at the end of the first day.[6] "Just observe and be with whatever's bothering you," directs the trainer. "Just let it be, and it will disappear." Mind states alter body states, according to such demonstration, confirming that the individual is the cause of his own world. "You're perfect," the trainer explains, "but your barriers block you from experiencing it. You try to change them or control them, but you can't. That's because resisting something makes it persist. Re-creating your experience of it makes it disappear."

On the second day, in "the anatomy of an experience," trainees are told that their problems take the form of physical sensations and emotional feelings ("upsets") psychologically associated with situational behaviors, attitudes, points of view, and ideas anchored in mental images of past experience. They are directed to locate, connect, and experience out these problematic "items," as they did their headaches of the night before, with the trainer's therapeutically detached, firm, and perceptive "assistance." Some trainees undergo and share intense abreactive experiences in public confrontations with the trainer. For example, the sensation of a clenched jaw is tied to feelings of anger and fear, tied to self-righteousness in marital strife, tied to an abusive parent in childhood: these elements of a psychic item are all recalled, vividly reexperienced, and apparently relieved. Others report strong feelings of identification in response to such exemplary cases, which they then follow out on their own in the "truth process." "If you can't recreate the experience and make it disappear, it's running you," warns the trainer. "And if you can make it disappear, then who's responsible for it, huh?" Semantically and mentally, trainees create their own problems by putting coexistent facts into conflict using *but*: "I want to go to the beach, *and* I don't have the time," is no problem at all. Trainees are next required to stand motionless, expressionless, and silent before the group, demonstrating that beneath the "act" of a composed social persona lie self-uncertainty and compelling fears of other persons and, beneath that, their true self. "Drop your shitty act," commands the trainer in the "danger process." "We can see right through it, and there's nothing behind it." Next, in the "fear process" trainees are instructed to enact their fears in terrified screams, and then reverse them into terrifying roars. "Who do you think everyone's afraid of?" asks the trainer. "They're afraid of you." By fully "experiencing your experience" in this way, trainees stuck at its effect come to be at its cause.

On the third day a pop Newtonian definition of reality, based on the "physicalness" of objects, is rejected and reversed to a Humean definition, based on the subjectivity of individual experience. "You are the one and only source of your experience. You created it." I experience, therefore I am, and so is my world. So goes the "suchness" of reality, which requires empathic, nonjudgmental "communication" if individuals are really to relate. Each must "harmoniously recreate the experience of another, intentionally." To this end trainees next experience out their embarrassment at looking foolish, a barrier to self-expression and communication, by histrionically enacting nonsensical and sex-role-reversed skits before one another. Women play tough he-men, for example, and men play cute little girls. They next visualize and enact the building of an "inner center" for communicating with their parents and significant others, wiring its modern audio-visual equipment to their own "wish switch." Finally they touch, taste, smell, and look at physical objects—cubes of pine and steel, a stone, strawberry, tomato, lemon slice, and daisy. Then they subjectively recreate and transform these objects in eyes-closed guided fantasies climaxed by a Mexican hat dance on the petal of a sixty-foot daisy.

On the fourth day the "anatomy of the mind" is exposed. "The mind is a linear arrangement of multisensory, total records of successive moments of now." It is an associative stimulus-response machine conditioned by birth and the chain of successively traumatizing and repressed experiences of pain that make human beings feel upset and act compulsively. The mind's "design function" is its own survival, a purpose it pursues by endlessly trying to prove itself right. In the training's final reversal this deterministic realization in itself proves humans to be self-aware, and thus unlike machines. "Enlightenment is knowing you're a machine." This insight leaves a person free to choose his conditioned responses consciously, experience them out, and thus dissolve his conditioning. "Whatever happens, choose it, and your life will clear up," concludes the trainer. "You *have* a mind that's a machine. And you *are* the perfect being that created it all." Experiencing this paradoxical fact constitutes "getting it": "I am. I am the context of my being me. I am the cause of my experience." After getting it, one can experience life and oneself in all their satisfying aliveness in a world without objectively fixed meaning, judgment, or purpose. The trainer unfolds the nature of reality from this viewpoint: Life is a game played for experiencing aliveness, not for believing you are right. Human choice is not reasonable, no more than choosing to eat chocolate instead of vanilla ice cream. "You choose it because you choose it. *You* cause choice, reasons don't." Successful activity consists of first *being* whatever you wish to be by mentally experiencing it, then *doing* it, then *having* it. (For example, first think of yourself being a millionaire, then borrow and invest, then have a million dollars.) There follows "everything you need to know" about sex ("When you're hot, you're hot. When you're not, you're not."), romantic love (a fantasy overlaid on a self-reinforcing cycle of interaction, affect, and sentiment), and truly "powerful relationships" (persons exchange power supporting each other's achievement of individual goals). At last the trainees graduate by intuitively "profiling" the personality and interests of strangers biographically sketched to them, thereby confirming their newly realized powers of experience and communication.

est graduates typically affirm that "*est* works!" and that "The training had value for me," although they may also complain of feeling manipulated by it. Several psychological surveys find graduates reporting positive changes in health and well-being, especially in psychological outlook, minor psychosomatic syptoms, and level of satisfaction. To date, only preliminary studies, without control groups or evidence besides retrospective self-reports, have investigated the training's results, largely bypassing its ideational content in the process.[7] No consistent correlation has been found between reported changes and use of *est* training processes. Nor, in fact, does *est* itself call for the repetitive practice of these processes outside the training, in contrast to TM or Zen Buddhist injunctions to meditate persistently. Instead *est* seems, as described, to employ these techniques to induce experiences that demonstrate to trainees the accuracy of its tenets, notably that the individual's consciousness creates her experience of the world and herself and is totally responsible for it, even at the level of physical sensation.[8] Like most human potential and therapeutic movements, *est* understands itself to be communicating epistemological, psychological, and psychosomatic facts about human existence, not teaching religious beliefs or moral systems; and doing so via experience, not ideas. Says Erhard, "The Training isn't a set of precepts or concepts or notions; it isn't anything we tell people.... It is the experience that the person has of himself."[9] The analysis to follow will suggest that *est* may be practically important to at least some of its participants, particularly sixties youth, for the system of moral norms, values, and attitudes it transmits to them.

Who are *est*'s clients? "Media coverage will sometimes imply that certain types of people take the training," cautions *est*'s president, "when in truth, *people* take the training."[10] These people are almost entirely white by race, middle-class by education, job, and income, and urbanized by outlook and residence.[11] Compared to the larger population, *est* numbers proportionately more women and fewer men, more divorced and fewer married persons, more young adults and fewer persons under twenty or over forty. The mean age of *est* graduates is 33.7, with sixties youth (now twenty-five to thirty-four) comprising nearly half their total. This is more than double their fraction of the Bay Area's population and four times that of the nation's. They also provide the bulk of *est*'s volunteer assistants. Many sixties youth in *est* saw themselves as members of the counterculture while going to college and for several years afterward, often living in modestly hip, dropout style during this time (living communally, working intermittently at casual jobs, using marijuana regularly and psychedelics occasionally). They have moved into apartments and tapered off their drug use since entering full-time white-collar jobs, around which their lives are now organized.

Caucasians make up 88 percent of *est*'s clientele; blacks comprise 1.3 percent. Minority members are usually upwardly mobile middle-class young adults. *est* graduates span the range of the middle class, with their educational level higher than average but their income lower. Nine out of ten graduates began college; less than six (57 percent) finished. More majored in psychology than in any other single discipline. Four out of ten began graduate or professional school; less than two (18 percent) hold advanced degrees or certificates.[12] Relatively few *est* graduates hold jobs as technically specialized professionals or blue-collar workers, perhaps 10 percent in each case. Only 0.4 percent of all graduates are lawyers, 1.4 percent are physicians, and 0.8 percent are laborers, for example, as opposed to 11.7 percent in clerical work—the largest single occupational category.[13] The great majority of *est* graduates (some 70 percent) work primarily with other people, not physical objects or abstractions. They do mainly white-collar work—clerical, sales, managerial, official, educational, and social work. They also do semiprofessional and professional work that puts a premium on interpersonal skills—as media and public relations professionals, executives and administrators, counselors and therapists. Their mean income was somewhere between $7,893 and $12,796 per year in 1974. Sixties youth in *est* tend to work in lower-status, nonprofessional jobs, earn less, and switch jobs more frequently than do older graduates, who switch jobs frequently themselves.[14]

Almost two-thirds of all *est* graduates are now unmarried. More than a quarter have never been married. Another quarter are presently divorced or separated, a rate three times that of San Franciscans and seven times that of Americans generally. Some 26.7 percent of *all* graduates, four out of ten ever married, have gone through such breakups within the year before or after taking *est*. The unreliably fluid, short-lived pattern of graduates' marital relationships carries over among sixties youth in *est*, whom one most commonly finds in nonexclusive, sexually active dating relationships or "living with someone," often for short periods in series and sometimes in tandem with outside dating. The pervasive sense in which *est* graduates live in a singles milieu, not isolated but moving rapidly among loose and shifting ties, is also suggested by the fact that fully half of them report having "different close friends" a year after the training as compared to the year before.[15] Most young graduates live alone with a lover or roommate in an urban apartment, changing addresses every few years. They rarely live in the same city as their parents, whom they see no more than a few times per year.

One out of three *est* graduates is affiliated with a conventional religious denomination, but less than one of ten participates weekly. Conventional religious affiliation among sixties youth in *est* is almost nonexistent. Many of them, however, are involved in spiritual and therapeutic disciplines (macrobiotics, yoga, TM, aikido, encounter groups), with which they tend to keep up after the training.[16] Roughly 60 percent of all *est* clients are women, who generally report themselves more influenced by the training than do men.[17]

LOVE AND SELF-INTEREST: EARLIER MORAL VIEWS

Younger *est* graduates, like their counterparts among Christian sectarians and Zen students, see their earlier moral views as confused and mistaken, describing a patchwork of consequential, regular, and expressive elements. The consequential style of the utilitarian ethic shapes the accounts of *est* graduates more clearly than it does the moral histories of Zen students or Christians. It is likewise seated in parental emphasis on individual achievement and success in school and work. Asked, "What was most important to your parents?" a graduate reflects,

I don't know. Money, I guess. Having a career. No, more the idea of making something of yourself in the world, and being independent.

What reasons did they give for what you were supposed to do? Did religion come into it?

No, there wasn't much of a God-trip. The Ten Commandments and the sayings of Jesus were occasionally hauled out as ways to behave, but only with a million other reasons, so Jesus wasn't really the source of it. He just happened to say it.

What were the other reasons?

Oh, like, "What will other people think of you?" or "You wouldn't want us to treat *you* that way," or "You won't get ahead if you're like that." That was a big one! It was as if by being moral, that was how you succeeded. Criminals are always failures. It was a marvelous universe. [laughing] Everyone got exactly what they deserved.

Here an ethic of self-interest seems to conflict less sharply with a regular ethic of obligation than it did for Zen students. Moral rules have a more de facto or merely conventional status within the family. Justifying doing one's duty as a means to winning approval and success tends to reconcile obligation and self-interest. The "marvelous" moral universe of such a success ethic, where everyone gets exactly what he deserves, seems laughable to the sixties youth as his parents defined it. (As *est* transforms it, however, it may come to seem self-evident.) Compared to the blue-collar parents of LWF youths, those of *est* graduates have made it into the white-collar ranks of the middle class, their efforts rewarded by success. Compared to the upper-middle-class parents of Zen students, they have not come so far nor arrived so securely. Less likely to have finished college, gone to an elite college, entered professional school, or pursued a professional career, the parents of *est* graduates have made their way in the world more by their own efforts on the job than by education and its disciplinary skills. Parental emphasis on getting ahead, while it clashed with hip love, created less conflict with traditional rules for *est* graduates than it did for Zen students. It likewise created less conflict with traditional authority than it did for LWF youth.

Graduates saw their countercultural allegiance to expressive ideals tending to collapse into egoism under the pressure of self-interest. Yet even in its extreme form, where the subject is unwilling to allow others to act on the same self-regarding motives as he does, some ambivalence toward the existence and binding meaning of moral rules seems to remain. One youthful *est* graduate formulates his earlier moral views as follows:

Before est what did right and wrong mean to you? What did you go by?

Before *est* I went basically by whatever I could get away with. I didn't try to hurt people; I wanted to be a good guy. But I didn't have any idea that I would have to pay a price, ultimately, for what I did. My parents were basically straight people, who got what they got by working hard and going by the numbers. But somehow I got a kind of devious way of dealing with things from them, too. I learned to manipulate other people to get what I wanted. If I wanted something, then it was OK. And I'd make up reasons to make it OK for me. Right was whatever benefited me. Wrong was what didn't benefit me.

Did you accept other people having the same idea, even when what benefited them got in your way?

No, then they were wrong. Otherwise it was OK, and both of us could be right.

Were there any set rules or principles tied up with your idea of right and wrong before?

There were rules and regulations from my parents. That was related to right and wrong, I guess, but I never felt the rules were right or wrong in themselves. They were just something I had to follow. I felt like I was gonna get punished if I broke the rules and got caught. I equated getting punished with being wrong. . . . I don't know, maybe I felt there *was* a moral code up there in the universe, a right way and a wrong way. But it was special for me. I was immune from other people's rules. Like with a lover, I'd feel, "I get to make it with whoever I want, but you don't." I wouldn't say that, but that's how I felt and that's what I did.

Outside of your family and personal relationships, how did you relate to rules?

All through school I always felt hassled by the rules and regulations. I was always against the institutions, always making them wrong, looking for shortcuts. They were all shit, the system was all shit. I felt a lot of tension and confrontation. I could never flow with it. Like my father would always tell me, "Jay, you gotta bend a little. You gotta eat some shit sometimes. It's OK to do that." It never used to be OK for me. I'd always rather be a martyr and stand out—"Fight for the right, for idealism. Fight for the truth."

What was the truth? Did it have anything to do with counter-culture ideas?

Yeah. Loving your brothers and sisters and grooving with them was right. And the Establishment was wrong, and the rules and regulations were wrong.

Where are you with all that now, since the training?

The rules are the rules. They're not wrong. They're not right, either. You see, I used to be very idealistic about being open and mellow. I was saying, "Let there be love—or else!" I was incredibly self-righteous and ready to put people down if they weren't "loving" enough. Meaning, if they didn't buy my act enough. *est* blew away all those standards I was carrying around. It gave me a chance to come from experience and deal with what's so instead of my pictures about it.

The utilitarian truth of the individual's natural rights and his freedom from restraint clash with the constraining bureaucratic regulations of modern society, which also conflict with expressive ideals of "flowing" with the situation, loving others, and expressing oneself. In this countercultural connection love and noninjury take on the obligatory weight of a regular ethic, yielding principled opposition to American public policy in the sixties, although *est* youths were less likely than Zen students to draw in issues of justice beside the obligation to love. Nonetheless, the same *est* graduate who fought against rules in the social system and personal life defended them as "idealism" in the political realm, with the value of the individual's freedom from restraint providing the denominator common to both stances.

Like Zen students, youthful *est* graduates generally see themselves as little influenced by "God-trips" or an authoritative ethic in the past. Before *est* they were ambivalent toward the conventional morality of rules, though more confidently opposed to its independent claims and more comfortably in favor of a consequential ethic of self-interest than the Zen students interviewed. Like Zen students and Christians, *est* youths professed an expressive ethic, but acted according to utilitarianism when the situation called for responses contrary to their own interests. Since *est*, moral values and judgments as a class, whether based on hip love or a conventional "act," appear as self-righteous and unworkable "standards." In their place the graduate sees no ethic of *est*'s making but simply "what's so," the self-evident facts of his own living experience, which transcends all ethical evaluation.

EST AND ETHICS

As we have seen, the predominant ethical styles of mainstream culture and sixties counterculture differed radically, and the imperatives of each clashed with the other's. The confusion of this differentiation and debate led the youths of the Christian sect to the shelter of its insulated moral absolutism, built around an authoritative ethic and warmed by expressive intimacy. It led Zen students to a synthesis of expressive and regular ethical styles based on meditation, moral rules, a monastic regimen, and their monistic interpretation. It led *est* youths to a consequential ethic that justifies compliance with conventional rules for the sake of self-interest defined in forms integral with self-expression and situational responsiveness.

Like utilitarianism, *est* rejects the deontological logic of the authoritative and regular ethical styles. Acts are not right or wrong in themselves. Acts are right only by virtue of the goodness of their consequences. What is good or intrinsically valuable, according to *est*, is the individual's experience of well-being and satisfaction. Acts of rule compliance and agreement keeping are right, because they produce such experiences in the agent. Likewise various attitudes, traits of character, and sorts of interpersonal relationships are praiseworthy because they contribute to producing these intrinsically valuable experiences. Thus the human potential *est* promises to realize is "your true potential for producing aliveness and satisfaction in your life."[18] Let us proceed through this reworking of utilitarian individualism more slowly, with reference to its felt meaning for sixties youth.

Felt Realization of Expressive Ideals: A Consequential Theory of Right and a Psychological Theory of Good

Like Zen students, youthful graduates see *est* enabling them to act appropriately on a reliable basis at last, realizing expressive ideals held

earlier. "Now I can actually *be* open to whatever comes up," affirms a graduate, "instead of *having* a position called openness that makes me right and
everyone else wrong. Being open is being appropriate. It means being here
now, with nothing added."[19] Expressive terminology permeates *est*'s moral
discussions. *Appropriateness* is the right-making characteristic of actions,
while the terms *right* and *wrong* are used derogatorily to designate deontological moral judgments as unsupported by experiential fact. *est*'s idea of
what it means to act appropriately, however, differs from the counterculture's and the Zen student's, since it continues to rely upon the consequential logic of utilitarianism. A graduate considers the question,

> *What does* acting appropriately *mean? Why should I do it, any-*
> *way?*
>
> Acting appropriately means playing for aliveness and getting
> what you want in life. When you act appropriately, your life
> works. You experience satisfaction and aliveness. You experi-
> ence completeness. . . . The reason why is because it works, not
> because it's right or wrong.

The appropriate action is the one that "works," that "plays for" and produces the fullest experience of "aliveness" for its agent. In other words, the
right act is the one that produces the greatest amount of good consequences
for the agent. Which consequences are good, and what makes them so? Ultimately, goodness inheres in certain *experiences* of well-being that the individual feels: aliveness, satisfaction, completeness, and the like.[20]
    According to *est*, an individual can assess not only her actions but also
the point of view from which she acts by the cost-benefit calculus and the
consequential logic of utilitarianism. Does a given point of view I hold yield
me the greatest payoff of aliveness for the least cost? *est* promises that "getting it" in the training will enable each individual to pose and act on this
question to transform her life:

> Every *context* or point of view we hold can be said to have a
> "cost" (reckoned in terms of aliveness) and a "payoff." "Getting
> it" means being able to discover that you are holding a position
> (a context) which costs you more in aliveness than it is worth *and*
> being able to choose to give up (or transform) that position. Liv-
> ing becomes a continuing and expanding discovery of positions
> or barriers to your and others' aliveness and the attendant oppor-
> tunity to give up (or "get off") those positions. The results of this
> continuing process of choosing or "getting it" is an expanded ex-
> perience of happiness, love, health, and full self-expression.[21]

Here *est* states its consequential theory of right in explicitly economic terms.
The worth of a viewpoint lies not in its truth or falsity, no more than the

worth of an act lies in its deontological rightness or wrongness. The worth of each lies only in the consequential payoff it makes to its holder or agent. As in classical utilitarian culture, the agent is calculating costs against payoffs in order to maximize or expand the satisfaction of her own wants. But *est* has carried this calculating activity inward, from the marketplace to the psyche. It is reckoning costs and payoffs in terms of *aliveness*, not money. It is analyzing points of view, not economic transactions. And it is seeking to expand experience, not capital.

While *est* shares the consequential theory of right action held by utilitarianism, it brings a more modern psychology to bear on the question of what makes consequences good. Its subjectivism is subtler in defining the good, its epistemology sharper in showing how actions produce these good consequences. Here *est* departs from the conventional ethic of utilitarian culture and has a revitalizing effect upon it. The usual utilitarian definition of what is intrinsically good fastens on notions like "pleasure and the absence of pain" or "happiness" derived from a mechanistic psychology and tending toward objectification in economic terms—material consumption and gratification, social status and power, and money itself. Tangible economic means displace relatively intangible psychic ends. Money comes to count for happiness. This displacement was cast in a harsh light for sixties youth by the counterculture's excoriation of utilitarianism and the contrast of its own self-consciously experiential definition of intrinsic value, drawn in specifically religious and psychological terms. Erhard makes a similar point: "Material success isn't all that bad a thing: however, it's only what people thought they wanted. When they have it, they often realize it's not what they thought it would be, and doesn't in itself bring them satisfaction."[22] A trainer dramatizes the point to his trainees:

> So now you have an all-electric kitchen and two cars, so you can put a TV dinner in the oven and drive around town in your Porsche. So what? How satisfied are you in terms of love and naturalness and full self-expression? How satisfied are you? Shit, you're right back there with the caveman, going out and clubbing an animal and dragging it back to the cave, and trying to get a fire going. No, you're worse. At least he's actually doing something. He's got that satisfaction.[23]

est defines what is intrinsically valuable in a form compatible with countercultural ideals, namely the individual's subjective experience of well-being and satisfaction—"aliveness," in short. *est* "is about an expansion of that area of life called aliveness—an expansion of the experience of happiness, love, health, and full self-expression," *est* literature announces.[24] Aliveness is further elaborated in the training to include "spontaneity, naturalness, centeredness, completeness, wholeness, awareness, fulfillment," and other personalist values. Maximizing these values justifies participation in *est*'s moral enterprise. "We *do* need to master life," Erhard concludes. "As you master life, what happens is that there's more living in life, more aliveness; more experiencing *here now*."[25]

The value of aliveness, like the conventional happiness that preceded it, appears empty of any objective content. Satisfying different wants, after all, makes different individuals feel happy or experience aliveness. This premise leads *est*, like utilitarian individualism, to see itself as neither normative nor evaluative. Thus Erhard explains, "To master life, you simply need to know what you want. There's nothing you *should* want. Whatever you want's fine."[26] Precisely by defining aliveness as what is intrinsically valuable, which is a specifically evaluative claim, *est*'s ethic can devolve on questions presumed to be exclusively empirical: how do I align actual means to the end of more aliveness? "*est* doesn't tell you what you should want," a graduate distinguishes, "it tells you how to get what you *do* want." Psychology and epistemology explain how and why actions produce certain experiential states as a consequence, thereby indicating which acts are to be performed in any given situation. Such is the function of *est*'s "body of knowledge," which the training seeks to reveal in a directly experienced, intuitively assimilated way that leaves the trainee able to perceive and do the appropriate action without consciously referring to or even recalling the gnostic corpus. "I don't understand anything that's happened and I can't remember concepts at the Seminars or Training," testifies a graduate. "But I'm able to Do and Handle and Create so much now."[27] Asked, "How do you know if an act is appropriate? Where does the knowledge come from?" another replies, "Ultimately, deep down, from your own experience of what actually works for you and contributes to your aliveness." This intuitive mode of operation resembles that of the expressive ethic, rather than the conventional utilitarian calculus, at least inasmuch as it is an experiential or affective calculus, not a mental one. But *est*'s consequential claim to have reduced moral action to purely empirical questions of ends-means alignment is similar to the utilitarian's. Once one knows that right actions are those which produce the fullest experience of aliveness for the agent, further recourse to moral standards or principles becomes pointless. One simply "plays for aliveness" by doing whatever produces this experience most fully.

Rule-Egoism

What sort of acts produce those states of experience that constitute the good? How do we come to do such acts? In answering these questions *est* graduates rely on empirical premises about human behavior and mental processes vital to the coherence of their ethic. First of all, the individual's experiences of well-being depend on and follow from the functional condition of her life, the state of "having your life work." This in turn results from "realizing your intentions and achieving your goals." "Love or money, you name it, whatever goal you set up in life, go for it!" urges a youthful graduate. "That's the only way you're gonna win the game." Intentions and goals refer to concrete events or conditions regarding social relationships, work, education, and lifestyle. By this logic the individual's felt well-being results from goal achievement. The possible contents of these goals have been expanded from the strictly social and economic ones of conventional utilitarianism. The individual may include self-awareness, meaningful love relationships, and other personal or private desiderata among her goals, even giving them priority. Nonetheless, the instrumental logic of utilitarianism is revitalized on this point. Feelings of individual well-being depend on achieving one's goals. They cannot be arrived at simply by "turning on, tuning in, and dropping out." For the sixties youth who has tried and failed to enact the expressive ethic by such direct means, this consequential reformulation of the counterculture's intrinsic values has a powerful appeal.

est's ethic explains the failure of the countercultural lifestyle to satisfy its own ideals of self-gratification, and it justifies dropping back in to middle-class social and economic life in order to do so. You must achieve your goals in order to experience satisfaction. *est* also allows for discomfort and exertion in the process of doing this, be it in striving for occupational success, developing personal capacities, or establishing certain sorts of interpersonal relations. "Life is a bitch sometimes," declares a graduate, paraphrasing Erhard, "*and* you can master it. You've just gotta get off it [your unworkable point of view] and get on with it. Werner says, 'Live your life as if your life depends on it.'" *est's* definition of the good as "aliveness" is less implicit than conventional utilitarian "happiness" and less liable to collapse into a purely economic instrumentalism. Its list of experiential states of inner satisfaction as the end of moral action is more integral with the central private-life and counterculture value of self-fulfillment, whose realization now hinges on the instrumental activity of goal achievement. Aliveness justifies goal achievement. Personal and expressive ends justify impersonal and instrumental means.

What must one do to attain his goals? In answering this second question *est* departs from the expressive ethic and from the usual utilitarian tactic of doing whichever particular act most directly serves one's self-interest. It posits that "following the rules and keeping your agreements" are necessary to achieve your goals. "Your life is based on breaking the rules. Cheating. Lying to yourself and conning your 'friends' into buying your lies," charges the trainer. "And then you wonder why you're never satisfied."[28] The individual cannot satisfy his "real" self-interest, as *est* defines it, by violating the rules and agreements bearing on him. Rule breakers experience no satisfaction. On these premises, the consequential ethic itself drives the self-interested individual to follow rules and keep agreements.

For *est* "the rules" possess no authoritative source, as they do for the Christian sect. Nor do they reflect in themselves the essential reality of existence, as in Western natural-law theory or its analogue in Zen Buddhism. *est* justifies following rules and keeping agreements because these practices produce good consequences for the agent: Follow the rules if you want to experience aliveness.[29] This constitutes what I will call *rule-egoism*. Compliance with rules is being justified on egoistic grounds. This formulation is consistent with utilitarian culture, inasmuch as it adheres to the consequential ethical style—right acts yield the most good consequences—and to an effectively egoistic reply to the question of whose good is to be sought— one's own. *est* invests the practices of following rules and keeping agreements with utility, thereby rerationalizing ethical elements of biblical religion in a way consistent with utilitarianism. It defines utility with reference to an ultimate good consisting of experiences such as aliveness, love, and spontaneity, whose subjective content seems compatible with countercultural ideals, even if the objective means to those experiences may not be. Aliveness seems to be a "groovie," so to speak, not merely a conventional "goodie," even if the means to experiencing it lie in achieving on the job instead of "grooving" as a dropout.

What are the rules to which *est* refers? Their identification outside the training itself is not precisely defined. They are "the rules of life," and examples range from codes of dress and etiquette through bureaucratic regulations to laws against speeding, tax evasion, and murder.[30] *est*'s discussions of the rules often draw analogies from them to physical laws like gravity. Breaking the rules is compared to "going out the window at the twentieth floor. Sure, you can do it, and five seconds later you hit the sidewalk— splat!"[31] While the analogy to physical laws calls to mind arguments for natural-law theory, the parallel can be misleading, because its moral gist in *est*'s usage is consequential, not deontological. "The rules exist for just one reason," a graduate emphasizes, "because they work to make your life work." The rules have no meaning in themselves, but only in their felt consequences for the individual. It follows that the egoistic agent may break the rules whenever he chooses, in *est*'s view, as long as he is willing to accept the consequences for doing so. And the consequences of doing so are invariably negative, according to *est*'s empirical premises, evidenced by the analogy to physical laws. A graduate underscores this reasoning:

Are there reasons for the rules in themselves, like "You should follow this rule, because it is such and such"?

No, the rules are just the rules. They don't have to have any reasons. That's just the way things are out there, and if you don't like it, OK, go ahead and break them—and take the consequences. And that means having a life that doesn't work.

So why not break them when you don't like them—and just take your chances?

Because, given that you have a choice about rules—you either stop at stop lights or you pay tickets—then you're gonna have a better, more

enjoyable time of it if you stop at the lights. That's all *est* is saying. The game's already been set up that way, so you get penalized when you don't stop. So why not play by the rules? Just
make them *your* rules and dig it.

Examples of the negative consequences that follow on breaking rules
include such external conditions as fines and arrest for law breaking, loss of
a job for laxity, disrupted relationships for breaches of interpersonal conduct. But such consequences do not always follow on breaking the rules—
sometimes the violator gets away with it—leaving open the question of why
a self-interested utilitarian should invariably follow the rules. In reply *est*
claims that negative internal or psychic consequences *do* invariably follow
on rule breaking. "You cheat on your taxes and you get the money," proposes the trainer. "They didn't find out. So what? Are you satisfied? No,
you asshole! You're scared shitless for the next seven years, waiting for the
audit, because they *could* find out."³² The uncaught highway speeder makes
himself feel tense and uneasy. The undiscovered adulterer lives in fear of
discovery or of being cheated on in turn. Not following the rules invariably
results in the agent's failing to experience those feelings of well-being that
constitute the ultimate good. Since this premise is empirical rather than
evaluative, *est* does not enjoin the agent from testing it for himself. Instead,
as one graduate puts it, "Whatever you want to do, it's OK to do it. Just
take responsibility for whatever comes up for you afterwards. If you break
the rules, you take what you get. If you're gonna feel guilty or bad, then
you're going to." Whenever he so desires, the agent is free to act contrary to
the rules for the sake of his perceived self-interest, on the assumption that he
will experience the negative consequences of so doing and revise his perceptions accordingly.³³
     While graduates affirm that an uncaught rulebreaker will feel guilty
and bad, they are less sure precisely why he does feel this way. The reasons,
however, seem psychological, not moral. "You feel guilty because the big
guys get you when you break the rules," answers one. "You grow up learning that. Even when you don't get caught, you're afraid you're going to." In
this view a person will *feel* guilty for breaking rules, but he will not *be* guilty
for doing wrong. Feeling guilty is not seen as the subjective accompaniment
to objectively being guilty, which implies the existence of a regular or
authoritative moral order. Instead moral guilt appears to stem from an idea
of punishability determined by prior conditioning, which is itself explicable
in the utilitarian terms of perceived interests or misguided moralism.
     By contrast to *est*'s indefinite references to the rules of life, the "ground
rules" by which the training itself proceeds are extraordinarily explicit, precise, and comprehensive. The *est* training is impressively and instructively
overorganized. Its procedural rules prescribe schedule, performance, seat-
ing, interaction protocols, physical movement, posture, and ideal attitudes
in exact and concrete detail. The trainees are told that in its rules, as it does

in every other respect, *est* parallels life. "If you follow the ground rules, you'll get value from the training. If you follow the rules of life, life will work for you." Taking this parallel concretely, the procedural rules that govern *est* as a bureaucratized voluntary association mainly reflect the bureaucratic regulations that govern public life in modern society, especially middle-class life centered on white-collar work. And indeed it is from this social setting, as we have seen, that *est* draws almost all its clients.

For the white-collar worker, in particular, bureaucratic regulations possess an external, objectively given quality. Unlike the policy-making executive, he does not participate in their formulation, and they act over against him, constraining his behavior. They exist as "social facts" in Durkheim's sense. But neither a divinely revealed, authoritative source nor the status of laws of nature is claimed for such regulations to legitimate their power. Instead they are justified by utilitarian efficiency. By following bureaucratic regulations, persons will be able to coordinate their activities most predictably to the end of maximizing productivity and its proceeds. Each individual should "go along to get along." His compliance is warranted because it promises to yield him the largest possible share of the proceeds that accrue from the collectivity's efforts.

Just as the rise of a market economy provided the social genesis and plausibility structure for the development of a utilitarian morality of action in general, so the rise of modern bureaucracy provided the social genesis and plausibility structure of a utilitarian morality of following rules. Classical economic man could pursue his self-interest directly, assessing each act according to its maximal market utility in satisfying his wants.[34] The modern organization man pursues his self-interest by complying with the rules of the bureaucracies that assess and reward his actions. "Pursue your own self-interest" remains the overriding utilitarian maxim. The classical popularization of utilitarian individualism (we might call it *act-egoism* in this context) translated this maxim into the advice to "Do whatever you want" or "Do your own thing," in its respective conventional and countercultural forms. Rule-egoism, in its vintage corporate formulation, advises the organization man to "Go along to get along." *est*'s counsel to "Follow the rules to get what you want in life" implies conventional socioeconomic success as a desideratum but makes it clear that it is not the only good nor, more importantly, the ultimate good. Individual experiences of well-being are what is ultimately and intrinsically valuable. Thus *est* takes an idea of the right (rule compliance) usually associated with the regular ethic and an idea of the good (feeling alive, natural, and so on) usually associated with the expressive ethic, and it subsumes them into the consequential ethical style of utilitarian culture in its bureaucratized version, rule-egoism.

In redefining the situational and expressive appropriateness of right action in terms of rule compliance for the sake of self-interest, *est* posits that situations are governed and defined by various sorts of rules. To respond appropriately to the situation, therefore, is to follow the rules governing it.

Unlike divine commands and natural laws, bureaucratic regulations and social etiquette are situationally variable, yielding a relativism that resembles that of the expressive ethic. A graduate explains,

> *What do you mean by* right *and* wrong *now, since doing the training?*
>
> I don't use *right* and *wrong* now. It's more *appropriate* and *inappropriate*. Being appropriate is, first of all, owning and taking responsibility for whatever the rules and regulations are in whatever situation you're in, and following those rules. That's being appropriate. Work with the system, and your life works. And the system can change, depending on whether you're at the *est* office or the university or the police station. Dress codes differ, the rules differ. So whatever's appropriate, that's correct.

Appropriateness, the right-making characteristic of acts in the expressive ethic, is affirmed over against conventional terms; while its meaning, still resonant with countercultural associations, is subsumed into rule-egoist discourse.

est's premise that situations are defined by rules is embodied in the paradigmatic case of the training itself. The situation is comprehensively and precisely structured by explicit rules, and compliance with them is strictly sanctioned. Consequently, the participant in the situation experiences as a fact that particular behaviors and attitudes clearly feel appropriate, and that they also comply with the rules. Like Zen's ritual and monastic orthopraxy, the *est* training constructs a highly regulated, totally institutionalized situation, in which certain actions are frequently repeated and consistently sanctioned.[35] Properly interpreted, participation in this situation produces the experience of realizing an expressive ethic. The rules are implicitly agreed to and internalized until they are felt to disappear, leaving only the intuitive familiarity of the situation itself and the smoothly intermeshing behavior of the participants within it.

A Morality Tale: The Rat and Cheese Story

Does *est* itself state a formal ethic corresponding to the rule-egoist understanding of right and wrong reported by its young graduates? *est* sees itself holding no tenets, let alone an ethic. "*est* doesn't have tenets, because it doesn't have a point of view," explains a staff member. It offers an "educational experience," whose data and processes are "not a system of beliefs or techniques to be learned and practiced."[36] Accordingly, *est* restricts formal statements of its body of knowledge to staff members charged with delivering the training. Significantly enough, given *est*'s nonethical and

nondoctrinal self-image, a widely circulated piece of its introductory literature, "The Famous *est* Rat and Cheese Story," offers a parable of human
life, and *est*'s role in it, freighted with moral meaning.[37] Before going on
with the main line of our analysis, we might make a short side trip to take in
this parable. It runs as follows:

The Famous *est* Rat & Cheese Story

One day, a rat found himself sitting in front of several
small tunnels. Curious, he studied them, and it wasn't long before his keen sense of smell told him that somewhere down one
of the tunnels, there was a piece of cheese.

Mouth watering, he raced up and down the tunnels looking
for the cheese. Nothing in the first tunnel, nothing in the second
tunnel, and nothing in the third tunnel. But when he got to the
fourth tunnel, there it was . . . a rich and succulent piece of yel-
low cheese which he gobbled down in an instant.

Each day, for many days after, the rat would then return
and zip down the fourth tunnel to claim his prize. He was a smart
rat, a happy rat! For he was a rat who knew where the cheese
was.

Then one day the rat raced down the fourth tunnel only to
discover, much to his dismay, that the cheese was gone. It was
nowhere to be found. He scurried back out of the tunnel, looked
around, made sure it was the same tunnel it had always been,
then raced back down for another look. No cheese. He ran out,
looked around, and ran back down again. No cheese. And again
he ran out, looked around very carefully, and ran back down the
tunnel. And still there was no cheese. Again and again and again
he scurried in and out of the fourth tunnel. He searched every
nook and cranny and corner and crevice. He was just about to
give up when all of a sudden it occurred to him, "Why, there is
no cheese in this tunnel!"

With that the little rat, excited but somewhat apprehensive
at the prospect of a new adventure, began cautiously exploring
the other tunnels. Sure enough, he found that at the end of one
of them was the biggest and best piece of cheese he had ever seen
and, smiling, he gobbled it down.

Now, up to a point, a human being will behave exactly like
the rat. The difference is that eventually the rat will stop going
down the fourth tunnel and will begin to look down the other
tunnels. The human being may go down the fourth tunnel forever.

Rats and human beings have one essential difference. Rats only know from cheese; humans want to be in the "right" tunnel. In fact, when humans come to believe in their tunnels, it is often a major achievement just to discover that there's no cheese there.

Among other things, the *est* training is about rats, cheese and tunnels. A tunnel is a context in which we hold the facts and circumstances (the content) of our lives. In the *est* training people have the opportunity to get in touch with their power to choose a tunnel that works.

What are we to make of this parable in ethical terms? Leaving aside the behaviorist slant suggested by its metaphoric ratomorphism (humans as rats, life as a maze), the parable's picture of reality includes some remarkable moral features:

1. There is a single solitary subject (the rat) facing a world of objects (a maze).

2. There is a single good (cheese). It is a goodie, an object "out there," like food, to be possessed and consumed.

3. It thereby makes its possessor happy. A praiseworthy agent ("a smart rat, a happy rat!") is the one who gets the goodie (claims his "prize") and knows where it lies.

4. The nature of the good (like the goodness of "rich and succulent" cheese) is a matter of taste and its capacity to satisfy certain wants or appetites.

5. We know what is good simply by sensing and desiring it. Our senses of themselves identify the good ("his sense of smell told him") and we desire it reflexively ("mouth watering").

6. Action (racing up and down tunnels looking for cheese) is driven or motivated by the actor's desire to satisfy his wants. It is a means or avenue to this end.

7. There are various possible means (tunnels) to the good end.

8. Doing the right act consists of finding the most effective means to the end of getting the goodie. The right act is the one that produces the most good consequences for the actor ("the biggest and best piece of cheese").

9. We identify the right act by trial-and-error coordination of means to end (checking out each tunnel for cheese)—that is, by technical reason.

10. Belief in "right" acts, identified apart from getting the goodie, hinders choosing the means that "work" most effectively to that end. Such technically irrational belief often distinguishes humans from rats, who "only know from cheese."

A single subject in a world of objects; the good as a goodie, known by the senses and desired by reflex; action driven by desire, calculated by technical reason, and defined as a means to getting the goodie instead of being right or wrong in itself: these features set out the ethic of utilitarian individualism in all its commonsense candor. *est* promises to enable its clients to "choose a tunnel that works," that is, to choose a "context" or worldview that will most satisfy their wants. In defining its own view of the world, *est* has chosen some fundamental features of utilitarian individualism. These features do not exhaust the synthetic, innovative whole of *est*'s ethic, nor do they account fully for its peculiar appeal. But they are present in *est*'s ethic, and they are necessary to make it "work" as a whole.

Moral Knowledge and Moral Responsibility

est's rule-egoism appears less accommodating to the self-expressive side of the counterculture than to its situationally responsive function. Following situational rules is justified more obviously as a means to self-gratification than to self-expression. However, *est* speaks of the individual's experiential states of aliveness and naturalness not only as the ultimate good which appropriate action yields, but also as the psychic source from which it arises. "When you come from aliveness," testifies a graduate, "you always act appropriately." In advocating this source and motive, *est* sponsors a facsimile of the counterculture's idea of appropriate action always arising from and expressing the individual's true inner self. Thus Erhard can assure trainees, "If you had even a glimpse of who you really are, you'd cry for joy." And he can promise them, "I don't think I know something that if you knew you'd be better off. I do think that you know something that if you knew, you'd be better off."[38]

Hip self-expression squares with the bureaucratic constraints of rule-egoism in light of *est*'s subjectivist epistemology and its related idea of moral responsibility as "the willingness to acknowledge you are cause in a matter." "You created the rules in the first place," a graduate affirms. "They wouldn't *be* the rules without the power of your agreement. The rules are part of the game you choose to set up. Following them just means playing the game, participating. That's how you express yourself." Social norms are interpreted as expressing the intentions and choice of each individual. He himself is seen to be the total cause of his experience, including the rules of society. The individual has created the rules by a process of self-expression and communication leading to interpersonal agreements, from which the rules have evolved. This position is reached by the following steps.

First, each individual defines the goals whose achievement will result in his feelings of well-being by fully experiencing and observing his subjective reality and his intentions. "Once you get what's so for you," says a graduate, "you can set up your intentions so you get what you want, and you want what you get." This process of "getting what's so for you" is seen to consist of an unclouded, nonevaluative intuition. It yields certain knowledge regarding what is good for a given individual—that is, what constitutes the concrete manifestation of his self-interest and the external form of his action. Such intuition is counterposed to received opinion or *belief*, which yields uncertain knowledge because its content is not experienced by the subject himself. "If you experience it, it's the truth," writes Erhard. "The same thing believed is a lie."[39] For this reason, "Belief is bullshit!" in *est*'s subjectivist view of reality, and "understanding is the booby prize in life."[40] *est* is less sanguine than the counterculture regarding the ease with which moral intuition can be exercised by all persons. It invokes psychoanalytic theories of traumatization and repression to account for difficulties in this regard, and it prescribes abreaction through therapeutic self-disclosure as the means to realizing and using one's intuitive self-awareness.

Second, in *est*'s post-Cartesian universe each person's experience is all that is real for that person.[41] "Experience is all you've got!" exclaims the trainer. "There ain't nothing but experience."[42] Each person perceives what is good for him or her and no one else. Various persons have various ideas of what particular ends are good and, therefore, which acts are right (that is, appropriate). *est* prescribes that these ideas are to be aligned not in themselves, which is impossible, but in their practical consequences, so far as possible, by self-expression and interpersonal communication leading to contractual agreements. *est*'s "What's So" seminars announce, "When you are clear about your intentions, you can communicate clearly and make agreements that are consistent with what you intend."[43] *est* delivers an emotivist attack on reason-giving moral discourse, painting it as a rationalization of one's personal tastes used "to make yourself right and other people wrong," while claiming to represent an illusory common reality. *est*'s empathic, encounter-style communication, by contrast, creates an intersubjective synthesis of "self's real" and "other's real" into "our real." True communication lies beyond "the exchange of agreed-on symbols or the development of understanding," Erhard explains. It is "the harmonious re-creation of one person's experience by another, intentionally."[44] In order to communicate in this way, each person must allow others to express fully their subjective reality, without questions as to its truth or falsity, and then she must re-create the expressed experience in her own consciousness. By exercising this sort of empathic imagination, practiced in the training, and by identifying with others, each person can expand her consciousness to accept and "flow" with their experience. By so communicating, each person abreacts and dissolves the intrapsychic barriers seen to block communication and cause interpersonal conflict.

Third, once intuitive self-expression and empathic communication have bridged the gap between individuals, then they are free to make agreements with each other that will serve the self-interest of each and will, therefore, be kept by both. *est* advises candor and vigor in asserting one's interests regarding a prospective agreement, care in making it, and fidelity in keeping it. When one's self-interest is insufficiently served, one should refuse without qualms to become involved in an agreement. Graduates report making fewer agreements than before, and keeping more of the agreements they do make.

Here we have reached a moral locale resembling the marketplace of classical economics and the focal situation of social contract theory. Mutually disinterested agents are each seeking to serve their own interests by mutual exchange. But in *est* the approach to this situation has been psychologized in a way echoing the expressive ethic, and the contract itself has been placed at the level of interpersonal relationships instead of social structure. *est*'s teaching on communication resonates with counterculture ideals of self-expression, interpersonal honesty and intimacy, and sensitivity to social situations as good in themselves. In the consequential logic of *est*'s ethic they appear, on one hand, as means to making viable agreements with others, in order to achieve one's own goals and experience aliveness. Thus expressive ends become rule-egoist means. On the other hand, *est* points out that satisfying interpersonal relationships, which may be chosen as goals in themselves, require the participant to keep agreements and follow rules. In this latter respect, *est* reinforces expressive ideals with elements of a regular ethic, as do Zen Center and the Christian sect. As a result, sixties youth experience countercultural ideals to be realized reliably for the first time in these alternative religious movements.

Resolving Disagreements

est's interlocking ideas of interpersonal communication and agreement define all social interaction not governed explicitly by "the rules." They also imply a strategy for resolving moral disagreements that leads us into considering *est*'s general conception of norms and the elaboration of moral responsibility from the individual to the interpersonal to the social level of analysis.

est sees moral disagreement as a fundamentally psychological issue involving the failure of two persons to communicate with each other. This failure is due to their individual intrapsychic barriers, raised by repressed contents of consciousness. Translating these individual biases into generalized judgments of right and wrong only exacerbates the conflict. "Instead of running your 'that's wrong because' tape," suggests a graduate, "why not just tell the truth and say 'I've got an upset on that.'" Instead of calling for moral reasoning, *est* calls for disclosure of the "real" psychological conditions and causes of one's "upset" at some behavior or situation. This leads to accepting others and going on to make relevant agreements or recognize relevant rules in relation to them. A graduate discusses this strategy:

What do right and wrong mean for you now?

They're ideas people have. Beliefs. They depend on where people are coming from, and everybody's coming from someplace different. I used to judge people on whether they were right or wrong, but it's a waste of time. Judging means putting extra bullshit on top of what's so. It's like lying.

Are there any acts that are right or wrong in themselves?

Sure there are, in my little universe, lots of them. Like if someone comes to my dinner table and farts, I consider that wrong.

What happens now when you disagree with someone about what he and you should be doing?

Right after the training I was coming from a place where I was right and everybody else was wrong. Then I got that and saw that when other people do stuff that's not OK with me, it's because there's something going on with me. Because it's OK with them. And it can be OK with me. At the time maybe I feel angry, then afterwards I look and see what was going on inside of me to make me feel that way. I just have to confront whatever's going on with me, get in touch with it, and get off it, so that whatever they're doing is OK with me.

When I relate to people now it's more for aliveness, instead of being right, so it's easier for them to be OK with me. They're not wrong if they're gay or something. It depends on whether it works for them or not, and that's up to them.

What if it's really not OK with you?

If it's really not OK, if it's just their act, well, that's beautiful, too, and I'll tell them that and give them the space to get off it.

What happens if they don't get that it's their act, or they just don't want to get off it?

That's OK, too. I acknowledge that's what's so for them, and all I can do is let them be the way they are.

Even if they're hurting you?

You're hurting you, they're not. When you let it be, they're just doing what they're doing. That's what the training is about, getting that nobody's doing anything *to* you. You're doing it to yourself. *You're* creating it.

All right. I guess I mean, what if it feels like you are *the victim? What if you get robbed and shot, or you're a black kid and you can't get a job. And you can't just let it be and go someplace else, because there's no place else to go?*

Look, if you're talking about murder or something, that's what the rules are for. *And* people get murdered anyway. We all know life ain't fair, and that doesn't change who's responsible for *your* life. You are.

From the emotivist viewpoint adopted by *est,* the bases of moral judgments do not inhere in any descriptive characteristics of acts or persons. Moral judgments originate in the subject's own psychologically conditioned beliefs and feelings. Attributing them to this latter source, disclosed by therapeutic introspection and communication, fosters interpersonal acceptance. To represent objects of moral judgment, *est* favors examples relating to standards of lifestyle, fashion, etiquette, or taste that tend to leave out considerations of overt injury or injustice (for example, homosexuality and table manners instead of murder or race discrimination). Indeed, the training's conclusive depiction of moral choice centers on the example of choosing to eat chocolate or vanilla ice cream, a matter of taste manifestly without moral value or reason. Such examples imply that the usual wisdom in matters of taste, *de gustibus non disputandum,* is to be followed in matters of moral choice as well.

Effectively, then, *est*'s memorable dictum that "Standards are bad" supports tolerance of various codes of personal behavior and lifestyle, thereby encouraging self-acceptance and acceptance of others in a pluralistic society, rather than licensing the amoralist to break laws. *est*'s critics charge that it also lends itself to toleration of injury and injustice to persons other than oneself and those with whom one interacts face to face.[45] Where the behavior of others does threaten one's own interests, they are to be asserted in the process of communication and agreement described above. If a mutually satisfactory agreement is not forthcoming, then withdrawal of one's emotion, interest, and involvement is justified.

The interpersonal mobility required by such an ethic is much more available to *est* graduates than to sectarian Christians or Zen students, given the circumscribed nature and time of their interaction, the relative permeability of the movement's boundary with the surrounding society, and the relative size of its clientele. Such mobility also characterizes the larger social milieu in which most of *est*'s youthful graduates live—urban, middle-class, white-collar, and singles-oriented—where decoupling from lovers and spouses, and leaving behind friends, neighbors, and coworkers are familiar facts of life. Where, for example, four of every ten married graduates left their spouses within a year of the training.[46] The relative economic security of this milieu, where most individuals can fend for themselves materially, likewise lends plausibility to the laissez faire aspect of *est*'s ethic.

Rules and Responsibility

est's ethic focuses on the individual actor pursuing her psychic, social, and economic interests through interpersonal relationships, not on social and political conditions. What relation does its adamantly psychological personal code bear to the requisites of a social ethic? *est*'s answer is couched in its conception of "the rules" and the proper attitude of the individual toward them.

The rules of society are agreements made by the individual at some time in the past, according to *est* tenets that echo social-scientific as well as religious and occultic sources.[47] By "choosing" to join a particular group, association, society, or species governed by given rules, each individual has "agreed" to and "created" the relevant set of rules, even if at present "you don't get to vote on it the way it is. You already did. You voted by getting born."[48] Taking the trainee's choice to enroll in *est* as the paradigm, *est* posits that individuals "choose" their birth and every condition of their lives. They "select" their parents, race, social position, and so on. In short, existing moral norms have been formed as consensual agreements, in which the individual is seen to have had an anthropologically and psychically active hand, even though she encounters the rules as accomplished social facts that constrain her agency. The idea recalls Locke's doctrine of tacit consent, as does its dramatization at the training's start, when trainees "agree" to its ground rules by sitting still and quiet. *est* defines responsibility as "acknowledging that you are cause in the matter." It specifies that "Responsibility is not fault, praise, blame, shame, or guilt. All these include judgments and evaluations of good and bad, right and wrong, or better and worse," which lie beyond causal acknowledgment.[49] It advises trainees to internalize the rules accordingly, not because rules-as-agreements are factual data, but because so doing will best serve their own interests.

A graduate reports on his experience of moral responsibility from the standpoint of rule egoism:

What does responsibility *mean?*

Being responsible means making the rules your own and being at cause with them, so they can serve you, instead of resisting them and being at effect.

How did you get that?

The training was the first time I ever took responsibility for rules I didn't make up myself. At first I was bitching and moaning. I couldn't stand the rules. They were driving me crazy. And the trainer kept saying, "These are your rules. Own them and follow them. You paid, this is your thing." I couldn't get that. Then I broke through it. I related to it by saying, "Look, I can choose to play the game the way they've set it up, or I can choose not to play it and leave. I'm here now because I want to get value out of the training. It's Erhard Seminars Training, not Fred's Seminars Training, so I'll play by Werner's rules, because I want it to work. Because I want my life to work." After that I owned the rules, and so it was no effort to follow them.

Now I own rules. I never even drive over fifty-five miles per hour. I own the rules. They're *my* rules. I know if I break a rule and the law doesn't get me, I get myself.

Has your idea of freedom changed along with that?

Before *est* freedom meant doing whatever I wanted to do, without having to answer to anybody. Now being free means keeping my agreements with myself and other people, and following the rules, 'cause that's the only way you're gonna feel satisfied.

The rules of a voluntary association, joined for the sake of individual self-improvement and claiming special expertise in effecting it, are offered as a model for norms generally. The trainee's self-interest dictates his discretionary choice in favor of *est*'s ground rules, which he could reject by walking out. This choice and its related attitudes are generalized to exemplify accepting and internalizing social norms per se. These include norms more heavily sanctioned and ineluctable than *est*'s, particularly the bureaucratic demands governing middle-class adulthood. Like the sectarian Christians and the Zen students, though with a peculiarly utilitarian twist, youthful *est* graduates have abandoned a negative concept of liberty as freedom from restraint for a positive concept that requires keeping rules and agreements.

Now it is possible to trace *est*'s elaboration of moral responsibility from the individual to the interpersonal to the social level of its extension. *est* defines moral responsibility as the acknowledgment by each individual that he is totally the cause of his own experience. "You're God in your Universe," writes Erhard. "You caused it."[50] Realizing and enacting this causal status requires a perfect state of consciousness, reached by a process of "transformation" resembling psychoanalytic abreaction and mystical enlightenment which the training occasions in the form of "getting it." The trainee "gets" the fact that he already is a perfect, universal, and omnicausal *being,* even as he appears phenomenally to be a discrete *mind* whose mental processes and behavior are entirely conditioned. The free and powerful "at cause" status of the responsible person, abreacted and enlightened, contrasts with the status of the person "at effect," who is still unconscious of all that he has repressed, and therefore compulsively repeats patterns of behavior determined by it. "At effect," says a graduate, "you're just so much stuff being knocked around by the forces of the universe, because you're pretending you didn't cause it. You're resisting life, and life keeps moving, so the next thing you know, you're the victim. At cause, there is no bitching or complaining. There's just observing, creating, and experiencing." The responsible person attributes whatever happens to him to his own ultimate doing, whether conscious or not, instead of blaming others. He acts directly to accept, then alter external conditions mediating his difficulties. How does he do this? He introspects his own consciousness to disclose the hidden motives for his difficulties. He acknowledges and experiences out these ultimate causes, thus allowing them to disappear and causing his problems "to clear up just in the process of life itself."

The responsibility each person bears toward others is simply to *assist* each of them in taking responsibility for himself in the abreactive fashion just described. This is contrasted with vain attempts at *helping* others, often associated with liberal "do-gooding," which attribute a person's difficulties to extrinsic causes, thereby degrading him and coddling him in "playing the victim." "Help someone," asserts the trainer, "and you just pat their ass and blow in their ear. Then they get to go right back to feeling sorry for themselves and running the same old act."[51] A young graduate expands the point:

> You're the person who has the most direct control over what's going on in your head, and what's going on in your head is, after all, what's determining whether you're experiencing aliveness and satisfaction. Nothing else is. Allowing someone to keep pretending that it is something else isn't doing them any favors.

> *What if someone says, "You're hurting me," and it's not just in their head? You are actually hurting them.*

> Well, if you're twisting his arm behind his back, that's one thing. That's the idea we usually have, but it's not usually what's happening. What's happening is more like the woman who says, "Why did you hurt me so? I sat up all night waiting for you to call." My answer to that is, "Look, why did you hurt yourself? Why did *you* sit up all night? *You* tell me."

> *What if you promised to call?*

> Ah, OK, so I promised to call. I broke my promise, for whatever reason. I acknowledge that. So then what? The fact is, I

haven't called. Now, you have a choice. You can either have
me not call and have a good time, or you can have me not call
and feel hurt. It's all up to you. Go for it.

est applies its analysis of moral responsibility to concrete cases drawn
almost entirely from the trainee's face-to-face interaction with lovers, family members, and work associates. Application to wider sociopolitical issues
—to conflicts between races, classes, interest groups, and nations as well as
lovers—is implied but not developed in the training.

Some young *est* graduates are aware that *est*'s emphatically individualistic conception of personal and interpersonal responsibility may seem
distant from traditional liberal ideas of social responsibility, and hip or
Christian ideals of love. One comments,

How you get from creating your own experience to caring for
your fellow human beings, I still don't understand completely.
I've seen *est* grads come off sounding very arrogantly individualistic and self-serving, while they were seeking to assist people.
I guess I even come off sounding like an arrogant bastard myself
when I tell people they're creating their own experience, and if
they're willing to, they can experience being the cause instead of
being the effect of their problems. But that's really the only way
you *can* assist them, because that's the only way you can change
what's so for them.

For its adherents *est* itself is the foremost example of this psychological ideal
of responsibility applied to interpersonal relationships. Graduates are encouraged to act out this ideal by recruiting others to take the *est* training
and "assisting" *est* as volunteer workers in delivering the training to them.
"In assisting," writes Erhard, "people move from being served to serving."[52]
Loyal graduates, such as those who assist regularly at *est*, testify that its
affectively detached yet therapeutically engaging style of relating to others
is the profoundest form of compassionate service one can render to them.
One quotes Erhard, "Love is giving someone the space to be the way they
are—and the way they are not." Other graduates, more former clients than
continuing members of *est*, are not so sure. One woman, a stewardess,
remarks in a discouraged moment,

Since the training I've realized everybody in a way doesn't care
about anybody else. They love you, but their own lives are more
important. Everything is sort of a projection of their own image
of themselves. And I'm the same way. It's a world of individuals.
That's why you've got to live for yourself.

But I'd like to have an outside-of-myself more and be thinking
of others more than just myself. You've got to give to others,

too, and that's one thing I kind of didn't like about *est.* They're stressing "Live for yourself," and that's what we're all doing anyway.

Here *est*'s ethic is perceived to justify the pursuit of self-interest at the expense of love and friendship in a universe of self-absorbed individuals, a view shared by *est*'s critics and rebutted as mistaken by *est* itself.

I. INTERPERSONAL RELATIONSHIPS: TOUCH-AND-GO

What effect does *est*'s model of interpersonal relationships have on its graduates? The rates at which they marry, divorce, and switch lovers and friends show no striking shifts, unlike the predictable increase in marriage and falloff in divorce among the sectarian Christians. At the same time, graduates credit the training with critically assisting them in choosing to leave old spouses, lovers, and friends, find new ones, and renew existing relationships. Says one, "I got that when I wanted a relationship to work, it worked. If it didn't, it was because I really didn't want it to." The high number and frequency of these interpersonal changes among graduates, coupled with their diverse directions, are significant in themselves. *est*'s ethic serves its clients in a social setting (the cosmopolitan city), social stratum (white-collar middle class), and age cohort (young adult) all characterized by extremely fluid relationships between spouses, lovers, friends, coworkers, and neighbors. A psychiatrist-graduate prefaces his recommendation of *est* by observing, "Nobody lives where they grew up. We're more a collection of individuals than ever. . . . People are realizing that in a fragmented, transient society, you have to depend on yourself, and they want to know how to better do that."[53] *est*'s clients are not social atoms or isolates of the sort often attracted to conventional cult movements. But neither are they persons bound to one another and a place by religiously weighted marriage, children, house ownership, compelling jobs, extended families, or a cohesive community. They are persons making their way through a large number of social contacts and relationships, many of short duration or low frequency of interaction, and seeking in their midst for love, intimacy, and honesty with others. "We're all looking for the fairy princess," laughs one. They see good love relationships as ends in themselves, not only means to the end of self-realization. They leave one relationship in search of another more satisfying one. This search has a special urgency for young adults no longer satisfied by casual relationships yet uneasy about the prospect of traditonal romance and marriage, daunted by their inaccessibility, or already discouraged by their failure.

In an associational society like our own, the differentiation of social roles makes common goals and meanings hard to arrive at with other persons. In their place it leaves the reciprocal exchange of instrumental support in a greater variety of interpersonal relationships, among which the individual can move and choose more freely. *est*'s ethic fits such social conditions, where "you have to depend on yourself." A young graduate reflects on his marriage and divorce with new insight:

> My old position on love was about giving and needing and having common goals. That's a myth. You can't make another person have your goals. *est* talks about *allowing*. You have to allow them to be who they are and want what they want. You support them in *their* goals, not yours.

The Christian sect and the Zen monastery offer communal contrasts to an associational society, which foster distinctive relationships between "brothers and sisters in the Lord" or in the dharma. *est* offers no comparable alternative setting. "You can't *belong* to *est*," comments a staff member. "There are no members." Instead *est* teaches its clients an interpersonal ethic directly attuned to the larger society's associational conditions. A graduate observes, "*est* enhances your ability to do things in the relationships you already have, where you can handle what's going on for you here and now. We're not trying to go up the country and get away from it all." Graduates may make acquaintances at *est* events who develop into friends and lovers. "Sure, I hustle at the seminars," says one. "It beats the bar scene." But *est* is primarily an ideological community that lends leverage to the graduate's activity in the larger touch-and-go social arena. It is a community of belief in nonbelief that comes to include those preexisting relations whom each graduate recruits to it, including her spouse or living partner in two out of every three cases.[54]

Since taking the training, *est* graduates report feeling more "closeness and fun," less "anger and boredom" in relation to spouses, living partners, friends, parents, and children.[55] Sixties youth see themselves being less judgmental and more accepting toward others, notably their elders. Says one:

> There were older, straight people in the training who revealed something of themselves and became more real for me. Now the guy in the leisure suit selling life insurance is much more human. He's got problems, too. Instead of relating to him like, "Well, I'm glad that guy's messed up because he's there wearing leisure suits and trashing the environment and, besides, he probably voted for Nixon," I'm willing to just look at him and experience sympathy. I got that my old self-righteous resentment was just a barrier to accomplishing things myself.[56]

Like the LWF and Zen Center, *est*'s age integration helps to reconcile sixties youth with their elders, removing barriers to cooperation and accomplish-

ment on the job, and to love at home. A young *est* graduate and one-time
staff member testifies that "You Can Go Home Again." He writes:

> When I left Chicago for San Francisco six years ago, I cut myself
> off from my family with a meat cleaver and disappeared. I would
> call home every couple of months with a new address and a new
> guru, as I floated around California trying to find out who the
> hell I was. . . .
>
> [Since taking the training] I realized that my parents loved me—
> that they always have and always will. I saw that all my parents
> ever wanted was for me to experience satisfaction in life. . . . The
> total source of the conflict, upsets, and noncommunication be-
> tween us had come out of the fact that I disagreed with the form
> they put their love in. My whole life had been organized around
> my attempts to prove I could make it "my way," whatever that
> meant.
>
> . . . [now] I am no longer coming from my past, no longer run-
> ning away from home, no longer trying to make it, trying to be-
> come a grownup. My parents know that they have completed
> their job with me. I am, and they know it. I love them totally
> and they know it. They love me totally and I know it. And all
> of us know that all of us know.[57]

Such reconciliations come as sixties youth are dropping back in to life plans
more continuous with their parents', among whom personalist values have
made complementary gains in the past decade. (Some young graduates, including one-fifth of those interviewed, report recruiting their parents to *est*.)
This reconciliation takes more than time and distance, a neat haircut and a
steady job. It also takes ideas that soften or discount the causes of rebellion
(whatever "my way" meant), redefine love's common ground, and reaffirm
the ex-rebel's independent identity even as they encourage his cooperative
behavior. Sixties youth have found such ideas in *est*.[58]

Young *est* graduates feel better, they say, because they are now more
assertive of their own interests and more accepting of others'. Women especially report greater assertiveness, rooted in self-acceptance and resulting in
felt satisfaction. Says one,

> In the training I got in touch with how I actually felt and what I
> actually want to do. Not what I'm *supposed* to do, not what
> somebody else wants me to do. *est* made it OK for me to do what
> *I* want to . . . I'm more forceful in the world. I see the people I
> want to see, I don't see the people I don't want to. I'm living my
> life more for myself, whereas before it was harder for me to say
> *no* to people. Now that I accept who I am, I can't be had any-
> more.

Psychological self-acceptance empowers effective social interaction, in which the interests at stake are inner satisfactions as well as external utilities. *est*'s ideal of "powerful relationships" (two persons exchange power supporting each other's achievement of individual goals) generalizes the market model of exchange to all social interaction. At the same time it psychologizes the content and medium of that exchange. This conflation of feelings and interests points to the merger of a utilitarian ethic based in public life and an expressive ethic based in private life.

est proposes a unified model of interaction—affectively expressive yet detached, therapeutically poised and engaging, and assertively self-interested—to apply equally to friends and lovers and to associates, clients, and strangers. The utilitarian logic of bureaucratic life defines interpersonal relations more calculably with reference to individual satisfaction, a function welcomed in a world where spouses, lovers, and friends circulate without the reliability of fixed rules, circumstances, and living groups to anchor impulse. Emotional fluency and detachment produced by therapeutic techniques are required in risking oneself to initiate tentative relationships, develop them into deep ones, and accept their failure to so develop, not merely to enjoy casual relationships. Does such therapeutic poise in itself help insulate the interpersonal seeker from those emotionally compelling relationships it was intended to uncover? A few youths think so, particularly those who have lost their earlier enthusiasm for *est*. One complains:

> You get this slippery kind of honesty in a lot of the human potential scene. You're peeling the onion of the self, and there's always another layer underneath. Sometimes I feel like my actual ability to find out what's happening inside me is less clear now, even though I'm more facile about it.

But most graduates answer this question by affirming their own increased capacity to experience satisfying relationships, and their release from fixed expectations of how others will respond to them and for how long, expectations they have found inhibiting and unmet in their past experience. Says one,

> I'm more realistic about relationships now. I don't put more value into them than there's really there. I can meet people and put it out there without having to have a lot of agreement out front. I don't get upset so easily, because I don't have so many pictures about the way it could be or should be. . . . I used to feel strange saying "I love you." I was always wondering whether I meant it, or they meant it. Now I can just say it. It's just another word in my vocabulary.

The all-or-nothing dilemma of romantic love leading to marriage is here replaced by a flexible openness to the sort of less committed, encompassing,

and reliable relationships that have become the norm in the social world
est's clients inhabit. Marriage itself takes on some of the same attitudinal
openness and the same contractual structure that permeate modern public
life. To explain "what it looks like when a relationship works," an *est*
trainer describes his marriage:

> First of all, when L—— and I got married, we set out a carefully
> created set of agreements, including an operating procedure and
> a divorce agreement. . . .
>
> . . . In order to have a workable marriage, it seems to me that
> you have to be willing not to have one. So we have already set
> up the whole divorce, as well as the whole marriage, to include
> all possibilities. It's a condition in which whatever happens is
> appropriate and okay. Out of that condition in which all possi-
> bilities are all right, we have created a strength in our relation-
> ship that allows us to be together at choice.[59]

Concludes a graduate, "We're getting away from those demanding, sacrificing kinds of relationships where you have to love me because I love you.
We're getting into more honest, open relationships where you're free to
choose to give each other support." Two individuals exchanging support to
maximize the satisfaction each feels: this utilitarian model achieves its interpersonal plausibility largely by making love, the heart of modern private
life, more adaptable to the conditions of bureaucratic public life that impinge upon it. In light of this adaptive function, *est*'s claim to enhance interpersonal sensitivity through the standardized techniques of a mass training
no longer seems so ironic. For it is increasingly in such bureaucratically
standardized settings that middle-class urbanites must exercise this virtue.

II. WORK: PLAYING THE GAME

The most obvious dimension of *est*'s merged ethic is the public utiliza-
tion of private emotions and expressive behavior in bureaucratic and
services-oriented work.[60] In such white-collar occupations the intimate side
of one's personality becomes part of the impersonal means of his livelihood.
The individual must sell his smile, not only his time.[61] At work as in the rest
of life, *est* holds the individual totally responsible for what he does and
what happens to him. "Either you get the job done or you don't," *est* volunteers are told. "There's no halfway and there's no such thing as trying."[62] *est*
echoes the buoyant affirmations of positive thinking, but qualifies them in
three important respects. Psychologically, it observes that internal barriers
can't be overcome simply by trying harder. They must be therapeutically
disclosed, accepted, and abreacted. "Trying to change it makes it persist.
Being with it makes it disappear." Bureaucratically, *est* observes that "Real-

ity isn't a democracy. It's a dictatorship." The individual agent makes the system work for him through learning to handle the physical and social universe by complying with its rules. Epistemologically, the apparent solipsism of the omnicausal agent, dualistically construed, dissolves into monistic self-awareness. "Your self is context rather than content." It is the ground of all being, from which emerges every particular manifestation of being.

est's central idea of the omnicausal agent relies in a peculiarly concrete way not on the mystical experience of the monist but on the interactive experience of the white-collar worker, especially the salesman, for its plausibility. Erhard's experience training door-to-door encyclopedia salesmen was applied directly during the first years of *est* to a franchise operation, owned by his wife, selling soap products and subsequently cosmetics and vitamins door to door. The business was run strictly according to *est* principles, and it was staffed exclusively by *est* graduates. A former employee recalls,

> When you went door to door, they said you only met one person behind every door—yourself. "There's nobody out there. It's all you." Whatever happened, you made it like it was. So if no one was home, it was because you weren't home. You could never say, "No one was home on my route today." It had to be, "Today all I did was create no one being home for me." Then they'd ask you, "Well, what's going on for you not to be home?" The idea that you created everything was like a law. You were never allowed to pass the buck—and you had some awfully shitty eighteen-hour days.

> The goal of the whole thing was to keep upping your sales volume, despite all the obstacles, and "go out the top" onto the *est* staff. It was all a game, right, but the atmosphere was very heavy there. We weren't people selling soap. We were perfect beings on the path of enlightenment. If you couldn't hack it, you were made to feel like you hadn't gotten it. You "went out the bottom."

> You were expected to give up all your outside life to get the job done. Then you could do anything you wanted. Only getting the job done was almost impossible. There were a few times, though, when I was really on, when it was like magic. All I had to do was be myself. Having no act was like the best act of all.[63]

> *est* showed me that I didn't have an outside life. It all entered into the job. How I felt, my relationships, everything. If I got angry, then people would come to the door already angry, before I'd even said a word. You're forced to look at that. The guy who delivered the soap said he could tell who had sold it without knowing, just from the way our customers were with him.

The door-to-door salesman incarnates *est*'s idea of the omnicausal agent. He sells products (soap, vitamins, encyclopedias) whose purchase is discretionary. His customers either have some on hand, have no specific need for the item, or can purchase it more cheaply at a store if they do. Consequently, their purchase depends entirely on the salesman's effectiveness at selling himself. The client buys in response to him, not the product. The appeal of the product itself follows from his success in attaching to it some supervenient state of being desired by the purchaser, whether erudition and self-advancement to encyclopedias, beauty to cosmetics, or health to vitamins. By effectively modulating his relation to others, that is, by first selling himself, the salesman makes the sale. From actually influencing the purchaser's behavior at the door, it is a short symbolic leap to "creating" him behind it. The door-to-door salesman creates from intrapsychic resources, through interpersonal means, the conditions of occupational success. In this sense the individual's inner state determines his external achievement, which in turn mirrors it. The result is positively neo-Calvinist. In fact, *est* has recast the classical Protestant ethic, after inheriting it through the hands of American evangelical religion (where success, once the sign of election, became the result of an experience of perfection) and a secularized commercial culture (where the believer who strives for salvation became the striver who believes in salvation on earth).[64]

According to *est*'s ethic, the individual's felt well-being follows from his having a life that works, which follows from his setting goals and achieving them. At the same time, according to its psychology, the converse is also true. Achievement follows from self-acceptance, that is, feeling good about oneself. Such acceptance is based on realizing one's inner identity as a perfect being, not one's external achievement or possessions—on who I am, not what I do or how much I have. If the individual has realized his true inner self by this account, he can achieve and gain whatever he wants, a dynamic made explicit in *est*'s sequential "be-do-have" formula for successful activity. The extent to which the individual achieves his goals mirrors the extent to which he has seen into and accepted himself, even as it produces the degree of aliveness he feels. The circular connection between the *est* graduate's psychic state, external achievement, and ultimate good recalls the Calvinist's. The predestined Calvinist, however, could only presume himself among the elect and achieve as if he were elected. He thereby reaped the rewards of this world but never enjoyed them, since those of the next remained ultimately unsecured. Blessed by secularized evangelical optimism and enlightened by psychologized oriental mysticism, the *est* graduate intuitively knows himself to be perfect and achieves accordingly. He thereby reaps the rewards of this world and enjoys them, since he also knows that this is the only world there is. In Calvinism's ethic success was the *sign* of a divine election that cannot be known until death. In *est*'s ethic success is the *result* of a transpersonal perfection that can be experienced here and now.[65]

Emotional Entrepreneurs

est takes the instrumental use of affective and expressive modes of behavior typified by sales and public relations work, draws in its managerial and therapeutic equivalents, and synthesizes a model of "high-tone" self-presentation and interaction for the wider arena of middle class life.[66] As in their private lives, *est* graduates report greater acceptance of others' interests and greater assertiveness of their own on the job. A psychiatric social worker remarks:

> People intimidate me less. I notice it at work, especially with my superiors. I feel stronger and more confident, I'm better at managing people. I'm less afraid of my clients, too. I feel less like a pretender or a hoax. I can really do it!

A sales representative elaborates the same theme in a corporate context:

> I work for a large corporation. I have managers and managers way above me, and I was really afraid of them. I'd almost shake when I'd get around my district manager, he was such a strong, aggressive man. I knew I had to play the role of a strong, capable woman out selling for General Consolidated, and I didn't know how to do it. It got so I was afraid to walk into the office. Even the secretaries frightened me.

> During the fear process I realized *everyone* was scared to death of other people, where before I thought I was the only one who didn't have confidence and was afraid. I went into the office the next day. I could see they were more afraid of me than I was of them. That's *why* I was afraid of them. Because we all see fear in each other's faces. We all put on our big show of being confident, when we don't know what to do. I just told my boss that I used to be scared to death of him and I wasn't any more. I told him how I felt about the company, I laid it on the line with him. That was worth $350 by itself, I felt so alive then.

> Now I can give myself the space to feel embarrassed or rejected without letting it run me. I let people have their opinions and I acknowledge them. And I can stand up to them. I can confront people face to face and tell them how it is; and just do it, knowing it's part of my job. I still feel nervous, but I don't get upset.

The same interpersonal medium that gives the white-collar individual such great power to create her external reality by influencing others also makes her utterly dependent on their responses to her for her own occupational identity and success. Because other persons are subjects like oneself, manipulating them is inherently less predictable than manipulating physical objects or abstractions. Making a sale or a psychotherapeutic cure is uncertain business in a way that making a car or a poem is not. Success in doing so seems to depend on the salesman's touch, as it were, with other persons, although overall shifts in supply and demand are determined by larger corporate and economic forces. A self-confidently relaxed and engaging salesman makes the sale and gets the girl, not the salesman who presses hardest. For such emotional entrepreneurs caught in the cracks of a corporate economy, success requires affectively attuned interaction, coupled with a certain relaxed detachment from it that enables the subject both to modulate his expressive behavior winningly and to accept the ever-likely outcome of losing a sale, or a girl, at another's discretion. Since such discretionary choice is a matter of taste, not reason, the customer is always right.

Work by *est*'s definition represents neither the Zen monk's practice nor the Christian's Pauline duty to provide for his family. It is "a game." What does this imply? It is to be played, not labored at or "efforted." It is played for fun but also for mastery. Indeed, as an *est* staff member points out to volunteers about to promote the training at a recruiting seminar, "Now relax and have fun, because it's all a game. *And* we want to play 100 percent. Play to win, because when you win, that's when it's the most fun."[67]

The individual detaches herself from her social activity in order to accomplish it more effectively, not to devalue its accomplishment. In advising this sort of instrumental detachment *est*'s psychologism folds a new wrinkle into the program of positive thinking if not into the history of religious renunciation. Says Erhard on the subject of making relationships work:

No matter what comes up, just absolutely be willing to let it be. Give it space and just continue moving on through the course. Whatever you can let be, whatever you can give space to, you've begun to master. What you can let be, allows you to be, and that's the beginning of mastery.[68]

A graduate puts it more succinctly: "When you let go of it, you get it all." Such detachment more closely resembles the psychological strategy of abreactively letting go repressed contents of consciousness in the interests of strengthening ego performance than it does the religious aim of nonattachment to self in the interests of loving God or compassionately identifying with the whole of existence.

Although *est* invokes both notions, egoless compassion tends toward egoist detachment as long as external achievement and ego performance remain the practical measure of personal worth. Take, for example, *est*'s idea of "giving space" to something. Now generalized to describe an ideal of nonjudgmental acceptance, the idea appears earlier and more specifically in Erhard's door-to-door sales psychology. A veteran employee recalls how he trained her to go to somebody's door:

We'd knock on the door, and then when it was answered we would step back. When you stand too close to the door it frightens people. It gives no space. So we stepped back. We went through our routine in a really respectful way, recognizing that they had pictures in their minds about what somebody is going to do with them when they come into their house.

Werner trained for hours just to handle that door and entrance business. We would work on that every night.[69]

Here the figure of speech takes on literal meaning, and the act of "giving space" to a prospective customer achieves a practical end. The salesman steps back in order to make an entrance, and then a sale.

A second example suggests how closely the dynamic of the salesman's exemplary experience carries over into *est* itself. A staff member describes the process of "discovering myself" while helping to invite thousands of graduates to enroll in a special course with Erhard:

So there I sat, dialing the telephone, hour after hour—nobody home. Finally, I realized that it was *me* who wasn't "home." I came face to face with myself and my willingness to relate with others. It was as if I discovered I was magical...and all that I required was me.

I dialed the phone, it rang and a voice said, "Hello." "Hi, this is B—— from *est*...," and so it continued for nine days, sharing with graduates, creating a personal relationship with each phone call.

I laughed, cried, and expressed myself without limits. I found out what Werner meant about living up to the magnificence that is in all of us, and that there truly is nothing but the battle that you carry inside yourself.[70]

Here again the "magic" of the omnicausal agent comes into play, performed by means of emotional self-expression in interpersonal relationships aimed at an occupational outcome.

A final example of the implicit link between inner detachment and external achievement comes from The *est* Academy. Staff members seeking to become trainers participate in this academy, where their personal development is publicly charted by the percentage of prospects each deals with who go on to enroll in and complete the training. Asked about this criterion, a trainer-candidate replies,

You see sales charts. I see the course of my movement from attachment to nonattachment. The less stuff of my own I'm attached to, the more totally I can communicate. The more I communicate, the more I can put people in touch with their own power to choose.

By such logic the evidence for monistic nonattachment can be found in per capita sales percentages.

Boot Camp for Bureaucracy

est adapts the entrepreneurial ideal of the salesman, that last American dreamer, to the corporate reality of middle-class work by emphasizing the need for bureaucratic cooperation and rule compliance in order to get the job done.[71] *est* makes explicit the individual's contractual agreement to comply with bureaucratic rules, invests them with the binding power of personal promises, and sanctions their violation accordingly.[72] To a generation of youth bred by liberal education and countercultural personalism to distrust the rationale and moral claims of bureaucratic work, yet now faced with the need to perform it for a living, *est*'s lesson carries a startlingly persuasive force.[73] Reports one former dropout, "Assisting is like a school for learning to keep your agreements. I always used to be the artist-hippie-weirdo doing my own thing. I'd cheat and lie to make the job someone else's problem. Now I take responsibility for me being the whole *est* organization and getting the job done."

Accused by critics of being an authoritarian army, the *est* organization is, in fact, a boot camp for bureaucracy. Hierarchical, tightly rule-governed, and meritocratic, it trains its young volunteers and staff to answer phones, write memos, keep records, promote and stage public events, and deal smoothly with clients. It explains organizational authority by locating its genesis within the psyche. "You created your boss to tell you what to do," explains a volunteer. "The same with the rules and Werner. The way you get power is by giving power to a source of power." By following this schema, sixties youth who have outlived their years of school, the summer of love, and the Revolution come to accept and "own" the bureaucratic organizations for which they now work, not by controlling an economic share of them nor politically formulating their rules, but by psychologically appropriating those rules. Says one young woman, an assistant buyer for a chain of retail stores:

I used to have a lot of trouble at work. It was my idea of honesty. I couldn't keep my mouth shut, and people don't like that, at least not in retailing.

Has est *changed that?*

It showed me my barriers about working with other people. It was my thing about being unique and individual, being one of the bright ones. I wanted to think things out and do them my way. I liked hard jobs, but it had to be *my* job.

est is serious about the rules and producing results, *and* they
know it's all a game. Sometimes assisting I'd get mad and wanna
know, "Why are we doing it this way?" They'd tell me, "Because
that's the way we're doing it." Everybody else is laughing about
it, so I can laugh, too, and just let myself have a good time playing the game.

Work as a white-collar game consisting of "appropriate nonsense" claims no
intrinsic meaning, unlike the professional's vocation, but its achievement is
necessary for the individual's felt well-being and social standing.[74] If she
plays at it with energy and detachment, the sixties youth doing such work is
assured by *est* of finding self-fulfillment as well as success. What has been
merely necessary now becomes worthwhile.

Before beginning *est*, Erhard similarly rationalized the work of door-
to-door sales for a similarly overeducated work force. Recalls one of the
young, college-educated women who made up most of his team selling
Parents magazine child development material for mothers to read to their
children:[75]

Werner devised a new approach to selling *Parents* material. He
trained us to communicate, not to sell. As a result, we sold better, *and* everyone involved felt much more satisfied about it. We
felt that what we were doing was worthwhile, and so did the
mothers who bought programs from us. This approach to selling
has now been carried over to other organizations that use direct
sales techniques.

It was this, more than anything else, that enabled Werner to recruit and keep the people who worked for him. Most of us were
overqualified for door-to-door selling. But we had our own
school, and our own community.[76]

Thus college-educated young adults, overqualified for selling but under-
qualified for the professions, come to accept routine white-collar work and
learn to live as emotional entrepreneurs. They perform better, and feel more
satisfied about it, once selling becomes "communicating," the office becomes a "school," and the employees an ideological "community." In one
sense, at least, white-collared sixties youth have become "graduates" of *est*
just as dropouts-turned-carpenters have become LWF "ministers" or Zen
"students." All of them have redeemed the meaning of mundane work by
coupling it with a sacred career.

For committed *est* graduates this sacred career centers around "expanding your aliveness," and mundane work becomes a means to this end.
The idea of work as a game goes hand in hand with the notion of one's own
life as a work of art. The enterprise of self-perfection, passed down from
philosopher and monk to bohemian dandy and hippie, now takes thera-

peutic form in "working on yourself." A young *est* graduate links his new sense of self and work in aesthetic terms:

> You know, there isn't a picture that anyone has painted in the world up to today that is any more magnificent than the picture I'm painting of me. Every brush stroke of me is perfect. It's full, it's complete, and it's magnificent. I just love it! The picture I'm painting of me is a masterpiece. Because now each brush stroke I do, each step I take, I'm experiencing it much more.
>
> See, what I realized in *est* is that when you get to the top of the mountain—it doesn't matter what it is: being a doctor, cleaning toilet bowls, writing a book—there ain't nothing there. You pick a mountain to climb and when you get to the top of the mountain, you get to the top of the mountain. That's it! There's nothing there except being at the top of the mountain. There's nothing to do. Once I really got in touch with that in the training, I realized the quality of my life for me is getting into each step I take. Just experiencing that and getting off on it—that's beautiful.

Sixties youth in the LWF and Zen Center devalued conventional work per se. Though much less radically, the graduate devalues its particular contents and prestige. For doctor, author, salesman, and toilet cleaner alike, "there ain't nothing there" in the idea of work as appropriate nonsense and the mountain-climbing metaphor for it. Thus the graduate restates the hippie's rejection of conventional work as the basis of his personal identity. Unlike the hippie, he then makes work into the mode of his own experiential self-creation. Exploded by the sixties counterculture, the old economic myth of the self-made man is recast into the new consciousness myth of the self-made Self.

Though compounded mainly from utilitarian and psychological common sense, *est*'s answer to the problems of bureaucratic work and middle-class life echoes religious attitudes described a half century ago by Max Weber commenting on Confucianism:

> The distinctive attitude of a bureaucracy to religious matters has been classically formulated in Confucianism. Its hallmark is an absolute lack of feeling of a need for salvation or for any transcendental anchorage for ethics. In its place resides what is substantively an opportunistic and utilitarian (though aesthetically attractive) doctrine of conventions appropriate to a bureaucratic caste.[77]

Yet however one evaluates *est*'s interpersonal ethic, it cannot simply be dismissed. Its emphasis on consciously poised relating to others—engaging yet detached, therapeutic yet utilitarian—responds adaptively to the social conditions permeating urban white-collar life, especially but not only for young adults. *est* presents a powerfully convincing model of and for interpersonal behavior in the urban office, schoolroom, sales conference, and singles bar. The appeal of this model, whatever its own merits, suggests how deep and troubling are the questions *est* addresses in contemporary American middle-class culture.[78] *est* appeals, says a psychiatrist-graduate, "because it's so middle-class, so all-American—like the Chevrolet."[79] Indeed it is such an ideological vehicle, but one redesigned for a society unsettled in new ways and now picking up freeway speed toward an end that may leave us far from home.

III. SOCIAL RESPONSIBILITY:
MAKING THE WORLD WORK

Controversy over *est*'s ethic grows sharpest in discussions of its implications for social and political responsibility. Youthful graduates usually disapprove of radical politics and liberal reformism of sixties vintage as inevitably vain attempts to force persons to change or to "help" them, instead of accepting them as they are and "creating the space" for them to transform themselves abreactively. What sort of concrete social activity is implied by the latter ideal? Graduates' views vary in reply. Some justify exemplary responsibility for oneself and for those with whom one normally interacts as sufficient. Most point to participation in *est* itself as the most effective contribution one can make to the future of American society, namely the transformation of its members and institutions in *est*'s image. They cite the growing number of educators, doctors, therapists, clergy, and other professionals who have taken the training, along with special trainings given for schools, prisons, and local governments, to show that progress toward such institutional transformation is already underway. Traditional forms of political participation and voluntarism are supported as secondary ways of "taking responsibility for the system, since you created it the way it is." Graduates often point to *est*'s nonpartisan voter registration drive among its members as an example of the latter sort of social concern, along with its Hunger Project. Since 1977 the Project has enrolled 1.7 million persons and raised 5.7 million dollars to publicize the idea that it is now possible "to end world hunger in twenty years."[80] (See n. 80 for a discussion of the Hunger Project, n. 89 regarding prison trainings, and n. 90 regarding psychiatric criticism of *est*.)

One young graduate, a veteran of antiwar demonstrations and campus politics though never arrested or affiliated with any radical political organization, characterizes his past and present political involvement in terms of *est*'s idea of responsibility:

During the sixties where did you stand on radical politics?

I was for it. I demonstrated. I marched on Washington in '68 at Nixon's inauguration. You know, "There ought to be a Revolution. Off the President. Kick the sonuvabitch out. Change the system. It's worthless, junk it. Let's take over, and start a whole new thing."

How did you see American society in the sixties?

I always pointed the finger at the system. "This is wrong. That's wrong." I blamed the Establishment, while I played the victim. I never took responsibility for anything. I wasn't responsible for the rules, I wasn't responsible for the laws. I wasn't responsible for the Vietnam War. I wasn't responsible for politics. I didn't own any of that shit. I didn't take responsibility for my choices. There I was trying to make the world work, and my own life didn't work. I couldn't even make a commitment to be on time before the training.

How does the system look to you now?

Totally different. Now I feel that the system is perfectly fine. What doesn't work is the people, because they don't take responsibility for it. Now I'm taking responsibility. I'm assisting [at *est*]. I'm gonna vote, because the system's set up to vote and it's my system, so I'm gonna take responsibility for it and vote.

What's responsibility then?

Owning my choices. Being more active, dealing with the system *in* the system, under the system. To me what's more important is conscious awareness, awakening. First you have to take responsibility for yourself, and from there it's an easy step to taking responsibility for the people around you and the whole system.

Sixties radicalism, which blamed and opposed the established sources of political power for conditions of social injustice, is now interpreted as self-righteous abnegation of one's own responsibility for these conditions. The graduate sees this to be especially hypocritical in view of his own irresponsibility in his personal life. He sees participation in *est* and cooperation with conventional politics at present to mark acceptance of responsibility for the existing social system. Its failures are due not to external structural conditions or to the concerted efforts of particular interest groups or classes, but to the universal unwillingness of individuals, first of all oneself, to take *est*'s kind of responsibility for themselves and the society as a whole. Typically, the young graduate has shifted from an attitude of outright alienation from the established social order during the sixties to mediated identification with it at present, from activities of overt opposition (more hip than radical in tenor) to modest participation. His present position is grounded less in any new faith in the established political structure than in commitment to *est*'s ideology of therapeutic change through abreactive acceptance, and the institutional promise *est* offers for the transformation of society from the inside out.

During the 1960s young *est* graduates shared the countercultural perception that American society was fundamentally wrong and in need of change. They usually subscribed to the hip view that America's "screwed-up values," more than its social structure, were to blame for its problems, which were approaching solution through cultural changes already underway. Many youths sympathized with political activists, some accepted radical diagnoses of what was wrong, why, and how it was to be changed. But virtually none committed themselves to enacting any such programs of change.[81] "I hung on the sidelines and watched the political game," concedes one. "I was interested but I wasn't ready to play it." *est*'s picture of society accounts for the futility of the hippie's version of a psychedelic utopia, while retracing its postmillennial shape in more conventional colors.

est agrees that American society is fundamentally faulty, but it blames the individual graduate. The trainer stresses,

> When you see why your lives don't work, you'll see why this whole fucking country doesn't work. Look at General Motors. That's the best this country can do. And look at one of their fucking cars. It's a piece of shit! I'm not blaming GM. I'm blaming you for being so stupid that you think it works.... Sure, you *understand* all the problems, you *want* things to get better. But not if it costs *you* anything, not if *you* have to take responsibility for it.[82]

The country is criticized for not working, just as its corporate representative is criticized for the inefficiency of its machinery, not for its mode of ownership and operation, its political influence or ecological impact. Such criticism leads to the conclusion that what must be done is to make the system work by accepting it as it is, acknowledging oneself as its cause, and participating in it according to its rules. Political activists failed in trying to make the system over by resisting it, blaming others for causing it, and dropping out of it, all according to their own rules. "How did the War end, anyway?" the trainer demands. "Did the kids running around with their little banners end it? No! All they did was get everyone else pissed off at them. What ended it was millions of ordinary people in this country going to the polls and voting it out."[83] *est* argues that the paradox of its psychological theory of change ("Trying to change an experience makes it persist, accepting it and being with it makes it disappear.") applies as powerfully to social institutions as to the individual mind. By heeding it first with themselves, then others, then everyone, individuals can "transubstantiate" social institutions, altering their essence while leaving their structural accidents unchanged. Thus psychologism defines both the mode and sequence of social change.

Transformation and Social Change

est presents itself as an agent of societal transformation whose success will enable "the institutions of man to deliver on their promises," in Erhard's phrase. "What I want is for the world to work," he says. "The organizing principle of *est* is: 'whatever the world is doing, get it to do that.'"[84] *est* is already acting to this end along two avenues. First, it is transforming an ever-increasing number of individuals, who will eventually make up a "critical mass" of the entire population, triggering its transformation by a chain reaction. A longtime *est* volunteer reports:

> There's a cumulative effect from graduates changing personally. They create the space for other people to get it. It's Werner's intention to give the training to forty million people in America, which would be like a critical mass. Everybody will be giving the training to everybody else just by living with them day by day.

By transforming individuals *est* is transforming society conceived as a collection of individuals. In this postmillennial vision no heroic efforts by a small elite of morally perfected Christians or enlightened Buddhists will be required to remake American society after it has been destroyed by divine or ecological catastrophes. Instead, the new age has already dawned and is now advancing, its continuous progress charted by the swelling curve of *est*'s mass membership.[85] In the process of its numerical growth *est* is "creating a context" to transform society, just as its Hunger Project is "creating a context" to end starvation. Project literature makes clear that "the process by which a context is created is communication and enrollment, communication and enrollment, communication and enrollment;"[86] while *est* points out that "numerical growth and international trainings represent, however, only one dimension of *est*'s development as a force for transformation in the world."[87]

Second, *est* is transforming the larger society's institutions of socialization—educational, therapeutic, medical, legal-penal, religious, governmental, and familial. They will take over the training's functions as their members assimilate its ethic, eventually permitting *est* itself to wither away. Erhard states that "the real thrust and goal of *est* is to put *est* in education. *est* will cease to exist somewhere along the pike. We've already begun to make inroads, we've already made good plans, we've demonstrated our effectiveness to the world, people will listen to us. We are starting to get into the education system. . . ."[88] Although *est* has yet to win over any insti-

tutional establishment, its pre-1976 graduates already included 9 percent of
all "educators" in the San Francisco School District.[89] The University of
California has offered academic credit for a course entitled "The *est* experience: Implications for Educators," with the training as a prerequisite. A
California state college has given credit for the training itself, conducted on
campus.[90] *est*'s advisory board numbers a score of distinguished doctors
and professors, including educators who have formerly been president of
Oberlin College, chancellor of the University of California at San Francisco
and HEW assistant secretary, and a Harvard Business School assistant dean.
It also includes entertainers John Denver, Valerie Harper, Suzy Chaffee,
and a vice-president of the National Broadcasting Company.[91]

Asked about *est*'s potential for transforming American institutions, a
young graduate replies with confidence, "It seems like it could happen. *est* is
growing faster than anything else and graduates are strategically located.
est doesn't make anything else wrong, so it can get along with anything. It
doesn't give you any answers, so its answers can't be proved wrong. It just
gives you a more open, useful viewpoint." The utility of *est*'s ethic for
bureaucratic work and social relations, the psychological content of its doctrine (high on epistemology, low on cosmology), and its streamlined delivery (weekend scheduling without "touchie-feelie" or religious props) do
indeed make *est* more appealing across the range of secular middle-class life
than such human potential competitors as Scientology and Arica, let alone
conservative Christian or neo-Oriental religion.

est's modest millennialism fits the social situation of its young graduates. Compared to their counterparts in the Christian sect and the Zen
center, they have dropped back in closer to the middle of mainstream work
and personal life. In fact, they had not dropped out so far nor burned their
bridges back so drastically in the first place. They did not use drugs so heavily, reject school so vehemently, nor so commit themselves to countercultural careers as drug dealers, rock musicians, hustlers, artists, craftsmen,
communards, or political activists. Nonetheless they shared countercultural
hopes whose disappointment was not painless for them. *est*'s ethic has
responded to the frustration and helplessness felt by college-educated
youths now stuck in white-collar jobs within the system they had hoped to
change. Says one resignedly,

> When I look at what we're doing in the world, it makes me feel
> helpless. There's nothing I can do about it, except accept it. *est*
> has shown me that's OK. At least after the training I felt a big
> burden of guilt removed toward people who were having prob-
> lems, whatever they were, because I got that *they* were respon-
> sible in a way.

> *Why do you think it looked different to you in the sixties?*

> We were all going to college then. The real world was outside.
> You could be outrageous, because you didn't have to deal with

it. In college everyone was young like me. They all did dope like me, wore long hair, and pointed out there at "them," the ones who were screwing everything up.

But then when I got out and started working, I found myself being one of "them." I wanted to get more for my efforts, you know, get ahead. I guess I'd gotten my hands dirty, so I wasn't so interested anymore in sitting around trying to figure out if it was left-wing dirt or right-wing dirt. [laughing] I found out you can't worry about saving the world. You have to just live your own life.

While it represents a reaction to cooled-off politics and a tightened economy in America since the 1960s, this shift of outlook—from seeking to understand the society to surviving in it, from making it over to making one's way in it—cannot be separated from the subject's age-related shift of position in the society: from studying in an age-segregated youth setting while being supported by others to working in an age-integrated adult setting to support oneself.

Following the line of such shifts of position, *est*'s ethic has also sustained hopes for social change, outside the context of radical or liberal politics, in a form compatible with a conventional career and lifestyle. A graduate seeking his first job as a corporate lawyer doing *pro bono* environmental work on the side suggests how closely *est*'s ideology suits his own situation:

When I was an undergrad I was involved in mildly radical politics. The War was a great rallying point for me, although I couldn't swallow the revolutionary rhetoric. I was coming from the place of "What you're doing, America, is wrong. You can't do that. It's evil." Which was absolutely ineffective. I was flailing around with my eyes closed.

Now instead of saying, "No, no, no," I say, "Yes, you're doing that." I'm seeing and dealing with what is, instead of wishing it were different. I'm coming to a place of acknowledging how things actually work, what the facts are, whether I like it or not, because it is what it is. It's not right or wrong.

In the past few years I've become more involved in my relationship to myself, the people around me, the earth. Social concern is there, but it's not the big issue. It's a question of putting it on a smaller scale, trying to change the energy instead of resisting it. *est* is like that. It's less defensive and more accepting than the radicals. And it's very centered and clear about where I am individually. You can accept opposition and not feel threatened about it. You can communicate with other people and see the world through their eyes, and then maybe you can do something better. It's like Werner saying,

The way it is,
is enough.
Who you are is enough.
The only thing you have to do
is be.[92]

I feel OK with a wait-and-see position on *est* and society, since I already see so much value in *est* for individuals.

For many who came of age in the sixties, *est*'s ethic of taking responsibility for the existing social order while pursuing one's own interests within it sounds sensible and straightforward. For many of their elders, once caught in the middle between the Establishment and the kids, *est* has opened up a new middle ground. An older businessman reflects on what *est* has meant to him:

> Where once I saw a bloated capitalist, an exploiter of the masses, now I see a man in a Lincoln.
> Where once I saw radical, hippie freaks, now I see four bearded men in a battered van. . . .
> When I had to understand everything, I didn't understand anything. When I needed to judge, I had no standards of my own.
> . . . When I knew what the world was supposed to be like, that's the way it was, whether I liked it or not, and I usually didn't.
> Since *est*, the world can be any way it wants. Fine with me. Here I am, then, with a wife who pats me on the leg, customers who want more work than I have time to do. I ride along the freeway and kids flash the peace sign, girls wave and two guys in the back of a pickup truck offer me a beer.
> So I don't understand it.
> So what?[93]

A social world that could not be understood or justified before can now be accepted. A society that could not be changed through politics, can now be "transformed" through *est*.

Individualism, Monism, and Moral Ambiguity

The ambiguity of *est*'s notion of moral responsibility derives ultimately from its binocular axioms, which are radically individualistic on one side and monistic on the other. *est* posits that each individual is the cause of all his experience, and it prescribes an attitude of responsibility as the acknowledgment of this fact. Construed dualistically (by distinguishing subject and object, self and other), this view can be generalized to mean that each and every person is "totally at cause" and therefore totally *and exclusively* responsible for his own situation and its difficulties. If A is subject to some difficulty, then by definition A willed it so. This inference can be used to excuse anyone else from seeking to alter the external conditions of A's predicament, since A alone is seen to have caused them and to have the capacity to change them. Now if A is a self-indulgent and self-defeating individual whom others have sought to help, only to be exploited and resented, this diagnosis of the situation is easy enough to accept as factual. More to the point, if A is the trainee himself in face-to-face relation to a lover, friend, family member, or work associate, this diagnosis may usefully motivate him to take the initiative to act to improve his situation, regardless of its factual accuracy. If, however, A is an individual or group relatively deprived of power to act on their own behalf by external conditions (whether social position, race, physical handicaps, or the like), then this diagnosis appears not only inaccurate but outrageously tolerant of social injustice and human suffering, according to *est*'s critics. They view it from a liberal-humanist or Judaeo-Christian vantage point, from which they perceive a laissez faire individualism, stripped now of even halfhearted attempts at liberal reform or Christian charity. Disillusioned by the frustrated efforts of sixties radicalism and liberalism, the middle class in this view has turned inward to self-realization and interpersonal intimacy in ways compatible with staying on the job and working toward incrementally greater status. Meanwhile the less advantaged continue to pay a disproportionate price for the existing order, and the more advantaged continue to enjoy its disproportionate profits.

More sophisticated adherents of *est* reject its characterization as a leading version of the "new narcissism," arguing that an exclusively individualistic construal of its concept of responsibility is mistaken. They offer, first, a social-psychological expansion of the concept, and then a monistic universalization of it. First, the individual is totally responsible for his own experience, and that experience includes all the other persons with whom he interacts. As a social self, then, each individual is totally responsible for everything that happens to others in relation to himself and, then, in relation to one another. If another person feels sad, angry, dominated, or whatever in relation to A, A is responsible for it. Second, *est* posits that while each individual experiences himself as a discrete *mind*, he exists ultimately as a *being* coextensive with all existence, conceived monistically. Therefore, each individual has "caused" and "created" every other person and everything that exists, and each individual is consequently responsible for everything and everyone else.

est's small staff and core of veteran volunteers, in contrast to its mass clientele, often interpret *est*'s ethic as deriving entirely from the transformation of self they take to be the training's essence. As Erhard defines it,

> Transformation is *the self as the self*, the self as the context of all contexts, everything/nothing. The self itself is the ground of all being, that from which everything arises. The self is pure context, it is everything/nothing, it is pure space. And out of the self

emerges a manifestation of it. That is, the self (context) *is complete;* the self manifests itself by *being complete,* and the manifestation is process or content.[94]

In other words, *est* shifts one's sense of self from the dualist's discrete ego to the monist's universal being. Echoing Zen's distinctions between small mind and Buddha mind or small self and Big Self, *est's* distinctions between mind and being, self and Self, content and context, position and space all rely on this dualist-to-monist shift for their meaning. So do Erhard's replies to his social critics:

> It is clear that people who think that transformation leads to narcissism and cuts you off from other people are confusing the "self" with a [dualist-realist] position, a body, an ego, an individual. The true experience of the [monist] self takes you out into the world to express the self.[95]

The monistic universalization of individual identity and moral responsibility takes form as an ethic of service to all humanity, which is often cited by Erhard in public statements of his own intentions and *est's* mission in society. He states:

> In *est,* the organization's purpose is to serve people, to create an opportunity for people to experience transformation, enlightenment, satisfaction and well-being in their lives. And to create an opportunity for people to participate in making the world work and to contribute to the lives of others. That's the purpose of *est.*[96]

Formal description of this service ethic, though sketchy, vaguely resembles the Bodhisattva ethic in Zen Buddhism, in which feelings of universal compassion and acts of exemplary service flow from monistic identification with all living beings.

Neither the *est* training nor its graduates elaborate this ethic of service in any systematic detail. They do often allude to it in connection with their appointed role of "assisting" others and with *est's* role in sponsoring the Hunger Project. To what extent *est* or its graduates enact this ethic, and with whom, remains a question open to debate, although *est's* social critics see monistic universalization of responsibility for social problems as obscuring their particular causes and dissolving focused efforts to resolve them. For example, while Erhard states that "Ultimately, the Hunger Project is about transformation of Self as Humanity—about making the world work,"[97] a critical food expert counters, "It's probably collected more money in the name of hunger and done the least about hunger than any group I can think of." He adds,

Anyone who has a real concern about hunger has to have some understanding and concern for social justice in developing countries, about existing inequitable structures, about rapid population growth. I can't see the Hunger Project doing anything about this.[98]

Its critics see *est* de-politicizing such issues by dissolving their social structure and moral substance into pure consciousness, thereby salving the consciences of its naive if well-meaning recruits and harnessing their volunteer efforts to the end of *est's* own numerical growth and legitimation.[99]

The ambiguity of *est's* ethic follows from its axiomatic assumptions. These axioms inform *est's* understanding of ethical evaluation, and fit with the social situation of its graduates. *est* interprets moral judgment as a function of the individual's subjective tastes, which are not subject to rational justification. And it issues no act-specific moral rules of its own comparable to the Christian's commandments or the Zen student's precepts. "We are not a source of rules. *Get it!*" insists a staff member. In the absence of any such rules, personal preference and self-interest tend to determine action more freely. Consciousness of the relativity of one's own tastes, and openness to the asserted interests of immediately present others function to make *est's* contractual ethic relatively feasible in interpersonal affairs. On the larger social and political scale, where others are not so immediately present or equally empowered to assert their interests, countervailing considerations of justice and noninjury may be discounted as mere expressions of taste or personal preference. Where a certain agent does not accept the empirical assumption that following the rules invariably results in his own interest being best served, other parties can exert no moral persuasion over against his empirical assessment. They can only seek to sanction him so as to cause him to revise his assessment of the personal consequences following on rule breaking.

Similarly, one may ask what happens if certain of the rules of society themselves appear to one group, A, to work systematically to their disadvantage and systematically to advantage another group, B. Faced with this question, a young graduate trained as a lawyer declares:

OK, they [the disadvantaged] aren't experiencing choice right now. *And* they actually chose what they got. They couldn't have gotten anything but what they chose. "Could have" denies reality, like "should have" replaces it with guilt. Let's just talk about "was, is, and will be," or better yet, just "is." If they choose what they got, then they can move on. If they keep bitching about it, they're stuck with it forever.

To be sure, the disadvantaged group, A, receives a promise of social change modeled on therapeutic abreaction—"choose, and move on." But this line of response can also allow the advantaged group, B, to discount A's perception as purely subjective and their appeals to justice as mere expressions of personal preference. The advantaged may avow in *est*-like fashion, "What you got is what you actually chose. The rules are just the rules. There are no reasons for them. Besides, since they govern the society you joined, you agreed to them beforehand, even if you don't get to vote now. So follow the rules."[100] Unless disadvantaged group A is somehow residually empowered to demonstrate empirically to advantaged group B that changing the rules will better serve B's own interests, then apparently arbitrary or unjust rules remain as they are. In areas of social action where existing laws and regulations do not reach or, worse, reach in and operate unjustly, we are left without deontological moral leverage to do anything about it.

An *est* graduate responds to the preceding line of criticism from the standpoint of rule-egoism and *est*'s idea of responsibility:

How do you respond to people who see est *being selfish and authoritarian in a way that looks to them like political fascism?*

I grant that the training itself is an authoritarian, law-and-order, "Werner knows best, so do what he says" setup. But you enter into it as a contract aimed at giving you what you want. And I don't see that authoritarian side of the training being held up as a model for society.

In *est* the majority doesn't make the rules. In the society it does, and *est* supports the majority making the rules by participating in the system, since it's your system. You created it, so you're responsible for it.

What about the radical who claims est *is really only holding up the status quo and helping the middle class adapt to it?*

I just don't feel like *est* is an adaptation. It's not repressive. It's *ex*pressive. When you accept the way it is and go with it, then it gets better. If you didn't have power before, you can get it. Not just power over your own individual life, but power in the system. You become the cause, instead of staying at the effect of it. Adaptation is saying, "Well, that's fate. It's determined," which is like being at effect.

How does that power work? Is it mostly power to change the system or to move up in it? I mean, when you go with it and it gets better, who does it get better for? Yourself? Other people who've already got a piece of the action, or everybody?

For everybody, I'd say, but I'm not sure I follow you, not if you're saying some people actually have more power because of class and money. I used to think that choice was impossible because it was conditioned by that kind of thing. And even more by random events and all the choices you've already made. That's what psychology's all about. It all depends on whether your mother dropped you on your head. You're programmed. Well, *est* accepts that. Everybody's a total robot. That means everybody can be totally free, too. If I accept it, then I'm free to choose. Now I know I can pick myself up by my bootstraps, even if I don't always choose to do it. Before I thought people couldn't do it. Maybe their bootstraps were damaged in infancy or they were lower-class and didn't have any.

OK. What's the difference then between going with it and going for yourself? The radical sees est *telling people that if they change their attitude and put out, they can do a little better for themselves than they're doing now and feel better, too, without changing the basic setup.*

Well, I think that's precisely where we have to start, since that's where we are now. The Revolution hasn't come, and a lot of the people who threw in with it are just the worse for wear now. Werner has talked about beginning with ourselves and coming from service. Forty million people down the road we're gonna see some big changes.

Aspen [Colorado] is a small example of what can happen when you get enough people in one place who've done the training. They're people with power, too. Twenty percent of the year-round population, the entire town council, the police chief. When people share the same experience and assumptions and vocabulary from the training, you get a very high level of communication and agreement. That enables graduates to work together very powerfully.

I experience *est* being concerned with how the society is, although it doesn't talk that much about what the society will look like in the future.

Wouldn't the radical say maybe that's because est *doesn't have any model for the future except more of the same?*

Maybe so, but that's missing the whole point between transforming something and trying to change it.

est advocates a form of "responsible" social participation to a white middle-class constituency that constitutes the majority of the society. It conceives the process of social change according to the paradoxical model of psychological self-transformation. Since it is so expressive, abreactive transformation appears to be a dynamic category distinct from mere adaptation to existing social conditions, whose psychological analogue is repression. Social power derives from psychologically generated personal power. It is exerted toward a utopia suggested more by a hip yet conventionally chic and thriving ski resort than by a communal sect or monastery.

Insofar as graduates' social participation rests on an ethic of subjectively defined self-interest, one can question how responsive they can be to the moral claims of other smaller and less powerful groups that lie beyond the interpersonal pale of face-to-face communication with them and possess interests unshaped by social experience specific to the middle class. *est* rests its ideological rebuttal, first, on the utilitarian assumption that mutual advantage and optimal societal conditions result from the psychologically rational pursuit of self-interest by each person, and the individualist assumption that each person is equally empowered to engage in it. A graduate writes, "Dear Werner, This week while driving around I realized that the world is shaped in such a way as to allow everyone to be on top of it at any given time."[101] The invisible hand extends its reach from the economic to the social-psychological sphere, creating bureaucratic regulations that benefit each and every agent as impartially as do traffic lights. Second, *est* professes a supplementary ethic of compassionate service based on the monistic identification of each individual with every other by reference to the universal *being* they all share. "Transformation of Self as humanity" will make the world work.

est's picture of reality may be highly conceptual for a popular movement, but it is not a conceptual system, either in its eclectic development or its presentation in the training. Its plausibility depends less on its philosophical logic than on the experienced power of the training itself in tandem with the social situation of the trainee. Sixties youth who have taken the *est* training span the middle class in their social background and usually hail from the cities and suburbs of major urban areas. Typically, they identified themselves as members of the counterculture while going to college and for several years afterward, often living during this time in modestly hip, dropout style. Now they have come of age and dropped back into the white-collar work force. Consolidating a career and a "relationship" have become their abiding concerns, both of which call for interpersonal fluency and emotional self-management in the white-collar singles milieu. They call, too, for an end to manifestos of radical social change. The need to make it in the world subdues the aspiration to make it over.

est's ethic responds to the predicament of sixties youth strongly exposed to the expressive values of the counterculture and conventional private life, yet now faced with the instrumental demands of adult middle-class public life. Its psychologized reintegration of personalism and utilitarianism also appeals, with different felt emphases, to older graduates moved by the same contrary cultural impulses. *est* defines what is intrinsically valuable in personalistic categories consonant with countercultural ideals. Then it uses these personally gratifying and expressive ends to justify the routine work and goal achievement of mainstream public life. "Work hard and achieve your goals in order to feel alive and natural," *est* advises in effect. This formula justifies sixties youth in dropping back in to middle-class economic and social life. And it motivates them to lead this life effectively, with an eye to inner satisfaction as well as external success. It also explains these youths' felt difficulty in continuing to be gratified by a countercultural lifestyle that did not fulfill residual middle-class expectations of social status, material comfort and stability, respectable work, emotional security, or the specifically ethical requirement that one must *deserve* feelings of well-being by virtue of first having achieved certain goals.

The counterculture's expressive ethic suited sixties youth experimenting with the possibilities of alternative states of consciousness and community in the expectation of a utopian social order to come. Its surrender was brought on by the disappointment of these expectations due both to changes in the society over a decade and to changes in the sort of life projects implied by passage from youth to adulthood. *est* has eased this passage and this surrender of one ethical outlook for another. Rule-egoism makes sense to the white-collar adult seeking self-fulfillment yet needing to consolidate a career and interpersonal relationships within the existing social order.

SUMMARY AND CONCLUSION
Moral Meaning in a Social Context

What are alternative religious movements about? What do they do? They enable sixties youth to make moral sense of their lives, I have answered, and they synthesize moral meanings important to the larger culture. Neither of these one-line answers has turned out to be as simple as it first sounded, however, for each refers to a complex of changes in religious and moral beliefs, ritual and practical activity, and the social context in which belief and action take form. Alternative religious movements have not overturned tradition and replaced it with something entirely new. Rather they have drawn out strands from traditional moralities and re-woven them into a fabric that ties into American culture as a whole yet differs in pattern from any one of its traditions.

As a romantic successor to modernism, the hip counterculture carried on the iconoclastic injunction to "Make it new!" in more radical form. The attempt to make life new in day-by-day experience and action, not just in art, poses problems for that side of the human condition that calls for order and regularity, for a measure that lasts. Though ever present, this call grows stronger as youth turns toward adulthood, and since the 1960s alternative religions have answered it as the counterculture could not. In doing so, these movements sustain expressive ideals by recombining them with moralities of authority, rules, and utility. Neo-Christian groups recombine the expressive ethic of hip culture with the authoritative ethic of revealed biblical religion, with particular plausibility for the lower middle class. Neo-Oriental groups recombine the expressive ethic with the regular ethic of rationalized religion and humanism, with particular plausibility for the upper middle class. The human potential movement recombines the expressive ethic with the consequential ethic of utilitarian individualism, with particular plausibility for the middle middle class. Such alternative religions are not rehearsing a new version of sixties iconoclasm, aimed at knocking over their predecessor along with its targets. Instead, these movements draw from the old targets of biblical religion, rational humanism, and utilitarian culture itself, as well as from non-Western traditions, in order to synthesize their ethics. In this respect they are *religious* in the literal sense that they bind together heretofore disparate elements within a pluralistic culture, revitalizing tradition as they change it. They are engaged in a constructive process of mediating and recombining existing meanings, not in the sort of prophetic breakthrough that began the great historical religions or triggered modern revolutions.[1] From diverse moral meanings these religions form alternatives to utilitarian culture (or variations of it, in *est*'s case) better adapted to survival within utilitarian society than was the counterculture, because their ideas are more coherent, their movements more stably institutionalized, and their members' lives more regulated.

Let us compare our cases, noting their common characteristics as a class of religious movements that change their converts' moral ideas and their way of life.[2]

CONVERSION AS ETHICAL RECOMBINATION

Alternative religions as a class lay out *a relatively detailed picture of reality* that is *analytically complete in its own terms.* So does every religion and in a more diffuse way every culture. But the typical alternative religious movement is remarkable for how well closed its reality picture is, how solidly it rests upon ritual experience, and in turn how solidly it supports *an explicit, unified ethic.* Norms, values, and moral attitudes are worked out in one piece. What ends are good in themselves? Which acts are right? What personal characteristics are virtuous? Alternative religions transmit coherent answers to these questions, along with clear ideas about what constitutes true selfhood, authority, love, work, and social relations.

The stock answers of utilitarian individualism begin to unravel when its adherent asks, "Why don't I feel happy?" This question presupposes, of course, the individual's right to possess happiness, not merely to pursue it— a shift in American expectations nowhere more dramatically visible than between sixties youth and the generation of their parents. Already possessed of much that money can buy and still unsatisfied, these youths found the meaning of conventional values and their logic of action undercut by the counterculture, which attempted to replace the instrumental values of wealth, power, and technical knowledge with the ultimate values of love and self-awareness. It sought to fill the subjective form of happiness left empty by utilitarianism with the expressive content of its own deeper feelings and closer intimacy with others and nature. It sought to intuit right action from whatever expressed one's inner self and fit the situation here and now, instead of calculating it from future costs and benefits to maximize want satisfaction. Yet these expressive alternatives, too, proved unable to stand up to experience on their own terms. "Money can't buy you love," it is true, but that doesn't mean that "love is all you need." You also need moral rules to live by, authority to respect, and contracts to keep— even to sustain your love. Alternative religions resolve this predicament by recombining elements of its opposed romantic, biblical, and utilitarian sides into unified ethics. By mapping out moralities of loving authority, antinomian rules, and rule-egoism through the middle of a conflicted culture, alternative religions have saved sixties youth caught between the devils of self-interest, law-and-order authority, and heartless rules on one side and the deep blue sea of boundless self-expression on the other.

As represented by the LWF, the conservative Christian offers a radically authoritative answer to the utilitarian question, "Why don't I feel happy?"—"Because you are sinning," he answers. "You are disobeying God's will, because you have turned away from God and are being possessed by the devil." By repenting his sins and being ritually reborn as a child of God, a person comes to recognize God's love and power to command right acts. An authoritative theory of right replaces a consequential theory: that act is right in itself which God commands. Good consequences follow on doing right acts. They do not define right acts. Obey God's will and then you will be a good person. As an aftereffect, affirms the Christian, you will feel good. Seek only to make yourself feel good, and then you will disobey God and be an evil person. Thus a theory of good follows on an authoritative theory of right. Relativism is rejected. God's will is read as an absolute in scripture, likewise proclaimed by the pastor, and recognized by the church as an orthodox unit.

At the same time, the Christian's authoritative ethic embraces expressive elements. He experiences the goodness of an intimately personal Jesus in ecstatic rites, responds to him with love, and follows him with gladness. Religious faith is the necessary condition of moral virtue. One must know and love God within a given church, and intend to obey him in order to do right. Sect members obey God because God is good but, finally, because God is God. They imitate the loving example of Jesus out of love for him. This morality of expressive aspiration based on love intertwines with a morality of regular obligation based on a covenant of reciprocal duties and rights between God and sect members as "God's chosen people." If they keep this covenant, God will reward them with everlasting life. If they break it, he will punish them with death.

The Zen student shares the deontological structure but not the content of the Christian answer to the utilitarian question, "Why do I feel unhappy?"—"Because you cannot get what you want," he answers. "You cannot satisfy your desires because by the very nature of desire they are inexhaustible and insatiable." He proposes practicing Zen according to its orthopractical rules in order to bring release from desires and so from suffering. In the course of such practice a regular theory of right replaces a consequential one. Release from suffering as the good consequence that makes acts right becomes release from delusion as the good state of consciousness that arises from acting rightly, that is, in accord with rules that follow the nature of reality. What does the Zen student advise us, then? Practice Zen (according to its rules) and you will become a good person who naturally acts rightly (as the precepts describe). Thus a theory of good both follows from and leads into a regular theory of right.

Zen's regular ethic can resolve itself into expressive terms. Acts are right or wrong in themselves, and they are so specified by moral precepts. Ultimately, however, acts appropriate to the moment arise directly from the ideal agent's non-attached state of mind and feeling of compassion for others and life itself. The good person, idealized by the Bodhisattva and embodied by the Zen master, feels and acts intuitively in response to the situation, as did the ideal hippie. But now the agent's feelings are shaped by meditation and monastic life. Through this experience his actions come to reflect the true nature of existence as an "inconceivable" unity. Moral relativism is rejected, albeit within a paradoxical dialectic that both recognizes moral rules and calls for non-attachment to them.

As represented by *est*, the human potential movement offers an analysis of the question "Why don't I feel happy?" within the consequential logic of utilitarian moral argument. Persons don't feel happy because they haven't figured out what they "really" want, which are experiences of aliveness and satisfaction in themselves. They mistake conventional "symbols of success" (i.e., traditional utilities) for these feelings of well-being. They try to manipulate themselves and others as mechanically insensitive objects in order to maximize the objective utilities they possess. Psychological self-clarification will enable persons to realize their full potential by identifying their real subjective interests and those of others. Then they can act directly to maximize their own felt well-being by playing for aliveness, and they can contract more effectively with others to do likewise. The human potential movement brings to bear a more subtle psychology on the utilitarian theory of good and further subjectivizes it: what is good in itself is experiencing aliveness, not having money. The human potential movement meanwhile retains utilitarianism's consequential theory of right: that act is right which yields the most good consequences to its agent.

Thus *est* merges an expressive theory of good with a consequential theory of right, in which rules play an instrumental part. Acts of rule compliance and agreement keeping are right because they enable the agent to achieve her goals and thereby feel aliveness. The expressive value of self-fulfillment justifies following the bureaucratic rules that govern the instrumental activity of middle-class adult life. The *est* training demonstrates that situations are governed by rules. To respond appropriately to the situation, therefore, is to internalize and intuitively follow its rules. Since bureaucratic regulations are situationally variable, *est* upholds a relativism that resembles the expressive ethic. *est* squares hip self-expression with the bureaucratic constraints of rule-egoism by positing that each person's subjective consciousness determines her experience, including her experience of rules. The omnicausal individual takes responsibility for the social rules that bind her by acknowledging herself as their cause and complying with them as a means to satisfy her own wants. She likewise engages others: individuals are to intuit their own subjective wants, empathically communicate them to each other, and then make contractual agreements that will serve the self-interest of each and will, therefore, be kept by both. In these ways *est* personalizes utilitarian exchange, while it invests rules and expressive values with utility.

CONVERSION AS A CHANGE OF HEART, MIND, AND WAY OF LIFE

Alternative religions change the ethical outlook of those who have adopted their teachings. They also change the experience and social situation of those who have joined their movements. These other changes give plausibility to the moral ideas that justify them. They fit into the biographical and social facts of converts' lives, often in fine detail. Yet for all its wealth of detail, the picture our case studies paint of getting saved from the sixties has a single discernible outline. It is one that departs at certain critical points from the conventional lines of American culture. At those points it signals more widely spread tension and movement in the culture, centered around the effort to mediate between its utilitarian and personalist impulses. Let us review the changes in experience, social relations, work, and politics that alternative religion has fostered in sixties youth from these three perspectives: the moral ideas they support, the biographical facts they fit, and the cultural trends they signal.

Ecstatic Experience

The LWF translates the disorienting psychedelic ecstasies of hip "dopers" into the devotional ritual ecstasy of Pentecostal Christians. Its doctrine interprets ecstatic ritual experiences, which validate the divine moral authority represented by the sect's pastor. For youths raised in lower-middle-class homes strong on authority, hip self-surrender to experience becomes Christian self-surrender to authority, and intuitive hip acceptance of moral truth as given by inner feelings becomes faithful Christian acceptance of moral truth as given by divine authority. Zen Center translates the solipsistic ecstasy of psychedelic seekers into a meditational enstasy that anchors monist beliefs, orthopractical rules, and moral precepts compatible with the humanism of their upper-middle-class families. Zen teachings, in turn, interpret the experience of meditation and elaborate a regimented monastic community around it. *est*'s abreactive "processes" guide the middle class through emotion-laden fantasies, thus offering modest psychodramatic facsimiles of drug experience to clients with comparably modest drug histories as sixties youth. *est* thereby confirms that the individual's subjective consciousness determines his experience. It does so without dissolving the discrete integrity of the experiencing agent (as do neo-Oriental groups) or fixing him in relation to a cosmic absolute (as do neo-Christian groups).

As a class, then, alternative religious movements of the seventies make *a directly experiential impact* on their members. Members do not *have* these experiences. Instead these experiences take hold of them: tongues "speak" the speaker; zazen "breathes" the breather; even the *est* training "takes you on a roller coaster ride." This results in *a softening up of the self* marked off as a unit by utilitarian culture. The hard edges of individualism, philosophical realism, and technical reason blur under the experiential impact of alternative religions. They conceive the self fought over by God and Satan, dissolved in the monist interdependence of Buddha mind, or divided and multiplied by the ambivalence of psychological forces. These religions take the individual self as subject separated from a world of utilitarian objects "out there," and they inextricably *relate or rejoin the self to the rest of reality.* The Christian's individual soul is created by God and remains God's "child." The Buddhist's "Big Self" is identical with "Buddha mind." The "being" of each *est* graduate is fused with all existence, and her social-psychological interests are interrelated with those of others. In *est* this interrelation remains formulated, however ambiguously, in the language of individual wants that justify contractual obligations. But in the neo-Christian and neo-Oriental groups rejoining the self to the rest of reality triggers an unambiguous ethical turnabout: the subjective and inexhaustible wants of individual persons give way to the objective (not merely collective) and therefore limited needs of persons in groups. Life is no longer a matter of wanting more and pursuing it, but rather of recognizing what is enough and accepting it.

Whether they consist of Christian tongue-speaking, Zen meditation, or *est* processes, alternative religions induce vivid experiences by ritual methods and use these experiences to anchor the teachings that interpret them. Rites induce experiences. Experiences prove teachings. Teachings interpret experiences. This circle of reciprocally reinforcing links is stronger in alternative religions than in conventional middle-class religion or culture, enabling them to overcome the conventional opposition between *ecstatic experience* and *technical reason.* In this way alternative religions carry ecstatic experience over into devotional, meditational, and psychodramatic ritual forms that reintegrate ecstasy into ordinary life. Through ritual modulation, ecstatic experience takes on ethical meaning in these movements and thereby comes to motivate their members to engage responsibly in practical pursuits. Experiencing and accepting the world instead of trying to control it remains a central theme in alternative religions. But they also justify diligently organized activity in the world to obey God, express compassion, or play for aliveness.

Social Relations

To street youths disillusioned by lovers lost to impulse and friends to circumstance, the Christian sect provides love and acceptance, friends and a spouse within a tightly regulated community. Social acceptance hinges on the moral choice to "decide for Jesus" and obey sect rules, not on external success or inner feelings. The sect controls courtship and reconciles youths to marriage and parenting. The sect's age integration smooths compromise by sixties youths with their elders and with conventional public behavior. The acceptability of the Christian ethic of work and love to the larger society allows sect youths to engage it more easily as Christians than as hippies, even as the sect sustains their alienation from utilitarian culture.

To college-educated youths relatively independent of friends and uncommitted to lovers, Zen Center provides acceptance and a side-by-side sort of intimacy, companions, and eventually lovers. It does so within a residential community regulated against intentional injury or deception but allowing a wide variety of interpersonal behavior and relationships, and transitions back and forth among them. It accommodates serious coupling, marriage, and children. It accepts divorce, supports single life, and respects celibacy. Social acceptance is based on dedication to meditation practice and commitment to monastic life, reinforced by the housekeeping interdependence of that life. Zen Center's own age integration and its teaching of nonjudgmental compassion for others eases relations among sixties youth and their elders. So does the diligent work and frugal way of life its ethic prescribes.

est's organization as a bureaucratic cult works no structural changes on the social relations of its clients (staff excepted), who remain living in the associational mainstream of urban society. *est*'s ethic adapts the middle class to the fluidity of their relationships there by using a cost-benefit calculus to assess interpersonal relationships for the felt well-being they offer the individual. *est* provides therapeutic techniques to give the individual the emotional fluency necessary to enact these calculations. Social relations do not rest on common tasks and goals but rather on the reciprocal exchange of instrumental support in achieving individual goals. The search for interpersonal satisfaction in middle-class private life is adapted to the bureaucratic conditions of public life that impinge upon it.

Alternative religions as a class *reconstitute community as the context of personal and social identity.* They soften the idea of the self as a unitized counterpart of the state and a cog in the mass machinery of utilitarian society, and they reconnect it to a more organic whole. The Christian rejoins his divine Father in the fellowship of the sect. The Zen student realizes his oneness with all existence in the sangha. The *est* graduate encounters others in the training, empathically joining them in a momentary community of two. The Christian sect knits its member families into a cohesive group of neighbors, coworkers, co-owners, of common property, and mutual providers of social services. Zen Center generates a similarly cohesive community, where the monastery not only frames but often replaces the family as the basis of social organization. Individuals remain discrete in *est* but they all come under one set of rules, one authority, and a single contract that links their feelings as well as their external interests.

Sect, monastery, and bureaucratic cult all possess an institutional rigor with an unmistakably moral quality to it. Each movement creates a world governed by detailed, clear-cut rules. Each engenders strict compliance with those rules and close agreement on certain values and goals. In the Christian sect and Zen monastery the rules take the form of categorical imperatives ("Do x."). There are objective values and common substantive goals. In *est* the rules take the form of hypothetical imperatives ("If you want to experience aliveness, do *x*."). There are contractually interlocking subjective values, and each person supports the other in reaching her own individual goals. These movements have also created stable forms of organization and authority that turn hip impulse into more reliable social virtues. Love and good vibes jell into Christian charity, Buddhist compassion-gratitude, and *est's* agreement to support powerful relationships.

For all their stability, however, alternative religions see their members engaged in an ongoing process of self-transformation, whether it be Christian perfection, Zen enlightenment, or *est* transformation. These organizations create a communal confluence of feeling, intuition, and will among their members that recalls the counterculture's ideal of society as an organism. They do so not by liberating individuals from conventional social roles and rules but by unifying private life, work, and interpersonal relations within a single system of moral meanings. They offer communal settings in which sixties youth can discover intimacy, reciprocity, and cooperation growing up in the middle of ordered work and public life, instead of undercutting them. In the sect or monastery all relationships are taken to be deeply and diffusely valuable, and all individuals are taken to have the same sort of status. Both social relations and status are based on moral virtue rather than occupational skills or personal attractiveness. Members of a single group fill and rotate different social roles. These roles are delimited and connected by function, but individuals are assigned to them by prophetic or communal agencies, instead of earning them directly by technical merit. In the encounter of two individuals, which *est* holds up as the paradigmatic social situation, different social roles and statuses all follow from a single psychological dynamic of communication and contractual agreement, whose outcome each participant sees herself creating.

In alternative religions diverse social roles remain secondary to an explicitly religious master role—the faithful sect minister, the compassionate Zen monk, the responsible, at-cause *est* graduate. These master roles secure the personal integrity of the individual in ideal form and motivate him to engage secondary roles as extensions of this master role, instead of playing them tongue in cheek in order to defend the integrity of his purely private self. Alternative religions thus loosen the role-playing dichotomy between private and public life in modern society, even when they locate the religious master role "in but not of" modern society. The leaders who exemplify these master roles are charismatic figures. Unlike bureaucratic or ritual office holders, they act as moral exemplars. They embody the norms, values, and virtues of alternative religions to their members. They make the ethic so entirely their own and they so give themselves to it that the gap between moral ideal and actual life appears to close. So, too, does the gap between virtuous personal character and legitimate social authority. The ethic exemplified seems to reach inside the outer, public surface of the leader's vocation to permeate his inner character. His followers see in him living proof that the ideals of a virtuous person and of a truly human society can be realized through each other.

In these ways alternative religions mediate the opposition between countercultural *holism* and the *analytic discrimination* of mainstream culture, while carrying on the counterculture's effort to unify all of life. First, they seek to reunite self and (a)cosmic other in ritual experience. Second, they seek to unify the diversity of modern meaning in a complete picture of reality and a comprehensive ethic capable of spanning intrumental work and expressive private life within an all-encompassing ideal of personality embodied by an exemplary leader. Third, they seek to reunify social roles and relations divided by modernization, either by regathering all of them into communal groups or personalizing all of them through social-psychological encounter. At the same time, alternative religions uphold deontological or contractual ethics that discriminate practically between right and wrong conduct in various kinds of relationships. Their members behave more reliably in specific roles than hippies ever did. They pay their creditors, satisfy their employers, keep their personal promises, and make their business appointments. In short, they fit in better as functionally related components of a complex society, but they do so more by virtue of their ethical convictions than their technical skills.

Education, Work, and Status

To hip youths who failed in school, dropped out of it early, and now work with their hands, the LWF justifies rejection of higher education as "worldly knowledge" that leads to moral corruption. Instead it engages in Bible study devoted to "spiritual knowledge" that endows the present with moral purpose and the future with millennial power. Zen "students" see their practice fulfilling a personalist ideal of education as an avenue of inner meaning and awareness. They held this ideal as upper-middle-class youths and found it unmet in their elite conventional schooling, which they came to reject. To middle-class youths who simply got through school instead of excelling or failing at it and who now find the abstract knowledge of their nonelite schooling to have little status and less practical use in their nonprofessional jobs, *est* offers self-help "data" in "seminars" that train "graduates" to "experience life more effectively."

To lower-middle-class youths who rejected conventional work and pursued countercultural careers in vain, the Christian sect justifies blue-collar work, motivates its reliable performance, and provides sacred careers that compensate for it. It justifies following orders on the job in order to obey God, regardless of the work's intrinsic meaning or prestige, to youths who feel their jobs lack both meaning and prestige. Zen Center justifies monastic labor to youths who have rejected the professional or executive careers of their parents on countercultural grounds. Within an ethic of this-worldly mysticism, all work becomes spiritual practice and service to others, the key link between meditation and everyday life. It stands severed from the rewards of consumption and leisure or prestige and achievement. A good job is one that offers a good opportunity for Zen practice, inverting the conventional hierarchy of headwork to handwork, permanent to temporary, and lucrative to subsistence work. *est* puts private emotions and expressive behavior to public use to manage interpersonal relations in white-collar work, while complying with the bureaucratic rules that govern it. *est* justifies work as a self-fulfilling game to college-educated sixties youths unconvinced that bureaucratic work has any intrinsic worth, yet faced with the need to perform it to make a living.

The LWF provides its lower-class members secure intrasect status and explicit status superiority to outside society. Both rest on moral rectitude and distinctive cultural values, not on job, education, or income. These same grounds earlier anchored the countercultural sense of moral superiority which sect members experienced as sixties youth. Zen Center provides secure status within a monastic community and implicit status superiority or independence in relation to the society outside. Both are based on commitment to meditation and monastic life. This is consistent with the status these youths enjoyed earlier as members of an educational and cultural elite who rejected conventional careers and their rewards. *est* gives its nonelite graduates a sense of gnostic superiority over outsiders and a loose sense of ideological if not social solidarity among themselves, based on sharing an enlightened state of awareness. *est* teaches techniques of poised self-presentation and directive face-to-face interaction that express such superiority to others in the behavioral lingua franca of the white-collar singles scene.

Alternative religions as a class, then, *rejustify the need to work* without insisting on the values of wealth, power, or social standing derived from work. Christians labor to obey God, provide for their families, and support their church. Zen students labor or do service work to follow their spiritual practice, serve others, and support themselves with "just enough." *est* graduates play the game of white-collar work to achieve experiences of individual well-being and to assist others. Such aims and values keep sixties youth at work despite their disillusionment with the traditional work ethic and their continued interest in expressive self-fulfillment. These alternative ethics also salve frustrated hopes for occupational importance and rewards. These are often held residually by youths who grew up in an era of booming affluence and now face downward social mobility, or none at all, in an era of economic constriction. But alternative religions do not simply compensate for shortfalls in conventional status. They reinterpret social success in terms of unconventional values that make work worth doing and make a place in society worth working for.

The middle course that alternative religions cut between countercultural attitudes of *acceptance* and the mainstream's *problem-solving activism* is clearest in regard to work and status. Usually located on the middle rungs of the job ladder with a chance to move up slightly, the *est* graduate accepts his job and the entire world of work as his own psychic creation and he complies with socially given rules in order to transform both for the better. He works to gain goods and advancement, but he sees such gains only as instrumental goals he himself has chosen on his undriven way to experiencing aliveness. Fixed in a blue-collar job with little chance of moving up, the sectarian Christian puts his work, like all life's problems, into God's hands. He knows its discontents come from the conflict of divine and demonic agencies and that, therefore, only God can resolve them. The millennial sect discourages careerism and individual achievement by casting work as each man's duty to obey God, while assuring him that God will reward his obedience by a radically moral redistribution of power at the apocalypse, when the faithful will inherit the earth.

Attitudes of acceptance among Zen students begin in the meditational experience of sitting through discomfort and desire and letting them come and go instead of acting directly to alleviate or satisfy them. Yet the meditator must give continuous attention to the process of sitting itself, which seeks to resolve the very problem of his own life (*genjo koan*). For educated youths who typically reject professional and bureaucratic work, or make it over in the monastery, Zen locates self-expression within monastic labor instead of leaving it as the hip alternative to work or the utilitarian reward for it. The Zen student works for just enough to live on, not for maximal profit or prestige. Rather than expanding the pie of economic goods, his ecological monism implies that activism should aim instead at trimming the pie's edges, equalizing its pieces, and assuring its future with greater care. Neo-Oriental religions in general espouse an attitude of mystical non-attachment and an ethic of compassionate service that call for working to help others rather than to advance one's own career.

Politics

The Christian sect makes a millenarian promise to sixties youths disappointed that neither radicals nor drugs transformed society in the sixties.

It offers symbolic political power to the powerless ex-hippie and the power-less lower middle class. It also gives them a proleptically moral and cooperative countercommunity in which to live until the millennial day arrives. The millenarian sect thus symbolizes the moral criticism, not merely the resentment, of its members toward the larger society. It reconciles them to living in that society for the present, and it sustains their faith in a radically different future. Zen Center offers its members the exemplary political power of a monastic community designed around eco-monist principles to set before an ecologically troubled society. It also gives them the chance to work in small-scale programs of neighborhood organization and improvement involving minorities and the poor. This appeals to youths concerned with social change yet unwilling to accept antagonistic conflict, pursue professional careers, or forego self-study in order to seek it. Zen Center enables these youths to live with the conventional society as they seek to influence its future course by living out an alternative to it.

est applies an abreactive model of psychological change to social institutions. One must accept the social system as it is, acknowledge oneself as its cause, and participate in it according to its rules in order to change it. This formula for social change from the inside out is compatible with the relatively conventional middle-class careers *est* youths are dropping back into. *est* discredits the politics of liberal reform, radical protest, and hip withdrawal to youths who feel disappointed with such efforts and unable to continue them. It promises that millennial social change is already under-way, as evidenced by its growing mass membership and its influence on conventional institutions of socialization. It invites its graduates to assist as volunteers in its work. *est* individualistically holds each person totally responsible for herself, and it monistically holds each person responsible for everyone else. The individual begins to take responsibility for others by "assisting" each of them in taking total responsibility for herself.

Alternative religions as a class proclaim or at least imply *a moral vision of society as a whole.* This vision is related to the exemplary image of their own ethic and organization. The experience of participating in these movements suggests to their members what social life in general can become. None of these movements has a comprehensive, concrete political program. But virtually all of them have a symbolic politics that relates their present organization and activity to the process of radically changing society for the better. All of them do something specific to give substance to their symbolic politics. The Christian sect is building and stocking an apocalyptic refuge in the mountains, while its members take loving care of one another in the present. Pacific Zen Center is working out an ecologically sound communal life, complete with such appropriate technology as windmills and compost toilets. *est* is delivering its trainings in prisons, and publicizing the idea that it is now possible to end world hunger in twenty years.

Each movement sees the society to come in explicitly moral terms. *est* perceives society already perfecting its contractual structure along lines that will yield greater personal fulfillment to its individual members through the greater efficiency of their collective efforts. The Christian sect awaits a theocratic state ruled by divinely revealed commands. Zen Center looks forward to an ecotopia whose natural-law-like principles are recognizable to all. The very existence of such symbolic politics in alternative religions points to the residual political concern of the sixties youth who belong to these movements. The indirect linkage between what these youths are now doing and the society's future transformation reflects their disillusionment with direct attempts at radical social change during the 1960s. To depict alternative religions as simply siphoning off would-be political activists or "cooling out" the politically disaffected oversimplifies the peculiar relationship of political concern and disillusionment in these sixties youths and, they would say, it oversimplifies the nature of social change itself. Few of the members of alternative religious movements committed themselves to radical political organizations or programs in the sixties, while now they see themselves as working for social change in the most effective ways possible. At least for them, if not for many of its other followers as well, the counterculture turned out to be less political than it once appeared and more religious than they once thought.

In the symbolic integrity of their political visions, alternative religions show their ability to find the sort of *intuitive certainty* the counterculture sought in the midst of the *pluralistic relativism* of modern society. These movements make singular sense out of the modern diversity of social worlds and their meaning. The Christian sect sweeps aside the many sectors of a differentiated society as morally irrelevant. Instead it divides the social world into two ethically armed camps, the society as a whole and the sect itself, one in thrall to the devil and the other in service to God. This division will culminate, it prophesies, in an apocalyptic battle and, afterwards, in the world's millennial reunification. One biblical God has created one world and each soul within it in his own image. The many remain, but they begin and end in the One. Their communion is to be lived out each day in the community of Christian love.

The possibility of an eco-millennial unification of society in the future is hinted at by some Zen students, while in the present diverse social meanings converge into the monastic *sangha* as an image for all of society, and into practice as a way of living all of life. Both can be generalized into any formal social setting, students believe, and both can be acted on without restructuring the setting. The lack of fixed content in the activity of meditation and in the figure of the monk-in-the-world accompany an ideological thrust to empty social structure and form itself of meaning. A verse much favored by Zen students advises:

> *As stars, a fault of vision, as a lamp,*
> *A mock show, dew drops, or a bubble,*
> *A dream, a lightning flash, or cloud,*
> *So should one view what is conditioned.*[3]

Through such renunciation a world of many things and many social realities becomes one.

est proposes that life is a game. It accepts the diversity of form and rules that obtain in the various games that appear to go on in a differentiated society. But it offers the training as a complete model for the rules of life. If all of life is a game and all of society is the *est* training, then differentiation arises with the different subjective forms that individuals' interests take and the different psychodramatic expressions they give to their interests—all within a procedurally uniform and objective bureaucratic social structure. Furthermore, the psychological dynamic that drives each self-interested individual is universal to all of them. Therefore, no stranger is unfamiliar to the *est* graduate, no personality is opaque to his ability to "profile" its interests. "There's nobody out there," *est* advises. Nobody, that is, but yourself.

Prospects for the Spread of Alternative Religious Ethics

Members of alternative religions usually see their movements as models for the entire society to follow in the future. What prospects *do* these models of understanding and organization have of spreading through the larger society? By what indicators can we assess their prospects? National statistics for involvement in alternative religions show a "continuing interest in the inner or spiritual life" into the 1980s, which has grown modestly since 1976.[4] In 1979 the percentages of Americans participating ranged from 22 percent in Bible study groups to 1 or 2 percent in "Mysticism" and "Eastern Religion," with those in neo-Oriental and human potential movements still tending to be college-educated young adults living in urban coastal areas. A qualitative clue to the prospects of alternative religions is the extent to which their ethics fit with and depend on out-of-the-ordinary social arrangements. There is a tight fit between the moral ideas of each movement and its social arrangements, the evidence reviewed below suggests, and some of these arrangements differ markedly from the ordinary social situation of nonmembers. This seems to limit the possibilities for diffusion of neo-Christian, neo-Oriental, and human potential ethics through American society in the undiluted forms they take within the movements described. But, I will argue in the following sections, such limits do not preclude these moral ideas exerting a strong if indirect influence throughout American culture.

The biblical ethic of the LWF depends on the conviction that there exists a personal God, all-powerful and all-good, who has created all persons, loves them, and uniformly commands them how to live. Communal rites engender immediate experience supporting this conviction. Sectarian social closure insulates its orthodoxy from the larger society's relativism. The pastor interprets God's will as revealed through scripture and visions. Conversely, close affective ties among sect members exemplify God's love, cement their agreement over the content of God's will, and underpin the pastor's authority to interpret it. The injunction to "Love thy neighbor as thyself" makes the most literal sense in face-to-face communal relationships like the sect's. Such diffuse relationships give social substance to the LWF's all-encompassing and absolutely relational definition of personhood: being "a child of God" among "your brothers and sisters in the Lord." The moral integrity of this definition comes from replacing the individual's subjective desires with cosmically and communally objective commands as the source of moral action. Instead of trying to make out his own wants and satisfy them, the individual looks with others to God's commands and obeys them. Freedom *from* restraint in a utilitarian society where the good remains as relative and varied as individuals' desires, becomes freedom *to* do the right act in a sectarian community where God reveals it uniformly. The social integrity of this definition of personhood as a child of God comes from regathering social roles and norms fragmented in the larger society and uniting them within a single "forever family" of coworkers and worshipers, neighbors, students, and spouses. Sectarian social organization, in sum, both follows on and maintains an authoritative ethic.

It follows that resurgence of an authoritative Christian ethic across American society can occur only with the revitalization and growth of congregational if not sectarian organizations. For they carry the sort of powerful ritual experience, affective communal ties, and prophetic leadership such an ethic requires. Evidence for the development of such organizations can be found in the recent resurgence of Evangelical, Pentecostal, and Fundamentalist churches, and the growth of charismatic movements within liberal Protestant and Roman Catholic churches. Such churches are far more traditional and socially adaptive than the LWF, in part because they allow for more outside social involvement and more ambitious work, while keeping ecstatic rites and millennial politics in tighter check. In these churches, personal experience of Jesus and belief in divinely revealed moral commandments have gained middle-class respectability outside their longtime rural and regional strongholds.[5]

Zen's ethic of antinomian rules relies on the collectively disciplined practice of meditation for the experience of non-attachment and compassion that leads to appropriate action. Zen's moral example comes across in face-to-face relationships among students and between student and master. The regimen of a monastic community generates rules to order the whole of everyday life, rites to establish its attitudinal texture, and social boundaries to protect its orthopraxy from deviant behavior. The monastic regimen bears out Zen's ethical assumption that persons continually face obligatory moral choices and responsibilities for one another that reflect their objective needs, not their subjective wants. The monastery bell rings, and everyone should respond as prescribed, whether or not each wants to. The monastery's housekeeping interdependence and its diffuse relationships allow for expressive resolution of disagreements. Negative liberty from restraints on satisfying individual wants turns into positive liberty to do the right act through the experience of meditating and living according to set rules.

In these various respects, the full impact of American Zen's ethic requires a monastic organization built around daily meditation and relationship to a master. As such it is likely to remain the province of relatively small numbers of monks, now little more than a thousand nationwide. But larger numbers meditate regularly in nonresidential groups or by themselves. They may meet with a master or hear a lecture on occasion, and they are usually familiar with Zen literature in English. The institutional location of these persons (in the arts, education, ecology, psychotherapy and the human potential movement, liberal denominations, and Catholic religious orders) will continue to give them a part in spreading Zen's ethic. To whom? To a larger and looser third circle of upper-middle-class urbanites for whom Zen's ethic stands as a personal ideal more thought-about than ritually practiced, and so more expressive and less regular in effect than it is for the monastic. For collective, meditation-based movements like Zen Buddhism, the greater the influence of monastic core groups on their wider circle of lay members, the greater ethical emphasis orthopractical rules will receive in relation to antinomian intuition.

Similar concentric circles of influence characterize other neo-Oriental religious groups, oriented either to meditation (e.g., Tibetan Buddhism) or to devotion to a guru (e.g., Meher Baba and Baba Muktananda). Many of these other groups rely less on monastic organization and seem more suited to developing a mass lay membership than does Zen.[6] How effectively they do develop as lay religions will be a key factor in the spread of neo-Oriental monist ethics. Perhaps so will the development of movements like TM which teach meditation techniques without direct reference to Oriental religions or ethics. They usually imply a monist view of the world that may carry over into intentions towards harmonious cooperation with others and service to them. But their monism may also be subsumed into a consequential ethic like *est*'s rule-egoism. This is particularly the case for the clients of such movements who respond to overt advertising or implicit promises of meditation's power as a technique to control stress and tension symptoms, and to increase ego performance in bureaucratic work, education, and interpersonal relations.

To establish felt conviction in its tenets, especially the principle that each person's consciousness determines her experience, *est*'s ethic requires the sort of temporary control over setting, behavior, and mood that the training offers. Beyond this the main requirements for *est*'s plausibility are met by middle-class urban life. Participants must feel the weight of bureaucratic regulation and the utilitarian rewards of bearing that weight, if they are to see themselves as creating the rules of life and gaining self-fulfillment through keeping them. The personal mobility and economic security of the white-collar singles milieu lend plausibility to *est*'s laissez faire individualism. So does *est*'s own organization as a bureaucratized cult with permeable boundaries and a mass clientele, mirroring the society around it instead of contrasting with it—as do the sect and monastery. Having to manage others and one's own emotions in bureaucratic work creates the need, which *est* answers, to put private feelings to public use and to calculate the costs and benefits of interpersonal relationships. Residual self-identification with America's white middle-class majority grounds acceptance of *est*'s political vision of "transubstantiating" society without changing its external structure. The tenet that each individual is totally responsible for herself yet responsible for every other being seems less puzzling to urban singles outside the mediating structures of family and community. For they find themselves on their own yet surrounded by a mass society presided over by the state, which is itself responsible for everyone (the welfare state) and no one (the laissez faire state), a state which in theory rests on their consent yet in practice proceeds without their active participation.

The growing influence of *est*'s ethic, unlike the neo-Christian and neo-Oriental ethics, does not depend on ongoing communal organizations as carriers. Although *est*'s staff shows many of the signs of a sectarian movement, the training is packaged and delivered by the bureaucratic methods of a sales-management or public-relations firm. *est* relies on each generation of its clients to recruit the next generation. Their success in doing so reflects the power of the training to interpret the conditions of urban middle-class singles life, where each individual, on his own from adolescence through middle age, negotiates the passages of his life from job to job, place to place, spouse to spouse, and lover to lover. It follows that the influence of rule-egoism will grow with the spread of these social conditions and with the recession of family, church, and related institutions that support moral authority, obligation, and self-expression within communal contexts. Will middle age and increased marriage among sixties youth lessen their loyalty to rule-egoism? Probably not, if the 40 percent of *est* graduates already over thirty-five and their high rates of divorce, remarriage, and job change are any indication. Will subsequent generations of middle-class youth, less exposed to countercultural values, prove less receptive to *est*'s pop monist and mystical tenets? Possibly, but *est*'s appeal lies in making mysticism the ally of a pragmatic common sense that seems common enough among post-sixties youth.

CULTURAL CHANGE IN A MODERNIZED SOCIETY

As long as the structure of American society continues to revolve around technological production, bureaucratic organization, and a massed urban population, outright rejections of the instrumental behavior rationalized by utilitarian culture are likely to flourish only within small subcultures or for short periods in the life cycle of their carriers. Otherwise adult Americans must respond to the practical demands exerted on them by the modernized society in which they live. Yet they must also respond to the integrity of meaning exerted by the different moral traditions with which they think. In this double-edged process, members of alternative religious movements carry nonutilitarian perceptions, assumptions, loyalties, and styles of evaluation out into a utilitarian culture that absorbs these contrary elements even as it dilutes and makes them over. Awareness, too, becomes a commodity to be merchandised for consumption. The good becomes still another goodie. Yet in the process the goodness of experience becomes less identified with the good *things* of life. The possession of happiness and the unrestrained freedom to pursue it become more elusive not only in fact but in meaning. This process of reciprocal cultural change will go on as long as utilitarian culture cannot justify by itself the dedicated work, cooperative behavior, and distributive justice that its political and social structure requires. It will continue, too, as long as utilitarian culture cannot symbolize the enchantment the human mind finds in the world around and within itself.[7] Alternative cultural views will inevitably rise up against the current of the utilitarian mainstream. They will be swept up in it and will influence its course in turn.

If the external conditions necessary to balance the production and consumption cycles of utilitarian society (for example, only moderate scarcity of energy, resources, and middle-class employment) should sharply deteriorate, whether for ecological, geopolitical, or economic reasons, then the utopian visions of alternative religions could conceivably inform deep changes in American's social structure as well as its culture. For the present, however, alternative religious movements influence the culture more directly than they influence the society's structure. They reintegrate the meaning of social life for sixties youth more directly than they reintegrate them into society. The cultural changes carried by alternative religions do help sixties youth adapt to adulthood in conventional society, but they also enable their alternative visions of that society to endure within it.

In some regards these movements find alternative grounds to justify conventional patterns of response to existing structures of opportunity: play the "game" of work for inner self-fulfillment; marry and raise a family to prepare for the millennium; leave off political struggle because "you are one with your opponent." But in other regards these movements back unconventiontal patterns of response to conventional job, education, housing, and other opportunities: live alone or coupled in a communal setting, serve people instead of a career, work on and off to buy time instead of things and space, learn from a master instead of a professor. In both of these ways alternative religious movements may signal wider trends in our culture.

Unconventional lifestyle patterns have begun to stake their public claims to normalcy, especially in metropolitan areas like San Francisco and its suburbs.[8] But in Des Moines, too, sixties youth have carried expressive lifestyles from the counterculture into mainstream institutions.[9] Having dropped back in and begun to interact as adults with their elders, they have introduced other generations to new attitudes toward marriage, work, and politics (not to mention sex, drugs, and dress). Meanwhile, more structural changes are underway. The stable, intact nuclear family with a working husband and a wife at home with the kids has ceased to be the modal household unit.[10] Indeed, only an estimated 7 percent of all American households now fit this pattern.[11] Singles, those "living with someone" or divorced, childless marriages, working women, and women with children and without husbands have all increased. Greater equality of opportunity for women and minorities since the sixties has enabled more persons to compete more equally for the rewards of the marketplace. This has stimulated utilitarian individualism and also strained its freemarket model of society on two fronts. First, economic dependence no longer reinforces marital stability so strongly. Working women are freer to lead lives of their own and negotiate egalitarian relationships with others, a fact with important implications for changing patterns of marriage, divorce, fertility, and child rearing. Second, if any competitor in the marketplace is to get a bigger piece of an economic pie trimmed by stagflation, her gain must come at the expense of someone else. This means that the key political value of equality comes under mounting pressure to shift, at least partly, from equality of opportunity to get ever more to equality of results pegged on a generalizable determination of just how much *enough* amounts to. This in turn means that some if not all persons must lessen their expectations, whether it is those with the biggest or the smallest belts who must tighten them the most.[12]

Changes in household formation and the family are tied to changes in the world of work. The labor force directly involved in industrial production keeps shrinking in relation to technological means and their management.[13] As a result, the influence of traditional work and its ethic continues to ebb, drained by structural unemployment at the bottom of the job ladder, overeducation and underemployment in the middle, and at the top an increase of fluidly interpersonal and knowledge-oriented jobs that require ongoing innovation, mobility, and learning. Emerging ideals of work and love characterize both as ever-unfolding processes of choice instead of once-and-for-all commitments. They counsel each of us to communicate sensitively and respond intensely in the present, taking as fully as we give. Over time they advise us to be flexible, to learn, and grow through crisis and change. They also encourage us to relax our demands for permanence and fidelity to past choices, whether it be our own fidelity or others'. Self-expression instead of self-restraint, self-realization instead of self-sacrifice: the counterculture has passed, but in the postindustrial mainstream personalist values continue to make headway against Protestant ones.

In general, the average person is now likely to spend much less of his life within a nuclear family than he was in generations past, and he is likely to undergo more changes in residence, income, job, and marital status with less linearity than before. As the course of work, marriage, and community life turns less continuous, persons grow more aware of themselves as individuals apart from their commitments to job and neighbors, spouse and children. They become more concerned with their own development—responding to their individual needs and rhythms, setting their own priorities and values. Yet their selfhood simultaneously becomes less secure, since it is less surely fixed by social institutions and less faithfully upheld by commitment to them. The individualist self, at once isolated and imperial, can look to no authority beyond itself for confirmation. We have seen how alternative religions rejoin the self to the rest of reality by conceiving it as a child of God, part of Buddha mind, or a transpersonal "being." These ideas of the self, backed by each movement's rules and authority, retie the individual to some form of ethical obligation not of his own making. Whether he wants to or not, he *ought* to obey God, live in accord with the precepts, or follow the rules of life. Duties rejoin rights. Deontological judgment of ends rejoins consequential calculation of means. Individual wants are not enough to justify action. They must be tested against common needs.

The quest for self-fulfillment seen spreading across America in the "Me Decade" carries with it questions about the ultimate usefulness of utilitarian goods and so about the ultimate meaning of utilitarian happiness. This has reopened the question of what is good in itself for an audience well beyond ex-hippies. Alternative religions have carried through the counterculture's recognition that getting the goods of affluence does not add up to feeling good. Nor does feeling good, they add, necessarily mean being good. The hip insight that "money can't buy you love" has been deepened by the religious truth that "man does not live by bread alone." These lessons have sharpened since the 1960s with the economic discovery that the goods of affluence may not grow ever more available to everyone in the society, not even to the middle class, and that getting such material goods may now confer fewer of the benefits of superior social position (such as the freedom to enjoy material goods in relative peace and solitary splendor) than before. In a society where material and positional goods become divorced, there is a loosening in the utilitarian linkage between getting the things you want and doing or feeling as you like.[14] Alternative religions respond to these problems with feelings and ideas, not things. The immediate personal experience they induce by ritual anchors a view of reality that gives substance to shared moral values.

The ultimate values of Christian salvation, Buddhist enlightenment, and even *est*'s rule-egoist aliveness deny radical subjectivism and materialism in defining what is good. These values justify compliance with social norms regardless of whether a person feels like it or reckons it advances her interests in a given case. Authoritative and regular forms of alternative ethics oppose head-on the utilitarian tendency to see rules and law itself merely as means to benefit oneself, or everyone, at best, and someone else at worst. *est*'s rule-egoism seeks to redefine the instrumental identity of social rules so that their self-interested violation can yield a person no real (psychic) good, though it may promise her mundane gains. The ultimate values of alternative ethics also support personal virtues—Christian charity, Buddhist compassion, and *est*'s "at-cause" responsibility—that help to objectify personal character in moral terms and likewise extend it into social relations. This has two positive effects. First, it makes the individual more accountable in interpersonal affairs. Second, it makes the legitimation of social authority more consistently open to claims and criticism of its representatives' moral character.

However little direct difference alternative religious movements may make to existing social or governmental structures, their political impact cannot be dismissed without gauging the secondary effects of the changes in moral and cultural meaning that they carry. The nature of selfhood, the individual in relation to the group, (inexhaustible) wants in relation to (limited) needs, rights in relation to duties, the legitimacy of moral authority and rules: redefinition of such ideas occurs at the foundation of social values and eventually makes itself felt in public policy. It does so by relocating the good ends at which policy aims and by reshaping the criteria of distributive justice which policy seeks to satisfy. Giving each person his due assumes that we know what a person is, what things are good, and what a person should do to deserve them. When such moral knowledge changes, so does the political exercise of social justice.

For those outside of alternative religious movements, even more than for those inside, the present importance of these movements lies chiefly in the ideas they carry, not in the social models they embody. Chances are that it will be an unforeseeable while before American society turns into a Christian theocracy, a monastic ecotopia, or one vast encounter group. This is just as well, given the nondemocratic structure of each. But the ideological upsurge of conservative Christianity, ecological monism, and psychologized individualism throughout American culture is already unmistakable. So is the weakening of liberalism, that synthesis of rational religion and humanism with utilitarian views that has long held sway over the center of American culture. This weakening has created a vacuum of meaning which these other three ideologies are expanding to fill. We are witnessing the beginnings of a postliberal culture, rooted in personal lifestyle but reaching through social values into the polity.

Whatever direction this new culture takes, however far it advances or is reversed, the initial lines between the would-be successors to liberalism have been drawn. Each of them already has an incipient constituency. Each also has influenced spokesmen in American public life, thereby bringing a new turn to our civil-religious rhetoric. This fact, apart from the political policies or prospects of these spokesmen, warrants our attention. Jimmy Carter has given voice to conservative Christianity, counterpointed by Ronald Reagan. Jerry Brown has given voice to ecological monism. Self-Determination, a state-wide "personal/political network" anchored by

California legislator John Vasconcellos, has given voice to human potential psychologism. What does each of these spokesmen have to say about morality and the shape of society? How have their distinctive ethics entered into the conventional climate of political opinion?

THE POLITICAL STATEMENT OF MORAL IDEAS

I. Presidents Carter, Reagan, and the Biblical Ethic

At the beginning of his 1977 inaugural address President Carter identifies the nation's needs in moral terms.[15] "We must adjust to changing times and still hold to unchanging principles." He defines those deontologically unchanging principles by quoting a "timeless admonition" from the biblical prophet Micah, just as John Winthrop did in 1630: "He hath showed thee, O man, what is good, and what doth the Lord require of thee, but to do justly, and to love mercy, and to walk humbly with God?" (Micah 6:8). This one verse states the authoritative essence of biblical morality. What is good consists of doing what God commands and "requires." What does God require? Just deeds, for one thing, but also merciful feelings toward others and humble obedience to his will. God commands intention as well as act. Being commanded by God makes an act right. Doing what God commands makes a good person. Biblical morality runs contrary to utilitarian individualism. What is good is not happiness derived from wealth, status, or power; and maximizing these utilities does not make an act right.

At the outset Carter has stated an ethic of duty as opposed to an ethic of want satisfaction. Having done so, he then recognizes the mixed moral genesis of American society, humanist and individualist as well as biblical:

> Ours was the first society openly to define itself in terms of both spirituality and human liberty. It is that unique self-definition which has given us an exceptional appeal—but it also imposes on us a special obligation—to take on those moral duties which, when assumed, seem invariably to be in our own best interests.

The passage is remarkable. Now moral action originates not from God's commandment but from society's self-definition. Obligation remains paramount, not want satisfaction, but now we are obliged "to take on those moral duties which, when assumed, seem invariably to be in our own best interests." What is happening here? Deontological duties are almost but not quite being justified on the consequential grounds of self-interest. John Locke is being read back in between the lines of the Bible and the Republic's lawbooks, held in check by the hedge that it is *only when assumed* that these moral duties seem invariably in our own best interests, not beforehand. Beforehand these duties may or may not seem this way, but we are obliged to take them on in either case. Their justification finally rests on the deontological ethic that first defined them. One assumes these duties because God, or at least the spiritual side of our nation's self-definition, requires it. Only then, when our perceived best interests have been deontologically defined to include doing our duty rather than consequentially defining which acts will be most useful to us, do utilitarian interests and biblical obligations lie coupled in one conception of what is right.

Carter goes on to qualify the utilitarian conception of the good, although he does not deny it outright:

> We have learned that *more* is not necessarily *better*, that even our great nation has its recognized limits, and that we can neither answer all questions nor solve all problems. We cannot afford to do everything, nor can we afford to lack boldness as we meet the future. So together, in a spirit of individual sacrifice for the common good, we must simply do our best.

Economic, fiscal, and political limits to growth hem in the "more is better" dream of the laissez faire economy and the liberal welfare state. Carter's call for "individual sacrifice for the common good" strikes a note more biblical than modern liberal (as in Kennedy's "Ask not what your country can do for you—ask what you can do for your country.") or laissez faire (as in Nixon's "Let each of us ask—not just what will government do for me, but what can I do for myself?"). Carter's call to "simply do our best," coupled with the admission that there are some things we may not be able to get done, turns self-evaluation away from the criterion of coordinating means to achieve utilitarian ends and toward conformity to regular moral principles.

Carter conceives American society chiefly as a moral community based on biblical spirituality and republic liberty, not as a collection of individuals under a liberal or laissez faire state. America faces objective moral duties given by God and law. The rightness of its actions and the goodness of its ends are likewise open to objective moral judgment. How, then, do we stand? "Let our recent mistakes bring a resurgent commitment to the basic principles of our nation," says Carter in the 1977 inaugural. The chapter of Micah from which he has quoted, however, goes further in this respect. In it God is condemning an often-blessed nation that has now disobeyed him, broken his Covenant, and brought down his punishment upon itself:

> Your rich men are full of violence; your inhabitants speak lies, and their tongue is deceitful in their mouth. Therefore I have begun to smite you, making you desolate because of your sins. You shall eat, but not be satisfied, and there shall be hunger in your inward parts; you shall put away, but not save, and what you save I will give to the sword. (Micah 6:12-14)

God calls on this nation to answer his charges not with the material goods of ritual religion, or of the utilitarian world—not with "burnt offerings" nor "rivers of oil"—but with the authoritative ethical good of biblical religion: just deeds, merciful intentions, and humble obedience to God's commands. (Micah 6:6-8) The ethical requirements with which Carter begins his inaugural are, in the biblical text quoted, those which God demands of a people who must repent their wickedness. Otherwise, God warns, they have turned from his law to follow false gods "that I may make you a desolation, and your inhabitants a hissing; so you shall bear the scorn of the peoples." (Micah 6:16)

The message carried by Micah's context was explicit in earlier drafts of the inaugural, which quoted 2 Chronicles 7:14 instead:[16] "If my people who are called on by my name shall humble themselves and pray and seek my face and turn from their wicked ways, then will I hear from heaven, and forgive their sins and heal their land." Carter switched verses after advisors opposed this message, causing him to comment later: "Sometimes we take for granted that an acknowledgment of sin, an acknowledgment of the need for humility permeates the consciousness of our people. But it doesn't."[17] Carter reflects on the connection between the nation's problems and the personal experience of sin and forgiveness in biblical religion:

But if we know that we can have God's forgiveness as a person, I think as a Nation, it makes it much easier for us to say, "God, have mercy on me."

A sinner, knowing that the only compensation for sin is condemnation, then he just can admit an error or a weakness or a degree of hatred or forego pride. We as individuals—and we as a Nation—insist that we are the strongest and the bravest and the wisest and the best. In that attitude, we unconsciously, but in an all-pervasive way, cover up and fail to acknowledge our mistakes and in the process forego an opportunity constantly to search for a better life for a better country.[18]

Carter's rewriting of the inaugural address and his later explanation of it at the National Prayer Breakfast indicate how strongly he sees American society in terms of biblical morality, even to the certainy of "condemnation" and the possibility of catastrophe if we do not repent our sins, or at least acknowledge our mistakes. The episode also indicates how strongly Carter sees the gap between the moral self-consciousness of Americans who recognize the biblical ethic and those who do not. The latter, he suspected, would take him to be playing "Solomon and saying that all Americans are wicked." That is why he dropped his call for national repentance into scriptural context, where only Bible readers would recognize it.

At several points in the 1977 inaugural address Carter's moral reasoning turns on the need for consistency and generalizability, conditions stressed by a regular ethic. He states,

> To be true to ourselves, we must be true to others. We will not behave in foreign places so as to violate our rules and standards here at home, for we know that the trust which our nation earns is essential to our strength.

And again,

> Because we are free we can never be indifferent to the fate of freedom elsewhere. Our moral sense dictates a clear-cut preference for those societies which share with us an abiding respect for individual human rights.

Here Carter is not simply attacking nationalistic hypocrisy but the moral relativism intrinsic to a consequential ethic based on self-interest, whether it is held by self-interested individuals or *realpolitik* nations. Here as in his earlier discussion of duty in general, Carter points out its congruence with interests: America's international trustworthiness is essential to its national strength. Elsewhere Carter recognizes that equality of opportunity has lagged behind personal liberty in America itself. He pledges to all citizens alike: "Our commitment to human rights must be absolute, our laws fair . . . the powerful must not persecute the weak, and human dignity must be enhanced."

To the American people Carter made an inaugural vow "to stay close to you, to be worthy of you, and to exemplify what you are." This moral sense of leadership owes much to the Baptist congregation, with its non-hierarchical intimacy, its stress on the autonomy of individual conscience in direct relation to God, and its view of church officers as servants.[19] Carter's campaign promise of exemplary political behavior rested on his code of personal behavior governed by the fixed prescriptions of biblical morality:

> I don't think I would *ever* take on the same frame of mind that Nixon or Johnson did—lying, cheating, and distorting the truth. Not taking into consideration my hope for my strength of character, I think that my religious beliefs alone would prevent that from happening to me.[20]

Post-Watergate voters welcomed the prospect of moral integrity in public affairs assured by an authoritative ethic, but some urban liberals feared that it might bring with it puritanical judgments of personal behavior. Asked during the 1976 campaign if he approved of laws against drug abuse, adultery, sodomy, and homosexuality, Carter responded:

I think the laws are on the books quite often because of their relationship to the Bible. Early in the nation's development, the Judaeo-Christian moral standards were accepted as a basis for civil law. But I don't think it hurts to have this kind of standard maintained as a goal.[21]

Carter goes on to reiterate Reinhold Niebuhr's view of law as a framework balancing conflicting social forces. He advises following civil law, except where it conflicts with "God's law." There "we should honor God's law. But we should be willing to accept civil punishment."[22]

Asked if he would *enforce* laws against victimless crimes forbidden by a biblical ethic as evil in themselves but permitted by an individualistic ethic as private contracts between consenting adults, Carter confronts the issue in more personal terms:

Committing adultery, according to the Bible—which I believe in —is a sin. For us to hate one another, for us to have sexual intercourse outside marriage, for us to engage in homosexual activities, for us to steal, for us to lie—all these are sins. But Jesus teaches us not to judge other people. We don't assume the role of judge and say to another human being, "You're condemned because you commit sins." All Christians, all of us, acknowledge that we are sinful and the judgment comes from God, not from another human being.[23]

Carter repeats the last point in closing this discussion of religious and social morality with journalist Robert Scheer:

Some people get very abusive about the Baptist faith. If people want to know about it, they can read the New Testament. The main thing is that we don't think we're better than anyone else. We are taught not to judge other people. But as to some of the behavior you've mentioned, I can't change the teachings of Christ. I can't change the teachings of Christ! I believe in them, and a lot of people in this country do as well. Jews believe in the Bible. They have the same commandments.[24]

The Baptist Christian's virtues of humility and not judging others are relatively adaptive to a pluralistic society. But, as Carter also affirms, the Bible's commandments are not themselves relativistic or subjective, leaving its ethic at odds with America's utilitarian culture though espoused by much of its population.

How much bearing did Carter's biblical morality have on his policies? Some critics saw him as more of an engineer than a Christian, more dependent on technocracy than morality in deciding policy, and unable to translate his private piety into public positions. Others found him a moralist first and last, moralizing and thereby oversimplifying complex technical and political issues like energy planning. Overall characterizations aside, Carter's biblical ethic did mark his view of some social issues, including human rights in foreign affairs, restricted abortion financing, and welfare reforms to favor marriage. To what extent his moral views determined his policy making is another question. To answer it one must weigh not only Carter's Christian convictions, but his respect for the nonbiblical ethics of other Americans and the laws of civil society. The lack of just such respect characterized the new religious right entering the 1980s, according to its critics, and made its political support for Ronald Reagan and selected Congressional conservatives seem ominous. Reagan's own moral rhetoric, however, differs significantly from that of his allies in the "moral majority" as well as from his Presidential predecessor.

Unlike Carter, President Reagan begins his 1981 inaugural address without reference to God or scripture. Instead he notes the "miracle" of America's Constitutional transfer of authority, the bulwark of a political system ordered by law and dedicated to individual liberty. Then he moves directly to "the business of our nation," finding the moral answer to our economic ills—inflation and unemployment, high taxes and higher public spending—in the individual's obligation to balance his own budget: "You and I, as individuals, can, by borrowing, live beyond our means, but for only a limited period of time. Why then should we think that collectively, as a nation, we are not bound by that same limitation?"[25] Respecting these economic limitations amounts to self-governance, according to Reagan, and this is the only solution to our present crisis, in which a profligate and intrusive "government is not the solution to our problem; government is the problem." For "if no one among us is capable of governing himself, then who among us has the capacity to govern someone else?" Self-governance in economic terms, Reagan promises, will have specifically political results, enabling us to "preserve this last and greatest bastion of freedom."

Individual freedom, the central political virtue for Reagan, rests on and makes possible individual industry and initiative, the central economic virtues that imply a self-reliant and self-disciplined ideal of character. In this sense "We are a nation that has a government—not the other way around. ...Our government has no power except that granted it by the people." Reagan describes "we the people" accordingly, as "a special interest group" that is "made up of men and women who raise our food, patrol our streets, man our mines and factories, teach our children, keep our homes and heal us when we're sick. Professionals, industrialists, shopkeepers, clerks, cabbies and truck drivers." Persons precede the polity in this Lockean view of civic association by contract and government by consent, and the economic realm likewise precedes the political realm. Persons defined by their

economic occupations make up a citizenry defined as an all-inclusive interest group, chiefly interested in "a healthy, vigorous, growing economy that
provides equal opportunity for all Americans." Conversely,

> If we look for the answer as to why for so many years we
> achieved so much, prospered as no other people on earth, it was
> because here in this land we unleashed the energy and individual
> genius of man to a greater extent than had ever been done before.

> Freedom and the dignity of the individual have been more avail-
> able and assured here than in any other place on earth.

This libertarian conceptual tie between political and economic freedom
from restraint underpins Reagan's diagnosis that "our present troubles
parallel and are proportionate to the intervention and intrusion in our lives
that result from unnecessary and excessive growth of Government," and his
proposal to "reawaken this industrial giant" composed of economic individuals by getting the government off their backs.

Reagan supports his counter-Keynesian call to increase economic productivity by cutting government spending, taxes, and regulation with a
Bunker Hill patriot's call to his colonial countrymen to "decide the important question on which rest the happiness and liberty of millions yet unborn." Like our original struggle for independence, our present effort to
prune the welfare state and achieve economic self-renewal will make
America "the exemplar of freedom and a beacon of hope for those who do
not now have freedom." Reagan promises our allies who share this ideal
that "we will match loyalty with loyalty." He warns the enemies of freedom
that no weapon in their arsenals is as formidable as "the will and moral
courage of free men and women." The price of this freedom is individual
responsibility and sacrifice, epitomized by military heroes who die for their
country. Reagan quotes one of their ranks, who pledged: "America must
win this war. Therefore I will work, I will save, I will sacrifice, I will endure,
I will fight cheerfully and do my utmost, as if the issue of the whole struggle
depended on me alone." Reagan unites military and economic heroes, who
likewise do their patriotic duty by working and saving in factories, on
farms, and across shop counters. As such patriots, Reagan calls on us to
"believe in ourselves and in our capacity to perform great deeds," since,
after all, "we are Americans."

References to God come late in Reagan's address, detached from any
explicitly biblical context and linked more specifically to the ideal of political freedom than to the foundation of moral authority. "We are a nation
under God, and I believe God intended for us to be free," Reagan avows.
Beyond this, religious references in Reagan's speech are emphatically civil.
After proposing that each Inaugural Day be a day of prayer, he directs our
attention to those "shrines to the giants on whose shoulders we stand"—

Washington, Jefferson, Lincoln, and those buried in Arlington Cemetery. He promises that "with God's help we can and will resolve the problems which now confront us," and then closes with a "God bless you." The rule of law appears briefly in allusions to America's Constitutional order, as does an ethic of principles with reference to "the idealism and fair play which are the core of our system and our strength," but Reagan steers clear of Carter's stress on human rights. He appeals most directly to expressive moral feelings, interestingly enough, in discussing the basis of social welfare action: "How can we love our country and not love our countrymen? And loving them reach out a hand when they fall, heal them when they're sick and provide opportunity to make them self-sufficient so they will be equal in fact and not just in theory?" Here the political ideal of equality less clearly implies obligations of social justice than it depends on opportunities to become economically self-sufficient, offered out of patriotic compassion. Throughout the inaugural address, Reagan's political stress remains not on equality but on the individual's negative liberty as it derives from and applies to his economic activities. We the people are described mainly in our occupational and economic roles, and *as such* we are revealed to be heroic patriots and citizens. Compared to Carter's inaugural address, Reagan's explicates little of the logic or ideas of an authoritative or regular ethic, although its rhetoric touches on them at points and implicitly relies on them throughout for its resonating chords of individual responsibility. Instead Reagan follows a libertarian logic, in which freedom *from* restraint comes before freedom *to* do our duty; even as he evokes traditional moral values which he elsewhere underscores.

In accepting the Republican nomination, for example, Reagan promises to "build a new consensus with all those across the land who share a community of values embodied in these words: family, work, neighborhood, peace and freedom." He explains that

> Work and family are at the center of our lives, the foundation of our dignity as a free people. When we deprive people of what they have earned, or take away their jobs, we destroy their dignity and undermine their families. We can't support families unless there are jobs; and we can't have jobs unless the people have both money and the faith to invest it.[26]

Political freedom rests on the social institutions of work and family, which in turn depend on private economic enterprise and capital investment. Reagan asks us to trust in these values and hold him responsible to them in order to renew the "American compact"—"the voluntary binding together of free people to live under the law"—first formed in Plymouth in 1620. On this Lockean view of civic association in America Reagan calls down God's blessing, and with it he justifies the economic if not military reforms his administration began by proposing in order to shrink the public sector and expand the private. In short, the mainstream of Reagan's own rhetoric flows much more directly from the libertarian right than the religious right, as do the economic items atop his policy agenda.

The chorus of conservative Evangelical and fundamentalist Christian groups supporting Reagan's candidacy was attracted not by the authoritative style of his moral argument but by his "pro-family" stands on such issues as abortion and the equal rights amendment, sex education, prayer, and creationism in the schools; and by Reagan's budget-bulging calls for "moral and military rearmament" against the godless immorality of Communism. Reagan's stands on such issues were clearly if often telegraphically signalled by his proclaimed support for the traditional moral values of *family*, work, neighborhood, peace, and freedom. He also gave deontological moral answers to campaign questions on such matters as abortion. "I believe that abortion is taking a human life," he typically declared, "and that can be done only in self-defense." In defending church involvement in political issues he affirmed,

I have found a great hunger in America for a spiritual revival, for a belief that law must be based on a higher law, for a return to traditions and values that we once had. Our Government, in its most sacred documents, the Constitution and the Declaration of Independence and all, speak of man being created, of a creator, that we are a nation under God.[27]

Pledging to use the bully pulpit of the presidency to maintain America's basic values, Reagan states a civil religious credo that at once remains distinct from and leaves room on the right for such Christian conservatives as Reverend Falwell to assert, "The authority of Bible morality must once again be recognized as the legitimate guiding principle for our nation."[28]

II. Governor Brown and the Eco-Monist Ethic

Jerry Brown is hardly a Zen Buddhist in the self-proclaimed sense that Jimmy Carter is a born-again Christian. Brown is perhaps even less a Buddhist than he is a lawyer raised a Roman Catholic and educated by Jesuits. Whatever his formal status, his working position as an eco-monist relies on a regular ethic whose natural-law premises characterize these two rationalized religions. This ethic clashes with the utilitarian view that each individual should act to satisfy his own wants. Asked whether American values need reform, Brown asserts the need for deontological principles opposed to both utilitarian individualism and the counterculture's ethic:

I think American values need reassertion in terms of fundamental roots. I think there has been an overemphasis on the ability of material comfort, on the ability of our economic machinery to provide human happiness. The growthmanship of the sixties, which equated growth in GNP with human happiness, I think, is far from the founding fathers.

I think the notion that human nature changes is a complete absurdity refuted by every chapter of history that I have ever read, and to that extent I would not call it a reform in the sense of something new, but it is a returning to a traditional view of human nature that looks to fundamental principles, to right, wrong, to ethics, to morality, to a sense that human nature is constant. It is weak, it needs a type of government that recognizes that mankind is really brought down by its own instincts.

If we think that just producing two and three cars apiece, and an economy of obsolescence and increasing mobility and material accumulation is the good life—I don't believe that, and I don't believe any society has ever survived on that basis. Every civilization that has gone through a sensate, sensual culture has fallen, and I think that is a real possibility; and to that extent I would like to see an austerer, leaner commitment on the part of the people of this country, yes.[29]

The means of utilitarian culture do not lead to its end: a growing GNP does not provide human happiness. Neither do self-expression and surrender to the senses, those hip alternatives to utilitarian accumulation. Why not? Because human nature is "weak." It is "brought down by its own instincts," not elevated and set free by them. Against the counterculture's Pelagian view that human nature is good in itself and corrupted only by its environment, and the mainstream utilitarian view that it is a mutable mixture of good and bad, Brown counterposes an Augustinian view of the evil inherent in our nature: "Can we alter the human condition? No. We can't make saints out of sinners. St. Augustine has something to say about that . . . we have to take the darker side into account in all that we do."[30]

Given Brown's view of human nature, which resembles Carter's Evangelical conviction that we are sinful yet we can be saved, Brown, too, arrives at the need for a deontological ethic that prescribes and forbids particular acts as right or wrong in themselves. Besides such fundamental principles to regulate human behavior, Brown calls for a type of government and culture that can curb our self-indulgence. He dismisses the life of utilitarian or expressive want satisfaction as a contemplative might, observing that "The contemporary search to satisfy every impulse that floats through your consciousness is doomed to failure—I don't think that's what people want, anyway."[31] He does not accept such wants as given, as would a utilitarian; instead he opens them to evaluation, as would a natural-law rationalist. Against individual want satisfaction, Brown counterposes the possibility of "a life of service and common purpose," and he talks with approval of a regular ethic able to resurrect "that sense of obligation and civic duty that appears to me to be diminishing through the society." He declares: "We have a great amount of work to do by way of assuring the rights of all citizens. But a right has no meaning unless there is a correlative emphasis on the responsibility, the obligation, and the duty of each of us to assume responsibilities."[32] Here Brown is rebutting a utilitarian view of each individual's natural or axiomatic rights with the classical and biblical view that rights depend on correlative duties to others.

Brown sees self-interested individuals in a mobile urban society convinced by utilitarian culture that they have the right to "go and come wherever they want" while dumping their social obligations into the lap of a welfare state. But people in families and churches, unions and small businesses, can take care of each other better than the state can, Brown argues. And the state can no longer afford to pay the rising costs of trying to care for people, since the period of economic growth that once filled its coffers has now ebbed into "an era of limits." Thus regular ethical assumptions of interlocking obligations underpin Brown's critical diagnosis of government spending and social services. He asks, "How do we strengthen, possibly recapture the values that a less mobile, less changing society had by way of obligation for others? . . . Because as the rate of [individual] mobility increases, the obligations that evaporate in the process do not disappear."[33] Traditionally conservative criticism of big government echoes here, but Brown isn't simply attacking the welfare state on behalf of the laissez faire individual once again. He is calling for a localized, communal cooperation among persons in terms that sound familiar to eco-monist and hip critics of bureaucratic society:

> We have centralized too much power, and we have to get back to neighborhoods and communities where people in face-to-face relationships can deal with the fundamental issues of justice, of education, of jobs, of birth, of death, of healing, of compassion, and of bearing one another's burdens that is done at the local level.[34]

Face-to-face relationships in a communal context encourage mutual aid, justice, and compassion. As in the Zen monastery, such expressive support for right action is now reinforced by an ethic of rules and obligation. The kind of compassionate service Zen calls for in work and everyday life Brown calls for in order to sustain society.

Brown reasserts the antiliberal wisdom of governmental inaction: "This administration is in the tradition of Thomas Jefferson, who said, 'He who governs best governs least.'"[35] Echoing Jefferson, such sentiments appeal to traditional conservatives. Echoing Lao-Tzu ("The way to do is to be"), they appeal to hip sixties youth. In describing his administration,.

Brown rejects a liberal approach based on legislative programs aimed at preset welfare goals. "I don't have any goals; they will evolve as we go along," he counters.[36] There is an unmistakably expressive ethical style to this evolution of truth from an empathically unified situation. "To be a leader you have to be at one with the people you lead. You have to feel it," Brown reports.[37] He affirms the expressive faith that "Life just is. You have to flow with it. Give yourself to the moment. Let it happen."[38] Such receptivity can turn into ascetic activity, however, at the drop of an issue. ". . . I'm relentless," Brown asserts. "When I get on an issue I can go fifteen hours a day. Seven days a week."[39] This admixture of passive and active attitudes signals more than the quick about-facing of a protean politician. It marks the political appearance of this-worldly mysticism, the approach to life taken by the neo-Oriental monk-in-the-world. "He is remarkably detached, and, at the same time, one of the most singleminded and intense people," admires Brown's state architect. "There are remarkably Buddhist things about him, even though he doesn't practice it. He approaches everything he does with incredible balance between utter detachment and total involvement."[40]

For all its expressive unfolding and situational emergence, the political process in Brown's view is not entirely free of regularity. In a line that recalls the beginning of Carter's inaugural, Brown remarks, "What we need is a flexible plan for an ever-changing world."[41] That plan rests on the assumption that human nature never changes. It is governed by a natural law that extends to social life, where it guides positive law and the dialectical process of making and enacting legislation. Brown explains how this dialectic functions:

> I think by asking people [questions], that's a way of slowing things down. If you ask something in a way that really seeks out the meaning of the situation or the assumptions on which a statement was made, that requires a pause and requires a reflection that would be missed. . . . That's the traditional *satyagraha*. Isn't that what Gandhi talked about—"expose the truth in the situation, and then the people by recognizing it are moved by it." That's the power of unarmed truth. I think it works in a situation where there's all this confusion, that truth has a power that it normally might not have. By truth I mean something that arises out of a situation, and people open their eyes, given the assumptions they all share, they'll perceive it to be the case. And oftentimes it's just there if you focus on it, and you get people to focus on it . . . by discussing it, by confronting some of the confusion, by pulling together concepts that are contradictory that people haven't perceived as contradictory.[42]

Brown names Gandhi as the patron saint of this dialectical method, but Socrates or St. Ignatius could claim some credit for it, too. The truth "arises out of a situation," and people will perceive it if they "open their eyes." But to do so, they must dialectically question the meaning of situations and discuss their assumptions about them, teasing out and resolving contradictory concepts along the way. Only then will the truth take casuistic form and move people in one direction.

Brown gives an example of his regular moral logic in evaluating Nixon's behavior. He refers not to any biblical commandment against lying, as Carter does, but to its contravening the nature of human relationship:

> I don't like lying under any circumstances. If we go back to our natural law, that's got to be one of the easy ones. You don't lie. Once you lie, you break the trust, you break the connection. Then there is no trust, there is no security, and how can you operate? It breaks down the whole basis of relationship.[43]

This line of natural-law reasoning recalls not only Scholastic arguments but the Zen student's explanation of his precepts (see chapter 3). Truth telling expresses the true nature of human relationship and makes it possible. Truth telling accords with the regularity of existence.

Brown's regular ethic stresses the need for rule of law in a pluralistic society. Defending the Supreme Court's claim to moral authority to intervene in issues like busing and abortion, Brown argues:

> We are now in a society where it is very hard to find a consensus. We are fragmenting, we're proliferating at every level of economics and morality and politics. The court is a unifying mechanism and a beacon of light if it acts wisely. I think by and large given the complexity of our country, the heterogeneity of our people, they're doing an excellent job . . . [of finding] this balance between the momentary perception of what needs to be done and the more elementary articulation of what the principles are by which we all live.[44]

Such confidence that situationally specific prescriptions can be generalized to consistent first principles "by which we all live" distinguishes the regular ethic. Formal rules made by government grow more critical as a society's informal consensus over moral values and norms grows looser and less effective. Muses Brown:

> If there was a social compact that basically threads everybody together, then [formal] rules would occupy a smaller part of the whole network by which people relate. Now, as this social compact appears to be breaking down a bit, then more and more rules are needed to glue everybody together. . . . I think you need more [formal] rules as the informal and internalized rules become less effective.[45]

Like Carter, Brown recognizes the importance of Durkheim's central problem: How does a differentiated society achieve normative integration? Neither Carter nor Brown is satisfied with reciprocal self-interest and "law-and-order" authority as sufficient answers to this problem.

As a political speechmaker, Brown's opening line states that "we are entering an era of limits," where we will have to lessen our expectations and tighten our belts.[46] As a moralist, too, this is Brown's opening line, for it constitutes the natural law premise for arguing the ethic of eco-monism against the relativity of moral values:

> You talk about the problem of the relativity and what sounds to me like the decline of the old values. And yet, one of the bases for an absolute commitment is the sense that resources are limited—that the world is a place with some kind of global relationship where people are part of a species or wider community that was not sensed before by the nation-states or ethnic groups. So some of the gaps in the relativity that's obviously part of modern technological society perhaps can be closed by this sense that there are limits. The limit is that you can wreck the place, you can blow it up, despoil it.[47]

Here the recognition of scarcity, that there are not enough resources for each self-interested individual to get his own satisfactory share, leads not to increased competition or to self-serving contracts, as it would for utilitarians, but rather to common sharing according to regular principles. It does so because eco-monists ideally recognize that all persons are "part of a species or wider community." Brown merges Carter's biblical theme of humility and mercy in the face of human weakness into the eco-monist theme of individual and technological limits in the face of all life's interdependence:

> I don't have a text today but if I did I might look to the Old Testament where it is written that pride comes before a fall. And also where it is said that past glory leads to present weakness. I think we have to walk with humility. I think we have to realize that our technology can only take us so far; that our government can only give us so much; that all of us are connected and dependent on one another; and that the apparent divisions in our country and throughout this globe are just that, apparent. And ultimately, and hopefully sooner rather than later, we'll come to see that we all depend on one another; and this planet and its water, its air and the fruits of its soil must continue not only in this generation but for those who must succeed it.[48]

The eco-monist ethic justifies protecting the environment and sharing its resources according to regular principles. These derive from the planet's ecological limits and the needs of its inhabitants as a community, not from the subjective wants of individuals.

To what extent has Brown's eco-monist ethic influenced his policies? Critics see him as an amoral "stimulus-response" politician, long on symbols and short on substance, whose "nothing for everyone" policies hit hard at have-nots while leaving haves in relative comfort. Brown's tight budgets and environmental protection laws, his support for localized social services, and even his administration's "creative inaction" have borne out aspects of his eco-monist ethic. On the other hand, his campaigns to stimulate business investment, foreign trade, and space technology funding in California appear more conventionally calculated. Brown boasts a nonprogrammatic case-study approach to particular policy issues, and he has mixed liberal and conservative elements in his policy decisions. Brown's general views and symbolic appeals, however, consistently reject utilitarian individualism in favor of a regular ethic with an eco-monist content.

III. Assemblyman Vasconcellos and the Human Potential Ethic

The human potential movement's moral ideas have found political expression in Self-Determination, a "personal/political network" that stretches across California from its base in the suburban Bay Area. Founded in 1975 by a group including State Assemblyman John Vasconcellos, Self-Determination is dedicated to a "humanistic politics" based on the premise that "self-realization is the path to political responsibility."[49]

Drawing more from the humanistic psychology of transactional, encounter, and body therapies than from est,[50] Self-Determination sees the problems of traditional politics coming from its "repressive, self-denying" cultural assumptions about human nature and human potential. Negative self-definition is at the root of institutionalized cynicism, says Vasconcellos: "My whole point is that if I'm still carrying a negative experience of myself, then I'll approach you that way and create laws based on that fact."[51] Vasconcellos puts the point in its cultural context:

> In traditional Western culture, man has been conditioned to see and experience himself in negative ways—with much fear and shame and guilt. Whatever the relationship (parent and child, teacher and student, priest and worshipper, politician and constituent), man was impressed to look outward and upward, to the authority figures, for instruction on how he ought to be.
>
> Today this relationship is radically changing. Many persons are looking inward and envisioning personhood in a positive way. And when I radically change my self-concept (or better, self-esteem), then all social structures and relationships built upon self-denial, repression and authority come sharply into question.

I challenge the assumption that someone else knows better than
I do what's best for me. I question those institutions that tell me
I need someone else to dictate to me how I ought to be.[52]

Here the individual is championed against an authoritarian social structure.
He is no longer "sinful, fallen, and shameful" by nature (as was Luther's
individual), nor self-interested (as was Hobbes'). Instead "human beings are
basically healthy" and "human nature is lovely rather than sinful in terms of
its ultimate capacity."[53] The only original sin is believing in original sin. Unlike Jerry Brown, Vasconcellos sides with Pelagius, not Augustine, in assessing human nature, thereby obviating the need for social control and discerning the promise of a nonhierarchical political order in pure self-expression. "What we are trying to do at this time," he explains, "is to give some
breath to those movements in which man is somehow exalted rather than
put down."[54]

Self-Determination proposes a positive and self-actualizing view of
human nature that will enable us to change ourselves *and* society simultaneously by "trusting our natural decency."[55] Its first principle states:

The individual human being is the basis of society, and the
source of all experiencing and valuing. Every person ... has inherent worth and dignity and trustworthiness. Every person has
the right and capacity and responsibility to know who he/she is,
to grow, to become a whole person (intellect, emotions, and
body), to be free and responsible and authentic and caring, and
to participate in decision-making that affects his/her life.[56]

Society and moral value are based in the individual. Right conduct consists
of acts that assure their agent of "becoming a whole person," one who is
"authentic and caring." Always cooperative and never competitive, good
social relationships are those that produce such individuals: "Every human
relationship, personal and political, should be built upon respect for the
integrity of each individual as a person, and be authentic, trusting, open,
and caring."[57] Like *est*, Self-Determination holds an implicitly consequential
theory of right action and an explicitly psychologistic theory of intrinsic
value, both hinged on the individual. It applies both to social institutions as
well as relationships: "Institutions consist *of* people, and exist *for* people,
and should always be person-centered and person-valuing. The purpose of
every human institution is to enable each person to develop all his/her
potential as a human being."[58] Each person's own feelings of authenticity
are what make the consequences of an act good. Yielding the most good
consequences to each person is what makes an act right. Unlike classical
notions of developing a virtuous character, these modern feelings of authenticity are subjectively given. They come from simply looking inward, not
from exerting oneself to conform to regular standards of excellence. Praiseworthy institutions, therefore, are those that enable each person to experi-

ence the most feelings of authenticity, whatever their objective correlate, right up to her full potential for such experience.

Recalling *est*'s idea of the omnicausal individual in more restrained terms, Self-Determination stresses the power of individual consciousness to determine the totality of experience:

> How we envision and experience ourselves affects all we feel and do, and what we expect of other human beings, relationships, institutions, and politics. Whether we see ourselves as inherently trustworthy and capable of freedom and responsibility determines our approach to other persons, relationships, institutions, and politics.[59]

This tenet draws political attention away from the public institutions, party organizations, interest groups, and leaders that concentrate and wield power. Instead it diffuses attention across the entire range of social interaction:

> Politics includes the total inter-actions of persons. Politics has been traditionally defined as those affairs which determine public policy. But public policy has meaning only insofar as it affects real human beings and real human needs. And in every human contact we affect each other, and each other's capacity to determine our own lives. Thus, politics necessarily includes not only every public place where decisions are made, but every place where human beings interact.[60]

Since "politics happens everywhere," political analysis tends to shift from the level of social structure to interpersonal relationships, much like *est*'s reworking of the social contract in terms of face-to-face encounters (see chapter 4).

Self-Determination acknowledges that self and society influence each other. Society is not simply a product of the psyche:

> Social conditions affect human growth, which determines personal attitudes and values; personal attitudes and values determine human activity, which in turn affects social conditions. This relationship is inherent and inescapable. A negative and repressive culture creates fear and guilt in persons, who thereby allow and recreate that repressive culture. A positive and nurturing culture strengthens freedom and responsibility in persons, who in turn create a freeing and nurturing culture.[61]

Self and society affect each other in this view, but "society" appears here chiefly as forms of culture that either repress or nurture persons, not as social structures that govern them justly or unjustly. Social structures lose their visibility because once persons set themselves free from the fear and guilt of a repressive culture, their natural goodness defines moral evil and injustice out of persistence. When evil is erased, so are its social symptoms and the apparatus of its social control.

Self-Determination sees many persons already living out a self-actualized vision of self and society. It seeks in its network to elaborate these persons into "a lateral and largely leaderless process for empowering persons in their own places to live more effectively in their personal lives and in the realm of 'politics.'"[62] Its program calls for "core groups" in local communities to link up through "a computerized, humanistic resource-exchange center." Workshops will educate local groups "to fuse personal growth and interaction techniques with problem solving, organizational development, and community-organizing skills." Publications will describe humanistic "methods for gaining access to bureaucratic and institutional decision-making processes." Questionnaires will ask candidates for public offices "to disclose themselves and their basic assumptions about people." By such therapeutic self-disclosure, interpersonal encounter, and affective education, Self-Determination seeks to translate the human potential movement's understanding of human growth into public policy. In this vision individuals leading self-determined private lives associate in an interpersonal network of collegial equals and encounter other individuals within the political bureaucracy. They experience one another face to face, thereby creating "person-oriented" institutions. Through this process Self-Determination promises something like the "transubstantiation" of society from the inside out which *est* describes.

In the first year of its existence Self-Determination made contact with some 4,000 persons in local meetings across California. It won sponsorship from a half-dozen California legislators and educational leaders, and it gained funding from several foundations, including the *est* Foundation. It has been endorsed by psychologist Carl Rogers as a political development that "comes closer to being an expression of, and an organization for, the persons of tomorrow than anything else I know."[63]

From the political podium in the late 1970s there began to ring out moral ideas already familiar from the pulpits of alternative religion. These politicians saw individualist selfhood as a problem, and they, too, sought to rejoin the isolated self to the rest of reality. They call on individuals to "walk humbly with God," act as "part of a species" in global relationship, or become "whole persons" who share the same potential. They reject the utilitarian view of human nature as an aggregate of wants beyond evaluation. Rather, they see it capable of good or evil in the light of objective moral values and rules. For Carter we are sinful as human beings yet we can be saved by obeying God and doing justice to one another. For Brown we are corruptible yet we can live "a life of service and common purpose" by recommitting ourselves to fundamental principles of right and wrong. For human potential politicians, we are repressed yet healthy enough to create a liberated society by "trusting our natural decency." These spokesmen derive moral values from a conception of divine authority, natural law, or human authenticity by which values can be objectively judged and universally applied. Contrary to conventional notions of "the good life" in America, and in view of our now-troubled economy, all three politicians stress the nonmaterialist essence of what is good. "More is not necessarily better," says Carter, nor can we "equate growth in GNP with human happiness," according to Brown. Human potential, adds Vasconcellos, lies in developing our psychic resources, not our material ones. Reagan, by contrast, bullishly reaffirms the supply-side bounty of a revived economy. But he emphasizes that we can revive it only by living within our means, working together with a sense of fair play, and saving and sacrificing for country as well as family.

To integrate a pluralistic society, both Carter and Brown advocate unchanging principles by which we all should live—the hallmark of a regular ethic—as opposed to reciprocal self-interest or law-and-order authority. With the market and the welfare state tightening up on traditional utilities, both men deny consequential ethics of maximizing want satisfaction and instead call on us to sacrifice self-interest for the common good and simply do our best according to an ethic of rules and authority. Human rights depend on correlative obligations to others, and our conscience cannot be cut to fit our interests. Both Carter and Brown also call for the revitalization of community institutions to provide the social context a regular ethic needs. Human potential politicians meanwhile propose to personalize bureaucracy in the service of self-expression. All three emphasize that legitimate social authority rests on and requires personal virtue, whether it develops through therapy, piety, or dialectical reason. Reagan agrees, albeit stressing self-reliance bred by budget-balancing industry and self-sacrifice inspired by love of country. He, too, would revitalize communities, counting on them to pick up social services a disarmed bureaucracy is forced to drop. Responsibilities and duties must accompany rights for Reagan, too. He appeals to principled idealism and to authority, divine and legal, as well as to reciprocal self-interest in hopes of regathering our society on the all-American main street of traditional moral values: family, work, neighborhood, peace, and freedom.

If the strengths of contrasting styles of ethical evaluation are evident in this sort of political statement, so are their weaknesses. Expressive values grow more important in an increasingly white-collar and professional work force, and in a postindustrial economy more oriented to services and knowledge. But full self-expression will not suffice to direct output, coordinate behavior, or curb conflicting interests, especially in large, complex social institutions. Consequential ethics have a genius for direction, coordination, and compromise in just such settings. Their calculations break down, however, when the payoffs and odds involved become incommensurable. Their·

appeal dies out, moreover, when the opportunity for individual profit is replaced by the need for individual sacrifice, and collective action must be taken for a common good. The consequential ethic is unable to justify substantive values, prescriptive norms, or legitimate authority by itself. When it tries to do so under the rubric of the greatest good for the greatest number, it poses unequalled problems of calculation and makes unequalled demands for altruism. Authoritative ethics, on the other hand, provide an absolute anchorage for values, norms, and authority, but to do so they must either disregard or merely tolerate the nonbeliever in pluralistic, relativistic societies like our own. Without a strong underlying consensus on the moral meaning of nature, self, and society, a rule ethic can neither appeal to natural law nor invoke reason very effectively. It must rely on formal law, the legislature that makes it and the judiciary that interprets it. No matter how ingeniously these legal institutions try to work around a lack of moral consensus, they cannot assure the social integrity of law, no more than their powers of enforcement can guarantee respect for it. The rule of law is far superior to the rule of force or interest, but it cannot replace morality, its cultural functions, or its religious foundations.

Moral meanings carried by conservative Christianity, eco-monism, and the human potential movement have already found their way into the political sector. There each has begun to build its own image of a newly coherent and cohesive society over against utilitarian individualism, or inside its psyche. Within the symbolic integrity of these images, trustworthy moral authority, rational principles, or authentic feelings will lead us as citizens to give up our individual interests for the common good, or at least to rediscover them there in enlightened form. In this translation from alternative religious movements into civil religious rhetoric, the process of getting saved from the sixties has become part of a larger cultural effort to save our selves from utilitarian society, and society from our self-interested selves.

HOW DO MORAL IDEAS CHANGE?

The Mutuality of Moral Choice

If persons choose ideas to live by, it is also true that ideas "choose" them.[64] Such choices do not occur in the thin air of ideal time and place. They occur in particular times in a person's life and in history, in a particular society and situation. These social conditions bear on the content and structure of the ethical outlook a person comes to hold. They make one idea more plausible than another to a given person. They make a given idea more plausible to one person than to another. For example, the child being commanded to obey by his parent, the soldier by his officer, or the lawbreaker by police must heed the voice of an authoritative ethic. The youngster learning the rules of games, the student learning the rules of disciplines, and those who interpret the law must face a rule ethic's demands for consistency and generalizability. Handling money and holding a job, managing a private, corporate, or public household bring adults into continual reliance on the cost-benefit calculus of the consequential ethic. Working within a bureaucratic organization reinforces respect for its procedural rules and contractual structure. Private life with lovers and friends, especially as it flourishes in youth, apart from family and job, supports the free-form intimacy of the expressive ethic.

Despite the close fit between such ideally typified social situations and styles of ethical evaluation, moral ideas do not derive simply from social structure or psychological development.[65] They come through culture itself, through tradition and language. We talk to one another and to ourselves through tradition. We grasp the meaning of things, including "social facts," through culture. We can feel things without thinking or talking about them. But we know what we are feeling only by thinking about it. Moral ideas possess an integrity, a self-reflexive autonomy that goes beyond any particular set of social conditions. One reason for this autonomy is the fact that the biblical, rationalist, utilitarian, and romantic traditions have all grown up across different societal and historical boundaries. They have developed in ways peculiar to each locale along the course of their growth, in the process evolving until they reflect no single set of social circumstances. It may be, too, that the integrity of ethics follows from constancies in social life and human thought per se, constancies reflected in the norm of reciprocity and the injunction against incest, for example, much as the universal obligation not to kill reflects the universal fact of humans' mortal vulnerability to each other. Thus the Mosaic covenant and moral philosophy, modern jurisprudence and structural-functional sociology can all be seen pointing out similar moral duties as institutional requisites of any community.[66]

Even when we affirm the ultimate integrity of ethical truth, however, we must still account for a wide range of variation in particular ideas of right and wrong. This becomes a practical problem precisely as the hidden power of language, symbol, and conceptual categories to make events what they are comes to light, that is, when a culture becomes pluralized and different systems of meaning compete to identify the same phenomena. Is the "low self-esteem" the psychologist finds in a person actually a matter of Christian "humility," or is it Buddhist "selflessness"? Is his strong conscience of "God's will" actually a "rigid cognitive defense mechanism"? Does he commit sins, miscalculate interests, exhibit neurotic tendencies, indulge dualistic delusions, or betray the revolutionary cause? Does he need to be punished, deterred, reindoctrinated, rehabilitated, or merely put in touch with his feelings? The answers we choose to such questions influence how we act and how we respond to others. The conditions of our social and cultural situation make certain moral ideas more plausible than other ideas to us, and more plausible to us than others. In this sense social and cultural conditions give certain ideas unequalled power to "choose" and move us. In the process of religious conversion the observer sees the convert choosing the beliefs, norms, and relationships presented to him by a given movement. The convert himself experiences these beliefs, norms, and relationships taking hold of him and taking care of his life.

Between *Is* and *Ought*

Every one of us must find a way to regulate our own conduct and our relations with others. When this breaks down, as it did for many sixties youths, we are driven to recover our moral balance, even if it means "getting saved" or becoming a world saver. Converts to alternative religion are people who experienced ethical contradictions of unusual intensity and as a result looked for unusually coherent solutions to them. Their conversions provide a particularly vivid picture of how moral ideas come together and change, but one that depicts a cultural process in which we all participate. If every person faces the need for self-regulation, so does every society. In traditonal societies and even now, less visibly but no less essentially in our own, religion makes morality possible. It does so by molding the fundamental order of reality—our deepest convictions about nature, self, and society —and deriving from it a feeling of commitment and a sense of intrinsic value and obligation.[67] We *ought* to act in accord with the way things actually are. So Christians ought to perfect themselves "in the last days," Zen students practice non-attached compassion in a reality without self or other, and *est* graduates take total responsibility for a world they totally created. Just as religious belief and ritual each borrow the other's authority to confirm their own, so together they enable our world view and ethic to confirm each other. The normative *ought* grows out of the factual *is* that grounds it and makes it intellectually reasonable. The general order of existence naturally accommodates the way of life that reflects it and makes it emotionally acceptable.[68] In so synthesizing *is* and *ought*, religion acts as a model *of* reality and a model *for* reality.[69] In the first role it shapes its symbolic structure to conditions "out there" in the world. In the second, it shapes those conditions to itself. Through this cultural process we make circumstances as much as circumstances make us.[70]

Religion ties the way a people live to the order they live within through sacred symbols. These are dramatized in rituals like tongue-speaking, meditation, and *est* processes. They are related in myths like the second coming of Jesus, the Bodhisattva's return from Nirvana to enlighten others, and even the success story of Werner Erhard. Religious rites and myths induce in those who worship and believe characteristic motives and moods, made in the image of their exemplar's virtues. These are habitual tendencies "to live like Jesus," that is, to act in certain ways toward given ends, and to feel in certain ways about given conditions.[71] Religious symbols, writes Clifford Geertz, "are felt somehow to sum up, for those for whom they are

resonant, what is known about the way the world is, the quality of the emotional life it supports, and the way we ought to behave while in it."[72] Thus
ontology and cosmology merge with morality and aesthetics in one seam-
less if circular web of meaning, spun from symbols. Fact and value come
together in common sense. *Is* and *ought* become one, married at the symbolic altar.

If moral meanings are so seamlessly maintained, why then do they
ever unravel, break down, and change? They do so because their web of
meaning is not entirely circular, in fact. It cannot be, for the nonsymbolic
structure of the world "out there" can never be manipulated entirely into
parallel with the symbol system.[73] Moral ideas make perfect sense in relation to other ideas, but not in direct relation to what goes on in the world
around us.[74] There exist certain conditions of human life, the singular fact
of death and every sort of undeserved suffering, that seem by their very
nature to constitute problems of moral meaning incapable of any neat, perfectly reasonable, once-and-for-all solution. Every culture offers answers to
these problems, to be sure, or it attempts to do so. Persons come to experience the unconditional truth of these answers through embracing their symbolic forms in particular rites and living them out under particular social
conditions. Thus they make the way the world ought to be into the way it
is. Apart from such efforts, ideal and actual remain different sorts of statements, one evaluative and the other descriptive. Ultimate answers remain
unable to resolve concrete problems of meaning with logical finality, since
the problems themselves are experiential, not just analytical. We must
suffer through them. We cannot simply think them through. "Accepting
God's will," for example, may answer the cry of faithful parents who have
lost a child, but this answer, like the problem, is physio-logical as well as
logical. Only when they surrender, in their hearts and on their knees, to its
symbolic affirmation of ultimate order will it enable them to account for
and even embrace what is concretely irrational, unjust, and insufferable.

Moral ideas do not make perfect sense out of life's events because ideas
must mean by virtue of their semantic constitution, while events need not.
Left unfinished by instinct, we must understand and regulate our actions in
order to act and interact, while events need only happen. They can be more
or less explained, but they happen nonetheless. Perhaps, then, things simply
happen to happen. Scientific explanations of cause and effect may account
for the physical conditions of an event like a crippling auto accident or the
death of a child. Such explanations can go on to find clues to the social, psychological, even cultural conditions of some such events. But they cannot
answer the most compelling questions we ask of life: "Why me? Why does
life have to be like this? *Is* it worth living? What should we do now, and
how should we live?"

Magic can explain a particular event more completely than any scientific concept of causality.[75] It can say exactly why a given accident occurred
to a given person at a given time and place. The question of whether or not

that person *deserved* to suffer the accident never arises. It is obviated by imputing to agents with supernatural powers the intent to harm him. Magic offers no morally coherent picture of life as a whole, but only a supernatural transposition of unresolved human conflict. Moral coherence comes to the whole of life when conflict between good and evil finds resolution in the unitary perfection of God, the cosmos, nature, or history. Such universal perfection is then reconciled with the world's particular imperfections in one of several ways. Religious millenarism promises to equalize the world's present injustices, the result of past sins, by rewarding saints and punishing sinners in a perfect kingdom to come upon the earth after the apocalypse. Historical millenarism promises to equalize injustices caused by social conflict by rewarding the oppressed and reforming the oppressor in a classless society to come after the revolution. Moral judgment of the dead offers a similar promise, with heaven and hell providing the retribution. Contemplating the world's finite imperfections in light of God's infinite power, knowledge, and love led to Job's conclusion that God's will is inaccessible to human understanding, even as human destiny is entirely dependent upon it. This conclusion detaches actual suffering from moral evil. It takes one classic form in the Calvinist notion that God inexplicably predestines human beings in this world and the next from all eternity. A second formulation is the Hindu-Buddhist notion that each person's good and evil deeds find karmic compensation in the successively reincarnated lives of his soul. However inexplicable what happens in the world may seem to be, the world itself is a perfectly closed cosmos of ethical retribution.

Notions such as these resolve problems of meaning in theory, but the power of such explanations rests on ultimate reference points removed from the common-sense experience that generated the problems in the first place. This distance leaves moral meaning vulnerable to life's misfortunes, especially to undeserved suffering and unpunished evil. That "the good die young and the wicked flourish as the green bay tree" may press one toward wider truths that redeem these facts by completing their context. Thus moral paradox may lead one person to renew his commitment to an ethic of faith, reason, efficiency, or self-expression for its own sake. But it may lead another to disillusionment and then to conversion. Received ideas lose their power to convince him, symbols to resound and move him, and ritual to reveal any authority beyond his own self. If enough persons undergo this process of disillusionment and conversion together, it can lead the culture itself to shift its ethical orientation, so that others find their ethical outlook changed without themselves experiencing any definite disjunction in the course of this change. Whether or not enough persons give up one ethic for another depends partly on the social conditions in which they seek to actualize their ideals and partly on their very effort to do so. If external structural conditions change so that a given symbol system cannot accurately shape itself to them (religion as model *of*), then it loses its power to motivate us to shape our lived reality to its pattern (religion as model *for*). The converse is also true. If our commitment to a given ethic slackens and it cannot shape social conditions so forcefully, then they become less susceptible to accurate reflection in its symbolic shape. On one hand, the more closely an ethic fits a set of social conditions—that is, the more plausible it seems under those conditions, and the more sensible they seem in its light—the more important that ethic becomes to live out and the greater adherence it gains. This holds true even when the ethic fits existing conditions by indicting them with such effective force that we can live out its ideas only by changing the world. On the other hand, the closer a society's institutions come to living up to its ethic, the greater commitment to them it can ask its members to make, and the more vigorous and coherent will be its life. In both respects the social significance of morality comes from its cultural functions.

Morality in Modern Society

Practically posed, moral questions are about one or another concrete activity. They are about learning, working, or loving; about family, communal, or political relations. The diversity of these activities and relations makes plausible diverse answers to what life means, how we should live, and how we should think out these answers. We have looked at four traditions of morality and styles of evaluation which begin to suggest this diversity. Tensions between these ways of understanding right and wrong are accompanied by tensions between different sectors of social life. Each way of understanding seems more plausible in one social sector than in another. The consequential style of evaluation, for example, seems particularly plausible in the experience of modern work and the economy, the regular style in learning and law, the expressive style in private life with friends and lovers, the authoritative style in parenting and the military.

In looking at alternative religious movements against the backdrop of the 1960s, we saw the strongest tensions between the consequential ethic of utilitarian individualism and the expressive ethic of the counterculture. But tensions also showed up between individualism and the authoritative and regular ethics of biblical religion. We have seen how closely the utilitarian ethic fits the technological, bureaucratic, and scientific conditions of a modern society built around economic production. As technology coordinates material resources to the end of greater productivity and bureaucracy organizes human resources to the same end, social life becomes more rational in coordinating means to ends. Technical reason orders external relationships between persons and things, and between persons in working relationships to things, ideas, and one another. As a model of meaning, technical reason enters other, noneconomic aspects of the lives of those who work with it. It enters their private, political, familial, sexual, psychic, and intellectual lives—with mixed results. It rationalizes the rest of their lives by discovering there the logic of want satisfaction in what were mysteries. In this very process, however, technical reason makes events and conditions irrational that once had authoritative, regular, or expressive moral meaning. Such events, like love and death, go on. Only now they simply exist or happen to happen. They no longer signify anything.

Conversely, the counterculture and alternative religion carry other ways of understanding right and wrong, which render irrational the utilitarian logic of want satisfaction and the instrumental behavior it justifies. Money does not count for happiness, protests the hippie, nor does careerist achievement add up to self-fulfillment. Maximizing utility does not assure a consistently principled moral life for the rational humanist, nor a life of obedience to God for the devout Christian: biblical believer, humanist, and hippie are not simply utilitarians disguised by their efforts to maximize obedience to authority, regular consistency, or situational self-expression instead of efficient want satisfaction. Their difference runs deeper than this, because all moral action is not goal oriented in the first place.[76] It is not necessarily a matter of aligning means to ends. Regular consistency, obedience to authority, and self-expression may be seen as values or virtues to which other ethics direct instrumental action much as utilitarian individualism directs it to the ends of want satisfaction. But this means-ends resemblance is itself the product of a moral outlook based on the consequential style of evaluation and its goal-oriented structure. In fact, the authoritative ethic is oriented primarily toward an authoritative moral source per se, not to the goal of obedience to it. The regular ethic is oriented toward consistent principles per se, not to the goal of compliance with them. The expressive style is oriented toward situational feelings per se, not to the goal of expressing them. In other words, each ethic works in its own authoritative, regular, or expressive style, with its own theory of what makes acts right. Each ethic does not work in the same consequential style toward different goals.

In a modernized society persons perform qualitatively different tasks and live in circumstances that differ in the access they offer to various tasks and to the rewards of work. Differences in social experience from person to person accompany different ideas about the moral meaning of their experience. Consider, for example, the moral differentiation of work itself. The unskilled laborer follows a foreman's orders, the skilled worker also refers to craft standards, the white-collar worker to bureaucratic regulations and interpersonal responses, the professional to disciplinary canons and collegial criticism. Each person tends to generalize the moral meaning of her own experience to social life and society as a whole. Those similarly situated in society tend to share their personal experience as a group and to fuse their interpretation of it into a consensual truth. This is the social-structural basis of moral disagreement among groups in a differentiated society, whether differentiated by class, sex, race, age, ethnicity, or region. Heterogeneity of tradition in modern culture and its pluralization into subcultures are the cultural bases of moral disagreement among groups in a complex society.

But differences in moral meaning do not exist only among persons of different classes, sexes, races, regions, and cultural backgrounds. They exist, to some extent, among sociocultural counterparts, by virtue of their biographical, temperamental, and intellectual differences as individuals. Finally, differences in moral meaning exist for each individual, because he experiences different moral norms, values, and attitudes in different sectors of his own social life, and within each sector at different times in his life. Both authority and self-expression are relatively strong for *any* individual within the family. Utilitarian individualism holds sway in business and much of public life, informing bureaucratic regulations and being circumscribed by law. In private life among friends, expressive feelings are the norm, while obligations arise between spouses. On one hand, the diversity of ethical outlooks surrounding each individual encourages him to distance himself from any single outlook and relativize all of them in order to enact each one in the social role specific to it: efficient worker, expressive lover, law-abiding citizen, authoritative parent, and so on. On the other hand, a diversity of ethical outlooks triggers a countervailing tendency toward convergence. The individual attempts to take the ethical outlook predominant in one sector of social life (whichever he is most involved in and identified with) and to generalize it to the whole.

Seen from this standpoint, sixties youth sought to expand the expressive outlook of private life with friends and lovers or the regular outlook of the student to take in the whole of social life. Even as they did so, they decried the utilitarian adult's attempt to do likewise with his market model of maximizing self-interest or the patriot's military model of unquestioning obedience to authority. In this fashion the tendency to generalize, in itself a characteristic of rationality, fuels social conflict when the experience from which each group generalizes lies in a different sector of social life and lends plausibility to a different ethical outlook on the whole of it.

The sector of social life which holds the most morally meaningful experience for a given person varies with cultural and historical factors, not only sociological ones. Among the latter, however, age has been fundamental to our inquiry. For age defines sixties youth as a generation, one which made fresh contact with aspects of American culture, reappropriating tradition in the light of changing social and historical conditions.[77] Age also defines youth as a stage of life. It begins with movement out of the family and into a peer group of age cohorts. This loosens the ties of tradition and the ideological power of parental authority. It makes youth more susceptible to ideological change and more able to act it out, since they are still unburdened by the constraints of economic self-support.[78] Youth's disengagement from the institutions of family, work, and political power, in which authoritative and utilitarian values are concentrated, and its involvement in educational institutions, which stress the disciplinary development of ideas, give youth a special concern for the coherence and regularity of cultural meaning. They also give youth the freedom to push that concern to its limits, however opposed to authority or utility these cultural meanings may appear.[79] Thus "the idealism of youth." To its critics in America during the sixties it appeared to be challenging the legitimate authority and disrupting the practical business of our society. To its sympathizers it appeared to be helping our society to generate changes it desperately needed yet could not calculate, legislate, or command.

The transformation of moral meaning evident in getting saved from the sixties reveals several aspects of the way in which moral ideas change. Besides the gap between moral ideas and the phenomena they seek to explain, moral ideas create internal tensions and inconsistencies of their own, amplified once they are socially enacted. At times, for example, the inspired commands of one authority clash with another's. Self-expression leads to conflict or a standoff instead of concord. Rationalists reason to different prescriptions, resist practical compromise, or surrender to self-interest in their actual behavior. Consequentialists confuse what they (or humankind) "really" want, miscalculate how to get it, or frustrate one another's calculated efforts to do so by their own. Tensions within moral ideas and in their relation to events both widen with the multiplication of experience and interpretation that goes on in modern society. This occurs among groups and classes of persons, and within each person's life. Cultural transformation follows on social change and leads into it, often in complex and diverse ways. Even when we cannot specify one-to-one correspondences or causal relationships between changes in culture and social structure, we can look for the breakdown and transformation of moral meaning to occur along the stress lines etched by tensions within the ideas themselves.

Different styles of evaluation tend to render one another irrational, yet syntheses occur among them. Which style of evaluation predominates for a given individual or group: Which of its tensions demand resolution most strongly? Does resolution come through conversion to another style of evaluation or synthesis with it? These are questions posed by this moral model. They can be answered only by locating evaluation within the social-structural, situational, biographical, and, most of all, the cultural factors that enter into it. Styles of ethical evaluation by themselves are empty analytical categories. They take on substance only when they are applied in turn to the different layers of moral meaning that make up social life. These include (1) cultural-historical patterns of morality, like biblical religion and utilitarian individualism, which support (2) the norms of social institutions, like government, education, and the family; and underlie (3) the formal ethics of ideological organizations, like religious movements, which inform (4) the ethical outlook of persons in a particular place in society at a particular time in their own lives and in history. Only when styles of ethical evaluation link the other elements that make up moral thought, that is, perceptions of facts, loyalties to others, and axial assumptions about the nature of reality, do these analytical categories reveal a living ethic by which persons make particular judgments.[80]

Without considering styles of evaluation, on the other hand, we are left with nothing but the particular judgments persons make. These appear as discrete "opinions" presumed to follow from the interests that their adherents' social conditions define. When persons act contrary to their interests, it can only be because they have miscalculated them. This pragmatic view of moral behavior has practical drawbacks that a more interpretive strategy can address by relating the process of evaluation to its outcome. Our inquiry has suggested that how a person thinks about right and wrong powerfully influences what he judges to be right or wrong, and what he decides to do about it. How a person justifies his moral positions and actions influences how he may be persuaded to change them. Styles of ethical evaluation are the necessary link between social and cultural conditions (which give these styles substance and plausibility) and particular moral positions and actions (which these styles generate and defend). Without taking ethical styles into account we cannot understand ethical outcomes nor can we change them, except by coercion or the manipulation of interests. This is because, once more, we think our way to moral actions. Social and economic circumstances influence our thinking, but they do not do it for us. Recognizing this fact makes it possible to enrich research that neatly correlates social and economic data with discrete opinions on concrete issues by exposing the interlocking assumptions, arguments, and modes of discourse that hold together these particulars. It also makes it possible to honor the commonsense conviction we have of our own moral views—that they come from our understanding, not our circumstances.

What do *we* go by? How do we think it out, and live it out? If we inquire into our own moral views as we have into the views of sixties youth in alternative religious movements, will we find traditional answers still clear and powerful? If so, then the voices we have heard here may sound curiously confused, the lives we have glimpsed may seem odd or obscure. But if instead we find ourselves unsure of what to go by, unmoved by our received ideas and symbols, and uneasy in the world around us, what then? Then we cease to be observers safely watching others search to get saved from the sixties. Eager or unwilling, we have already joined them in a cultural drama where their efforts to renew tradition or transform it offer us cues. Whether we take their example as paths to follow or avoid, possibilities to test, or puzzles to solve, the answers they give us about how we should live cannot simply be dismissed. For the questions are our own. Let us face them.

APPENDIX 1
Typology of Styles of Ethical Evaluation

This typology distinguishes four ideal styles of ethical evaluation, as distinct from the contents of an evaluation. These four types are: (1) authoritative; (2) regular (i.e., constituted by fixed rules); (3) consequential; (4) expressive.

I. These four styles constitute a taxonomy along the following dimensions:

A. General Orientation and Mode of Knowledge

1. The authoritative style is oriented toward an authoritative moral source known by faith.

2. The regular style is oriented toward rules or principles known by reason.

3. The consequential style is oriented toward consequences known by cost-benefit calculation.

4. The expressive style is oriented toward the quality of personal feelings and of situations known by intuition.

B. Form of Discourse

In posing the moral question, "What should I do?"

1. The authoritative style asks, "What does God command?" and answers with which act is "obedient" and "faithful."

2. The regular style asks, "What is the relevant rule or principle?" and answers with which act is "right" or "obligatory" according to the rules.

3. The consequential style asks, "What do I want? What act will most satisfy it?" and answers with which act will be most "efficient" or "effective" in producing the consequences that satisfy a given want.

4. The expressive style asks, "What's happening?" and answers with which act is most "fitting" in response.

C. Right-making Characteristic of an Act

1. Authoritative: an act is right because the authoritative source commands it.

2. Regular: an act is right because it conforms to the relevant rules and principles.

3. Consequential: an act is right because it produces the most good consequences; that is, maximizes satisfaction of wants.

4. Expressive: an act is right because it constitutes the most fitting response to the situation and the most appropriate or honest expression of one's self.

D. Cardinal Virtue

1. Authoritative: obedience to moral authority makes a person most worthy of praise.

2. Regular: rationality in discerning and enacting moral principles makes a person most worthy of praise.

3. Consequential: efficiency in maximizing the satisfaction of his wants makes a person most worthy of praise.

4. Expressive: sensitivity of feeling and situational response makes a person most worthy of praise.

E. Resolution of Disagreement

1. Authoritative: moral disagreement is resolved by literal exegesis of scripture and increased familiarity with it; and, ultimately, by conversion.

2. Regular: moral disagreement is resolved by reasoning dialectically (from problem to solution to generalized, consistent principles to other problems, and so on) to increasingly abstract principles consistently generalizable to the most cases.

3. Consequential: moral disagreement is resolved by review of the pertinent empirical evidence; and, ultimately, by social-scientific explanation of alternative perceptions of the facts.

4. Expressive: moral disagreement is resolved by exchanging discrepant intuitions within the context of ongoing social interaction, thereby reshaping the situation (or community), and the agents' consciousness as formed by the situation.

F. Degree of Specificity of Prescription (ranked from most to least specific)

1. The authoritative style yields the greatest possible specificity of prescription or proscription of particular acts by means of commandments and regulations that can be casuistically applied to particular cases.

2. The regular style provides less specific prescription of acts by ruling out certain acts because they fail to meet prior fixed criteria of right conduct—regardless of their consequences.

3. The expressive style yields still less specific prescriptions of right acts, derived from the intuited moral sense of the relevant (reference) group or community regarding the most

fitting feeling within a given situation and the most fitting
act in response to it.

4. The consequential style yields the least specific prescriptions regarding right acts, since it judges acts solely by their
effectiveness in producing given consequences or achieving
given goals. It does not judge acts qua acts, viewing them
as instrumental procedures for effecting desired consequences.

II. Relationship of the Four Styles to Deontological and Teleological
Theories of Right:

Both the authoritative and the regular styles employ a *deontological*
theory of right to define right acts. This means they assert that there are
characteristics of an act that make it right besides the goodness of its consequences. These are features of the act itself, other than the results it produces—namely, that it is commanded by God, or it conforms to the rules.
The regular style justifies the rules themselves not by the consequences of
their recognition, as would a rule-utilitarian, but by their inherent features
—that they are just, consistent, reflect the true nature of existence, and
the like.

This stands opposed to the consequential style of ethical evaluation,
which employs a *teleological* or *consequential* theory of right, by which it
defines right acts. (I will use these two terms as equivalent, *from* a viewpoint described below.) This theory asserts that there is only one right-
making characteristic of acts, namely the comparative goodness or value of
their consequences. An act is right if and only if it produces at least as great
a balance of good over bad consequences as any available alternative act.
(See William K. Frankena, *Ethics*, chapter 1, esp. pp. 13-16.)

The expressive style of evaluation appears somewhat ambiguous
regarding its use of a deontological or a teleological theory of right acts. The
characteristic that makes acts right in its view—their self-expressive and
situation-fitting character—may seem to inhere in the act itself, not in its
consequences. But then why is it that no particular act is consistently or
inherently right or wrong? Because, this style answers, situations change,
and so do feelings of the agents in situations, though their inner selves may
remain constant in some significant sense. So the appropriateness of acts,
and therefore their rightness, varies according to the situation and the
agent's feelings. If we consider this characteristic of appropriateness attrib-
utable to the variable effect or consequences of a given act rather than to its
situationally invariable identity in itself, then the expressive style of evaluation seems to be using a teleological or consequential theory to define right
acts by reference to the goodness of their consequences. Even granting this
ambiguity, the expressive style yields more specifically prescriptive acts
than does the consequential style (at least in its countercultural use) by virtue of its conception of the self.

In modern philosophical usage, a deontological theory holds that at least some acts are morally right and obligatory not only because of their consequences (or, more strongly, apart from or regardless of their consequences) for human weal or woe. Kant is usually seen to be the first modern philosopher to propose such a theory in holding that moral rules are universally valid and admit of no exceptions. W. D. Ross is a twentieth-century deontologist, who admits of (intuitive, not consequential) exceptions to rules in cases where two or more moral rules conflict. I usually describe the deontological position by saying that it holds that acts are right in themselves, as opposed to the consequential or teleological position of utilitarianism, which holds that acts are right by virtue of their consequences. The distinction, in fact, is not always so neat, since some acts that are right in themselves are right because of the consequences they entail. Not harming, for example, is right because it refrains from bringing about certain results. That refraining is right in itself, but it is partly defined by the anticipated results of an act of harming. A second factor enters into the consequential-deontological distinction, namely that deontology attends to the moral significance of the past in a way that consequentialism does not. Promise keeping, for example, is right because I have made a promise. It remains a right-making consideration, even if there are consequences of keeping that promise that are wrong-making. (I am indebted to Arthur J. Dyck for these last two points.)

This strictly consequential construal of teleological ethics, the larger deontological-teleological dichotomy, and indeed this whole typology of evaluative styles implies a viewpoint in philosophical ethics that is more modern than classical and a viewpoint in Christian ethics that is more Protestant than Catholic. Aristotle, for one, proposes a eudaemonistic sort of teleology that spans regular and consequential styles of evaluation as I define them. His ethic rests upon a concept of virtuous character in harmony with nature (not a concept of obligatory acts), whose practical reason conjoins rules with a situational and expressive sense of human needs that transcends desire. St. Paul, for another, makes no distinction between what is commanded by God and desired by man, after his repentance and redemption. Indeed, until the twelfth century, Christianity merges God's will and human desire in a single transcendent conception of the Good. Stoicism begins the deontological opposition between duty and inclination that culminates in Kant after the conciliatory Thomist view that "grace perfects nature" gives way to the Protestant view that grace makes up for nature.

III. Assignment of Styles to Cases

These characterizations of four styles of ethical evaluation refer to ideal typifications, construable as extending to the *predominant* ethical style of an actual cultural system, in which some or all of the other styles nonetheless play a part. This taxonomy is drawn with some modifications from an apparatus developed by Ralph B. Potter (see n. 2, chap. 1) to interpret moral debate over a particular public policy issue, nuclear arms. For the general difficulties of this typological usage and the particular difficulties of so typifying the cultural-historical and case material analyzed here the present writer is, of course, solely responsible.

APPENDIX 2
Schematic Presentation of Cases

I. LIVING WORD FELLOWSHIP

1. belief system:	cosmological dualism
2. organization:	sect (conversionist-introversionist)
3. leadership:	ethical prophet
4. rites:	tongue-speaking; demon expulsion and spirit filling; baptism, faith healing, and prayer
5. membership:	lower-middle- and working-class hip dropouts, with conservative Christian parental backgrounds and high-school education; small upper-class minority of inherited wealth with elite liberal arts education; countercultural alienation; blue-collar work.

ETHIC: authoritative/expressive

1. chief orientation:	divine authority
2. mode of knowing:	faithful conscience
3. right-making characteristic of acts:	commanded by God, intent to love God
4. cardinal virtues:	obedience, love
5. moral example:	Jesus/pastor
6. formal statement:	Ten Commandments Greatest Commandment

TENETS:

1. personhood:

cosmological—individual eternal soul

2. human nature:

evil but perfectible

3. theory of personal change:

a volitional-affective process: soul suddenly receives God's grace, "decides for Jesus," and repents; person is saved, "filled," then gradually perfected morally, until becoming millennially immortal.

4. politics:

millenarian; right-wing conservative

II. PACIFIC ZEN CENTER

1. belief system:

epistemological monism

2. organization:

monastic community (with sectarian and churchly traits)

3. leadership:

exemplary prophet

4. rites:

zazen meditation, master-student relationship, monastic regimen

5. membership:

upper-middle-class bohemian-hip seekers; secular humanist parental backgrounds; elite liberal arts education, blue-collar and service work.

ETHIC: regular/expressive

1. chief orientation:

situation and "no-self"
orthopraxy and precepts

2. mode of knowing:

meditational intuition; reason

3. right-making characteristic of acts:

one with situation, accords with rules

4. cardinal virtues:

non-attachment, compassion

5. moral example:

Bodhisattva/Zen master

6. formal statement:

precepts

TENETS:

1. personhood:	phenomenological—"no-self"
2. human nature:	at once deluded and aware; gradually perfectible
3. theory of personal change:	an epistemological-volitional process: student begins to sit, gradually deepens practice, suddenly attains enlightenment experience (*kensho*), then gradually integrates this into ordinary behavior.
4. politics:	eco-millennial; left-liberal/monist conservative

III. ERHARD SEMINARS TRAINING

1. belief system:	psychologized monist individualism
2. organization:	bureaucratic cult
3. leadership:	mystagogue
4. rites:	*est* training—guided fantasy "processes," therapeutic "sharing," encounter-style confrontations with trainer
5. membership:	middle-middle-class whites, less alienated than neo-Christians and neo-Orientals; wider age and class range, much lower demands; white-collar parental backgrounds; nonelite education and white-collar work.

ETHIC: consequential/expressive

1. chief orientation:	felt consequences; situational rules
2. mode of knowing:	affective calculus; psychological intuition
3. right-making characteristic of acts:	produces most felt aliveness, follows situational rules
4. cardinal virtue:	responsibility (being "at cause")

5. moral example: Werner Erhard/*est* trainer

6. formal statement: "rules of life" (*est* training ground rules)

TENETS:

1. personhood: psychological—individual "mind"
pop mystical—universal "being"

2. human nature: at once completely determined and completely causal; immediately perfectible

3. theory of personal change: a psychological-epistemological process: trainee gradually acknowledges he is "an asshole" and abreactively "experiences out" his self-caused problems, then "gets it" after some 60 hours; he then "enhances" this enlightenment through meetings of denominational frequency over an indefinite period of time.

4. politics: post-millennial; middle-of-the-road/ psychologized laissez faire

APPENDIX 3
Methods

Research for this study began in 1972 with fieldwork and informal interviewing in a series of preliminary visits to the Living Word Fellowship, a Pentecostal sect, and ended in 1979 with several followup interviews for each case study.

Throughout the summer of 1973, I worked as a researcher in the LWF with the pastor's permission, "since this is the Lord's way of bringing you to himself." During this three-month period I participated in the full round of services, instruction, and fellowshipping required of every sect member, although I did not undergo or feign conversion. After several benignly inconclusive attempts at demon expulsion and an affirmative "vision from God" and "word of knowledge" concerning my case, the pastor allowed me to remain formally unsaved yet informally accepted in the LWF. Nonstop proselytizing efforts directed at me diminished in intensity thereafter, although they never ceased.

Taped formal interviews began in the LWF during a week-long "camp" in 1973, eventually including forty persons and totalling some 150 hours. The last such interview was done in late 1978. While most persons were interviewed for two to three hours, some youths were interviewed three or more times during this period, some for as long as six hours at a sitting. Although most Christians were interviewed singly (as were all Zen and *est* informants), seven interviews were done with married couples and three others with groups of three or four. Much the same format was used for almost every person in the initial interviews, for Zen students and *est* graduates as well as for Christians: A "moral biography" was elicited (see Preface and pp. 297-299), usually turning on the problems that led each person to the religious movement and the answers she found there. In the case of the LWF (and *est* as well), where stylized conversion stories are part of each member's religious repertoire, each person was encouraged to deliver her usual version of this biography and to elaborate its normative side as well. Key issues and cases were followed out dialectically against the background of this moral biography. I asked for reasons and premises; concrete examples for generalizations, and generalizations from examples to set against counterexamples. I used no notes and followed no fixed protocal in my questioning, and these interviews often constructed themselves, covering my list of intended questions (see pp. 295-299) and then some, in their own sequence and with their own emphases. I would then check over my list, sometimes resuming the interview to raise or return to additional items.

As I listened to, transcribed, and filed material from each interview, new questions and details were raised which found their way into subsequent interviews with others, or followup interviews with the same person. Followup interviewing allowed this cumulative process to continue into the period of drafting and revision of each case study. If I was unclear about a point, I sought to go back and check it with at least two informants. This meant that I asked or reformulated a given question or series of related questions several times with some youths. Most extended quotations (for example, on page 44) represent a single continuous statement made by one person in a single interview. In perhaps one case in ten I have spliced one person's responses to the same question in two different interviews; or, more rarely, the responses of two different persons to the same question. Some ellipses or paragraphlike separations in quoted material mark such splicing. More often they merely indicate gaps or shifts in the response of a single speaker during the same interview.

Since I was not given access to church records or a directory, quantitative data for the LWF (see pp. 35-37) were gathered largely through formal and informal interviewing and direct observation. A listing of social characteristics (age, education, occupation, marital status, age and date of conversion, and so on) was worked up bit by bit for each member of the LWF, using annual church camp photographs of the entire congregation together to help keep track of their overall numbers. From June, 1974 through May, 1975 I attended LWF services, Bible classes, and special events (baptisms, weddings, picnics), taking notes and/or taping almost all of these events. From this material, from the interviews, and from LWF literature, I wrote a 300-page monograph in 1975-76, on which I drew for chapter 2 of the present study. The substance of this chapter has been reviewed verbally with several young LWF members in taped interviews. A former LWF minister read and commented on it in draft form.

My interest in Zen Buddhism as practiced in the San Francisco Bay Area began earlier than did my research into it. That interest was both intellectual and personal, and I participated in one such group in 1970-71. In June, 1975, I began participating in a second Bay Area Zen group with the announced intention and the master's permission to pursue research among its younger members. I participated regularly for the following year and irregularly thereafter. Ten Zen students were formally interviewed between 1976 and 1978, with several being interviewed repeatedly. Informal interviews were done with twenty to thirty additional students, including members and former members of three other Zen meditation groups, San Francisco Zen Center among them. Quantitative data related to "Pacific Zen Center" (see pp. 103-105, 322-323), a composite of several Bay Area Zen groups, were based on information provided by the officers of the groups selected, their records and literature, augmented in a few instances by David

Wise's "Dharma-West," which studied San Francisco Zen Center prior to 1971. The Zen chapter was read in draft form by masters of two of the groups described, and by several sixties youth involved in them as priests or veteran members.

I began participant observation in *est* in December, 1974, and I attended the *est* standard training program in San Francisco in 1975. (The fee was afterward refunded to me by *est* as a "scholarship.") I took extensive notes during breaks scheduled in each day of the training and immediately afterward, and compiled a 100-page account of the training in the week after it ended. I then enrolled in three graduate seminars involving twenty-three weekly meetings, in which I took field notes. I did informal interviewing along the edges of the training program schedule, in the graduate seminars, and while serving as a volunteer assistant on and off at *est*'s San Francisco offices and at events it staged between October, 1975, and May, 1976. I interviewed some fifty persons informally and recruited formal interviewees from these three venues. This enabled me to talk with persons from one month to five years after they had taken the *est* training. Among the twenty *est* graduates I interviewed formally were persons who had enthusiastically dedicated months of volunteer labor and recruited every available relative, friend, and associate to *est*; and others who had done no more than attend the sixty-hour training over two weekends. I interviewed one person who had defected during the training and was outraged by *est*, as well as several who had sat through it, felt depressed and confused by it, and then had nothing more to do with *est*. However, my sample was intentionally weighted toward persons who felt sufficiently positive toward the training to subsequently espouse its point of view and remain engaged in its seminars, if not its organization.

I interviewed several *est* staff members informally before requesting and being denied permission to do formal staff interviews. Several senior staff members read the *est* chapter in draft, and one of them commented on it extensively. Since *est* clients spend only sixty hours before graduating from its training while its core staff are often involved with *est* over several years on an almost-daily basis, we should expect much greater subtlety and possibly major differences in the respective interpretations of *est* clients and staff regarding its ethic. (The chapter's staff reviewer argued that *est* should be interpreted as a deontological ethic of universal compassion based on a monist world view; he objected to any view of it as consequential, utilitarian, or individualistic. He also allowed, however, that some persons might be vainly trying to use *est*'s ethic in such fashion. See pp. 225-226; p. 333, n. 20. Since *est*'s clientele is roughly 1,000 times larger than its staff, the fact that its clients' view of *est*'s ethic is more fully represented here than is its staff's is, I would argue, no great liability.

Most quantitative data regarding *est* graduates come from Robert Ornstein et al., *A Self-Report Survey: Preliminary Study of Participants in Erhard Seminars Training*, and from raw data compiled for that study in

1974. Data from both sources are used with the permission of the study's project director, Charles Swencionis. Data codebooks stored in the *est* archives and additional *est* research records were examined in 1978 with the permission of *est*'s Office of Research, then headed by Kenneth Anbender.

Let me conclude by acknowledging my own point of view, and bias, toward each of the cases studied. Although I shared relatively little common cultural or social background with most of the LWF's members, found certain of their cosmological and millenarian beliefs impossible to credit literally, and sometimes felt uncomfortable under the pressure of their aggressive proselytizing, I was moved by the genuine love LWF members showed for one another, for me, and for the God they served. "By their fruits" I knew them as persons I could trust and respect. This applies both to the minority of upper-class sixties youth who provided my initial access to the group and to the lower-class youth with whom I did most of my subsequent research.

With many Zen students, by contrast, I shared a social and cultural background similar in many respects. I also found Zen's practices and tenets in themselves more appealing than those of the other two cases. (This does not necessarily apply to all of Zen Center's characteristics as compared with the LWF's; its marital instability, for example, seems less desirable on the face of it than does the LWF's familism.) I have sought to hedge against my greater personal interest and involvement in Zen in describing and especially in judging its ethic, although the tone of the chapter reflects my relatively favorable attitudes toward it.

During the *est* training I found myself moved by many of the trainees, impressed by the efficiency with which they were managed by the *est* staff, and intrigued by the eclectic yet commonsensical quality of *est*'s tenets. Although I took part in all of the training's "processes," I participated only minimally in its confrontational dynamic, and I remained unpersuaded to suspend moral disbelief in it. Most if not all of *est*'s staff, and virtually all of its volunteers, appear to me to believe most sincerely that *est* "creates value" in the lives of its clients and in their society. For all their interpersonal astuteness and effectiveness in performance, however, *est*'s staff and its clients also appear to be almost entirely unaware of the meaning of what they profess, either practically, intellectually, or morally. I have sought to hedge against my relative lack of sympathy for the movement per se (as distinct from its clients), and to limit my criticism to those substantive issues that deserve it on their own merits.

Interview Reference Questions

How should we live?
How do you decide what you should do?
What do you go by? How do you live it out?

Right and Wrong

1. What does it mean to say "that's wrong" or "that's right" about something a person does?
2. What do *you* mean when you say it?
3. What characteristic of a right act makes it right?
4. Are any acts absolutely wrong? Which? Why/Why not?
5. If someone says, "What's right and wrong is relative to how each person feels about it," do you agree? Why/Why not?

Value

1. What is the most important thing in life?
2. What is good in itself? What is intrinsically valuable? Why? What do you mean by *happiness*, (or *love, pleasure*, or whatever is good in itself)?
3. What do you want? How do you know what you want?
4. What makes you feel good? What does it mean to feel good? Is it the same as being good?
5. What should we do in order to realize what is good in itself? (Obey God, follow certain rules, be here now? . . .)

Styles of Evaluation

1. How do we know what's right or wrong? Are there specific moral commands we should obey? Where do these commands come from? How do you know them? Do you need to know God or obey God to do what's right? Why/Why not?
2. Are there fixed rules you should follow? What are they? Where do they come from? From some first principles? What? How do we know them?
3. What sort of acts produce good consequences? What consequences are good? How can we tell which acts will produce the most good consequences? Whose good should the consequences advance? Our own, everyone's, certain others'?
4. When you respond to a situation appropriately, do you have any particular idea of what you should do, like "Don't hurt anyone"? How does this feeling come about? Can you do anything to uncover or strengthen it?

Moral Feeling and Will

1. How do you feel when you do something that's right? Something that's wrong? Do you ever feel guilty? When? What does it mean when you do?
2. Why don't people always do the right act? Why don't people always do what they know is right, or think is right? How can they become more able to do it? Do you ever do something even if you don't want to? How does this feel? Why do you do it?

Moral Disagreement

1. Why do people disagree about what's right and wrong? What can they do about it? Can persons prove their views? Can they give reasons for them? What does it take for you to be persuaded to change your mind? When you disagree with someone in movement X, compared to an outsider, do you work it out differently? How?

The Good Person

1. What is a good person like? What qualities does she/he have? Examples?
2. Can a person change her life? How? (Change consciousness, relationships, social situation, societal structures? Which is most basic?)
3. How does a person learn to do what's right? How can you educate them?

Interpersonal Relationships

1. What's important in your relationships to the people around you? What would you like to change or strengthen in your relationships as they are now? How should they be? What rules, ideas, models should they have?
2. What social arrangements and institutions (e.g., marriage, communes) best fit the way relationships should be? How?

Work

1. What's most important in a job? Pay, creativity, helping others, security, advancement potential? Is one kind of job any better than another? Why?
2. Do you have a career or vocation? Describe it.

The Good Society

1. What is a good society? What makes society good?
2. What should we do in relation to other people in society? How are we

responsible for one another? Are we "our brother's keeper"? What does that mean? How does this relate to the law?

3. What do you see most Americans going by in their behavior? How do they decide what to do? How does this compare with your own case? With movement X? Does movement X have some way or message to help society change for the better? What is it?

4. What is authority? How do we recognize true authority? What makes it legitimate?

5. What is the meaning of *freedom, justice, social equality*? (Equality of opportunity or of results? What is a fair share? Of what?)

World View

1. What does *God* mean for you? Has this meaning changed over time? How?

2. What is a person? Is there such a thing as "human nature"? Is it basically good, bad, neutral? Fixed or mutable? How does it change?

3. How should we relate to the world of nature? Master it, follow it, harmonize with it, etc.?

4. How should we orient ourselves in time? Be here now, plan for the future, learn from the past, etc.?

5. What kind of process does human activity represent? Being, becoming, doing? How do these fit together?

6. What are social relationships based on? Are they essentially vertical, horizontal, individual?

7. Is life worth living? Why?

Social Identity—A short autobiography: What was it like growing up?

1. Age
2. Sex
3. Ethnicity
4. Religious background; present affiliation and participation?
5. Residence? Now? Growing up? Moves?
6. Family: composition, values, religion, parental schooling and work?
7. Schooling: where, what studied, how long?
8. Work: doing what, feeling about it, plans?
9. Marital status: single, married, divorced, living with someone?
10. Want to have kids? What would you like them to do?
11. Social standing, class background?

Moral Biography

1. Looking back at your family, what did they place the most value on, what was central in their lives? What did they go by?
2. Was your family religious? How so? How did they live out their beliefs?

3. What experiences have been the most important for you? Religious experience, drugs, art, etc. What have they meant for how you live? Has movement X changed this? Before and after?
4. How would you describe your relationships before movement X and now? With parents and family, friends, lover/spouse, boss, etc.?
5. How do you see yourself as a woman/man? What does it mean to "act like a woman/man"?
6. Have you ever lived communally? How was that? How would you compare and judge the different arrangements or ways you've lived?
7. How should you raise children? Compare this with how you were raised.
8. Was school important to you? How? What did learning mean to you before, now? What is the purpose of it?
9. What kind of work are you doing now? Why? How do you feel about it? About past work? Plans for the future? To what end?
10. What does success mean to you? What is a successful person?
11. When you look at this society, what do you see? What is wrong, right with it? What should we do about it?
12. Have you ever been involved with any social or political activity? What, when, why? What about now? How do you see the change?

Conversion

1. What were you doing before you joined movement X? Did you have any particular problem or needs then? What was bothering you? How did you see it then? What were you trying to do about it? (other movements, therapy, career?)
2. How did you first hear about movement X? What was your first contact? First impressions? How did they change?
3. Was there a turning point, a point of no return, as you were getting involved in movement X? What was it? When?
4. Did you make friends at X? How, with whom? Did you keep seeing old friends, or other nonmembers? How did you come to see less of them? How are your relationships with other members different from relationships with outsiders?
5. When did you really commit yourself to movement X? When did you feel you were really a part of it?
6. Is there anything else you ever experienced, before or since, that's at all like your experience in X? (e.g. drugs in relation to meditation?)
7. Compare the organization of movement X to the way you were living before.
8. Since joining movement X, what have been the main changes, the biggest ups and downs? What rules at X were easiest, hardest for you to accept? What beliefs, practices? Which have changed your life most? How? Has X changed your feelings about rules and authority in general, like in school, work, or politics?

9. Describe your relationships with Pastor/Guru/Master X. Does it have an ethical or moral side to it? How so?
10. How is he/she an example of how to live? How does he/she relate to people? How would you compare this to other religious leaders or ministers you have known?

APPENDIX 4
Buddhist Sutras

THE MAHA PRAJNA PARAMITA HRIDAYA SUTRA

(The Heart Sutra)

Avalokiteshvara Bodhisattva
When practicing deeply the Prajna Paramita
Perceived that all five skandhas are empty
And was saved from all suff'ring and distress.

"Shariputra, form does not differ from emptiness;
Emptiness does not differ from form.
That which is form is emptiness;
That which is emptiness, form.
The same is true of feelings, perceptions, impulses, consciousness.

Shariputra, all dharmas are marked with emptiness;
They do not appear nor disappear,
Are not tainted nor pure
Do not increase nor decrease.

Therefore in emptiness, no form,
No feelings, perceptions, impulses, consciousness;
No eyes, no ears, no nose, no tongue, no body, no mind;
No color, no sound, no smell, no taste, no touch, no object of mind;
No realm of eyes and so forth until no realm of mind-consciousness;
No ignorance and also no extinction of it, and so forth until
    no-old-age-and-death and also no extinction of them;
No suff'ring, no origination, no stopping, no path;
No cognition, also no attainment.
With nothing to attain
The Bodhisattva depends on Prajna Paramita
And his mind is no hindrance.
Without any hindrance no fears exist;
Far apart from every perverted view he dwells in Nirvana.

In the three worlds all Buddhas depend on Prajna Paramita
And attain Anuttara-samyaksambodhi.

Therefore know the Prajna Paramita
Is the great transcendent mantra,
Is the great bright mantra,
Is the utmost mantra,
Is the supreme mantra,
Which is able to relieve all suff'ring
And is true, not false.
So proclaim the Prajna Paramita mantra,
Proclaim the mantra that says:
Gate, gate, paragate, parasamgate! Bodhi! Svaha!"

DŌGEN'S FUKANZAZENGI AND SHŌBŌGENZŌ ZAZENGI

Translated by Norman Waddell and Abe Masao

1   The Way is basically perfect and all-pervading. How could it be
contingent upon practice and realization? The Dharma-vehicle is free
and untrammelled. What need is there for man's concentrated effort?
Indeed, the Whole Body is far beyond the world's dust. Who could
believe in a means to brush it clean? It is never apart from one right
where one is. What is the use of going off here and there to practice?

2   And yet, if there is the slightest discrepancy, the Way is as distant as heaven from earth. If the least like or dislike arises, the Mind is
lost in confusion. Suppose one gains pride of understanding and in-
flates one's own enlightenment, glimpsing the wisdom that runs
through all things, attaining the Way and clarifying the Mind, raising
an aspiration to escalade the very sky. One is making the initial, partial excursions about the frontiers but is still somewhat deficient in the
vital Way of total emancipation.

3   Need I mention the Buddha, who was possessed of inborn knowledge?—the influence of his six years of upright sitting is noticeable
still. Or Bodhidharma's transmission of the mind-seal?—the fame of
his nine years of wall-sitting is celebrated to this day. Since this was
the case with the saints of old, how can men of today dispense with
negotiation of the Way?

4   You should therefore cease from practice based on intellectual
understanding, pursuing words and following after speech, and learn
the backward step that turns your light inwardly to illuminate your
self. Body and mind of themselves will drop away, and your original

face will be manifest. If you want to attain suchness, you should practice suchness without delay.

5   For *sanzen*, a quiet room is suitable.* Eat and drink moderately. Cast aside all involvements and cease all affairs. Do not think good or bad. Do not administer pros and cons. Cease all the movements of the conscious mind, the gauging of all thoughts and views. Have no designs on becoming a buddha. [*Sanzen*] has nothing whatever to do with sitting or lying down.

6   At the site of your regular sitting, spread out thick matting and place a cushion above it. Sit either in the full-lotus or half-lotus position. In the full-lotus position, you first place your right foot on your left thigh and your left foot on your right thigh. In the half-lotus, you simply press your left foot against your right thigh. You should have your robes and belt loosely bound and arranged in order. Then place your right hand on your left leg and your left palm [facing upwards] on your right palm, thumb-tips touching. Thus sit upright in correct bodily posture, neither inclining to the left nor to the right, neither leaning forward nor backward. Be sure your ears are on a plane with your shoulders and your nose in line with your navel. Place your tongue against the front roof of your mouth, with teeth and lips both shut. Your eyes should always remain open, and you should breathe gently through your nose.

7   Once you have adjusted your posture, take a deep breath, inhale and exhale, rock your body right and left and settle into a steady, immobile sitting position. Think of not-thinking. How do you think of not-thinking? Non-thinking. This in itself is the essential art of zazen.

8   The zazen I speak of is not learning meditation. It is simply the Dharma-gate of repose and bliss, the practice-realization of totally culminated enlightenment. It is the manifestation of ultimate reality. Traps and snares can never reach it. Once its heart is grasped, you are like the dragon when he gains the water, like the tiger when he enters the mountain. For you must know that just there [in zazen] the right Dharma is manifesting itself and that from the first dullness and distraction are struck aside.

9   When you arise from sitting, move slowly and quietly, calmly and deliberately. Do not rise suddenly or abruptly. In surveying the past, we find that transcendence of both unenlightenment and enlightenment, and dying while either sitting or standing, have all depended entirely on the strength [of zazen].

Sanzen, Zazen, and *wall-sitting* all refer to Zen meditation.

10   In addition, the bringing about of enlightenment by the opportunity provided by a finger, a banner, a needle, or a mallet, and the effecting of realization with the aid of a *hossu*, a fist, a staff, or a shout, cannot be fully understood by man's discriminative thinking. Indeed, it cannot be fully known by the practicing or realizing of supernatural powers either. It must be deportment beyond man's hearing and seeing—is it not a principle that is prior to his knowledge and perceptions?

11   This being the case, intelligence or lack of it does not matter; between the dull and the sharp-witted there is no distinction. If you concentrate your effort singlemindedly, that in itself is negotiating the Way. Practice-realization is naturally undefiled. Going forward [in practice] is a matter of every-dayness.

12   In general, this world and other worlds as well, both in India and China, equally hold the Buddha-seal, and over all prevails the character of this school, which is simply devotion to sitting, total engagement in immobile sitting. Although it is said that there are as many minds as there are men, still they (all) negotiate the Way solely in zazen. Why leave behind the seat that exists in your home and go aimlessly off to the dusty realms of other lands? If you make one misstep, you go astray from (the Way) directly before you.

13   You have gained the pivotal opportunity of human form. Do not use your time in vain. You are maintaining the essential working of the Buddha Way. Who would take wasteful delight in the spark from the flint-stone? Besides, form and substance are like the dew on the grass, destiny like the dart of lightning—emptied in an instant, vanished in a flash.

14   Please, honored followers of Zen. Long accustomed to groping for the elephant, do not be suspicious of the true dragon. Devote your energies to a way that directly indicates the absolute. Revere the man of complete attainment who is beyond all human agency. Gain accord with the enlightenment of the buddhas; succeed to the legitimate lineage of the patriarchs' samadhi. Constantly perform in such a manner and you are assured of being a person such as they. Your treasurestore will open of itself, and you will use it at will.

APPENDIX
Demographic Representation
of EST

5

Comparisons Between the Ornstein Study's
1973 Questionnaire Respondents and the
1970 Census for the Bay Area

Census figures are for San Francisco-Oakland SMSA (Standard Metropolitan Statistical Area), including the five Bay Area Counties (a population of 3,109,519), and for the nation. Source: 1970 Census: *Population and Housing*, issued April, 1972, U.S. Department of Commerce.

In sum, there appears to be a higher proportion of women in the *est* population than in the Bay Area at large. The *est* population seems younger. Thε *est* population has a higher proportion of divorced people and lower proportion of married people. The "living with someone" category is not strictly comparable to any census category. Income seems close, and educational level is higher.

TABLE 1

Sᴇx

(persons 16 and older)

	Questionnaire respondents	Questionnaire nonrespondents	SF SMSA
Males (16 yrs. +)	41.4%	46.5%	48.2%
Females (16 yrs. +)	58.6%	53.5%	51.8%
	(1,204)	(741)	

TABLE 2

AGE

Ages 16-75 +	Major Q respondents	SF SMSA	US
16-19	2.0%	9%	
20-24	11.2	13	
25-34	46.7	19	12.3%
35-44	19.9	16	11.3
45-54	11.5	17	
55-64	6.4	13	
65-74	1.2	8	
75 & over	1.1	5	
Missing	0.2	—	
Mean:	35.11 yrs.*	42 yrs. approx.	

*Mean age falls to 33.7 by 1978, according to *est* records.

TABLE 3

INCOME CHARACTERISTICS
(families and unrelated individuals)

	Major Q (1973)* respondents	SF SMSA (1969)
$ 1- 4,999	17%	13%
5,000- 9,999	27	25
10,000-14,999	27	30
15,000-24,999	20	24
25,000-50,000	7**	7
50,000 +	2***	1
	100% (710)	100% (776,750)
No response	(494)	
Mean income	$ 12,796	$ 13,429

*Possibly underestimates income for families where there are two earners and respondent replies for own income only.
**Mean for *est* 25,000-39,999
***Mean for *est* 40,000 +

TABLE 4

EDUCATION

(persons 25 or older)

	Yrs.	Major Q respondents	SF SMSA	US total
Some grade school	(1-7)	0.3%	10%	14.3%
Finished	(8th)	0.5	8	13.4
Some high school	(1-3)	3	16	17.1
Finished	(12th)	8	33	34.0
Some college	(1-3)	31	16	10.2
Finished		17		
Graduate or Professional School after College		40	17	11.0
		100%	100% (1,783,717)	

TABLE 5A

MARITAL STATUS
(raw data*)

	Major Q respondents
1. Married, widowed and remarried	38.0%
2. Separated	6.2
3. Divorced (annulled)	13.3
4. Widowed	1.9
5. Never married	26.7
6. Living with someone**	9.7
7. Separated/divorced and living with someone	2.5
8. Never married and living with someone	1.6
9. Divorced and remarried	0.1
	100.0 (n = 1,179)

*Variable W81, File SYS8, 10/11/74, p. 64.

**The "Living with someone" (LWS) category is ambiguous in table 5B and, to a lesser extent, in 5A, since it contains persons never married, separated, or divorced, and it conflates them. 5A gives a partial breakdown (#7, 8) of the LWS category, but a residual category (#6) remains. Assuming one-half of those reporting themselves simply LWS without reference to being never married or divorced/separated are, in fact, divorced/separated, then 27 percent of all *est* graduates turn out to be divorced/separated [6.2 + 13.3 + 4.9 + 2.5] instead of 19 percent or 22 percent; with 33.1 percent of all graduates never married. Then 40.4 percent of all those ever married are now separated/divorced [27/(100-33.1)], instead of 26.6 percent [19.5/(100-26.7)] or 30.7 percent [22/(100-28.3)].

TABLE 5B

MARITAL STATUS
(14 years and older)

	Major Q respondents	SF SMSA	US total
Married	38%	60%	71.8%
Separated	6	2	—
Divorced	13	6	3.2
Widowed	2	7	8.6
Single	—	27	16.4
27			
Never married	27	—	—
Living with someone*	14	—	—
	100%	102%	

*The "Living with someone" (LWS) category is ambiguous, since it contains persons never married, separated, or divorced, and it conflates them. See note to table 5A.

NOTES

1. CULTURE AND COUNTERCULTURE

1. See Daniel Yankelovitch, *The New Morality: A Profile of American Youth in the 70's*, especially chapter 1. From national survey data and 3,500 interviews done in 1973 and compared with studies in 1967, 1969, and 1971, Yankelovitch reports that certain new values associated with the counterculture in the 1960s and especially with upper-middle-class college youth have since spread to the entire youth generation, i.e., middle-, lower-middle, and working-class youth, and thence to older upper-middle-class urbanites. As schematized by Yankelovitch, these new values include: (1) Moral Norms: (1) more liberal sexual mores; (b) lessening of compliance with and respect for established authority in the form of the law, the police, the government, and one's boss; (c) waning influence of organized religion and churches on moral behavior; and (d) waning of traditional uncritical attitudes of patriotism. (2) Social Values: lessening loyalty to the work ethic, marriage and family, and the value of money as a measure of success. (3) Self-Fulfillment: increasing concern with life as a search for self-fulfillment as opposed to a pursuit of economic security. Also see Yankelovitch, *New Rules in American Life*.

2. This chapter draws its overall approach and argument from Robert Bellah, "New Religious Consciousness and the Crisis in Modernity," chapter 15 of Charles Y. Glock and Robert N. Bellah, eds., *The New Religious Consciousness* (hereafter cited in its draft form as Bellah 1974), and less directly from his *The Broken Covenant: American Civil Religion in Time of Trial*, esp. chaps. 1, 2, 6. It rehearses Bellah's interpretation of the historical relationships involved, while slanting his typification of biblical, utilitarian, and countercultures toward their specifically normative aspect. The taxonomy of styles of ethical evaluation is taken from Ralph B. Potter's paradigm of the ethical system in his "The Structure of Certain Christian Responses to the Nuclear Dilemma, 1959-1963" (Th.D. thesis, Harvard Divinity School, 1965), pp. 363-398. The typifications of utilitarianism and, to a lesser degree, of the counterculture borrow freely from chapter 3 of Alvin Gouldner's *The Coming Crisis of Western Sociology*, "Utilitarian Culture and Sociology." The discussion of modernization and the counterculture follows Peter Berger's in parts I and III of *The Homeless Mind*, though not quite to his conclusions. See note 41 below.

3. See Bellah 1974, p. 3.

4. See Bellah 1974, pp. 3-5. Also see Talcott Parsons, "Utilitarianism: Sociological Thought" in David L. Sills, ed. *International Encyclopedia of the Social Sciences*, 15:229-235. Also see Max Horkheimer, *The Eclipse of Reason*, chap. 1.

5. See Bellah 1974, pp. 4-5. Also Alasdair MacIntyre, *A Short History of Ethics*, pp. 119-123.

6. See Appendix 1, section ii, for a discussion of deontological and teleological theories of right in relation to the four styles of ethical evaluation. Also see William K. Frankena, *Ethics*, chap. 1, esp. pp. 13-16.

7. See Robert Bellah, "Religious Evolution," in William A. Lessa and E. Z. Vogt, eds., *Reader in Comparative Religion* (New York: Harper & Row, 1972), pp. 36-50, esp. "Early Modern Religion," section, pp. 45-47. Also see MacIntyre, *Ethics*, chaps. 9-10.

8. Talcott Parsons, "Christianity," in Sills, ed., *Encyclopedia*, 2:438.

9. See Michael Walzer, *The Revolution of the Saints: A Study in the Origins of Radical Politics* (Cambridge, Mass.: Harvard University Press, 1966), p. 1.

10. Max Weber, *The Protestant Ethic and the Spirit of Capitalism*, p. 121. Here I am paraphrasing Weber's reference to Sebastian Franck's characterization of the Reformation.

11. John Winthrop, "A Modell of Christian Charity," pp. 41-43 in Conrad Cherry, ed., *God's New Israel* (Englewood Cliffs, N.J.: Prentice-Hall, 1971). Cf. Jimmy Carter, "Inaugural Address," chap. 5.

12. In the following remarks, as in those above typifying biblical religion, I am not addressing myself to a moral theory, theology, or a philosophical system per se, but to a more diffuse and mundane notion of the biblical or utilitarian *culture* which spans religious meanings, norms, and ideas of the social order. These typifications are intended to sketch a cultural matrix consistent with the general shape of the philosophical theories involved, but they do not deal distinctly or systematically with the substance, detail, or terminology of particular theories. Throughout I have conflated contractarian, utilitarian, and egoist philosophical ethics under the terms "utilitarian individualism," "utilitarian culture," and "utilitarianism." I may appear to treat all of them as if they were equivalent to the philosophical position termed General Impersonal Ethical Egoism ("Everyone ought to act so as to produce the greatest balance of good over bad consequences for him or her, and any choice that doesn't affect him or her is morally indifferent.") They are not. But in practice the morality of utilitarian culture is, in my view, closer to this philosophical position than any other; and so I have interpreted it, often with reference to Hobbes. My nonphilosophical usage of the term *utilitarian* follows directly on that of Bellah 1974 and his *The Broken Covenant*, and on Alvin Gouldner's *The Coming Crisis of Western Sociology*. It stems from a tradition of sociological and social theory that includes Talcott Parsons, Max Weber, Emile Durkheim, Marx, and Hegel. In philosophical usage, *utilitarianism* can be defined in its most general generic form to mean largely what I am using it to mean: "The doctrine which states that the rightness or wrongness of actions is determined by the goodness or badness of their consequences." (J. J. C. Smart, "Utilitarianism," in Paul Edwards, ed., *The Encyclopedia of Philosophy*, 8:206.) This doctrine is then interpreted in either an egoistic or nonegoistic/universalistic fashion: Are the good consequences which must be considered, consequences to the agent himself (e.g. his own happiness) or to everyone? The latter alternative yields universalistic utilitarianism, the form of it with which philosophical discussion is usually concerned, and which Bentham and Mill advanced. The latter alternative yields egoistic utilitarianism, with which our discussion is clearly but not exclusively concerned.

13. See Bellah 1974, p. 5.

14. By use of the term *technical reason* I refer to the rationalization of means —that "functional rationality," associated by Max Weber with modernized society,

which consists of conceptually separating means from ends, and calculating the arrangement of means so as to maximize given ends. This term distinguishes the rationalization of means from "reason" generally, and particularly from that reflective rationality associated with the rationalist philosophical tradition. Max Horkheimer draws much the same distinction between a "subjective reason" concerned with coordinating means to ends that are taken for granted and an "objective reason" aimed at evolving a comprehensive system of all beings and judging the goodness of ends. See *The Eclipse of Reason,* chap. 1, esp. pp. 1-12, 21. Note Horkheimer's parallel between subjective reason and Weber's functional rationality, and his qualification of any comparison between his category of objective reason and Weber's more relativistic "substantial rationality," (p. 6, n. 1).

15. See Alvin Gouldner, *The Coming Crisis of Western Sociology,* pp. 61-65 (cited hereafter as Gouldner 1971).

16. See Louis Dumont, *From Mandeville to Marx,* pp. 93-97.

17. Utilitarian individualism posits a timelessly determined human nature in conceiving human wants and interests as an inner physics of forces and drives largely unorganized into a theory of personality. For Hobbes each individual is motivated basically and most powerfully by the desire to preserve himself. To this end he seeks to dominate others, giving rise to a war of all against all in the absence of authoritarian political rule, to which men resort out of calculated self-interest. For the sake of self-preservation they enter into a social contract, submitting to a sovereign authority who by force guarantees order and "so much liberty [to each man] against other men, as he would allow other men against himself." (Michael Oakeshott, ed., *Leviathan,* p. 104.) In Hobbes' view there are no shared rules or moral standards, indeed no social life, prior to the social contract that establishes political authority. Feelings of social obligation result from qualities that society superimposes upon man's nature by a long process of habituation. Locke's milder state of nature is neither entirely premoral nor presocial. The natural right of self-preservation has been expanded to life, liberty, and property. Men live in families and possess the property of their own labor, and make and acknowledge claims on one another. They enter into a social contract to establish a minimal government to safeguard each other's rights by due process. Valid laws are those passed by a majority vote, and the legitimacy of the political authority requires the (tacit) consent of the governed, making Locke the ancestor of liberal democracy. Locke sidesteps the Hobbesian problem of each individual's pursuit of self-interest leading to conflict with others by simply assuming the harmonious identity of individuals' self-interest. This accounts for the existence of mutual advantage in exchange. See MacIntyre, *Ethics,* chaps. 10, 12. Also Willmoore Kendall, "Social Contract" in Sills, ed., *Encyclopedia,* 3:376-381.

18. See Dumont, *From Mandeville to Marx,* chap. 6, esp. p. 97.

19. Thus Hume held that morality could not be deduced a priori from reason, but only inductively, by inspecting and seeing the consequences of behavior. Kant contended that "from the critical standpoint . . . the doctrine of morality and the doctrine of nature may each be true in its own sphere," while maintaining that morality was a species of rationality. (See Gouldner, 1971, p. 67.)

20. On this last point I am paraphrasing Robert Merton's discussion of the social sources of anomie in *Social Theory and Social Structure,* p. 157, while following the argument of Gouldner 1971, pp. 65-73.

21. See Frankena, *Ethics,* chap. 3, esp. pp. 30-35. Also see John Rawls, "Two

Concepts of Rules," *Philosophical Review* 64 (1955): 3-32; and R. B. Brandt, *Ethical Theory* (Englewood Cliffs: Prentice-Hall, 1959), chap. 15.

22. Cf. *est's* "rule-egoism," chap. 4.

23. Hobbes and Locke differ on the substance of this identity, and so on the nature of society. See n. 17 above.

24. Gouldner 1971, p. 69.

25. Bellah 1974, p. 5.

26. This description pertains to the norms or consciously shared common understandings in a culture of what transpires in social relationships, not to what an outside observer might perceive to be happening in actuality. It asserts no empirical claims about the actual effects of reciprocity of exchange in any given societies.

27. See Gouldner 1971, pp. 72-73.

28. See Bellah 1974, p. 4.

29. See Kendall, "Social Contract," in Sills, ed., *Encyclopedia*, 3:376-381.

30. See n. 17 above and sources cited there. Bentham attacked the idea of natural rights, arguing that rights are calculable in exactly the same way as are duties. He treated as rights those human needs or capacities, the realization or protection of which would maximize good consequences for everyone.

31. See Bellah, 1974, pp. 3-6. also his *The Broken Covenant*, esp. the preface and chaps. 1, 2; and his "American Civil Religion in the 1970s," in Russell E. Richey and D. G. Jones, eds., *American Civil Religion*, pp. 255-272.

32. Bellah 1974, p. 4.

33. For the purposes of comparison with the biblical and utilitarian traditions my interpretation of the counterculture will proceed as if it were a single unified viewpoint. In fact, it consisted of several wings, notably the hip-psychedelic and the radical political. Their differences stand out most clearly if we conceive of the two as being involved in two different kinds of revolution, one primarily political and the other primarily cultural. (See Kenneth Keniston, "You Have to Grow Up in Scarsdale," in *Youth and Dissent*, pp. 303-317.) The political revolution of the sixties radicals was concerned mainly with redistributing traditionally conceived moral goods (i.e., the utilities supposed to effect them). It demanded that existing sorts of material rewards, political freedoms and powers, socioeconomic opportunities *and* results heretofore concentrated among the upper and middle strata of American society be shared equally among all its members. The guiding value of counterculture radicalism, then, was the central *political* value of equality, brought to bear on issues of distributive justice. It thereby continued the heritage of the liberal-democratic-egalitarian revolution that began in eighteenth-century America and France. The second revolution was less concerned with the *amount* or distribution of socioeconomic goods than with the *quality* of personal and social life in itself. That is, it was less concerned with the redistribution of goods than with the redefinition of what was good. The guiding value of the second revolution was the central cultural and personal value of self-realization and self-fulfillment. Its predecessors were to be found among religious revivals, and in romantic and bohemian culture reaching back almost to the beginning of industrial society and up to the Beat subculture of San Francisco in the 1950s. Having made this sharp distinction, let us look more closely at those sixties youth involved in political protest activity but not in its ideological or organizational core groups. The good society at which most of these youths aimed their efforts was, in fact, largely drawn from the redefinitions of the hip-psychedelic wing of the counterculture rather than from classical liberal or

Marxist social theory. Here the difference between the two wings of the counterculture was largely over how that good society was to come about. (See Bellah 1974, p. 8.) Radicals held to the need, first, for revolutionary political change in order to realize a fully human society. Hippies saw no need to act over against the existing social structure directly, but simply to withdraw from its life programs and enact a new style of life in the present, which would spread of its own loving momentum from the interstices of the old society to the whole of a new one in a process of transformation from the inside out. To accomplish "the greening of America" the hippie had only to enact and celebrate the cultural end, and the political means would take care of themselves. Be-ins, love-ins, and rock festivals were such celebrations. Sitins, marches, and demonstrations, by contrast, were political tactics that often resembled those of earlier political movements or even the old society itself in their instrumentalism, but they were seen by radicals to be justified by qualitatively different ends—overthrowing the existing order instead of maintaining it. Similarly, many radicals personally resembled their "uptight" conventional antagonists. They were oriented toward work, organization, and control, while the "hang-loose" hippie represented an unmistakable counterdefinition to the conventional personality ideal. Whatever their differences with each other, both political radical and hippie were united in opposing utilitarian culture, and they both tended to dismiss the biblical tradition, even though they espoused certain attitudes akin to it, as the Jesus movement later made clear.

34. For discussion of the expressive style in relation to deontological and teleological theories of right action, see Appendix 1, section ii.

35. Here again I am referring to ideals, postponing for ethnographic treatment the actual interpersonal problems posed by attempts to enact the counterculture's expressive ethic and its spiritual quest. Cf. David McClelland et al., *The Achievement Motive* (New York: Appleton-Century-Crofts, 1953).

36. In the 1950s American religious organizations expanded their membership dramatically, outstripping the population growth rate by 12 percent. In the early 1960s their growth rate had slowed down to about that of the population. Around 1965 major liberal Protestant denominations (characterized by an orientation toward social action and ecumenism) began to show losses, for reasons that may have little to do with their liberalism, while conservative groups (focused on personal rather than social issues and holding to doctrinally distinctive identities) continued to gain. Some of them, notably the Pentecostal movement, have not abated to date. But in 1971 or so major conservative churches—such as the Catholic, American Lutheran, and Southern Presbyterian Churches—began to experience the same patterns of decline evident earlier among their liberal counterparts. Falloffs in religious participation also occurred in this period, especially among Catholics, led by young adults in their twenties. (See Constant Jacquet, *Yearbook of American and Canadian Churches.* Also see Dean Hoge and David Rosen, eds., *Understanding Church Growth and Decline.*) According to Gallup data for 1957-71, church attendance declined 23 percent among persons between the ages of twenty-one and twenty-nine, but it fell only 11 percent among those thirty to forty-nine and 4 percent among those fifty and over. Other longitudinal data point to comparably outsized declines in conventional religious belief among youth during the 1960s. (See Robert Wuthnow, "Recent Patterns of Secularization: A Problem of Generations?" *American Sociological Review* 41 (1976): 850-867, esp. pp. 856-857.) Youth also led a shift in perceptions of conventional American religion's influence as declining.

Since 1957 the Gallup Poll (George Gallup, Jr., *Religion in America*, 1979-80, p. 27) has asked, "At the present time do you think religion as a whole is increasing its influence on American life, or losing its influence?" A national sample has responded as follows:

	Losing	Increasing
1957	14%	69%
1962	31	45
1965	45	33
1967	57	23
1968	67	18
1969	70	14
1970	75	14
1974	56	31
1975	51	39
1976	45	44
1977	45	36
1979	48	37

37. Distinguishing between the counterculture and contemporary American Christianity (see Bellah 1974, pp. 9-11) raises the question of the counterculture's relationship to earlier sociopolitical movements and to Romanticism (see Gouldner 1971, pp. 78-80). Unlike earlier radical political protest in America, for example in the 1930s, the sixties counterculture rejected the central values of modern industrial society per se, not just its capitalistic or American variant. It rejected the maximization of utility in its fundamental social forms—the achievement ethic enacted in routine industrial, white-collar, and professional work; the inhibition of expression and impulse—not just class-biased ownership of the means of production and the like. Gouldner sees the psychedelic counterculture as "a new wave of an old resistance to utilitarian culture" that crystallized in nineteenth-century Romanticism. These antecedents make the counterculture no less important. Indeed they indicate that its concerns go back to the emergence of industrial society. The counterculture's indifference to Christianity contrasts with earlier versions of Romanticism, which often employed Christian values consciously as a standpoint for social criticism. Moreover, early Romanticism rejected an immature industrial society, full of promises but offering relatively little bounty or justice to most of its members. The sixties counterculture rejected the ripened fruits of an affluent society, the expanded rights and opportunities of the Welfare State, and the proffered personal compensations of mass leisure. In short, the counterculture rejected an industrial society and a utilitarian culture that had already succeeded (for the middle class) by its own standards.

38. For a quick sketch of this history see Raymond Prince, "Cocoon Work: An Interpretation of the Concern of Contemporary Youth with the Mystical," in Irving I. Zaretsky and M. P. Leone, eds., *Religious Movements in Contemporary America*, pp. 255-271, esp. 258-263.

39. This refers to normlessness strictly on the level of the culture's ethical system and intentionally leaves aside the matter of *anomie* as a lack of social integration.

40. See, for example, Daniel Bell, *The Coming of Post-Industrial Society.* Also see Ann Swidler, *Organization without Authority: Dilemmas of Social Control in Free Schools*, chap. 7.

41. This section follows the analysis of Peter Berger, Brigitte Berger, Hansfried Kellner, *The Homeless Mind*, esp. chaps. 8-10 (hereafter cited as Berger 1974). It assumes the general viewpoint of the sociology of knowledge, although it attempts to present Berger's findings without explicit recourse to the Schutzian phenomenological apparatus used to derive them in chaps. 1-4. My position differs from Berger's mainly in developing the normative dimension of utilitarian culture and counterculture, in which the counterculture acquires a positive identity beyond that of a form of "demodernizing consciousness." I attribute to the "private sphere" of modern society not only a new sociopsychological "softness" and personalism, as does Berger, but (especially to the family) a rather old sense of moral obligation and universalism and virtue as well. This is the heritage of biblical and rule-oriented moralities elsewhere in recession, and now at odds with the expressive moral style sponsored by the private sphere generally and particularly prevalent outside the family. Conversely, I give more weight to the ambiguously utilitarian *and* expressive character of the public sphere in "postindustrial" society and its new professional-managerial class than does Berger's more dichotomous treatment of utilitarian public and expressive private life. Also I conceive of alternative religious movements as mediative successors to the conflict between mainstream culture and counterculture in the 1960s, rather than as synchronic expressions of the counterculture itself, as Berger seems to (see Berger 1974, p. 205). Finally, I have shied away from some of Berger's terminology in the interests of ease of usage, even at the expense of systematic clarity.

42. The dissenting young were not against reason but only against a utilitarian definition of reason as a quantitative calculus that ignores expressive human values and needs. (See Keniston, *Youth and Dissent*, p. 380.) Neither were they neo-Luddites opposed to technology per se, but they were opposed to the imposition of the ends-means logic of technology and the overriding criteria of efficiency and productivity on human life in general. See n. 14 above.

43. See Berger 1974, chap. 2, for a detailed treatment of bureaucracy. The point on limited reciprocity appears on p. 59. Also see C. Wright Mills, *White Collar*, pp. xv-xviii, 63-70.

44. See Berger 1974, chaps. 4, 9, especially pp. 112, 205-206.

45. Gouldner 1971, p. 74.

46. Berger 1974, pp. 205-206.

47. Ibid., p. 208.

48. The "role-distance" concept is Erving Goffman's. See Berger 1974, p. 114.

49. See Berger 1974, pp. 114-115.

50. Ibid., p. 208.

51. Cf. Berger, who sees the counterculture opposed to order and institutionalism per se, or at least opposed with less qualification than I find. (See Berger 1974, pp. 212-214.) I would be cautious in accepting Victor Turner's liminal "antistructure" characterization of it for much the same reasons. The distinction made between relatively structured society and relatively unstructured community implies Toennies' *Gesellschaft-Gemeinschaft* distinction. It could also be made in terms of Durkheim's organic and mechanical solidarity, or Talcott Parsons' pattern vari-

ables, which are implied by the contrast between commune and bureaucracy discussed on p. 18. On the whole, this chapter's discussion of culture and social modernization centers on the process of functional rationalization as interpreted by Weber, as do the discussions in Bellah and Berger.

52. The picture of the Earth was, predictably, taken from a rocket-propelled vehicle, by a highly sophisticated camera, and so on. Such irony recurs throughout culture/counterculture oppositions, especially in considering the counterculture's attempt to liberate the individual from those social-structural conditions of modernity that have bred the peculiar individuality of our times as well as its alienation.

53. See Berger 1974, p. 113. Also Horkheimer, *The Eclipse of Reason*, p. 19: "The pattern of the social division of labor is automatically transferred to the life of the spirit, and this division of the realm of culture is a corollary to the replacement of universal objective truth by formalized, inherently relativistic reason."

54. Berger 1974, p. 185.

55. See Berger 1974, pp. 186-191, with reference to the following treatment of the private sphere. Regarding shifts in occupational structure see Mills, *White Collar*, pp. 63-65, on the growth of "the new middle class," especially office workers. Also, for example, Peter Blau and O. M. Duncan: "Technical improvements in production and farming have made possible the tremendous expansion of the labor force in tertiary industries—those other than agriculture or manufacturing—and, particularly in [salaried] professional and semiprofessional services since the turn of the century," in *The American Occupational Structure*, p. 428. I have lifted the phrase "game between persons" from Daniel Bell's characterization of postindustrial work, but I mean it to span the bureaucratized middle level of modern social organization, and so as a more ambiguous mixture of instrumental reciprocity and management than Bell's view of cooperation and communal reciprocity among the professional elite in postmodern society. At least in the former context work as "a game between persons" ambiguously implies a game of persons against one another as well as with one another.

56. See Appendix 1, section ii.

57. See Berger 1974, pp. 185-188.

58. Besides their expressive aspect, note the regular aspect of the counterculture ethic and the familial private sphere as defined by Appendix 1 and the discussions on pages 3, 5, 15.

59. The output of industrial production in America has expanded since the 1920s, while both labor and capital inputs per unit of output have remained constant or declined. Technology and organizational expertise have more than made up the difference. See Fred Block and Larry Hirschhorn, "New Productive Forces and the Contradictions of Contemporary Capitalism: A Post-Industrial Perspective," *Theory and Society* 7 (1979): 368-371. Also see Ann Swidler, "Love and Adulthood in American Culture," in Neil Smelser and Erik Erikson, eds., *Themes of Love and Work in Adulthood*. This paragraph and the next two draw on these sources.

60. Here I am following the historical conclusions of Philippe Ariès, *Centuries of Childhood*, as used by Berger 1974, pp. 191-195.

61. This view departs from the Oedipal interpretation of Lewis Feuer in *The Conflict of Generations*; it fits with empirical evidence of relatively happy relations between campus rebels and their parents, as in Daniel Bell and Irving Kristol, eds., *Confrontation*. See Berger 1974, p. 247 n. 9.

62. See Keniston, *Youth and Dissent*, pp. 391-392. Also Ronald Inglehardt, *The Silent Revolution*, pp. 28, 60-61, 79, 286, which ties expressive "postmaterialist" values to conditions of increased education and economic affluence during the formative years of sixties youth in both Europe and the U.S.

63. John K. Galbraith's *The Affluent Society* can be read as a formalization of these shifting perceptions as discussed below (see esp. chaps. 1, 2, 22-25). It argues that affluence as an accomplished fact makes possible and necessary a shift away from continued investment in increasing material production and instead calls on society to "invest in people" (p. 332) as the key to eliminating both poverty and the social imbalance in the distribution of goods, services, and opportunities. It is, in short, an agenda for liberal reforms attempted in the 1960s.

64. At least for the upper-middle-class vanguard of the counterculture, the classical philosophical and scientific functions of education predominated over its function as socialization or the technician's simple absorption of applied science.

65. From 1940 to 1960 the fourteen to twenty-four age cohort remained constant at about twenty-four million. In the sixties it swelled to forty million. Daniel Bell analyzes this same demographic condition in making an "organizational harness" argument for youth's alienation from the increasing demands of technological society. He sees it as directly increasing competitive pressure on youth and thereby contributing to their alienation. I have interpreted it as first invigorating and then deflating the counterculture, though in both respects contributing to their alienation. (See Bell, *The Cultural Contradictions of Capitalism*, p. 189, including n. 4.)

66. Bellah 1974, p. 8.

67. See Bell, *Contradictions*, p. 190.

68. This mood, epitomized by Nixon's overwhelming victory in 1972, carried through the later 1970s and into the 1980s as tax-cut movements gained momentum among middle- and upper-income voters pinched by inflation, a form of privatism and "middle-class hedonism" also expressed in growing opposition to spending for social services and its liberal Democratic justification. The most successful candidates in the 1976 and 1980 campaigns were those who built constituencies around single issues and personal appeal, not institutional commitments or party loyalties, the "new" Republican Party notwithstanding. They ran "against Washington," appealing to both the skepticism and the moral outrage of voters directed at governmental institutions. For consideration of the meaning of moral ideas in political rhetoric of this period, see chap. 5.

69. See n. 1 above and Yankelovitch, *The New Morality* and *New Rules*.

70. The depressing and disorienting aftereffects of the sixties are obvious enough in the extreme cases of the dysfunctional drug user, SLA terrorist, and Jonestown suicide, but there has also been a much broader fallout. For example, the *New York Times* reports "Many Rebels of the 1960s Are Depressed as 30 Nears" (29 February 1976, pp. 1, 40):

> The rebellious idealistic generation of adolescents who reached maturity in the 1960s is now approaching 30 and, for many, according to the psychiatrists and mental health counsellors, the trip into adult life is being dogged by disillusionment and depression... reflected in an increase in the number of people in their late 20s and early 30s receiving psychiatric help; by a rise in suicides and alcoholism in this age group; and a boom in the popularity of certain charismatic religious movements, astrology, and pop psychology cults....

2. COMMUNAL LOVE AND ORDER

1. This chapter refers to one particular congregation. Names and minor historical details have been altered to protect the anonymity of its participants.

2. The pastor's history turns on a rite of passage much like the ecstatic journey that qualifies a shaman for his role and legitimates extraordinary status for women in some traditional societies. See Arnold van Gennep, *The Rites of Passage* (1909) and his modern elaborators, particularly Victor Turner; Mircea Eliade, *Shamanism*, chap. 4; I. M. Lewis, *Ecstatic Religion*, chaps. 3-4. This history also describes a series of social passages and structural reversals: (1) from orphan and ethnic outsider to a worldly success of sorts; (2) from the conventional status of wife (but not mother) through small businesswoman to sectarian Christian; (3) from the usual woman's religious role of Bible teacher to the unusual one of pastor and minister; (4) from small sect to millennial world government, in LWF doctrine.

3. Unless otherwise attributed, all doctrinal quotations in this chapter come from "The Notes" (some 500 pages of instruction to LWF members written or edited by the pastor and mimeographed ad seriatim through the mid-1970s), or from taped commentary on them by LWF Bible class teachers or the pastor.

4. More sect youths work as carpenters or apprentices than any other occupation. Unemployment rates are often high in the LWF, especially among the large number of its members in the building trades. During 1975, for example, unemployment ran at about 40 percent in the carpenter's union local to which sect members belonged, with 60 percent or so of the apprentices unemployed. Single young males doing unskilled blue-collar work tend to move back and forth between jobs, which the LWF discourages, and which it succeeds in cutting back sharply after marriage. (Age and other demographic data were calculated in 1978. For a note on how data regarding the LWF were gathered, see the methodological appendix.)

5. This generalization does not apply to a dozen or so youths who came to the LWF not from the counterculture but from more denominational Pentecostal and conservative Christian churches. These they abandoned for having "compromised the pure Christian spirit" they feel the LWF has brought to life. Such sectarian revitalization and the LWF's absorption of countercultural motifs, attractive yet unacceptable outside a Christian context, play major roles in their affiliation. Two of this group are ministers' children, and almost half of them were recruited en masse from Oral Roberts University.

6. This divorce rate compares with a San Francisco area average of 8 percent in the 1970 United States Census. (See tables 5A, 5B, Appendix 5).

7. Common indicators of this shift are cases of parents who stopped going to church, switched from conservative Protestant or ethnic Catholic churches to more liberal denominations, or withdrew their children from parochial schools, often when they moved up from working-class city neighborhoods to the suburbs, and from being carpenters, for example, to being small contractors. Recalls one young woman, "When I was little my mom made me go to Sunday School. I could never understand why, because my dad didn't go to church and after awhile my mom stopped, too. I remember asking her why she didn't have to go. She said she just didn't have to—no answer, really—and that stuck in my mind."

8. LWF doctrine defines *koinonia* as "fellowship." "It expresses partnership, togetherness, a common sharing of all life, not only of privilege but of responsibility. This word is used to denote what we are supposed to be as the Body of Christ."

'And all that believed were together, and had all things common; and sold their possessions and goods, and parted them to all men, as every man had need (Acts 2:44-45).'"

9. A woman recounts, for example, how

one of the closest friends I ever had in the world almost let me die. I was already up on crystal [heroin] and I just had to have some speed. This guy tried to hit me up but he couldn't get the vein, because he was really loaded. I was bruised all up and down the arm, my arm was just ashen. I told him to pull out, I just couldn't handle it. Instead he rammed in the hammer [of the syringe] all the way. It busted everything. In seconds my arm swelled up purple. He'd over-amped me, and I knew as soon as I'd started rushing that I was gonna die. My best friend was in the bathroom with us, and I said to her, "Linda, call a doctor, I'm gonna die." And she goes, "You're not gonna die." She covered the arm with a cold washrag and says, "Now don't look at it, 'cause you're just gonna freak out. You're not gonna die. Just let me get off first, then I'll see what I can do." And she was my closest friend.

10. Hobbes makes the point: " . . . there is no such thing as perpetual tranquility of mind, while we live here; because life itself is but motion, and can never be without desire, nor without fear, no more than without sense." (*Leviathan*, Pt. I, chap. 6, "Felicity.")

11. This constitutes a form of rule-utilitarianism, as opposed to act-utilitarianism. (See chap. 1.) Spiritual instead of material ends—salvation instead of pleasure—make it a form of "ideal utilitarianism," not hedonism. Its collective instead of individual scope makes it a form of universal utilitarianism, not egoistic utilitarianism. (See chap. 1 n. 12.)

12. The utilitarian observer sees a compensatory substitution of one kind of outcome for another, all within the consequential style of evaluation: heavenly or millennial rewards are claimed in place of worldly ones, which the millenarian usually failed to achieve before renouncing.

13. For the LWF the wages of sin *is* death, quite literally. Job's crisis and the dissociation of the ethical world from the physical world of suffering are overridden in spirit by the millennial merger of heaven and earth. So far only one committed sect member has died, triggering a crisis of belief that the pastor dealt with by reversing the causal linkage between doubt and death: "Some of you are thinking, the Great Deceiver is whispering in your ear, 'Look! Ada died. God let her die.' And you're doubting God. Well, that's *why* Ada died, because she doubted God. And if you doubt God, that's what will happen to you."

14. See Kenneth Keniston, "The Speedup of Change" in *Youth and Dissent*, pp. 58-80.

15. See n. 2 above.

16. Conventional sorts of social stratification admittedly persist in the LWF, and its members are admonished to do away with them in the process of self-perfection demanded by premillennial conditions, which the sect's mountain enclave anticipates: "Down here in the city everybody's making good money, carpenter's wages, a nice apartment. But we're holding back, too. . . . It's gonna come to a time, during tribulation, where people are gonna be *forced* to be so close together, it will mold into a brotherhood fellowship for the whole church."

17. Sociological interpretations of traditional Pentecostalism have tied its patriarchal familism to questions of power, hearing in Pentecostal descriptions of the male's worldly role the lament of the lower middle class which arises from its subordinate occupational status. See Gary Schwartz in *Sect Ideologies and Social Status*, p. 177: ". . . there is an element of status compensation in this strong emphasis on the patriarchal family. It gives men a position of influence and importance in their own homes, even though they may very well occupy a subordinate position in the occupational realm." For countercultural youth, the experience of relative powerlessness also followed from their failure to realize countercultural ideals—political, hip, sexual, and communal—in their own life plans, let alone in the society as a whole. This includes the special failure of upper-middle- and upper-class women to establish themselves by careers and relationships as liberated women in the world.

18. Ongoing counseling and monitoring of sect members, including unannounced home visits, implement the LWF's marital norms. The pastor's interventionary discretion extends to the physical separation of couples in others' homes and to binding judgments on the temporary custody of children with either or neither parent. The sect is strenuously natalist and very firm yet loving in its childrearing. The faithful should extend God's gift of life to their children, and the elect should increase and multiply to prepare for their theocratic responsibilities.

19. All of the LWF's high-school and junior-college dropouts come from lower-middle-class and working-class backgrounds. Many attended high schools oriented to upper-middle-class students, compared to whom they found themselves unsuccessful students. Some of them were functional illiterates. All used drugs regularly, which made schoolwork difficult, and they subscribed to the drug ideology, which made it irrelevant and stifling. "I couldn't trip on schoolwork," says one; "and I didn't go for the drill-sergeant bit they pulled in class." The LWF strongly encourages high school graduation for its youngest members, but does not demand it. Two-year programs at a local junior college are mildly encouraged, but only where an A.A. degree leads directly into a practical occupation, for example, practical nursing for women or law enforcement for men. Higher education is rejected, since it is a full-time activity that interferes with sect participation, and it is a "vain philosophy" whose intellectualism clashes as much with sect tenets as it does with the counterculture's. Sect youths typically recall the creative activities of art, music, and literature as their favorite subjects in high school. Of those who attended junior college or college, more majored in English than any other field. One of them complains: "They say college is a learning institution, but what you're supposed to learn was all empty for me. All the literature I read led me to believe there was just more literature to read, and so on. One guy said one thing, and the next guy said the opposite, and maybe they were right and maybe they weren't, but you should learn the argument anyway. Everything I ever read was academic suggestion about how the world was—maybe—and most of it was so difficult I couldn't understand what they were talking about, or so existential it didn't make any difference. And all the time my life was going haywire, because I had nothing to ground it." In search of certain moral knowledge, this youth found only intellectual speculation and disagreement in college. Neither universalizable nor prescriptive, this gave him no foundation for moral principles, nor did it convey the sect's sense of certainty, clarity, and symbolic power sufficient to motivate him to a particular course of action.

20. The most important auxiliary justification of conventional work is the

husband's obligation to provide for his spouse and family. The Pauline admonition is often repeated that the man who does not so provide is worse than a blasphemer. By locking all sexual relationships into marriage and requiring steady jobs for men to marry, the LWF mobilizes powerful motives for accepting and staying with otherwise unappealing work.

21. Not all LWF youths sympathized with the political wing of the counterculture. A vehemently antiradical minority was composed largely of working-class males who used hard drugs and alcohol, not psychedelics, and felt ambivalent about the hip ethic of peace and love. Significantly, their experience of sixties political strife suggests that it was effective in undermining the legitimacy of established social authority for the reactionary as well as the radical. Says one self-styled "greaser": "Here there's all these young people out on the street yelling for rights, man, when they've got the rights they're yelling for! I don't know what they're screaming about. Here we are, beating them up, and we got nothing. And the cops, the guys that pull us in for burglaries, they're telling us, 'That's OK, you can beat on 'em. We'll bust them, because they're the weird ones. You guys just boogie on down the street.' In jail everybody praised us, but the political guys always got beat up, like 'What more do you want, Commie?' So I always thought this world was pretty weird. I was wondering where does the truth start, and where does love start? Because that's what I really wanted."

22. See George Sorel's discussion of religious and political pessimism in his "Letter to Halevy," pt. I; in *Reflections on Violence*.

23. See Robert Welch, *The Blue Book of the John Birch Society*, especially sections 2, 3, in which Welch analyzes the political weakness of the United States as a result of its loss of religious faith.

24. For discussion of this tension in terms of ideal-typical Christian church and sect see Ernst Troeltsch, *The Social Teachings of the Christian Churches*, summarized on pp. 993-1013.

25. For example, "briarpatch" cooperative grocery stores, auto repair garages, day-care centers, schools, and bookstores have grown up around Western University, nearby the LWF, fed by ex-radicals, hippies, and street people. This philosophy was exemplified by the Whole Earth Truck Store community, whose catalogue articulated it. Other neo-Christian as well as neo-Oriental religious groups sponsor organic grocery stores, restaurants, bakeries, and similar small businesses, in addition to farms and ranches doubling as religious settlements.

3. ANTINOMIAN RULES

1. "Zen in America: An Unconditioned Response to a Conditioned World," a brochure published by San Francisco Zen Center, 1968, not paginated. "Pacific Zen Center" is a composite constructed to represent sixties youth practicing Zen Buddhism in selected groups in the San Francisco Bay Area. It shares certain characteristics with San Francisco Zen Center, but it does not correspond entirely or exclusively to that institution, whose current members were not among those formally interviewed. While encouraging interest in its activities, San Francisco Zen Center maintains a long-standing policy against research on its members.

2. *Windbell*, a periodical publication of San Francisco Zen Center, 12 (1973): 30. Also see "Mountain Gate: Community Work," a brochure published by San

Francisco Zen Center, 1976, not paginated. Demographic data were calculated or checked in 1978.

3. David Wise, "Dharma West: A Social-Psychological Inquiry into Zen in San Francisco" (Ph.D. diss., University of California, Berkeley, 1971), pp. 54-55.

4. Wise, "Dharma West," p. 71.

5. *Windbell*, 14, 1 (1975): 11-12.

6. A small but growing minority of students are in college or conventional careers. This group includes proportionately more persons younger and older than sixties youth than does the Zen Center population as a whole.

7. See, for example, Richard Robinson, *The Buddhist Religion*, pp. 26, 94.

8. Katsuki Sekida, *Zen Training*, pp. 41, 43.

9. Koans are experientially and contextually meaningful questions without answers reasonable in themselves. Thus, to take an example much quoted out of context, "What is the sound of one hand clapping?" The student recites and works on a koan with his mind, breathing, and respiratory muscles during meditation. For discussions of koan practice, which is not done generally at Zen Center, see Sekida, *Zen Training*, chapter 9; and Philip Kapleau, *Three Pillars of Zen*.

10. "Just sitting" describes the relatively formless meditation known as *shikantaza*, in which there is no particular point of mental focus such as breath counting or a koan. It is characteristically associated with the Soto School of Japanese Zen Buddhism, while the *kanna* Zen ("seeing into the topic") of koan practice is associated with the Rinzai School.

11. Every "4 and 9 day" on the calendar marks a day off, during which students are free between breakfast and dinner. They generally bathe, wash clothes, hike, read, and so on, before gathering for conversation over a sit-down dinner.

12. "Zen in America."

13. Ibid.

14. Richard Baker-roshi, "Sangha-Community," in Michael Katz et al., eds., *Earth's Answer*, p. 46.

15. "Zen in America."

16. Ibid.

17. Ibid.

18. See Shunryu Suzuki, *Zen Mind, Beginner's Mind*, p. 31.

19. See, for example, Paul Reps, ed., *Zen Flesh, Zen Bones*.

20. Haiku Zendo/Bodhi, Los Altos, Ca., undated xerox.

21. This data comes from formal interviews averaging four hours each with ten Zen students, done in the San Francisco Bay Area in 1976 and followed up in the period 1977-1979, and earlier informal interviews with twenty or so others done over several years of participant-observation. As calculated in 1978 the average age of formal interviewees is representative of sixties youth practicing Zen, as is the sex ratio of the group, their marital status, social class, religious-ethnic background, and employment. All come from upper-middle-class backgrounds. Three are WASP, five Jewish, and two Catholic. Five do unskilled blue-collar work (gardener, housecleaner), two do skilled blue-collar work (carpenter, mechanic), two are schoolteachers, and one a lawyer. All but one had used marijuana and psychedelic drugs, several of them steadily. Compared to other Zen students of this age group, these interviewees are among the most highly educated, verbally articulate, and politically active. Six had been active in political protest. Four hold advanced degrees (three M.A.'s, one J.D.), another three B.A.'s, and three had two or more

years in elite colleges. Of twenty-five students interviewed by David Wise at San Francisco Zen Center in 1970, three-quarters had used LSD more than once. Half had B.A.'s and one-fifth M.A.'s. One-fifth had participated actively in radical politics, and two-fifths peripherally. The average age of this group was twenty-eight. Sixty percent were male and 40 percent female. Almost half were Jewish, a quarter Catholic, and a quarter either Protestant or from nonreligious family backgrounds. Three-quarters held part-time menial employment like house cleaning. (See Wise, "Dharma West," chap. 3.)

22. See Wise, "Dharma West," p. 94.

23. A sociologist might argue that conventional social demands on upper-middle-class males are greater than those on females in American society—and so are the rewards for complying with them. Men over forty, who are most likely to comply with these demands, are better rewarded and better integrated into conventional society than their female counterparts, and therefore they are less likely to be affiliated with an alternative religious movement. Of those who refuse to comply, chiefly sixties youths, men are more clearly penalized than women by reference to their usual social rewards and self-expectations, and more impelled towards an alternative social setting like Zen Center and an alternative career and social identity like that of Zen monk or priest. See Wise, "Dharma West," pp. 93-94. The disproportion of men at Zen Center has increased since the early 1970s, as full-time membership has become defined more in terms of a monastic career.

24. See *Windbell* 12 (1973): 13.

25. See Wise, "Dharma West," pp. 94-97.

26. Ibid., p. 105.

27. Ibid., pp. 102-105.

28. Ibid., p. 106.

29. Ibid., p. 107.

30. See Robert Wuthnow, "The New Religions in Social Context," in Charles Y. Glock and R. N. Bellah, eds., *The New Religious Consciousness*, pp. 276-278, for general Bay Area population survey data correlating radical politics and "attraction to religious movements."

31. Wise, "Dharma West," p. 94.

32. Ibid., pp. 109-110.

33. The Four Noble Truths constitute a consequential, indeed egoist argument for following the Eightfold Path defined by Zen's moral rules. See following note.

34. Buddhism's Four Noble Truths make up a sort of practical syllogism seen as expressing the experiential truth of Buddha's enlightenment. The first tenet posits that life is suffering. The second attributes this suffering to desire for or attachment to certain conditions of life (pleasure, security, health, youth, meaning, and so on) and to life itself in forms that human existence inherently does not satisfy. Since life is suffering and suffering is caused by desire, the third tenet concludes that if desire is dissolved, then suffering will cease. The fourth prescribes a method for ending desire and suffering, the Eightfold Path: (1) right views; (2) right intentions; (3) right speech; (4) right conduct; (5) right means of livelihood; (6) right effort; (7) right mindfulness; (8) right meditation.

35. These phrases allude to the Heart Sutra, an essential passage of Buddhist wisdom literature chanted daily by many American Zen students. Its text (Appendix 4) extols the wisdom (*prajna*) of meditation, because it truly embodies the truth of acosmic monism, and because it relieves all human suffering. Deontological and

consequential justifications intermingle in its lines. Its paradoxical logic finds the senses (*skandhas*) and phenomenal manifestations (*dharmas*) of universal existence to be "empty," without negating that emptiness takes form.

36. Baker-roshi, "Sangha," pp. 50-51.

37. Ibid., p. 49.

38. A thirteenth-century Japanese Zen master, founder of one of the two principal schools of Japanese Zen Buddhism, whose adherents accord his teaching a central place in their study. See his remarks on Zen practice (Appendix 4), noting the combination of (a) assertion of the unconditional truth of acosmic monism (#1) and the conditional possibility of its nonrealization (#2); (b) exhortation to emulate past religious virtuosi and attain or express a state of consciousness realizing that truth (#3, 4, 12, 13, 14) in meditation (#3, 4) and the activity of daily life (#10, 11), particularly monastic life; (c) concretely detailed instruction, uttered in the imperative mood of an orthopraxy, designating posture, dress, diet, setting, and a nonevaluative, noncognitive, self-disinterested attitude for meditation (#5, 6, 7).

39. Baker-roshi, "Sangha," p. 50.

40. *Ecstasy* refers to a state in which the self or soul is placed *outside* the body or ordinary reality, usually in contemplation of divine things or in a transport of rapturous feelings. As used here, *enstasy* refers to a state in which attention or consciousness is placed entirely *within* the phenomenal reality given by meditation, focused on the body's posture, muscle tension, and breathing, its immediate circumstances and undirected mental events.

41. Wise, "Dharma West," p. 87.

42. Suzuki, *Zen Mind*, pp. 89-90.

43. See the Heart Sutra (Appendix 4), especially stanzas 1 and 4. The ideal meditator has "perceived that all five *skandhas* are empty / And [is] saved from all suffering and distress." / He "depends on *Prajna Paramita* [the wisdom of meditation] / And his mind is no hindrance. / Without any hindrance no fears exist; . . ."

44. Sixties youth experienced with psychedelic drugs often found easier entry to zazen practice than those who were not. But a tendency to model their zazen experience according to psychedelic patterns later made special problems for drug veterans, since Zen meditation, in fact, diverged from the psychedelic pattern. Youths who had used drugs most heavily and whose social identities depended most on drugs, like dealers, had the greatest problems of adjustment and were most likely to leave Zen Center on this account.

45. See Albert Stunkard, "Some Interpersonal Aspects of an Oriental Religion," *Psychiatry* 14 (1951): 419-431, especially p. 430.

46. See Sekida, *Zen Training*, chaps. 1-3, especially pp. 31, 47.

47. Ibid., chap. 3; also Stunkard, "Oriental Religion," p. 422.

48. Suzuki, *Zen Mind*, p. 98.

49. Ibid., p. 22.

50. See Sekida, *Zen Training*, pp. 49-59.

51. Akira Kasamatsu and Tomio Hirai, "An Electroencephalographic Study on the Zen Meditation," in Charles Tart, ed., *Altered States of Consciousness*, p. 493.

52. Samadhi is also described as a "fullness" or "totality of which there is no outside," a meaning that shares with emptiness the "nondiscriminating" quality of a monist reality indivisible into constituent elements.

53. Suzuki, *Zen Mind*, p. 63.

54. The neurophysiological response of monks in zazen to repeated sound stimuli consists of sensation without association which does not become habituated. Comparison between Zen and Yoga indicates how closely such response corresponds to Zen teaching: "The adept practitioners of both forms of meditation show almost continuous alpha waves (normally associated with a state of relaxed alertness in ordinary Ss) during meditation. This is particularly startling in the case of the Zen monks because their eyes are open: one almost never sees alpha rhythm in the eyes-open condition in ordinary Ss. The Zen monks also show normal blocking of the alpha rhythm in response to stimulation which does not adapt with repeated trials as it does in ordinary Ss. The Yogins, on the other hand, show no response to stimulation at all . . . these differences may be quite consistent with the differing philosophical outlooks of Zen and Yoga. The Zen monks are striving to exist in the here-and-now, in the immediacy of the phenomenal world; thus if one interprets the adaptation to stimulation invariably seen in ordinary Ss as the substitution of abstract cognitive patterns for the raw sensory experience, the Zen monks are apparently managing to stay in the here-and-now of immediate sensory experience. Yoga philosophy, on the other hand, has a strong world-denying quality, a belief that the phenomenal world is all illusion and ensnarement (*maya*), which the yogin must learn to transcend. Thus it makes sense that they show no EEG response to stimulation and also report being unaware of the stimulation when questioned after the meditative state is terminated." (Tart, *Altered States*, pp. 485-486.) For a discussion of the implications of such responses as a class see Arthur Deikman, "Deutomatization and the Mystic Experience," in Tart, *Altered States*, pp. 23-43.

55. Sleep deprivation, a standard element of monastic training (see schedule, p. 97), restricts the subject's time for dreaming, thereby "pushing the contents of our dreaming up into meditation, where we face them wide-awake." This process aims at producing a person "free of self-clinging but not dissociated or alienated," emphasizes a priest. That is, Zen's ideal person is non-attached but not psychologically separated from his ego as a realist frame of reference for action.

56. Suzuki, *Zen Mind*, pp. 30-31. Another moral can be drawn in terms of Western psychology, in which zazen appears as a de-repressive psychotherapy. See Wise, "Dharma West," chap. 5, for such a picture.

57. American Zen students rarely do consider Zen practice a form of moral education, or a method for developing moral virtue. For them it is a source and expression of the fundamentally enlightened nature of human beings. Yet they recognize the Aristotelian quality ascribed to it here. Comments a priest, "Dogen said Zen practice is magical, like the Dragon Gate. You're just this deluded character, then you go into a monastery and follow the rules, and then without fail you become a Buddha." The passage referred to (see *Shobogenzo Zuimonki*, Reiho Masunaga, trans., p. 105) parallels a fish being transformed into a (fishy) dragon by swimming through "a place where great waves rise," and a human being transformed into a (human) Buddha by practicing as a Zen monk.

58. Stunkard, "Oriental Religion," pp. 427-429.

59. Wise, "Dharma West," p. 86.

60. Suzuki, *Zen Mind*, p. 14.

61. A master emphasizes the relational rather than exemplary character of the master's identity: "A teacher is a spiritual friend who's entirely willing to be there for you and put up with you the way you are. He doesn't have to be a good person, although if he is, all the better. In one sense a roshi is someone whose teacher has

acknowledged him as having received the teacher's understanding. Because of that ability to understand someone else thoroughly the roshi is a fully realized person. But anybody can be your teacher. *You* make him your teacher by choosing him. The point is that he understand you thoroughly and you come to understand him, not that he be perfect. The emphasis is not so much on the teacher being a perfect person as being a perfect mirror. This makes the Zen master different from the guru."

62. Suzuki, *Zen Mind*, p. 14.

63. Zen Mountain Center Library, "Warm-Hearted Practice," xerox, February 23, 1971.

64. The actual structure of routine and policy-making authority at Zen Center also aids in interpreting its exercise according to an expressive ethic. Routine supervisory roles are explicitly defined and interconnected, but with a short span of control at their lower levels and wide-ranging personal interaction among their occupants at daily meetings. Policy-making authority is more concentrated and less situationally diffuse than routine authority, but it reflects a central ambiguity in the Zen tradition, namely that the master constitutes the charismatic axis of a highly rationalized monastic institution. He does not decide all major policy issues for Zen Center, but such issues are decided in accord with his views. This process of making policy draws on that of Japanese organizations in general, not only Zen monasteries. See, for example, Chie Nakane, *Japanese Society*, pp. 63-86; R. P. Dore, *British Factory—Japanese Factory;* and Ezra Vogel, *Japan As Number One.* Major issues to be decided are circulated as questions through a relatively wide compass within Zen Center and among its supporters. Opinions and advice are sought out informally, but no special committees are appointed nor are contending positions worked out for general debate. Instead, a relatively small leadership group, a "council" centered around the master and sensitive to his views, gradually reaches an informal agreement taken to represent the community's consensus. It does so in the course of prolonged discussion, integrating or neutralizing disagreements along the way. "Because no one will go ahead as long as you disagree," recalls a former participant, "you disagree only when you have a strong feeling of the integrity of your own view. This makes some pressure to agree, but since everyone will listen to you, it also gives you a lot of power to disagree." Members of this leadership group then review the issue and propose a solution for further discussion and ratification by an official board, apprised that the proposal would meet the master's approval.

65. See Wise, "Dharma West," p. 163.

66. Suzuki, *Zen Mind*, p. 29.

67. Ibid., p. 28.

68. To resolve disagreements with persons beyond the community of shared religious experience, one strategy of Zen students seeks to include such persons within the existing community or to establish a facsimile of it with them: ". . . find out where that person is working and go and work with him and function with him, and finally find out yourself where the reality of practice is in his own experience, and find the reality that you meet at. You can't always communicate that in words. In fact, you can lose it in the words." A second strategy accepts the limited (by time, circumstance, and others' disinclination) extension of such communal intimacy, but it still interprets moral disagreement as a conflicted encounter between persons, to be harmonized, rather than the engagement of various positions, to be thrashed out. A Zen student formerly involved in nonviolent political radicalism describes such an encounter with friends who are still politically active: ". . . the energy they released,

the anger and all, didn't stick on me. My ego wasn't so attached to any particular result or feeling that had to come out of it. I didn't have to win or get to some final truth, so they could come at me and I could still accept them and see them as people. Every so often, when they let me, I asked them why they felt they had to attack me. They couldn't answer that question then, because of the strong emotions, but it seems like the real question. After the argument, when nothing was really resolved, I called them the next day, just to make some contact. Not about the argument, but just to touch each other."

69. See Max Weber's distinction between social action rationally calculated to achieve the actor's own chosen ends (*zweckrational*) and action rationally oriented to embody an absolute value (*wertrational*), for its own sake. (*The Theory of Social and Economic Organization*, p. 115.)

70. "Zen in America."

71. Baker-roshi, "Sangha," p. 48.

72. See Wise, "Dharma West," pp. 98-102.

73. By its tight value consensus, highly regulated ritual and practical activity that is retributively sanctioned by censure and expulsion, and by its relatively undivided labor, the monastery creates a facsimile of social solidarity through "the likeness of consciences" or "mechanical solidarity" in Durkheim's terms. He notes, "The similitude of consciences gives rise to juridical rules which, with the threat of repressive measures, impose uniform beliefs and practices upon all. The more pronounced this is, the more completely is social life confounded with religious life, and the nearer to communism are economic institutions." (*The Division of Labor in Society*, p. 226.) Interpersonal acceptance at Zen Center rests on the basis of "likeness of conscience," backed by the face-to-face meshing of housekeeping roles, rather than the complementarity of individual traits produced by a differentiated society.

74. Wise, "Dharma West," pp. 166, 169, 170.

75. Wise, "Dharma West," p. 106.

76. Ibid.

77. Youths who have established religious careers at Zen Center—becoming ordained, going on scholarship, and taking a secure place in its administration—have a rate of marriage 1.7 times higher than other serious students. Of sixteen established priests in the mid-1970s, nine were married (although four have since separated).

78. Quoted phrases allude to the Prajna Paramita. See stanzas 2 and 4 of the Heart Sutra, Appendix 4.

79. Wise, "Dharma West," p. 89.

80. "Zen in America."

81. *Windbell* 13, 1-2 (1974): 23.

82. Petr Kropotkin, *Mutual Aid, a Factor of Evolution*, especially chaps. 7, 8, and conclusion. Note his association of mutual aid with the village community, as opposed to the contractual relations of the State.

83. See Wise, "Dharma West," p. 104.

84. Dick Anthony and Thomas Robbins, "The Meher Baba Movement: Its Effect on Post-Adolescent Social Alienation," especially pp. 504-508, in Irving Zaretsky and Mark Leone, eds., *Religious Movements in Contemporary America*, pp. 479-511.

85. A Japanese master interprets the American Zen student's career as a

hybrid: "Here in America we cannot define Zen Buddhists the same way we do in Japan. American students are not priests yet not completely laymen." (Suzuki, *Zen Mind*, p. 129.) For all except Zen Center's small paid staff, the permanent institutional status of monks and priests is unavailable, because of Zen Center's relatively limited resources and following, even if they wished to claim it. On the other hand, serious students are not content merely to attend occasional lectures, rites, and meditation periods like the laity of a Japanese temple or a middle-class American denomination.

86. See Rosabeth Kanter, *Commitment and Community*, chaps 3-4.

87. See n. 77.

88. "Mountain Gate: Community Work."

89. "This-worldly mysticism" is the least discussed category of the four possibilities generated by Max Weber's paired characteristics of religion—other-worldly/this-worldly, asceticism/mysticism. He mentions in passing "an inner-worldly religion of salvation . . . determined by contemplative features: A mystic of the type of Tauler completes his day's work, and then seeks contemplative union with his God in the evening, going forth to his usual work the next morning, as Tauler movingly suggests, in the correct inner state." See *The Sociology of Religion*, pp. 166-183, esp. 175-176.

90. Suzuki, *Zen Mind*, p. 129.

91. Baker-roshi, "Sangha," p. 56.

92. Wise, "Dharma West," p. 161.

93. *Windbell* 14, 1 (1975): 13.

94. Baker-roshi, "Sangha," p. 56.

95. E. F. Schumacher, *Small Is Beautiful: Economics as if People Mattered*, pp. 52, 54.

96. See Ernest Callenbach, *Ecotopia*, a utopian novel favored by some Zen Center students, in which northern California, Washington, and Oregon secede from the U.S. to found an ecologically stable-state, communitarian, and hip-humanitarian nation of their own.

97. See *Windbell* 14, 1 (1975): 16-23.

4. EST AND ETHICS

1. From "What is the purpose of the *est* training?" a four-page pamphlet published by *est* (#680-3, 13 January 1976).

2. *est* began and is based in San Francisco. It expanded first to Los Angeles, Honolulu, and Aspen, Colorado; then to New York, Washington, D.C., and Chicago. By 1978 it was offering trainings in eighteen of the nation's top twenty-five population areas. *est* estimates that in the San Francisco Bay Area one out of every nine persons aged twenty-five to thirty-nine who are college graduates has taken the training. In Los Angeles, one in twenty; in New York, one in thirty-three. (*est, The Graduate Review*, February 1978, p. 3.) *est* grossed $9.3 million in 1975, $10.9 million in 1976, $13.2 million in 1977, $16 million in 1978, $20 million in 1979, and $25 million in 1980, according to *est* trainers V. Gioscia and K. Anbender. Graduate volunteers effectively tripled the size of *est*'s staff by contributing some 20,000 hours per week in 1977 (*est, The Graduate Review*, June 1978, p. 2), mostly in recruiting, logistical, and administrative services. See "A Report on the Legal and Financial

Structure of *est*" (a fourteen-page document published by *est* in June 1976) for a description of *est*'s corporate structure in detail sufficient to engross a tax lawyer without disclosing its overall assets and profitability, or the extent of Erhard's effective ownership. Compare Arnold Levison, "Where Erhard Launders the Money," *Mother Jones*, December 1978, pp. 52-53. In essence, Erhard sold his "body of knowledge" to an overseas holding and licensing corporation, to which *est* pays a maximal portion of its gross income in the form of pretax royalties. Now located in the Netherlands, this holding corporation pays 7 percent in Dutch taxes and then sends all its profits to the tax-exempt "Werner Erhard Foundation for *est*" in Switzerland, which owns the holding corporation outright. *est*, meanwhile, pays 30 percent in American taxes on its minimal postroyalty income. All the remaining profits go to The Werner Erhard Charitable Settlement, a tax-exempt trust on the Isle of Jersey, which owns *est*. Devised on the pattern of tax shelters common among high-profit, low-overhead entrepreneurs like best-selling authors, this arrangement is justified by Erhard on the grounds that "you maximize your assets in an organization by paying the least amount of taxes." (Suzanne Gordon, "Let Them Eat *est*," *Mother Jones*, December 1978, p. 54.) It has so far withstood the IRS, which had six income tax cases lined up against *est* and Erhard in the U.S. Tax Court in 1978, pending the outcome of pretrial negotiations.

3. Erhard has described his experience as follows: "I had a direct experience of myself. That means I no longer identified myself with my body or my personality or my past or my future or my situation or my circumstances or my feelings or my thoughts or my notion of myself or my image or my—I think that covers it." (*San Francisco Chronicle*, 3 December 1974.) Note the resemblance between this negative definition and that of enlightenment in the Buddhist Heart Sutra, especially stanza 4 (see Appendix 4). Erhard calls Zen Buddhism the "essential" one of all the disciplines he has studied. (Adelaide Bry, *est—60 Hours That Will Transform Your Life*, p. 99.) Perons involved in Scientology and Mind Dynamics call much of *est*'s data and processes direct copies of their material. (See Mark Brewer, "We're Gonna Tear You Down and Put You Back Together," *Psychology Today*, August 1975, p. 88; and R. C. D. Heck and J. L. Thompson, "*est*: Salvation or Swindle?" *San Francisco*, January 1976, p. 70.) Erhard was an instructor in Mind Dynamics (a now-defunct program devised by autodidact Alexander Everett to teach people how to control their minds more efficiently, reportedly through self-hypnosis and visualization) immediately before starting *est*, and his delivery of the Mind Dynamics course closely resembled *est*, according to some clients of both. (See Ornstein, p. 11, cited in n. 7 below.) Various observers of *est* have traced its ideas to Zen, Vedanta, and Christian perfectionism; behaviorist determinism, Freud, Maslow, Rogers, and Perls; Korzybski's *General Semantics*; Dale Carnegie's *The Power of Positive Thinking*; Napoleon Hill's *Think and Grow Rich*, and the self-image psychology of Maxwell Maltz's *Psycho-Cybernetics*. Its methods have been traced to hypnosis, autosuggestion, revivalism, psychodrama, encounter, Gestalt therapy, and behavior modification; Subud and yoga; military, monastic, and penal institutions; sales and business motivation courses. An *est* staff member describes Erhard's pragmatic use of such sources: "Werner has done just about every discipline and religion and philosophy there is to do. He took the part of each one that really works and cut out the trappings. . . . Once back when Werner was training businessmen, he asked the boss of this company if he could use Zen on them. 'Just as long as it's not blatantly illegal,' the guy said; 'and you don't get any on the walls.'" (D. Percy, *est* guest seminar,

Palo Alto, California, December 1974; also Bry, *60 Hours*, p. 153.) Erhard managed door-to-door salespersons for the *Encyclopedia Britannica's* Great Books Program; then for a division of *Parents' Magazine* and later for a subsidiary of the Grolier Corporation, both of which marketed "child development materials" for parents to read to their preschool and early-grade school children. (See William W. Bartley, III, *Werner Erhard: The Transformation of Jack Rosenberg*, Part II, for an account of Erhard's pre-*est* studies and employment.)

4. From "What is the purpose of the *est* training?"

5. For official descriptions of the *est* training see Werner Erhard and Victor Gioscia, "The *est* Standard Training," *Biosciences Communication* 3 (1977): 104-122, and "*est*: Communication in a Context of Compassion," *Current Psychiatric Therapies* 18 (1978): 117-125. For an enthusiastic description of the *est* training by a non-staff member see Bry, *60 Hours*. For an appreciative, Zen-slanted description see Luke Rhinehart, *The Book of est*. For a critical description of the training as pop psychology, see Sheridan Fenwick, *Getting It*. For a critical description of the training as "brainwashing" see Brewer, "Tear You Down." I have compared these descriptions with a 100-page account of my own training and detailed taped accounts of several interviewees in trainings other than my own.

6. *est* holds that upsetting physical sensations and emotions are linked to memories of painful experiences in the past that have not been fully experienced. During the training these memories, along with their physical and emotional symptoms, come up to be experienced. Once fully experienced, they disappear. The entire psychic and psychosomatic constellation can be "experienced out" by directing non-evaluative, all-accepting attention to the symptoms and then to their causes, that is, by "accepting it, being with it, observing it." This model resembles Freud's notion of abreaction: If repressed memories of traumatic past events are recalled and vividly reexperienced, their associated psychic and psychosomatic conditions will be relieved. (See Ornstein, p. 58, cited in n. 7 below.)

7. Robert Ornstein (principal investigator), Charles Swencionis (project director), Arthur Deikman, Ralph Morris (consultants), *A Self-Report Survey: Preliminary Study of Participants in Erhard Seminars Training* (The *est* Foundation, 1975) (hereafter cited as Ornstein). In 1972 Behaviordyne, Inc. of Palo Alto, Ca. conducted psychological testing for personality changes among a smaller group of graduates, concluding, "the psychological picture that emerges is that of a happier, psychologically sounder, and more responsible person" (quoted in Bry, *60 Hours*, p. 213). These studies have not been able to weigh the hypothesized influence on their self-reported results of the placebo effect (participants feel better after completing a therapeutic program, regardless of its content, because they expect to) or the phenomenon of regression on the mean (persons tend to seek therapy at some low point in their lives and subsequently to report feeling closer to the mean, regardless of the therapy's content). Expectations of positive change are widespread among those enrolling in the training. Such expectations are vigorously encouraged by promotional and application procedures designed by *est* and by those enthused members of each wave of graduates instrumental in recruiting the following wave. Many if not all of the persons delivering the training share these expectations. Perhaps most significantly, the training's own tenets and techniques appear to mobilize the placebo effect by affirming and demonstrating the power of expectations (states of consciousness and choice, perhaps mediated by the autonomic nervous system) to determine outcomes (experience, particularly its psychological and psychosomatic

dimensions). (See Ornstein, pp. 8, 15, 17, 62, 63.) Graduates' retrospective self-reports show no neat correlation between precisely what and how much they expected to improve beforehand, and what and how much they afterward felt to have improved. (Earl Babbie and Donald Stone, "What Have You Gotten After You 'Get It':" Paper presented to the American Psychiatric Association, 13 May 1976, in Miami Beach.) This does not, however, preclude inferring that the placebo effect may be at work, since the data indicate that diffuse prior expectations of positive change and subsequent self-reports of it are consistently high.

8. Ornstein, pp. 6-9, 62. Also Donald M. Baer and Stephanie B. Stolz, "A Description of the Erhard Seminars Training (*est*) in the Terms of Behavior Analysis," *Behaviorism* 1, 1 (1978): 45-70, esp. 52-54, 56-58.

9. *est*, "Werner Erhard: 'All I Can Do is Lie,'" reprinted from an interview in the *East-West Journal*, September 1974, p. 2.

10. Donald Cox, *est* mailing, p. 2, par. 2, of a 1976 letter announcing establishment of an "*est* Public Information Office."

11. These data are drawn from Ornstein, pp. 25-27, 34-36, 59; supplemented by reference to Ornstein data sets in File SYS8, 10/11/74, Variables W29-88; and to twenty sixties youths formally interviewed by the writer. Tables from Ornstein, p. 59, are attached as Appendix 5 herein, with 1970 Census figures for the nation added alongside those for the San Francisco Area. The Ornstein sample (surveyed in 1973) showed an average age of 35.1 years; *est*'s own records showed the average age of all graduates falling to 33.7 by 1978. Only 25 percent of all graduates were then over forty. (*est, The Graduate Review*, February 1978, p. 3.) Persons twenty-five to thirty-four years of age comprise 46.7 percent of *est*'s clientele and 19 percent of the San Francisco population, a ratio of 2.45 to 1. By the author's informal count of volunteers at *est* graduate seminars, guest seminars, special events, and the like, at least 70-80 percent range from twenty-five to thirty-four in age. (See Brewer, "Tear You Down," p. 36, for a corroborating observation.) Youths interviewed averaged 30.3 years of age, as calculated in 1978, were equally divided by sex, and were all Caucasians. Eighteen of twenty had used marijuana, fourteen LSD. Nine had been in political demonstrations. Eleven of twenty had lived communally; three now did so. Fifteen of twenty had worked irregularly since school; three were now unemployed, one by choice. Ornstein's 1973 sample shows that 39.5 percent of *all est* graduates had used marijuana, but only 14.4 percent had used LSD. Since *est*, 49.8 percent reported using less marijuana and 56 percent reported using less LSD. (File SYS8, 11/22/74, pp. 27-30.)

12. Ornstein File SYS8, Variable W85, pp. 69-71. Teaching credentials far outnumbered any other category of "graduate degree" held by *est* clients; for example, eighty-five credentials versus twenty Ph.D.'s. Psychology majors accounted for 6.4 percent of all college-educated *est* clients. Then came Education, 6.1 percent, and Business Administration, 5.7 percent; "Liberal Arts" or "Two Majors" made up 8.1 percent. Few majored in technical or preprofessional areas: Premedicine, 2.2 percent; Engineering, 2.9 percent; Law, 1 percent; Economics, 1 percent. Interestingly, nonpsychology majors close to *est*'s subject matter are among those least represented: Philosophy, 0.3 percent; Religion, 0.3 percent; Theology, 0.1 percent.

13. Occupational data come from Ornstein File SYS8, Variable W88, pp. 76-78. This file includes sixty occupational categories in six groupings: professional, technical, business, arts and media, trades, and labor. From these data I estimate that 69.3 percent work mainly with other persons (including students and house-

wives; excluding them, the estimate is 61.8 percent), as opposed to physical things or abstractions. White-collar workers make up the largest grouping of occupational categories, some 32.7 percent of *all* graduates (including students, housewives, retirees): clerical workers, 11.7 percent; "executives," 9.7 percent; non-college teachers or instructors, 7.4 percent; business owners, 4.4 percent; salesmen, 4.3 percent; media and arts, 6.9 percent. Students made up 9.6 percent of all graduates and housewives 8.6 percent. Professionals comprise roughly 10 percent of all *est* graduates, including: college teachers, 1.8 percent; architects, 1 percent; clinical psychologists, 0.3 percent; psychiatrists, 0.3 percent; clergy, 0.5 percent. Less educated therapists or counselors make up 3.3 percent. Persons working with things make up less than 10 percent of all *est* graduates. They include: artisans and skilled manual workers, 4.7 percent; general service workers, 3.2 percent; and unskilled labor, 0.8 percent.

14. Ornstein, pp. 25, 36, 59. The lower figure for mean income in Ornstein takes in all nonresponses to the question as equaling zero; the higher figure simply excludes them. The latter method appears to yield the figures in column 1 of the table for income on page 305. Nearly half of all *est* graduates reported increased job satisfaction since *est*, and half of this number—one quarter of the entire Ornstein sample—attributed it to getting a new job since the training (an average of eleven months previous). (Ornstein, p. 25.) Of twenty interviewees, fifteen had switched, left, or entered a job within a year of taking the training. Only three such moves constituted a clear-cut advancement or promotion. Interviewees earned an average of $8,150 in 1975. Interviewees were employed as follows:

retail clerk	elementary schoolteacher (M.Ed.)
corporate sales representative	psychiatric social worker (M.S.W.)
shoe salesman	dentist (D.D.S.)
store manager	educational administrator (Ed.D.)
2 secretaries (1 part-time)	lawyer (unemployed by choice) (J.D.)
office clerk	law student (J.D.)
office manager	housepainter/carpenter (self-employed)
car rental agent (unemployed)	nurse (R.N.)
purchasing agent	custodial services manager
assistant buyer (unemployed)	

15. Ornstein, pp. 27, 36, 59. See Tables 5A, 5B, Appendix 5. (Cf. Babbie and Stone, pp. 14-17.) Forty-seven percent of 1,063 respondents reported different close friends, with only seventy-five admitting to having none at all (Ornstein, p. 27.) Regarding marital status:

6.2 percent of graduates divorced the year before *est* (n=1,138)
8.5 percent separated the year before *est* (n=1,065)
4.3 percent divorced the year after *est* (n=1,130)
7.7 percent separated the year after *est* (n=1,050)

26.7 percent divorced or separated in this two-year period, yet only 19-22 percent (see Tables 5A, 5B, Appendix 5) are presently divorced or separated, suggesting a rapid remarriage rate (and/or re-cohabitation rate for those living with someone) as well. No exact figures for those who have *ever* divorced are available; but in light of the existing data, they should be sizable. (See Ornstein, pp. 27, 36.) Fourteen percent of all *est* graduates report themselves "living with someone." (Ornstein, p. 36.)

Thirty percent of the sixties youths interviewed were living with someone, with four of the six couples maintaining exclusive sexual relations. Two were married, one with a single child. Another four were previously divorced. Four persons were regularly dating one other person, two of them to the exclusion of others; five were dating two or more persons at once. Three reported dating only occasionally. Fifteen of the twenty had lived with someone for at least several months at some time in the past, and only two were still living with their first such partner. (According to surveys reported in *Time*, 10 January 1977, p. 43, more California residents aged twenty-one to thirty are now living together than are married.) Twelve of the twenty had changed their residence within a year of taking the training. Six had moved to San Francisco within a year before *est*, and one within a year after taking *est* elsewhere.

16. See Ornstein, pp. 35-36. Religious affiliation of all graduates (n=1,188): Protestant 17.8 percent; Catholic 10.5 percent; Jewish 6.4 percent. Religious participation: never 65.6 percent; several times a year 20.2 percent; monthly 6.4 percent; weekly 7.8 percent. Mean number of disciplines practiced: before *est* 1.24; after *est* 0.95. Twelve of twenty interviewees practiced macrobiotics, Rolfing (massage), yoga, aikido, or the like both before and after the training. Afterwards one person took up TM and another started going to a Protestant church for the first time since leaving home, both attributed to ambivalent experiences of *est*. A third interviewee had earlier experimented with Zen meditation, "got" that it was unnecessary in the training, and then stopped it. No other interviewees reported any religious affiliation or participation.

17. According to the Behaviordyne study of *est* (see Bry, *60 Hours*, p. 213). My interviewees support this finding, as does the differential response rate by sex to mailed questionnaires in the Ornstein survey: of respondents 58.7 percent were women, 41.3 percent men (n=1,113); of nonrespondents 52.6 percent were women, 47.4 percent men (n=576). (Ornstein, p. 61.)

18. *est*, "Questions People ask about The *est* Training," an unpaginated brochure #1474-1, 1977.

19. Cf. William W. Bartley III, *Werner Erhard: The Transformation of Jack Rosenberg*, pp. 212-222. (Hereafter cited as Bartley, *Erhard*; all page numbers refer to the uncorrected proofs of this authorized biography.)

20. Erhard and *est* staff members often distinguish between (monistically real) "experience" and (dualistically apparent) "feeling" in explaining *est* tenets, but *est*'s clients rarely do. Sixties youth used the two terms interchangeably, and so will I in following their accounts. In referring to relatively formal or official statements of *est* ideology the nominal distinction is maintained where ease of usage permits. The formal conceptual distinction rests on the difference between the monistically "transformed" and omnicausal "being," which experiences; and the dualistically limited and determined "mind," which merely feels. See pp. 225-226.

21. *est*, "Questions People Ask about the *est* Training." The same brochure explains that a point of view or *context* consists of "the often hidden, tightly woven fabric of assumptions, opinions, rules, values, concepts, habits, beliefs, patterns, positions, and points of view with which we frame or hold the facts and which actually shape much of our perceptions of and response to life." Note that even "values" can themselves be evaluated by their payoff in terms of aliveness. That is, *only* aliveness is an intrinsic value, good in itself. All other values are merely instrumental values, means to the ultimately good consequence of experienced aliveness. Rules

are evaluated and justified in similar style—by the aliveness they pay off to their recognizer. This constitutes rule-egoism.

22. *PSA Magazine* (Pacific Southwest Airlines) June 1978, p. 13.

23. Trainer R. McNamara, day 1, San Francisco "A" Training, September 1975. (Hereafter cited as R. McNamara, day—.)

24. *est,* "Questions People Ask About The *est* Training."

25. *The Graduate Review,* a periodical published monthly by *est,* July 1976, p. 5. (Hereafter cited as *Graduate Review.*)

26. Ibid., p. 3.

27. Ibid., September 1976, p. 16.

28. R. McNamara, day 1.

29. The deontological ethic prescribes, for example, "Keep your promises." Why? "Because promise-keeping is right." Why? "It is God's will." Or, "It accords with the true nature of existence." *est*'s consequential ethic asserts, "If you want to experience aliveness, keep your promises." The imperative is conditional upon particular desires or goals of the agent. In Kant's terms, there are no unconditional or "categorical imperatives" for *est* ("Keep promises!"). There are only "hypothetical imperatives" ("*If* you want to experience aliveness, keep promises.").

30. For all its examples of "the rules of life" and allusions to them, *est* takes pains to reject any objectified general definition of them. See Earl Babbie, "You Can't Apply *est,*" in *Graduate Review,* August 1978, p. 18, which also proclaims:

> The Rules of Life
>
> by
>
> Werner Erhard
>
> 1. Life doesn't have any rules.
> 2.

31. R. McNamara, day 1. *est*'s emphasis on rules, accepting things as they are, and determining one's own experience of them has led some observers (see, for example, Sheridan Fenwick, *Getting It,* pp. 40-41) to detect in it traces of Stoicism. Despite echoes of Epictetus' "Men are disturbed not by things, but by the views they take of things," *est* contrasts with Stoicism in denying (1) the centrality of reason, (2) a rational cosmic order or *Logos,* and (3) a character ideal of rational self-control. Instead *est* emphasizes (1) an intuitive affective calculus, (2) the mystical acosmic integrity of existence, and (3) a character ideal of therapeutic derepression.

32. R. McNamra, day 1.

33. The agent's freedom to violate the rules in his perceived self-interest in the *est* ethic, allied with its fundamentally egoistic viewpoint, distinguishes it critically from rule-utilitarianism (see chapter 1), which likewise justifies rules by the consequences of their recognition but obliges the agent, once he has assessed which complete set of rules produces the greatest amount of good consequences for *all* persons, to act according to the relevant rule of that set in every particular case.

34. To be sure, the classic utilitarian (an "act-utilitarian") followed the "rules" of the cost-benefit calculus, just as the classic economic man followed the "rules" of the market in *rationally* pursuing his self-interest.

35. Compare, for example, timely adherence to a precise schedule in both cases; prescribed posture in zazen and in certain *est* processes; restricted conversation and physical movement.

36. *est*, "Questions People Ask About The *est* Training."

37. *est*, "The Famous *est* Rat and Cheese Story," an undated single-sheet brochure.

38. *est*, "Special Guest Seminar" mailer #599, 1976.

39. Werner Erhard, "Up to Your Ass in Aphorisms," 1973. An unpaginated booklet published by *est*. (Hereafter referred to as Erhard, "Aphorisms.")

40. R. McNamara, day 1; see also Erhard, "Aphorisms."

41. For *est*, statements are not *true* or *false*. They are only "real" (fully experienced) or "unreal" (believed, not fully experienced) for their speakers. *est*'s own statements constitute "facts" or "data" that are "so;" that is, epistemologically accurate.

42. R. McNamara, day 3.

43. *est*, "Graduate Seminar Series" announcements, 1977.

44. *Graduate Review*, June 1978, p. 6.

45. By "*est*'s critics" I refer, notably, to Peter Marin ("The New Narcissism," in *Harper's*, October 1975, pp. 45-56), Edwin Schur (*The Awareness Trap: Self-Absorption instead of Social Change*), and a slew of journalists, including Mark Brewer ("We're Gonna Tear You Down and Put You Back Together," in *Psychology Today*, August 1975), Tom Wolfe ("The Me Decade," in *New York*, 23 August 1976), and Kenneth Woodward ("Getting Your Head Together," in *Newsweek*, 6 September 1976).

46. See p. 181 and n. 15 above.

47. See, for example, *Society By Agreement: An Introduction to Sociology*, authored by Earl Babbie, a professor of sociology and *est* graduate. As excerpted in *est* publications (*Graduate Review*, July 1977, pp. 1-4), the text suggests the affinity between *est*'s view of social norms and sociological views drawn from utilitarian and contractarian theory. Note the following interpretation of "Agreements: a Balance Sheet—Every time you make an agreement with someone else, you both win and lose. Every benefit comes at a cost, and every cost has some benefit attached to it. . . . You don't have to make agreements unless the gain at least equals the loss and preferably exceeds it. . . . The gains we realize in agreements extend well beyond such obvious commodities as money, food, physical pleasures, and the like. Prestige, love, respect, obligations due to us, the inner glow of charity and altruism, thoughts of divine reward, the cessation of pain or its threat, and countless other immeasurable rewards and anticipated rewards tip the balance in favor of this agreement or that."

48. R. McNamara, day 1; see also Erhard, "Aphorisms."

49. *est*, "Definition of Reponsibility," publication #137-a, 1973.

50. Erhard, "Aphorisms." Drug experience of sixties youth in *est*, compared to those in the LWF and Zen Center, provides an interesting biographical correlate to the appeal of *est*'s idea of responsibility, with its emphasis on the individual as omnicausal. All three movements teach the priority and power of consciousness or spirit over matter or external event and circumstance. In general, this fits with the

hippie's experience on drugs that what's inside his consciousness is more real than what's outside, or, more strongly, that all reality is a function of consciousness. In contrast to the LWF and Zen Center, *est* emphasizes the individual's power to "choose" consciously the tenor of his consciousness and to "create his own experience" intentionally. This fits with the biographical fact that most sixties youth in *est* used drugs, but few of them were heavy users (see n. 11 above), far fewer than among the LWF's "dopers" or Zen Center's psychedelic seekers. Nor do many *est* graduates recount the sort of drug episodes common among LWF and Zen Center youths on psychedelic bad trips, who intensely experienced the *un*chosen, *un*controllable, *un*willed aspects of their consciousness. Instead, says one, "I started smoking grass in '67 and I tried acid a few times, but I never had anything like a religious experience on drugs. I was just getting high." Uncontrollable "religious experiences" lead toward doctrines emphasizing self-surrender to God or self-dissolution in Buddha-Mind, and away from stress on the individual's power to create his experience and his "universe" entirely by choice.

51. R. McNamara, day 2.

52. *Graduate Review*, June 1978, p. 5.

53. Dr. Joe P. Tupin in *Graduate Review*, June 1977, p. 12 (excerpted from the *Sacramento Bee*, March 1977).

54. Ornstein, p. 26.

55. Ibid.

56. Some youths report disrupted relationships after they take the *est* training, especially with those who resist being "assisted" to take the training themselves. A loyal graduate explains why he broke off with a resistant girlfriend: "People whose lives work are a threat to people whose lives don't work. People who can accept and cope with many different points of view are a threat to people who have rigidly structured lives and hold on tight to one point of view. Even our tolerance seems intolerant to them." Here the LWF's self-image is reversed, as the *est* graduate sees his nonjudgmental pluralism threatening the moral absolutism of more "rigid" others. Yet both graduate and sectarian Christian share the conviction that their lives "work" or please God as the lives of others do not, which causes some others to resist instead of imitate them, a conflict focused by proselytizing activity. An *est* trainer interprets this conflict: "It's not yet safe to express enlightenment. People poke fun at it. The world of 'endarkenment' is set up to invalidate people's experience. When you're enlightened, you share yourself, you're very open, so people's criticisms and evaluations are often invalidating for your experience." (*Graduate Review*, October 1978, p. 19.) Such reformulation of the sectarian Christian's polarization between "the children of light" and "the children of darkness" hints at the sectarian side of *est*'s own relationship to the larger society, which echoes the counterculture's sectarianism for some sixties youth in *est*. "I don't experience a whole lot of difference between *est* and the hippie thing in the sixties," says one. "*est*'s an ingroup, too, you know. . . . We're enlightened and you're assholes."

57. *Graduate Review*, October 1976, pp. 2-3.

58. *est* teaches that parents are "the two most important people in your life." Each person must "complete" his relationship to his parents—that is, resolve its difficulties by disclosing, abreacting, and communicating them—in order likewise to complete all his other relationships. Although the training induces psychological revelations of how powerfully one's parents have affected him, *est* argues that they can't be blamed for doing so, since, "you're the one who chose them." Says one

young graduate, "My father and mother didn't do it to me. *I* did it to me. I've let go a lot of my case against my parents. In the game they set up—money, job, house, security—they're successes. All I have to do is let them be who they are and accept that they love me, because they do." Roughly 60 percent of all *est* graduates say they feel closer to their parents and less angry at them since the training (Ornstein, pp. 26-27).

59. *Graduate Review*, June 1977, pp. 3-4.

60. How were sixties youths educated before they entered the job market and *est*'s seminars? Fourteen of twenty youths interviewed hold B.A. degrees, and seven also hold advanced degrees. Five of twenty dropped out a year or two short of finishing college, and one never began. Of nineteen college students, nine majored in humanities, six in social sciences, three in natural sciences, and one in business. Although they include some highly educated professionals, *est* youths typically report "getting through" in school, without the antipathy and failure reported by the Christians or the intellectual-artistic passion reported by some Zen students. Most *est* youths studied humanities and social sciences undirected at a career. Says one, "I thought people who were into becoming engineers were crazy. After four years I'd had it with school, but I didn't have a clue about what I was gonna do. I spent a few years hanging out, then I sort of gave up the idea of 'It's better to have hair on your face than not to.' I shaved and put on a suit and went around to places looking for a job, any job, 'Hello, I am a college graduate. I am looking for a job.' Nothing. I was out of it, totally unprepared. I've wound up doing things I never thought I would, that I didn't like doing. Selling shoes, working in a rent-a-car agency. All of a sudden I feel like I'm getting old and I have to get going." Meaningfully for such a clientele, *est* identifies itself as an "educational corporation" whose clients "enroll" in "seminars" from which they "graduate" in four days to "graduate seminars," as opposed to Zen's lifelong "students." *est* refers prominently to highly educated members of its advisory board and staff, and cites educational data as evidence that "*est* graduates are smart. . . ." (*Graduate Review*, June 1976, p. 5.) But *est* distinguishes its directly experienced knowledge of how to live and work (knowing how) from rationally understood propositional knowledge that explains life (knowing that). Thus, "understanding is the booby prize in life," claimed by those who have not experienced it. Those who have, like Erhard himself, succeed through their personal power, not through institutionalized learning.

61. See C. Wright Mills' classical analysis of this phenomenon in his *White Collar*: "In many strata of white collar employment, such traits as courtesy, helpfulness, and kindness, once intimate, are now part of the impersonal means of livelihood. . . . When white collar people get jobs, they sell not only their time and energy but their personalities as well. They sell their smiles and their kindly gestures, . . ." (p. xvii).

62. R. Bruce, *est* staff member, San Francisco, April 1976, paraphrasing briefing notebooks for *est* assistants. Trying (and failing due to circumstances beyond one's control or intention) is not a legitimate category in *est*'s subjectivist theory of causality. The trainer dramatizes this concept (R. McNamara, day 3) by dropping a book on the stage, calling on a trainee to "demonstrate *trying* to pick up this book," and then explaining the impossibility of doing so as proof that belief in "trying" lacks actuality in experience. Note that to make this lesson plausible, the object to be acted on is located within a face-to-face interpersonal relationship: what one person drops, another can pick up without even trying, if he is willing to do so. But what if

the object to be picked up were not a book on the stage but the stage itself? Or if the problem to be resolved were not part of a social interaction but a complex mathematical proof? Then, of course, an actor does have to try in order to succeed. Even so, he may try and fail, through no lack of his own willpower, as distinct from muscle or brainpower. In short, the concept that "there's no such thing as trying" depends on an interpersonal, interactive social context for its plausibility. It becomes implausible as soon as the example shifts from such an interpersonal context to one of abstractions or physical objects in themselves. Sociologically, *est*'s idea likewise loses plausibility when it shifts from the interpersonal, interactive work and lifestyle experienced by *est*'s urban middle-class audience to professionals committed to intellectual-technical abstraction or to workers laboring with material things. See n. 90 below.

63. Erhard has similarly described his first experience of higher consciousness (Bry, *60 Hours*, p. 155), manifested as a prolonged charismatic hot streak as a salesman, which presaged his enlightenment experience: ". . . my life totally opened up. I could produce fucking magic . . . I ain't kidding about it. It was that space where you cannot miss. I walked into an office and they said, 'Here comes Werner Erhard.' Just by my presence things got better. What happened is I got arrogant and in three months it was all gone." (San Francisco *Chronicle*, 3 December 1974, p. 5.)

64. See Max Weber, "The Protestant Sects and the Spirit of Capitalism," in Hans Gerth and C. W. Mills, eds., *From Max Weber*, pp. 302-322; and his *The Protestant Ethic and the Spirit of Capitalism*.

65. For comments leading me to sharpen these last two sentences, I am indebted to Victor Gioscia.

66. The human-relations approach to management has long recognized the utility of personal attention, open communication, and friendly feelings for engendering cooperative informal ties among coworkers in order to increase the productivity of their formal organizations.

67. J. Palmer, Fairmont Hotel, San Francisco, March 1976.

68. From "Making Relationships Work II," quoted in graduate information briefing notebooks in use April 1976, San Francisco.

69. Bartley, *Erhard*, p. 141.

70. *Graduate Review*, September 1978, p. 6.

71. In 1950 C. Wright Mills could write: "Only a fraction of this population consists of free private enterprises in any economic sense; there are now four times as many wage-workers and salary workers as independent entrepreneurs." (*White Collar*, p. xiv.) As these corporate trends continue, the salesman remains an entrepreneurial survivor in his ideas and in some of his circumstances. He may work for a large corporation and draw a base salary from it, but the salesman, unlike advertising or public relations men, spends most of his time on his own in the field, not in the office. He makes most of his living from commissions hinged entirely on performance, not from a bureaucratically fixed salary.

72. For example, each latecomer to an *est* seminar is taken aside individually by a volunteer, who faces her steadily and gravely asks: (1) Are you late? (2) Did you agree to be at the seminar on time? (3) Are you breaking your agreement? (4) Who is responsible for you breaking your agreement? (5) Are you willing to recreate your agreement at this time and be responsible for it? Until the often-squirming graduate satisfies her interrogator with straightforward acknowledgments of her breach of promise instead of polite excuses for it, she is not allowed inside.

73. Instrumental argument for middle-class work (you have to put in your time to make a living) proved convincing to the Depression-bred parents of sixties youth, whose success in following it helped undercut its force for their children. *est* has transformed and revitalized it. A young graduate ponders his own history as a dropout handyman in light of his father's life in business: "It's funny. Everything I've ever done for money, like carpentry, was the stuff my father used to do around the house on weekends, the stuff he enjoyed. He never talked about his business, like he didn't feel that good about it. I asked him what he did once, and he said, 'I go to the office and kiss ass on the telephone all day.' That was what he had to do to make money to raise us. It wasn't really what he wanted to do. . . . Since *est* I see it kind of differently. He was a poor kid who worked his way through college and got himself a job and made damned good money. He made it."

74. Erhard compares assisting at *est* to mountain climbing. "There's no point to it beyond getting to the top and back down again with the most efficiency. . . . Assisting is for people who want to get to the top." He also observes, "There's no point to life. There's only nonsense. However, there's appropriate nonsense and inappropriate nonsense. The nonsense that's appropriate to the moment is the moment's nonsense." (Paraphrased from briefing notebooks for assistants, April 1976.)

75. The original core of *est*'s staff consisted of three such women, carried over from Erhard's sales corporation, whom he had recruited through newspaper ads. Recalls one of them, "Werner wrote brilliant ads. He appealed to educated women who at that time were not particularly accepted in key contributory jobs." (*Graduate Review*, January 1977, p. 2.)

76. Bartley, *Erhard*, p. 144.

77. Weber, *Sociology of Religion*, p. 90.

78. See Christopher Lasch, "The Narcissist Society," *New York Review of Books*, 30 September 1976, pp. 5-13; also Otto Kernberg, *Borderline Conditions and Pathological Narcissism*.

79. *Graduate Review*, June 1977, p. 12.

80. In February 1977, Erhard declared, "I take responsibility for ending starvation within 20 years," to members of the *est* Foundation. The Foundation then granted $100,000 to begin The Hunger Project, incorporated independently of *est* but largely housed in *est* offices, staffed by *est* personnel and graduate volunteers, and indebted to *est* for a $400,000 interest-free loan. In the fall of 1977 Erhard presented the Project in eleven cities (at a cost of $518,000 to the Project) to 40,000 persons, most of them *est* graduates, and thus to the media and to the public. By 1979, 180,000 persons had enrolled in the Project, two-thirds of them nongraduates. (See *Graduate Review*, September 1977, p. 2; also The Hunger Project, "A Shift in the Wind," *The Hunger Project Newspaper*, 1, May 1978.) "Ultimately, the Hunger Project is about transformation of Self as Humanity—about making the world work," writes Erhard. "It is about creating the end of hunger on our planet as an idea whose time has come." (*Graduate Review*, September 1977, p. 5.) What does this mean in organizational terms? "The Hunger Project is not about feeding people," explains one official. "All the Hunger Project does," says its Boston chairman, "is enroll more people. What we are doing is using money to create growth." (Mac Margolis and R. Hornung, "An Idea on Every Plate," in *Nightfall*, October 1978, pp. 15-22, quoted from p. 18.) Project literature states, "Your donation will be used for the project. The project is not about researching new technical solutions, growing food,

or feeding people directly—but rather creating a context of commitment to eliminate starvation on the planet in two decades. The process by which a context is created is communication and enrollment, communication and enrollment, communication and enrollment." (The Hunger Project, "It's Our Planet," p. 5.) The idea of "creating the context to end hunger" is thus identified with the action of "communicating" about and "enrolling" in The Hunger Project. By 1979, each of 180,000 enrollees had been asked to donate at least five dollars to the Project, enroll others, volunteer for its staff, and fast for a day. By this time, the Hunger Project had raised $880,000 and spent over a million, gaining recognition from the media, government officials, and established hunger organizations. Some experts and officials have welcomed the Project's publicity for the issue of world hunger. Others adopted a wait-and-see attitude, or expressed uncertainty about what the Project actually does. Critics have charged that it does little besides publicize itself and recruit new members, thereby performing the same functions for *est* itself. Such critics point to the Project's initial budget: 57.6 percent ($518,000) went to pay for Erhard's presentations; another 26.6 percent ($238,000) went to produce Project literature and films; 15 percent ($135,250) went for the Project's own administrative, organizational, and miscellaneous expenses. This left 0.8 percent ($7,500) to support other hunger organizations, which actually feed people. Critics also point to reports of nongraduate Project volunteers being pressured by its *est*-trained staff and assistants to take the training. (See Suzanne Gordon, "Let Them Eat *est*," *Mother Jones*, December 1978, pp. 42, 44, 50.) Through 1980 the Hunger Project enrolled 1.7 million persons and raised $5.7 million, according to *est* trainer K. Anbender.

81. If we define the committed political activist by such indicators as leading or regularly participating in radical political activity, being arrested for so doing, belonging to a radical organization, mastering its formal ideology, resisting the draft or filing for CO status, then none of those formally interviewed could be classified as a committed activist. Of thirty additional graduates informally interviewed, only one, an early sixties civil-rights worker and CORE member now turned massage teacher, would qualify, the case of *est* graduate Jerry Rubin notwithstanding. Seventeen of twenty interviewees reported sympathizing during the sixties with the view that American society seemed fundamentally in the wrong; only four of the seventeen accepted a full-blown radical political analysis of what was wrong, and none acted on it.

82. R. McNamara, day 1.

83. Ibid., day 3.

84. Bartley, *Erhard*, p. 221.

85. This postmillennial optimism began to fade in 1975-76 among insiders aware of *est*'s slowing rate of recruitment and profit in its original Western markets, staff defections; and staff morale, legal, media, and public image problems. In a videotaped staff meeting in March, 1976, Erhard acknowledged that *est*'s goals of training forty million persons and transforming American society might not, after all, be possible within one generation. *est* subsequently reincorporated itself more effectively and entered large urban markets in the eastern United States. *est*'s enrollment and profits rebounded after 1976, and its organization stabilized. (See Jesse Kornbluth, "The Führer over *est*," *New Times*, 19 March 1976; and *Graduate Review*, November, 1976.)

86. The Hunger Project, "It's Our Planet-It's Our Hunger Project," (a 10-page brochure, published May 1978), p. 5.

87. *Graduate Review*, July 1978, p. 16.

88. *est*, "Werner Erhard: All I Can Do Is Lie," (an undated reprint of an interview published in the *East-West Journal*, September 1974), p. 5.

89. *est* has had mixed success with professionals, winning the loyalty of some individuals, notably clinical psychologists and physicians, but not the approval of any professional establishment. *est has* won over elements of the middle echelons of certain educational, business, and administrative institutions, in which its ethic is particularly applicable. At the end of 1975 *est* claimed 8.83 percent of all "educators" in the San Francisco Unified School District among its graduates. (R. C. Devon Heck and J. L. Thompson, *San Francisco*, January 1976, p. 22.) Disproportionately women, schoolteachers must present themselves to large groups, motivate their efforts through interpersonal means, and manage their behavior within the constraints of a bureaucratized setting, to which youngsters are especially resistant. Special *est* trainings have reportedly had the clearest institutional impact in prisons. Because these prison trainings are often cited to counter indications that *est* appeals predominantly to middle-class whites, it is worth noting that prison inmates—though predominantly poor, black, and male—can be particularly receptive to rule-egoism. They usually hold an individualistic ethic overtly antagonistic to the conventions and rules of "straight" bureaucratic society, yet they find themselves imprisoned within the most totally constraining of all bureaucratic institutions. They are there for trying to beat the system by bucking it. Being there offers strong evidence that their attempts have been unsuccessful. Now the system is beating them, sometimes literally. Rule-egoism sensibly advises that the only way to beat the system, in one's own interests, is to go along with it. One inmate translates *est*'s ethic to another: "What the man is tellin' you is that you don't need to get your head knocked doin' what you're gonna end up doin' anyway." ("The *est* Standard Training at San Quentin Prison," *est* publication #1391, November 1976.) Dropout rates in prison trainings appear to be way above the 3-5 percent middle-class average outside. From Bry, *60 Hours*, p. 125, it seems that 67 percent of those who signed up for the Lompoc Prison training did not complete its first delivery there. Similarly, more than one-third of the prisoner-trainees at San Quentin dropped out by the end of day 3; sixty-one remained of ninety-four who had begun, including eight prison staff members. (*Graduate Review*, September 1976, pp. 1-7.)

90. Robert W. Fuller and Zara Wallace, *A Look at est in Education* (San Francisco: *est*, 1975), pp. 62-63. The sharpest institutional debate over *est*'s meaning and effects has so far occurred among psychiatrists, centered around the possibility of harm raised by apparently rare but nonetheless serious cases of post-*est* psychotic episodes. Several psychiatrists treating such persons concluded: "We are impressed that an authoritarian, confrontational, aggressive leadership style coupled with physiologic deprivation fosters an 'identification with the aggressor.' The inability of this defense mechanism to contain overwhelming anxiety aroused by the process may lead to fusion with the leader, ego fragmentation, and psychotic decompensation." (Leonard L. Glass, M. Kirsch, F. Parris, "Psychiatric Disturbances Associated with Erhard Seminars Training: I. A Report of Cases," *Am. J. Psychiatry* 134 (1977): 245-257.) *est* responded by (1) denying any "causal relationship between taking the *est* training and the occurrence of psychotic problems"; (2) arguing that the incidence of psychotic episodes after the *est* training is 0.8 percent, "less than the number of people having episodes in college classrooms or just walking the street"; (3) citing *est* policy to screen from the training all persons ever in a mental hospital or

not currently "winning" in therapy. (*est*, "Statement on article in the *American Journal of Psychiatry*," 1977.) Four of the five psychotic cases reported in the Glass article had no histories of psychiatric disturbance or treatment. Neither side in the debate touched on the apparent congruity between the cognitive content of the psychiatric symptoms reported—grandiosity, paranoia, delusions of influence and reference—and those of *est* tenets. Yet in one case a person, convinced he could live without air, jumped into a swimming pool and tried to breathe under water. Another, convinced "nothing was real," put his hand through a window and severed tendons in his wrist. A third was convinced he could read others' minds, and feared they could control his own mind. These symptoms appear to dramatize, however extremely, such familiar *est* ideas as the omnicausal yet entirely determined self, creating his experience of others yet being created by them, accomplishing all things without "efforting" or "trying" (see n. 62 above).

91. *Graduate Review*, June 1978, pp. 15-17.

92. *est* "Special Guest Seminar" announcement, February 13, 1976.

93. *Graduate Review*, June 1976, p. 11.

94. Ibid., November 1976, p. 3.

95. Ibid.

96. Ibid.

97. Ibid., September 1977, p. 5.

98. Lester Brown, director of the Worldwatch Institute, quoted in Gordon, "Let Them Eat *est*," p. 52.

99. See n. 80 above.

100. See, for example, Erhard, "Aphorisms," page beginning, "Life is a ripoff."

101. *Graduate Review*, June 1978, p. 22.

5. MORAL MEANING IN A SOCIAL CONTEXT

1. The *prophet* is an individual bearer of charisma, "the gift of grace" borne out by exceptional sanctity, heroism, or exemplary character. By virtue of his mission he proclaims a religious doctrine or divine commandment. (See Max Weber, *The Sociology of Religion*, chap. 4; also *Social and Economic Organization*, part III, especially pp. 358-363, Free Press edition, 1964.) As opposed to the priest, who claims authority from his official service to a sacred tradition, the prophet claims it from personal revelation and inner power. Moreover, the prophet sets his authority over against tradition and seeks to break through it with a new doctrine. Thus the biblical Jesus prefaces his preaching, "It is written, but I say unto you. . . ." Leaders of alternative religious movements at present in American society tend to be charismatic figures, not ritual or legal officeholders. Even those who hold ritually transmitted status (e.g., Buddhist masters and Christian ministers) built their own movements from the ground up. But neo-Christian and neo-Oriental movements renew older revelations, which they set against or apart from utilitarian individualism. Part of the impulse and attitude necessary to define their posture of opposition or independence derives from the romantic tradition of the counterculture. Yet the persistence of utilitarian society is a necessary condition of their formation. Their sectarian and monastic communities suggest alternative models of society, but, unlike Calvinism's reformed church, sect and monastery cannot be translated directly into public policy nor used directly to cement a new social order. Visions of a "postmod-

ern" or "postindustrial" society notwithstanding, the larger social-structural stage has not yet been set for a new "revolution of the saints." A structural parallel to the transition from traditional (feudal, hierarchical, patriarchal, or corporate) to modern society, which set the stage for the radical politics of Calvinism and Puritanism, has not arrived for sixties youth. (See Michael Walzer, *The Revolution of the Saints*, chaps. 1, 9, esp. pp. 310-330.) What they have experienced, however, is the problematic unsettledness of their "identity" or moral character and of their own place within a modernized society. Conversion to alternative religious movements, as to sixteenth-century Calvinism, expresses the drive to become a new person. But a different sort of anxiety drove sixties youth, and getting saved from the sixties turned out to be a process of neo-Oriental self-transcendence, human-potential self-integration, or Pentecostal self-surrender, not Calvinist self-conquest. Few of these converts (with the notable exception of the Moonies) see themselves at society's center stage dismantling the old order and constructing the new. But they do see themselves setting the stage of the self for a new social order. The old utilitarian order has lost its legitimacy for these sixties youth, and a new order could draw for its legitimation on the ideals of the small-scale alternative institutions to which they are now committed.

2. See Appendix 2 for a schematic presentation of the three cases.

3. Quoted in *Windbell*, a publication of San Francisco Zen Center, 13, 1-2 (1974): 34 (trans. E. Conze).

4. George Gallup, Jr., *Religion in America 1979-80*, p. 34.

5. Almost needless to say, none of these developments should be misconstrued as presaging societal adoption of an authoritative Christian ethic along the lines envisioned by Rev. Sun Myung Moon's Unification Church. Such a merger of church and state would require, for starters, a nationally organized political movement based on anti-Communist, right-wing fundamentalism, capable of remaking or suspending the Constitution. Moral and political authority would have to fuse in a theocratic state whose officials would prescribe moral behavior with the force of law. Although it claims biblical authority, Rev. Moon's Unification Church contrasts with neo-Christian groups in several respects: 1) It recruits across a wider class range than most neo-Christian movements, with a core of upwardly mobile lower-middle-class urban youth, and it includes more Jewish, Catholic, urban, and non-white minority members. 2) The Moon church is governed by a totalistic moral and social authority that aggressively seeks to change society, organizing nationwide political activity to this end. Thus it resembles a reformed church, like Calvin's, fighting "a revolution of the saints" to reconstruct society directly, instead of a millenarian sect receptively awaiting God's apocalyptic intervention to make over the existing order. (See n. 1 above.) 3) The Unification Church's millenarism, though based on the Bible's cosmological dualism, gives a specifically anti-Communist and nationalistic definition to the conflict between good and evil, foreseeing its resolution in a noncompetitive, nonindividualistic, and ascetic form of godly socialism. (See Dick Anthony and Thomas Robbins, "A Typology of Non-Traditional Religious Movements in Modern America," a paper delivered at the American Association for the Advancement of Science, February, 1977; also their "The Decline of American Civil Religion and Development of Authoritarian Nationalism: A Study of the Unification Church of Rev. Sun Myung Moon," a paper delivered at the Society for the Scientific Study of Religion, 1975.)

6. Dick Anthony and Thomas Robbins (see "A Typology of Non-Traditional

Religious Movements in Modern America," 1977; also "Youth Culture, Religious Ferment, and the Confusion of Moral Meanings," a paper presented at the Society for the Scientific Study of Religion, 1974) interpret monistic neo-Oriental religious groups as implying a qualified moral relativism more directly attuned to the pluralism of contemporary American society, especially its bureaucratic urban settings, than I have suggested in connection with Pacific Zen Center. There are two reasons for this. First, devotional-charismatic movements, especially the Meher Baba movement, figure centrally in Anthony and Robbins's description and analysis of neo-Oriental groups, not meditational-monastic groups like Zen Center. The former do indeed appear less rule-oriented and more directly integrative to the larger society, especially to bureaucratic and professional work, than do Zen Center and other meditational-monastic groups. Second, Anthony and Robbins contrast the moral absolutism of neo-Christian groups based on dualism and the moral relativism of neo-Oriental and human potential groups based on monism. I have contrasted the human-potential movement, whose relativism derives from the consequential ethic of utilitarian individualism, to the authoritative absolutism of neo-Christian groups, and to the paradoxical position of Zen Center, which combines the absolutism of a regular ethic and the relativism of an expressive ethic. Somewhat different conceptual categories as well as empirical cases distinguish Anthony and Robbins's studies from this one, but the overall arguments seem to run closer to parallel than to cross purposes.

7. See Max Weber, *The Protestant Ethic and the Spirit of Capitalism*, pp. 181-182; also "Science as a Vocation," pp. 155-156 in H. H. Gerth and C. Wright Mills, eds., *From Max Weber*.

8. For survey research evidence of substantial change in these directions, and a discussion of the San Francisco Bay Area as a setting favorable to sociocultural innovation, see Robert Wuthnow, *The Consciousness Reformation*, especially pp. 11-57, 215-224.

9. "Spirit of 60s Generation Still Alive in American Society," *New York Times*, 12 August 1979, pp. 1, 38.

10. See Larry Hirschhorn, "Urban Development and Social Change: the Demographic Dimension," xerox, Childhood and Government Project, the Earl Warren Legal Institute, School of Law, University of California at Berkeley, 1976, especially pp. 73-79.

11. See the *New York Times*, 10 April 1977, p. 26.

12. See pp. 258 and 260-267 for political calls to lower our economic expectations in one such fashion or the other.

13. See Fred Block and Larry Hirschhorn, "New Productive Forces and the Contradictions of Contemporary Capitalism: A Post-Industrial Perspective," *Theory and Society* 7 (1979): 368-371. Also see Ann Swidler, "Love and Adulthood in American Culture," in Neil Smelser and Erik Erikson, eds., *Themes of Love and Work in Adulthood*. This paragraph and the following two draw on these sources.

14. For an economist's analysis of this predicament see Fred Hirsch, *Social Limits to Growth*, especially pp. 1-12, 117-158.

15. Inaugural address of President Jimmy Carter, January 20, 1977, as reprinted in *Vital Speeches*, 15 February 1977, pp. 258-259.

16. "Remarks of the President at the 25th Annual National Prayer Breakfast," xerox, Office of the White House Press Secretary, 27 January 1977, p. 1.

17. Ibid., p. 1.

18. Ibid., pp. 1-2.

19. "Playboy Interview: Jimmy Carter," *Playboy*, November 1976, p. 86.

20. Ibid.

21. Ibid., p. 68.

22. Ibid., p. 69.

23. Ibid., p. 68.

24. Ibid., pp. 69-70.

25. Inaugural address of President Ronald Reagan, January 20, 1981, as reprinted in *New York Times*, 21 January 1981, p. 13.

26. Republican National Convention Presidential Nomination Acceptance address, July 17, 1980, as reprinted in *Vital Speeches*, 15 August 1980, pp. 642-646.

27. *New York Times*, 22 September 1980, p. B7. Also see *New York Times*, 29 February 1980, p. B1, for the text of Reagan's stock campaign speech.

28. Jerry Falwell, *Listen, America!*, p. 265.

29. NBC's "Meet the Press," 5 October 1975, transcript, p. 5. Quoted in *Thoughts: Edmund G. Brown, Jr.*, ed. N. J. Peters. (Hereafter referred to as *Thoughts*.) This collection of excerpts from Brown's speeches, interviews, and press conferences has circulated widely in California. Although it leaves the original context of quoted remarks unspecified, it alphabetizes them under such headings as "Human Nature and Values." This arrangement, for better or worse, has become the context that remains visible to the public eye.

30. *Thoughts*, p. 52.

31. "Playboy Interview: Jerry Brown," *Playboy*, March 1976, p. 72.

32. Brown, Edmund G., "Speech to the Commonwealth Club," April 15, 1977, California Governor's Office transcript, p. 10.

33. Brown, "Speech to Commonwealth Club," pp. 5-6.

34. Public Broadcasting System, "Agronsky at Large," 1 April 1977, producer's transcript, p. 8.

35. *Thoughts*, p. 14.

36. Ibid., p. 15.

37. Ibid., p. 14.

38. Ibid., p. 14.

39. Ibid., p. 15.

40. David Broder, "The Canniness of the Long Distance Runner," *The Atlantic Monthly*, January 1978, pp. 38-39.

41. Thoughts, p. 12.

42. Ibid., pp. 11-12.

43. Ibid., p. 65.

44. Public Broadcasting System, "Firing Line," 11 October 1975, producer's transcript, p. 6.

45. *Coevolution Quarterly*, Spring 1977, p. 25.

46. *Thoughts*, p. 7.

47. *Coevolution Quarterly*, Spring 1977, p. 26.

48. *Thoughts*, p. 47.

49. Self-Determination, "Why Self-Determination?" xerox, 1975. Vasconcellos chairs the Ways and Means Committee and the Subcommittee on Higher Education of the Education Committee of the California State Legislature's Assembly. His largely suburban district (Santa Clara and part of San Jose) includes a high proportion of college-educated, white-collar young adults. It lies in one of the three

U.S. counties in which *est* recruits most heavily. A lawyer by training, Vasconcellos is also a student of humanistic psychology (Abraham Maslow, Carl Rogers, and especially Sidney Jourard's *The Transparent Self*) and a veteran of encounter groups, Esalen, and neo-Reichian body therapy. An increasing number of California legislators share such interests. One of them, himself involved in Transactional Analysis, estimates that 25 percent of his colleagues have had "similar personal growth experiences." (See Ralph Keyes, "The Case of the Liberated Legislator," *Human Behavior*, October 1974, p. 27.) As a state legislator active in educational planning and budget review, Vasconcellos has sought to introduce human-potential insights and methods into the state's classrooms, and to establish "self-esteem" as an educational goal.

50. See n. 3, chap. 4.

51. *Sacramento Union*, 21 March 1976, p. 1.

52. John Vasconcellos, Foreword to *Your Perfect Right: A Guide to Assertive Behavior*, by Robert E. Alberti and Michael L. Emmons.

53. John Vasconcellos, "Education for What?" address given to the New Consciousness Education Conference, 1973, transcript, p. 6. Though quoted out of context, the meaning of the phrases quoted seems nonetheless clear. After hailing the progress of humanistic psychology in education, Vasconcellos cautions, "I don't think that it is realistic at this point in time for anyone to expect that all the schools are tomorrow morning going to have the goal of new consciousness or assume that human beings are basically healthy or that human nature is lovely rather than sinful in terms of its ultimate capacity."

54. Vasconcellos, "Education for What?", p. 4.

55. Self-Determination, "Why Self-Determination?"

56. Self-Determination, "Principles of Self-Determination," a two-page xeroxed "discussion document," April 1974.

57. Ibid.

58. Ibid.

59. Ibid.

60. Ibid.

61. Ibid.

62. Self-Determination, "Second Report on Self-Determination," xerox, December, 1975. This is the source of the organizational information that follows in the paragraph.

63. Carl Rogers, *Carl Rogers on Personal Power*, p. 277.

64. See Weber's use of the concept of "elective affinity" in "The Social Psychology of the World Religions," in *From Max Weber*, pp. 284-285; and in "Castes, Estates, Classes, and Religion," in *The Sociology of Religion*, chap. 6; and, of course, in the Protestant Ethic argument.

65. See Lawrence Kohlberg's cognitive-developmental theory of moral reasoning in, for example, "From Is to Ought," in his *Cognitive Development and Epistemology*, pp. 151-235. For an analysis of the ethical oversimplification of this theory see Ralph B. Potter, "Justice and Beyond in Moral Education," Andover Newton *Quarterly*, 19, 3 (1979): 145-155.

66. See Arthur Dyck, "Moral Requisites of Community: Love of Neighbor," chap. 5 in his *On Human Care*. Also see, for example, W. D. Ross on "prima facie duties" located in various sorts of social relationships in *The Right and the Good*, esp. pp. 19-22; H. L. A. Hart's discussion of "the minimal content of natural law" in

The Concept of Law, esp. pp. 189-190; David Aberle et al, "The Functional Prerequisites of a Society," *Ethics* 60, 2 (1950): 100-111.

67. The following view of religion's role in constituting and maintaining morality receives its classic statement by Clifford Geertz in "Religion as a Cultural System" and "Ethos, World View, and the Analysis of Sacred Symbols." This paragraph and the next rely on the ideas, and the felicitous phrasing, of these two essays, reprinted in Geertz, *The Interpretation of Cultures,* pp. 87-141. Max Heirich points to the need for some such interpretation of conversion in "Change of Heart: A Test of Some Widely Held Theories about Conversion," *American Journal of Sociology* 83, 3 (1977): 658-680.

68. See Geertz, "Religion," pp. 89-90.

69. Ibid., pp. 93-94.

70. Karl Marx, *The German Ideology:* ". . . circumstances make men just as much as men make circumstances." (In Robert C. Tucker, ed., *The Marx-Engels Reader,* p. 165.) My intent is not to argue against Marx but to complement his argument by emphasizing the dynamic of cultural meaning also necessary to constitute the relationship between culture and social structure, though likewise insufficient by itself to complete it.

71. See Geertz, "Religion," pp. 95-98.

72. Geertz, "Ethos, World View, and the Analysis of Sacred Symbols," p. 127.

73. See Geertz, "Religion," p. 93.

74. This discussion rests on Weber's concept of theodicy in chap. 9 of *The Sociology of Religion* and Talcott Parsons's commentary on it in the Introduction to the 1963 Beacon Press edition (trans. E. Fischoff), pp. xlvi-ix.

75. See Max Weber, *The Sociology of Religion,* p. 125; also E. E. Evans-Pritchard's use of the granary example to compare the explanatory powers of magic and science in *Witchcraft, Oracles, and Magic among the Azande,* part I, chap. 4, esp. pp. 69-70.

76. See Weber's definition (*Social and Economic Organization,* p. 93 in the Free Press edition) of all human action susceptible of meaningful interpretation in terms of a means-end scheme: ". . . processes or conditions, whether they are animate or inanimate, human or non-human, are in the present sense devoid of meaning in so far as they cannot be related to an intended purpose. That is to say they are devoid of meaning if they cannot be related to action in the role of means or ends but constitute only the stimulus, the favouring or hindering circumstances." Talcott Parsons, the editor, notes: "Surely this passage states too narrow a conception of the scope of meaningful interpretation. It is certainly not *only* in terms such as those of the rational means-end schema, that it is possible to make action understandable in terms of subjective categories. This probably can be called a source of rationalistic bias in Weber's work. In practice he does not adhere at all rigorously to this methodological position."

77. See Karl Mannheim, "The Problem of Generations," chap. 7 in his *Essays on the Sociology of Knowledge,* esp. pp. 293-294 on the notion of "fresh contact." Quantitative evidence exists linking sixties youth as a generation, via their countercultural involvement (in contrast to their stage in the life cycle or exposure to ongoing secularizing trends), to a greater decline in traditional religious commitments than preceding generations exhibit. See Robert Wuthnow, "Recent Patterns of Secularization: A Problem of Generations?" *American Sociological Review* 41 (1976): 850-862, for an analysis of this data in light of Mannheim's "generation-unit" theory.

For an application of Mannheim's theory to an alternative religion, see Jack Balswick, "The Jesus People Movement: A Generational Interpretation," *Journal of Social Issues* 30, 3 (1974): 23-42.

78. See S. N. Eisenstadt, *From Generation to Generation*, chaps. 1, 3, 4, 6. Also his "Archetypal Patterns of Youth," in Erik H. Erikson, ed., *The Challenge of Youth*, pp. 29-50. Also Kenneth Keniston, "Youth as a Stage of Life," in his *Young Radicals*, pp. 264-272.

79. In defining those groups most sensitive to ideological changes carried by prophetic movements, Weber stresses three conditions typical of youth in a modern society: (1) lack of responsibility for existing social institutions (military, political, bureaucratic, economic), and therefore little investment in maintaining the established order and little personal identification with it; (2) a sufficient sense of economic security to break with the existing order, even if it impairs their economic interests rather than advances them; (3) occupational involvement entailing some form of rationalization. The student's work entails rationalization on intellectual grounds, the early Christian artisan's on technological grounds, the early Protestant merchant's on economic grounds. In considering the content of different prophetic movements in relation to the social position of their proponents, Weber rejects any unilateral causal link between the two. But he describes constant conjunctions borne out by the types of alternative religious movements joined by sixties youth. In connection with early Christianity, he notes that the urban lower middle class tend toward a "pneumatic-enthusiastic congregational religion" of salvation, based on belief in a transcendental divinity who created and controls the world. Considering Buddhism, he finds that intellectual elites, by contrast, are drawn to forms of "illumination mysticism," often institutionalized monastically, based on belief in an immanent divinity at one with the world. Considering Confucianism, Weber sees the bureaucratic middle class drawn away from salvation to the values of disciplined "order" and security, which underpin "a utilitarian doctrine of convention." (See *The Sociology of Religion*, chaps. 6-8, and Talcott Parsons's Introduction, pp. xxxviii-xlv.)

80. See Ralph Potter, "The Logic of Moral Argument," pp. 93-114 in Paul Deats, ed., *Toward a Discipline of Social Ethics*.

BIBLIOGRAPHY

I. PRIMARY SOURCES

Unpublished Documents

Erhard, Werner. "Up to Your Ass in Aphorisms." San Francisco: *est*, 1973.
———. "The Evil of *est*" videotaped staff meeting. San Francisco: March 1976.
est. "Definition of Responsibility," *est* document #137-a, 1973.
———. "The *est* Standard Training at San Quentin Prison," *est* document #1391, November 1976.
———. "The Famous *est* Rat and Cheese Story." An unnumbered *est* document, undated.
———. "Graduate Seminar Series" announcements. San Francisco: offset, 1977.
———. "An Idea Whose Time Has Come." A "special source document" contributed to The Hunger Project from *est*, replacing *The Graduate Review* of January 1976.
———. "Assistants Notebooks." In use in *est*'s San Francisco office, April 1976.
———. "Questions People Ask About The *est* Training." *est* document #1474-1, 1977.
———. "A Report on the Legal and Financial Structure of *est*." *est* document #1301-1, June 1976.
———. "Statement on article in the *American Journal of Psychiatry*." Xerox, 1977.
———. "Werner Erhard: All I Can Do is Lie." undated reprint from the *East-West Journal*, September 1974.
———. "What is the purpose of th *est* training?" *est* document #680-3, 13 January 1976.
Fuller, Robert W. and Z. Wallace. *A Look at est in Education.* San Francisco: *est*, 1975.
Haiku Zendo/Bodhi. "Dōgen's Fukanzazengi and Shōbōgenzō zazengi." Translated by Norman Waddell and A. Masao. Los Altos, Ca.: Xerox, undated.
———. "The Heart Sutra." Los Altos, Ca.: Xerox, undated.
———. "The Precepts." Los Altos, Ca.: Xerox, undated.
The Hunger Project. "It's Our Planet-It's Our Hunger Project." San Francisco: May 1978.
———. "A Shift in the Wind." *The Hunger Project Newspaper* 1 (May 1978).
Living Word Fellowship [pseudonym]. "The Notes." San Francisco Bay Area: Mimeograph, 1971-1976.
McNamara, Randy. "*est* Standard Training Program." San Francisco: verbally presented, September 1975.

Ornstein, Robert, et al. "File SYS8, Codebook for Variables W29-88." San Francisco: The *est* Archives, 11 October 1974.

San Francisco Zen Center. "Mountain Gate: Community Work." San Francisco: letterpress, 1976.

———. "Zen in America." San Francisco: letterpress, 1968.

Zen Center Mountain Center Library. "Warm-Hearted Practice." Xerox, 23 February 1971.

II. SECONDARY SOURCES

Books

Ariès, Philippe. *Centuries of Childhood.* New York: Knopf, 1962.

Aristotle. *Nichomachean Ethics.* Indianapolis: Bobbs-Merrill, 1962.

Babbie, Earl. *Society by Agreement: An Introduction to Sociology.* Belmont, Ca.: Wadsworth, 1978.

Back, Kurt W. *Beyond Words.* Baltimore: Penguin, 1973.

Barker, Sir Ernest. *Social Contract.* New York: Oxford University Press, 1975.

Bartley, William W., III. *Werner Erhard: The Transformation of Jack Rosenberg.* New York: Clarkson Potter, 1978.

Bell, Daniel. *The Coming of Post-Industrial Society.* New York: Basic Books, 1973.

———. *The Cultural Contradictions of Capitalism.* New York: Basic Books, 1976.

Bell, Daniel, and Irving Kristol, eds. *Confrontation.* New York: Basic Books, 1969.

Bellah, Robert N. *The Broken Covenant: American Civil Religion in Time of Trial.* New York: Seabury Press, 1975.

Bellah, Robert N., and Phillip E. Hammond. *Varieties of Civil Religion.* San Francisco: Harper and Row, 1980.

Bentham, Jeremy. "Principles of Morals and Legislation." *The Utilitarians.* Garden City, N.Y.: Anchor-Doubleday, 1973.

Berger, Peter; Brigitte Berger; and Hansfried Kellner. *The Homeless Mind.* New York: Vintage Books, 1974.

Blau, Peter, and O. M. Duncan. *The American Occupational Structure.* New York: Wiley, 1967.

Brown, Edmund G. *Thoughts.* Edited by N. J. Peters. San Francisco: City Lights, 1976.

Bry, Adelaide. *est—60 Hours That Will Transform Your Life.* New York: Avon Books, 1976.

Callenbach, Ernest. *Ecotopia.* Berkeley: Banyan Tree, 1975.

Dōgen. *Shōbōgenzō Zuimonki.* Translated by Reiho Masunaga. Honolulu: University Press of Hawaii, 1975.

Dore, Ronald P. *British Factory-Japanese Factory.* Berkeley, Los Angeles, London: University of California Press, 1973.

Dumont, Louis. *From Mandeville to Marx: The Genesis and Triumph of Economic Ideology.* Chicago: University of Chicago Press, 1977.

Durkheim, Emile. *The Division of Labor in Society.* New York: Free Press, 1964.

Dyck, Arthur J. *On Human Care: An Introduction to Ethics.* Nashville: Abingdon, 1977.

Eisenstadt, S. N. *From Generation to Generation.* New York: Free Press, 1956.

Eliade, Mircea. *Shamanism: Archaic Techniques of Ecstasy.* Princeton: Princeton University Press, 1970.

Evans-Pritchard, E. E. *Witchcraft, Oracles, and Magic among the Azande.* Oxford: Clarendon Press, 1937.

Falwell, Jerry. *Listen, America!* Garden City, New York: Doubleday, 1980.

Fenwick, Sheridan. *Getting It.* Philadelphia: Lippincott, 1976.

Feuer, Lewis. *The Conflict of Generations.* New York: Basic Books, 1969.

Frankena, William K. *Ethics.* Englewood Cliffs, N.J.: Prentice-Hall, 1963.

Galbraith, John K. *The Affluent Society.* Cambridge, Mass.: Riverside. 1958.

Gallup, George, Jr. *Religion in America, 1979-80.* Princeton, N.J.: The Princeton Religious Research Center, 1979.

Geertz, Clifford. *The Interpretation of Cultures.* New York: Basic Books, 1973.

Gennep, Arnold van. *The Rites of Passage* (1909). Chicago: University of Chicago Press, 1960.

Glock, Charles Y. and Robert N. Bellah, eds., *The New Religious Consciousness.* Berkeley, Los Angeles, London: University of California Press, 1976.

Goffman, Erving. *Encounters: Two Studies in the Sociology of Interaction.* Indianapolis, Ind.: Bobbs-Merrill, 1961.

Gouldner, Alvin. *The Coming Crisis of Western Sociology.* New York: Avon Books, 1971.

Hart, H. L. A. *The Concept of Law.* London: Oxford University Press, 1961.

Hirsch, Fred. *The Social Limits to Growth.* Cambridge, Mass.: Harvard University Press, 1976.

Hobbes, Thomas. *Leviathan.* Edited by Michael Oakeshott. New York: Collier Books, 1974.

Hoge, Dean, and David Rosen, eds. *Understanding Church Growth and Decline: 1950-1978.* New York, Philadelphia: The Pilgrim Press, 1979.

The Holy Bible. King James Version. Cleveland: World Publishing Company, 1966. Also, Revised Standard Version. Cleveland: World Publishing Company, 1964.

Horkheimer, Max. *The Eclipse of Reason.* New York: Oxford University Press, 1947.

Inglehardt, Ronald. *The Silent Revolution.* Princeton, N.J.: Princeton University Press, 1977.

Jacquet, Constant H. *Yearbook of American and Canadian Churches.* New York: Abingdon Press, 1973.

Jourard, Sidney. *The Transparent Self.* New York: Van Nostrand, 1971.

Kant, Immanuel. *Foundations of the Metaphysics of Morals.* Indianapolis: Bobbs-Merrill, 1959.

Kanter, Rosabeth. *Commitment and Community.* Cambridge, Mass.: Harvard University Press, 1972.

Kapleau, Philip. *Three Pillars of Zen.* New York: Harper and Row, 1966.

Keniston, Kenneth. *Young Radicals.* New York: Harcourt, Brace, and World, 1968.

———. *Youth and Dissent.* New York: Harcourt, Brace, and Co., 1971.

Kernberg, Otto. *Borderline Conditions and Pathological Narcissism.* New York: Jason Aronson, 1976.

Kohlberg, Lawrence. *Cognitive Development and Epistemology.* New York: Academic Press, 1971.

Kropotkin, Petr. *Mutual Aid, a Factor of Evolution.* Boston: Extending Horizons,. 1955.

Lewis, I. M. *Ecstatic Religion: An Anthropological Study of Spirit Possession and Shamanism.* Harmondsworth, England: Penguin Books, 1971.

Locke, John. *Two Treatises of Government.* Edited by Peter Laslett. New York: Mentor Books, 1965.

MacIntyre, Alasdair. *A Short History of Ethics.* New York: Macmillan, 1966.

Mannheim, Karl. *Essays on the Sociology of Knowledge.* New York: Oxford University Press, 1952.

Merton, Robert. *Social Theory and Social Structure.* Glencoe, Ill.: Free Press, 1957.

Mills, C. Wright. *White Collar.* New York: Oxford University Press, 1951.

Nakane, Chie. *Japanese Society.* Berkeley, Los Angeles, London: University of California Press, 1970.

Ornstein, Robert, et al. *A Self-Report Survey: Preliminary Study of Participants in Erhard Seminars Training.* San Francisco: The *est* Foundation, 1975.

Parsons, Talcott. *The Structure of Social Action: A Study in Social Theory with Special Reference to a Group of Recent European Writers.* New York: Free Press, 1966.

Rabinow, Paul, and William M. Sullivan, eds. *Interpretive Social Science: A Reader.* Berkeley, Los Angeles, London: University of California Press, 1979.

Reps, Paul. *Zen Flesh, Zen Bones.* Rutland, Vt.: C. E. Tuttle, 1957.

Reich, Charles. *The Greening of America.* New York: Random House, 1970.

Rhinehart, Luke. *The Book of est.* New York: Holt, Rinehart and Winston, 1976.

Robinson, Richard. *The Buddhist Religion.* Belmont, Ca.: Dickenson, 1970.

Rogers, Carl. *Carl Rogers on Personal Power.* New York: Delacorte Press, 1977.

Ross, W. D. *The Right and the Good.* London: Oxford University Press, 1930.

Rousseau, Jean-Jacques. *The First and Second Discourses.* Edited by Roger Masters. New York: St. Martin's Press, 1964.

Rubin, Jerry. *Growing (Up) at 37.* New York: Warner Books, 1977.

Sanders, Ed. *The Family.* New York: Avon Books, 1972.

Schumacher, E. F. *Small is Beautiful: Economics as if People Mattered.* New York: Harper Torchbooks, 1973.

Schur, Edwin. *The Awareness Trap: Self-Absorption Instead of Social Change.* New York: Quadrangle Books, 1976.

Schwartz, Gary. *Sect Ideologies and Social Status.* Chicago: University of Chicago Press, 1970.

Sekida, Katsuki. *Zen Training.* New York: Weatherhill, 1975.

Smelser, Neil and Erik Erikson, eds. *Themes of Love and Work in Adulthood.* Cambridge, Mass.: Harvard University Press, 1980.

Sorel, George. *Reflections on Violence.* New York: Collier Books, 1961.

Suzuki, Shunryu. *Zen Mind, Beginner's Mind.* New York: Weatherhill, 1970.

Swidler, Ann. *Organization without Authority: Dilemmas of Social Control in Free Schools.* Cambridge, Mass.: Harvard University Press, 1979.

Tart, Charles, ed. *Altered States of Consciousness.* New York: Wiley, 1969.

Troeltsch, Ernst. *The Social Teachings of the Christian Churches.* New York: Macmillan, 1931.

Tucker, Robert C., ed. *The Marx-Engels Reader.* New York: Norton, 1978.

Turner, Victor W. *The Ritual Process.* Chicago: Aldine, 1968.

Vogel, Ezra. *Japan As Number One.* Cambridge, Mass.: Harvard University Press, 1979.

Walzer, Michael. *The Revolution of the Saints.* New York: Atheneum, 1976.

Weber, Max. *From Max Weber.* Edited by H. H. Gerth and C. Wright Mills. New York: Oxford University Press, 1958.
———. *The Protestant Ethic and the Spirit of Capitalism.* New York: Scribner's, 1958.
———. *The Sociology of Religion.* Boston: Beacon Press, 1964.
———. *The Theory of Social and Economic Organization.* Translated by A. M. Henderson and T. Parsons. New York: Free Press, 1964.
Welch, Robert. *The Blue Book of the John Birch Society.* Belmont, Mass.: John Birch Society, 1955.
Wuthnow, Robert. *The Consciousness Reformation.* Berkeley, Los Angeles, London: University of California Press, 1976.
Yankelovitch, Daniel. *The New Morality: A Profile of American Youth in the 70's.* New York: McGraw-Hill, 1974.
———. *New Rules in American Life: Searching for Self-Fulfillment in a World Turned Upside Down.* New York: Random House, 1981.

Articles

Aberle, David et al. "The Functional Prerequisites of a Society." *Ethics* 60, 2 (1950): 100-111.
Anthony, Dick, and Thomas Robbins. "The Meher Baba Movement: Its Effect on Post-Adolescent Social Alienation." In *Religious Movements in Contemporary America,* edited by Irving Zaretsky and Mark Leone. Princeton: Princeton University Press, 1974.
Baer, Donald M., and S. B. Stolz, "A Description of the Erhard Seminars Training (*est*) in the Terms of Behavior Analysis." *Behaviorism* 1, 1. (1978): 45-70.
Baker-roshi, Richard. "Sangha-Community." In *Earth's Answer,* edited by Michael Katz, W. P. Marsh, and G. G. Thompson. New York: Harper and Row, 1977.
Balswick, Jack. "The Jesus People Movement: A Generational Interpretation." *Journal of Social Issues* 30, 3 (1974): 23-42.
Bellah, Robert N. "American Civil Religion in the 1970's." In *American Civil Religion,* edited by Russell E. Richey and D. G. Jones. New York: Harper and Row, 1974.
———. "New Religious Consciousness and the Crisis in Modernity." In *The New Religious Consciousness,* edited by Charles Y. Glock and Robert N. Bellah. Berkeley, Los Angeles, London: University of California Press, 1976. Reprinted in Rabinow and Sullivan, *Interpretive Social Science,* and in Bellah and Hammond, *Varieties of Civil Religion.*
Brewer, Mark. "We're Gonna Tear You Down and Put You Back Together." *Psychology Today,* August 1975, pp. 35-89.
Deikman, Arthur. "Deautomatization and the Mystic Experience." In *Altered States of Consciousness,* edited by Charles Tart. New York: Wiley, 1969.
Eisenstadt, S. N. "Archetypal Patterns of Youth." In *The Challenge of Youth,* edited by Erik H. Erikson. New York: Anchor Books, 1965.
Erhard, Werner, and V. Gioscia. "The *est* Standard Training." *Biosciences Communications,* 3 (1977): 104-122.
———. "*est*: Communication in A Context of Compassion." *Current Psychiatric Therapies,* 18 (1978): 117-125.

Glass, Leonard L., M. Kirsch, and F. Parris. "Psychiatric Disturbances Associated with Erhard Seminars Training: I. A Report of Cases." *American Journal of Psychiatry* 134 (1977): 245-247.

Gordon, David. "The Jesus People: An Identity Interpretation." *Urban Life and Culture* 3, 2 (1974): 159-179.

Gordon, Suzanne. "Let Them Eat *est*." *Mother Jones*, December 1978, pp. 40-54.

Heck, R. C. D. and J. L. Thompson. "*est*: Salvation or Swindle?" *San Francisco*, January 1976, pp. 20-71.

Heirich, Max, "Change of Heart: A Test of Some Widely Held Theories about Religious Conversion." *American Journal of Sociology* 83, 3 (1977): 658-680.

Jacquet, Constant H. "Statistics of Organized Religion in the U.S.: A General Appraisal." *Sociological Analysis* 33 (1972): 34-40.

Kasamatsu, Akira and Tomio Hirai. "An Electroencephalographic Study on the Zen Meditation." In *Altered States of Consciousness*, edited by Charles Tart. New York: Wiley, 1969.

Kendall, Willmore. "Social Contract." In *International Encyclopedia of the Social Sciences*, edited by David L. Sills. New York: Macmillan-Free Press, 1968, 3: 376-381.

Keyes, Ralph. "The Case of the Liberated Legislator." *Human Behavior*, October 1974, pp. 25-30.

Kornbluth, Jesse. "The Führer over *est*." *New Times*, 19 March 1976, pp. 36-52.

Lasch, Christopher. "The Narcissist Society." *New York Review of Books*, 30 September 1976, pp. 5-13.

Lindsey, Robert. "Many Rebels of the 1960s are Depressed as 30 Nears." The *New York Times*, 29 February 1976, p. 1.

Margolis, Mac, and R. Hornung. "An Idea on Every Plate." *Nightfall*, October 1978, pp. 15-22.

Marin, Peter. "The New Narcissism." *Harper's*, October 1975, pp. 45-56.

Parsons, Talcott. "Utilitarianism: Sociological Thought." In *International Encyclopedia of the Social Sciences*, edited by David L. Sills. New York: Macmillan-Free Press, 1968, 15:229-235.

Potter, Ralph B. "Justice and Beyond in Moral Education." Andover Newton *Quarterly* 19, 3 (1979): 145-155.

―――. "The Logic of Moral Argument." In *Toward a Discipline of Social Ethics*, edited by Paul Deats. Boston: Boston University Press, 1972.

Prince, Raymond. "Cocoon Work: An Interpretation of the Concern of Contemporary Youth with the Mystical." In *Religious Movements in Contemporary America*, edited by Irving I. Zaretsky and M. P. Leone. Princeton: Princeton University Press, 1974.

Scheer, Robert. "Playboy Interview: Jerry Brown." *Playboy*, March 1976, p. 69.

―――. "Playboy Interview: Jimmy Carter." *Playboy*, November 1976, p. 63.

Seligson, Marcia. "*est*―The New Life-Changing Philosophy That Makes *You* the Boss." *New Times*, 18 October 1974, pp. 165-205.

Smart, J. J. C. "Utilitarianism." In *The Encyclopedia of Philosophy*, edited by Paul Edwards. New York: Macmillan-Free Press, 1967.

Stunkard, Albert. "Some Interpersonal Aspects of an Oriental Religion." *Psychiatry* 14 (1951): 419-431.

Trippett, Frank. "Going Our Own Way―at 65 m.p.h." *Time*, 21 November 1977, p. 95.

Vasconcellos, John. Foreword to *Your Perfect Right—A Guide to Assertive Behavior*, by Robert E. Alberti and Michael L. Emmons. San Luis Opispo, Ca.: IMPACT, 1974.

Woodward, Kenneth. "Getting Your Head Together." *Newsweek*, 6 September 1976, pp. 57-62.

Wolfe, Tom. "The Me Decade." *New York*, 23 August 1976, pp. 35-87.

Wuthnow, Robert. "The New Religions in Social Context." In *The New Religious Consciousness*, edited by Charles Y. Glock and Robert N. Bellah. Berkeley, Los Angeles, London: University of California Press, 1976.

———. "Recent Patterns of Secularization: A Problem of Generations?" *American Sociological Review* 41 (1976): 850-862.

Periodicals

Coevolution Quarterly, Sausalito, Ca.

The Graduate Review, a monthly publication of Erhard Seminars Training, San Francisco, 1975-.

Newsweek Magazine, New York.

PSA Magazine [Pacific Southwest Airlines], Los Angeles.

Time Magazine, New York.

Vital Speeches, Southold, New York.

Windbell, a publication of Zen Center. San Francisco, 1961-.

Newspapers

Chicago *Daily News*, Chicago.

The *New York Times*, New York.

Sacramento Union, Sacramento, California.

San Francisco *Chronicle*, San Francisco.

Dissertations and Unpublished Papers

Anthony, Dick and Thomas Robbins. "The Decline of American Civil Religion and the Development of Authoritarian Nationalism: a Study of the Unification Church of Rev. Sun Myung Moon," a paper delivered at the 1975 Annual Convention of the Society for the Scientific Study of Religion, Milwaukee, Wisconsin.

———. "Youth Culture, Religious Ferment, and the Confusion of Moral Meanings," a paper delivered at the 1975 Annual Convention of the Society for the Scientific Study of Religion, Milwaukee, Wisconsin.

———. "A Typology of Non-Traditional Religious Movements in Modern America," paper delivered at the Annual Meeting of the American Association for the Advancement of Science, Miami, February 1977.

Babbie, Earl and Donald Stone. "What Have You Gotten After You 'Get It'?" paper delivered at the Annual Meeting of the American Psychiatric Association, Miami, 13 May 1976.

Hirschhorn, Larry. "Urban Development and Social Change: The Demographic Dimension," Childhood and Government Project, the Earl Warren Legal Institute, School of Law, University of California, Berkeley, Ca., 1976.

Vasconcellos, John. "Education for What?" address delivered at the New Consciousness Education Conference, Monterey, Ca., 1973.

Potter, Ralph B. "The Structure of Certain Christian Responses to the Nuclear Dilemma, 1959-1963." Th.D. dissertation, Harvard University, Cambridge, Mass., 1965.

Wise, David. "Dharma West: A Social-Psychological Inquiry into Zen in San Francisco." Ph.D. dissertation, University of California, Berkeley, 1971.

INDEX